D1034771

SUNRISE TO ETERNITY

OTHER BOOKS
BY JOHN JOSEPH STOUDT

Consider the Lilies How They Grow—An Interpretation of the Symbolism of Pennsylvania German Art

Jacob Boehme's The Way to Christ *in a New Translation*

Pennsylvania Folk Art—An Interpretation

Pennsylvania German Poetry, 1685–1830—An Anthology

Private Devotions for Home and Church

JACOB BOEHME ACCORDING TO THE 1715 EDITION

"The stature of his outward body was almost of no Personage; his person was little and leane, with browes somewhat inbowed; high temples, somewhat hauk-nosed; his eyes were gray and somewhat heaven blew, and otherwise as the windows of Solomon's Temple: He had a thin beard; a small low voice. His speech was lovely. He was modest in behaviour, humble in his conversation and meek in his heart . . ."

—*From the* Life, *1644, London.*

SUNRISE TO ETERNITY

A Study in Jacob Boehme's Life and Thought

JOHN JOSEPH STOUDT

Preface by
Paul Tillich

PHILADELPHIA
UNIVERSITY OF PENNSYLVANIA PRESS

Published in Great Britain, India, and Pakistan
by the Oxford University Press
London, Bombay, and Karachi

Library of Congress Catalogue Card Number 56-11804

PRINTED IN THE UNITED STATES OF AMERICA

TO MOTHER

PREFACE

An extensive, scholarly, and readable book on Jacob Boehme in English has been long overdue. It has now been provided by John Stoudt in *Sunrise to Eternity*. For many years his interest was centered around the life and the work of the mystical and philosophical shoemaker and shoetrader of Görlitz in eastern Germany. As a result of the author's work, we have a concrete and vivid picture, not only of the personal affairs of his hero, but also of the spiritual and cultural situation of Protestant Germany in the early sixteenth century. One of the achievements of the book is that it reports in an interesting way the destruction of the Boehme "legend," which has dramatized, as well as distorted, the unique figure of Boehme in the traditional view.

But the main purpose of the book is an analysis of the development and structure of the philosophy and theology of Boehme. This is not an easy task, for although Boehme's thoughts have changed during his writings from a stage of crudity to a stage of comparative clarity, they are always expressed in a language which mirrors speculative vision, mystical experience, psychological insight, and alchemist traditions. It is often difficult to uncover the rational element in this mixture, but it is there and it had an astonishing influence on the history of Western philosophy. One need only mention Schelling's famous book on human freedom which is thoroughly dependent on Boehme's vision of the genesis of God, world, and man. From here, Boehme's indirect influence reaches Hegel and Schopenhauer, Nietzsche and Hartmann, Bergson and Heidegger. He also was a power in the speculative theology of the nineteenth century, especially through his ideas concerning creation and evil. If Protestant theology wants to penetrate the ontological implications of the Christian symbols, it would do well to use the ideas of Boehme more than those of Aristotle. In contrast to the *actus purus* of Aristotle, Boehme tried to describe in metaphysical-psychological symbols the *living* God in whom the roots of every life must be sought.

John Stoudt's book will be a help to all philosophers and theologians who desire an introduction to one of the most profound and strangest systems of Western thought—strange in comparison to the prevailing method of modern philosophy—profound in comparison with much theism in modern theology.

PAUL TILLICH

Harvard University

CONTENTS

CONTENTS

ILLUSTRATIONS

ACKNOWLEDGMENTS

Dr. Rufus M. Jones first lighted our Boehme candle in our years at Haverford College and we are in increasing debt to him.

Dr. Will-Erich Peuckert led us to the newly discovered biographical materials, thus enabling us to shake off the dust of old legends.

Dr. Ernst Benz gave valuable help in clarifying several points.

Dr. Hugh Watt and Dr. John Baillie aided in structural arrangement.

The Schwenkfelder Historical Library, Pennsburg, Pennsylvania, allowed use of extensive Silesian materials.

The British Museum gave many favors during the trying war years.

Dr. Alexander Koyré's book proved provocative.

Dr. Howard Brinton and Dr. Anna Brinton shared our Boehme "concern."

Mr. Geoffry Watkins enabled us to acquire the older Boehme editions.

Dr. Paul Tillich, with graciousness, helped us relive Boehme's spirit.

ABBREVIATIONS

THE German text herein used and cited is that of the 1730 edition, edited by Johann Wilhelm Ueberfeld and published in ten volumes under the over-all title of *Theosophia Revelata.*

All references to Boehme's works are given within the text itself. The abbreviations are the standard ones adopted by the early editors. The *Epistles* are numbered and so cited as in the 1730 edition which offers the largest number of letters.

There follows a list of Boehme's writings in the probable order of their composition with German title and standard abbreviation of each:

Die Morgenröthe im Aufgang	*Aurora*
Von den drei Principien Göttlichen Wesens	*Princ.*
Vom Dreyfachen Leben des Menschen	*Dreyfach*
Vierzig Fragen von der Seele	*Seel. Frag.*
Von der Menschwerdung Jesu Christi	*Menschw.*
Von Sechs Puncten, or *Sechs Theosophische Punkte*	*Theos. Punkt.*
Eine Kurze Erklärung or *Sechs Mystische Punkte*	*Myst. Punkt.*
Vom Irdischen und Himmlischen Mysterium	*Ird. u. himl. Myst.*
Unterricht von den Letzten Zeiten I	*Letzte Zeit I*
Unterricht von den Letzten Zeiten II	*Letzte Zeit II*
Erste Schutzschrift gegen Balthasar Tilke	*I Apol. Tilke*
Von vier Complexionen	*Complex*
Bedenken über Esaias Stiefels Buchlein	*Bedenk. Stief.*
Zweite Schutzschrift gegen Balthasar Tilke	*II Apol. Tilke*
Von der Geburt und Bezeichnung aller Wesen	*Sig. Rer.*
Erklärung über Stiefels Auslegung	*Irrth. Stief.*
Von Wahre Busse	*Busse*
Von der Wahren Wiedergeburt	*Wiedergeburt*
Von der Wahren Gelassenheit	*Gelassen.*

Vom Uebersinnlichen Leben	*Uebersinn. Leb.*
Von Gottlicher Beschaulichkeit	*Beschau.*
Von der Gnadenwahl	*Gnad.*
Schlüssel zum Verstand Gottlicher Geheimnisse	*Busse II*
Erklärung über das Erste Buch Mosis	*Myst. Mag.*
Tafel Göttlicher Offenbarung der Dreyen Welten	*Taf.*
Von Christi Testamenten	*Test.*
Tafel der Drey Principien	*Tab. Princ.*
An eine Hungrige und Durstige Seele, or *Gespräch einer Erleucht- und Unerleuchteten Seele*	*Gespräch 2er Seel.*
Schlüssel der Vornehmsten Punkte	*Clav.*
Schutzrede gegen Gregor Richter	*Apol. Richt.*
Ein Gebet Buchlein	*Gebet*
Von 177 Theosophischen Fragen	*Theos. Frag.*

Abbreviations of the standard biographical and critical works used in this work:

Francis Okeley: *Memoirs of the Life, Death, Burial, and Wonderful Writings of Jacob Behmen . . . ,* Northampton, 1780; (translations of the early biographical materials)
Okeley: *Memoirs*

Richard Jecht: *Jakob Böhme, Gedenkgabe der Stadt Görlitz,* Görlitz, 1924; (Publication of newly discovered biographical materials)
Jecht: *Böhme*

Will-Erich Peuckert: *Das Leben Jakob Böhmes,* Jena, 1924; (The one usable, standard modern biography)
Peuckert: *Böhme*

Alexander Koyré: *La Philosophie de Jacob Boehme,* Paris, 1929; (The standard work of exposition)
Koyré: *Boehme*

Werner Buddecke: *Verzeichnis von Jakob Böhmes Handschriften;* (The critical analysis of the newly discovered manuscripts)
Buddecke: *Verzeichnis*

Ernst Benz: *Der vollkommene Mensch nach Jakob Böhme,* Stuttgart, 1937; (The sharpest modern insight into Boehme)
Benz: *Böhme*

Im Innern ist ein Universum auch
Daher der Völcker löblicher Gebrauch,
Das Jeglicher das Beste, was er kennt,
Er Gott, ja seinen Gott benennt,
Ihn Himmel und Erden übergibt,
Ihn fürchtet, und wo möglich liebt.
—GOETHE: *Sprüche in Reimen*

AUTHOR'S PREFACE

THE TURBULENT SEVENTEENTH CENTURY saw the birth of the modern world, for when Francis Bacon destroyed ancient, stubborn idols, trusted experiment, and established the empirical method our technical civilization arose on the debris of medieval culture. It gained impetus—this scientific world of ours—from René Descartes who, though skeptical, was discovering new certainty in a mathematically grounded rationalism which even then was enriching Scholastic systems with Galilean methods of research. For modern science was being born in a world which was seeking the unity of spirit, a sunrise to eternity, and this longed-for cohesion of man's knowledge was expressed by Descartes in these words of his *Principes de la Philosophie:*

> The whole of philosophy is like a tree, the roots of which are metaphysics, the trunk is the science of physics; and the branches shooting from that trunk are all the sciences.[1]

And the road here laid out goes straight from Descartes to Einstein—a highway which more lately passed through Hiroshima, Nagasaki, and Bikini too!

Several years before Descartes had likened the sciences to a branching tree, Jacob Boehme, known as the German philosopher, had employed the same metaphor, but in a far different connotation. Boehme had said:

> I liken . . . philosophy to a precious tree which grows in a lovely garden. Now the earth in which the tree stands continually gives sap to the tree from which the tree gets its living quality. But in itself the tree grows from the earth's sap, increases, and broadens out with its branches. Now, just as the earth works on the tree with its vital force so that it grows and increases, so also the tree continually works with its branches . . . ever to produce much good fruit. (*Aurora,* Preface, 1, 2, 3)

Descartes' tree is metaphorical, expressing the sought-for rational unity of technical civilization; Boehme's tree, however, is symbolic, asserting the inner connection between the order of being and the content of theological discussion. For Boehme, philosophical theology is not *like* a tree—it *is* a living, vital, fruit-bearing organism!

Here with Jacob Boehme, then, we come to grips with a theological and philosophical—and perhaps even a religious—tradition different from that which now dominates within Western culture. It is a philosophical theology which subjugates the tables and formulae of the scientist to life's vital force. For with Jacob Boehme the philosophy of life (*Lebensphilosophie*) reasserted its ancient, compelling claims against Western culture's dominant rationalism. He stressed once again those feelings for life's primitive vigor which the Renaissance had cherished and which then were pouring forth—no, bursting out—into new and broader channels. He expressed these intuitions not by orderly exposition but through a fragmentary vision which was at once the vital as well as logical center of his thought. His exposition lent itself to flashes of genius, to aphorism, to cryptic insight, and to bold and far from meaningless symbolism.

Much has been written on Boehme. His place in Western culture's history has become obscured by the exalted reputation some have given him and by the Faustian quackery associated with his name. The extravagant praise heaped upon him has led to wild claims and to wilder writing; he has been called "God-taught," "God-illuminated," the "man who walked with God," and "our blessed Jacob." Indeed, Boehme's obviously meaningful religious experiences have been dismissed as gossamer and fancy while Descartes' visionary bout with the German stove is allowed the substance of truth! Already in the first generation of men after Boehme's death—and to some degree while he was yet alive—there were those, like Abraham von Franckenberg, his first editor, who surrounded his name with hagiographical adoration, ascribing to him an authority which he, in humility, would have been the first to deny. Indeed, a Boehme "folklore" has arisen which suggests "amazing private visions and direct heavenly dictation"—myths which careful reading of Boehme's writings dispels.

Some of this confusion comes from Boehme's way of writing. He was no word-artist. His vocabulary was sometimes barbaric—at least in his earlier and best-known works. On the whole, though, he developed a German which became an adequate instrument for conveying his meaning, even rising at times to high cadence, developed rhythm and outer ear-quality. Yet language obscurities render his thought so opaque that Émile Boutroux, himself an admirer of Boehme's achievement, confessed that he found his language

> a mixture of abstruse theology, speculations on the indiscernible and the incomprehensible, fantastic poetry and mystic confusion; in fact, a dazzling chaos.[2]

Gerhard Tersteegen, devout eighteenth-century mystical poet, wrote:

> I cannot say that I understood, but I read [Boehme] until I was filled with strange fears and bewilderments. . . . At last I took the books to their owners, and it was like a weight lifted off my heart.[3]

John Wesley, founder of Methodism, was somewhat more emphatic, saying that Boehme's writings were the

> most sublime nonsense, inimitable bombast, fustian not to be paralleled.[4]

However ill Boehme's spirit may have been communicated by his words, nonetheless, it has become a force and field of influence within Western culture, even spilling over to the

East. Hegel consecrated an elegiac although not always accurate chapter to him in his *Vorlesungen über die Geschichte der Philosophie,* considering him father to German philosophy.[5] Schelling, much moved by Boehme's spirit, believed that he was a miracle in human history,[6] and Boehme's influence on Romantics like Coleridge, Tieck, and Novalis is obvious.[7] Boehme's philosophical impulses, as his view of the "original craving" and his anticipation of the modern view of existence, became influential for modern philosophy, mediated by Schelling, Kierkegaard, Nietzsche, and Bergson to Heidegger and Jaspers.[8] While historians seem to agree that in Boehme's speculations

> religious thought is carried to a limit, a limit which no subsequent attempt of a similar kind has succeeded in transcending,[9]

there is by no means agreement on the exact element or on the nature of that significance. Hegel believed that Boehme was a pantheist-idealist.[10] Franz von Baader believed that Boehme's realism earned him his reputation as *the* Christian philosopher.[11] Baur reproached Boehme for his gnostic Manicheanism.[12] Bréhier links Boehme with Weigel in introducing his chapter on Leibnitz.[13] Lord Russell does not mention Boehme in the index of his *History of Western Philosophy.*[14] While somehow agreeing that Boehme is significant, historians of philosophy read their own systems in him [15] and so, anomalously, Boehme remains vaguely significant in the history of Western thought.

However, if philosophers agree at least that Boehme is somehow significant, churchmen, more confident, have violently disagreed. Gottfried Arnold, prince of Pietist historians, gave Boehme large place, but then Arnold's penchant for heresy made his historiographical principles unique.[16] Mosheim lumped Boehme together with chemists, *Rosenkreutzer,* fanatics, fire-philosophers and other venom.[17] The Commission of the Churches of Berne, February 8, 1699, condemned Boehme's works as enthusiastic and fanatical books.[18] Dorner saw in Boehme only fermenting speculative chaos.[19] Max Göbel gave Boehme place in the Rhineland's spiritual history even though detailed analysis lay beyond his scope.[20] Ritschl opposed Boehme because he believed that the shoemaker had presumed to oppose evil in the Lutheran churches and Ritschl argued that Boehme's *The Way to Christ* was used as a foil to parry established Lutheranism's thrusts—as it was—and he concluded that it was impossible to know Boehme's meaning because his writings were not clear.[21] R. Seeberg mentions Boehme but twice in his two volumes on Protestant doctrine.[22] The Quaker, Rufus M. Jones, however, claimed that Boehme's influence on the radical left-wing groups was strong and he saw in Boehme a man of towering stature.

We propose now to add another book on Boehme—to confound the confusion, if that be possible—by turning iconoclast and breaking the traditional image of venerated sainthood in a heretical eternity which his well-meaning but misguided admirers have formed. Moreover, we propose to give Boehme his rightful place, as we see it, within the history of Western culture by an objective exposition of his mature doctrine. Nor do we propose to walk a middle road, for we know that he who walks down the middle of the road gets shot at from both sides! We are seeking facts and, although positivism is now old-fashioned in historical scholarship, it may prove feasible to present what is surely known. Who was he? What did he write, and in what order? What were the lines of his growth? What did he really mean to say? For we are seeking neither a heaven-blessed saint nor a baroque Faust but a man who saw the sunrise to eternity.

Two basic problems appear and our book's two parts are attempts to answer these problems: first, Boehme's life, age, region, and spiritual growth; and second, his mature religious thought.

Charting Boehme's intellectual development rests on what we can learn from external source materials combined with informed reading of his works. Before 1924 our knowledge of Boehme's life depended upon the biographical materials gathered together by Abraham von Franckenberg and other early admirers. These documents are not always reliable. Discovery of new biographical matter by Jecht and Peuckert, rediscovery of the original manuscripts by Buddecke, new knowledge of the background, and careful reading of

Boehme's letters in their proper chronological order, allows a new picture of Boehme, the prosperous merchant, to supplant that of the simple, stuttering cobbler who dreamed doctrines from vision-stuff. We propose to try to paint this new portrait on the basis of the evidence now available, one which may, perhaps, project Boehme as the proponent of a theology which stresses feeling and intuition instead of reason and intellect.

Expounding Boehme's doctrine, which is our second task, remains hopeless as long as we are so naive as to accept everything that he wrote, at every stage of his life, as of equal value; for no hope seems to exist for us if we do not see his astonishing capacity for growth. His was a restless mind which never really found a static, stable, "systematic" point of view; his thought was ever mobile and alive; and he grew from what he himself called a "childlike beginning" to deep maturity. We have chosen 1623, the last full year of his life, during which he wrote *Gnad.* and *Myst. Mag.*, as his finest mature period. His works of 1624, some of which remained incomplete, presaged a still higher synthesis yet to come and he died just as his profoundest thought was emerging in clearly expressed ideas. His promise was great. Our exposition of his views, then, is an attempted cross-section of his thought during the year 1623 which is, we believe, his finest period. Astute scholars will be able to discover passages in his earlier works which seem to contradict our exposition; but, we believe, these contradictions were ultimately resolved in his last synthesis.

Moreover, Boehme's doctrine, never fully systematized, emerges from matter which may, perhaps, defy rational order. His earlier periods were the least lucid, marked by efforts to adopt terms and symbols foreign to his thought which were being urged on him by his friends. The Pietist Spener wanted someone to wade through the swamp of Boehme's terms to the dry land of clear ideas. Boehme did this himself; he threw off the foolish jargon of alchemy and the Cabala as he matured, and, while ideas from such sources continued to influence his doctrine, their terms were being rejected by Boehme himself as he wrote to Christian Bernhard:

I am sorry that you find my writings so difficult in some points, and I wish I could impart my soul to you so that you may grasp my meaning . . . for I understand that it deals with the deepest points where I have used some Latin words; but my sense rests in truth, more in the natural language than in the Latin. . . . (*Epist.* iv, 25, 26)

Slowly he gained courage to reject the foreign terminology which his friends urged on him and the works of his maturity are as clear as they need be.

Boehme's mature system—if such it be—was not Spinoza's: tight, logical, orderly, and static. His expressed words emerged from what may be called mystical vision—and we have sought to reconstruct that vision of the sunrise to eternity from his own accounts—for he sought to expose the mystical analogue. Moreover, he was part poet, enamored of metaphor, and we must not confuse poets' words with theological substance. He was prophet, too, and we ought not to mistake prophetic passion for religious insight.

Untrained in the schools, free as only Renaissance men were free, unhindered by the past yet with a sense of history, Jacob Boehme approached old, old problems with a new sincerity. Like Clement of Alexandria Boehme was driven by an individualizing freedom which places him, with Bacon and Descartes, as one of the founders of modern culture. The scientists, who with formula and tables have split the atom, have only proved in the laboratory what Jacob Boehme saw in that fire-flaming quarter of an hour—his sunrise to eternity —that in Yes and No *all things* consist!

JOHN JOSEPH STOUDT

Norristown, Pennsylvania
Nineteen Fifty-Six

NOTES TO PREFACE

1. As quoted by Lucien Lévy-Bruhl, *A History of Modern Philosophy in France,* Chicago, 1924, p. 8.

2. *Historical Studies in Philosophy*, London, 1912, p. 171.
3. Quoted by H. E. Gowan, *Life of Gerhard Tersteegen*, London, 1898, p. 42.
4. Quoted by G. C. Cell, *The Rediscovery of John Wesley*, New York, 1935, p. 117.
5. *Vide: Werke*, xv, Berlin, 1936, p. 297, *et passim*. In 1809 Van-Ghert, the Dutch philosopher, presented Hegel with a "beautiful edition of Jacob Boehme's writings in two volumes." This was doubtless the 1715 edition. Cf. *G. W. Fr. Hegels Lebensbeschreibung durch Karl Rosenkranz*, Berlin, 1844, p. 284.
6. *Philosophie der Offenbarung*, in *Werke*, II, iii, Stuttgart, 1858, p. 123.
7. O. Walzel, *German Romanticism*, New York, 1932, pp. 6, 66ff, 86, 98ff, and 92.
8. Cf. Paul Tillich, "Existential Philosophy," in *Journal of the History of Ideas*, January, 1944, I, pp. 44ff.
9. H. Höffding, *A History of Modern Philosophy*, tr. Meyer, London, 1924, I, p. 78.
10. *Werke*, xv, pp. 301ff.
11. *Vorlesungen über J. B. Theologumena und Philosophie*, in *Werke*, III, Leipzig, 1853, p. 357.
12. *Die Christliche Gnosis*, Tübingen, 1835, pp. 586, 591.
13. Émile Bréhier, *Histoire de la Philosophie*, II, i, pp. 231ff.
14. *A History of Western Philosophy*, New York, 1945.
15. A Koyré, *La Philosophie de Jacob Boehme*, Paris, 1929, pp. ixff.
16. Gottfried Arnold, *Unpartheyischen Kirchen- und Ketzer Historei*, Franckfurt, 1579, pp. 1130–1155a. *Vide:* Erich Seeberg, *Gottfried Arnold, Die Wissenschaft und Mystik seiner Zeit*, Meerane, 1923, pp. 35ff.
17. *Vollständige Kirchengeschichte*, Heilbronn, 1780, IV, pp. 67–69.
18. Hadorn, *Geschichte des Pietismus in dem schweitzerischen Reformirten Kirchen*, Konstanz, 1901, p. 82.
19. *History of Protestant Theology*, Edinburgh, 1871, II, p. 184.
20. *Geschichte des Christlichen Lebens in der rheinisch-westphälischen Kirche*, II, Coblenz, 1852, pp. 608ff.
21. *Geschichte des Pietismus*, I, Bonn, 1880, p. 96, and II, Bonn, 1894, pp. 301 and 902.
22. *Lehrbuch der Dogmengeschichte*, IV, i, Leipzig, 1917, and IV, ii, Leipzig, 1920.

Write the things which thou hast seen, and the things which are, and the things which shall be hereafter.

—THE REVELATION OF ST. JOHN, i, 19

HISTORICAL INTRODUCTION

IF IN his experience which was for him a sunrise to eternity Jacob Boehme saw good and evil, Yes and No, in all things; if his mystical knowledge embraced dialectic, then he was his age's sensitive son reflecting in his vision the bitter factional disputations of the age of the religious wars.

Already in 1528 Caspar Schwenkfeld had written that a new world was arising.[1] Scholasticism, chivalry, feudalism, monkish asceticism, other-worldliness, courtly love were passing. The bourgeoisie, like Boehme himself, were arriving with their wide-eyed interest in this world's wonders. A new life was waiting, a new birth portending. But of what? [2] Even in its first meaning, Renaissance had embraced Joachim of Flora's religious hopes, dreams more sharply defined by Franciscan spirituals and Dominican mystics [3] as combining new birth with cultural regeneration. This desire for renewal was in accord with the Renaissance veneration of classical form, for Renaissance man found himself attracted by ancient culture's incomparable simplicity and purity, by its precision of expression and conceiving, by its easy, natural ways of thought.

Saint Francis had sought renewal by restoration of apostolic living, a new birth which was for history as well as for individual man. Both a new world and a new man were waiting to be born in the purest of Apollonian forms.

Life was no longer simple and violent, centered in the next world. Medieval brusqueness had given place to endless searching. This led to science. Even humanist Erasmus and theologian Melanchthon had searched the skies to know the future. This was significant because the medieval mind had been incapable of imagining spirit as spirit inhabiting this world. But the men of the Renaissance trusted their own experience, relied on their own minds, disciplined their fantasies by study of nature, and supplemented the upsurging medieval gothic with the ideas of a single natural scheme and with a this-world culture.

So the Renaissance world view began with man, thus sharply contrasting with medieval theocentrism. Instead of conceptions the men of the Renaissance demanded things:

> instead of artificially constructed words, the language of the cultivated world, instead of subtle proofs and distinctions, a tasteful exposition that could speak to the imagination and heart of living man.[4]

Scripture and nature were twin sources of revelation: one told of the macrocosm, the other of the microcosm. The idea of God thus retained a point of unity for the diverging branches of science, spiritual and secular.[5]

During the early years of the sixteenth century, Theophrastus Paracelsus von Hohenheim had melted Renaissance impulses into one fused system of thought [6] and transmitted it to German minds. He had been a lone genius, a compassionate, devout physician of original ideas, a man whom Sebastian Franck called a "strangely wonderful man." [7] He was humanist, reformer, original thinker, but above all consecrated physician and healer. By birth a Swabian physician's son, he had traveled to Italy, France, Russia, Egypt, Arabia, and Asia before settling down.[8] Speculative problems interested him because he wanted to heal and to do so he had to know the causes of disease.[9] He found Hippocrates and Galen unsatisfactory and he sought a new master in nature. He said that life must be based on Scripture and on Christ's teachings, and that there were three corner stones: prayer, faith, and imagination: [10]

> In consciousness we come to God, in faith to Jesus Christ, and through the imagination we receive the Holy Spirit.[11]

To heal, Paracelsus believed, the physician must enter into his heart, know the origin of disease, and experience the cure. Nature breeds disease; nature cures, too. How do health and disease exist together? How are they cured?

> First the physician must know heaven and earth in their material, species, and essence, and when he is educated into this, then he is one who may practice medicine, for in such experience, knowledge, and art medicine begins.[12]

Here is yet another motive to study nature. The Florentine Platonists had sought God within nature; the alchemists had sought by knowledge to control nature; Paracelsus sought to cure disease by knowing nature.

Paracelsus' light of nature, as he named it, brought the physician more knowledge than he needed to heal for the more he knew of nature the deeper his faith in God became. This was a different way to knowledge of God than the Thomistic and Neoplatonic way of negation—the notion that God is known by negating the world.[13] Rather, in Paracelsus' words,

> He who understands and knows much of nature's work is high in faith, for the Creator is his teacher. What sanctified Peter but Christ's works which made him believe? What [sanctifies] nature? The activities of the plants. The greatest one is he who knows, learns, and experiences natural wonders. Each believer should be such a philosopher, or have a neighbor who is such, so that he knows what maintains the health of his life. . . . He should know what it is that he eats and drinks. . . . He should know all the impressions so that he may know how it is possible to make something out of nothing. . . . He should know about the earth, what grows on it, of the sea and sky, so that he knows the Creator of all things . . . Then is he wealthy, for he knows Him through His works, and believes from them to Him.[14]

God is hidden in nature and to find Him therein is man's task.

Paracelsus also transformed Jewish Cabalism, accepting, however, its profound theology. If Jews were looking for God's own esoteric name, then Paracelsus boldly proclaimed it—*Jesus!* He accepted Jewish mysticism's epistemological insights but believed, as also did Boehme, that the hidden God has stepped out from anonymity in the word *Jesus.* Cabalism is possible only where the incarnation is denied and Jewish mysticism therefore could not reap the full harvest of its own profound religious insights. Paracelsus incorporated medieval Jewish mysticism into Christian nature philosophy and so deepened the traditional Logos doctrine.

The sixteenth century had also been the time of Martin Luther, a Roman monk who had met mysticism in all its characteristic forms—Dionysian, Augustinian, Bernardine; Tauler, the nameless Franckfurter who wrote the *Theologia Germanica,* Thomas à Kempis, and the Vicar Staupitz. Luther had met God face to face and then he wrote:

> *Come, Holy Spirit, God and Lord!*
> *Be all Thy graces* now *outpoured*
> *On the believer's mind and soul,*
> *To strengthen, save, and make us whole. . . .*

Now! Not later! Not in heaven! For Luther wanted no secure berth in heaven and he knew that no penny-pinching Johann Tetzel could control the Holy Spirit's coming and going. This was the same German lay mysticism and piety which during the fourteenth and fifteenth centuries had worked in broad and increasing circles, infecting the towns with an independent, anti-ecclesiastical Christianity, freed from hierarchies, the main points of which were personal religious experience, inwardness, ethical regeneration, religious reformation, and social change.[15] Staupitz too had taught that God's love was in man prior to man's love for God. This lay mysticism had leavened the lump [16] and Luther's break signified the coming of a new, though perhaps only revived, religious ideal.[17] With the northern Renaissance and the Reformation older ideas of an inward spirituality again made themselves felt: Sebastian Brandt had written:

> *Gott hat uns darum nicht geschaffen*
> *Dass wir Mönche werden oder Paffen;*
> *Und zumal, dass wir sollten entschlagen*
> *Der welt.*[18]

Ulrich von Hutten had written:

Mut, Landsleute, gefasset! Ermannen wir uns zu dem Glauben,
Dass wir das göttlichen Reich durch redliches Leben erwerben.[19]

More important for Boehme, who had not read these writers, was the expression of such universal theism and the new religious ideal in the sixteenth century's popular art and poetry.[20] Pictorializations of the dance of death portraying man as controlled by dark powers were supplanted by Dürer, the Holbeins, and the Cranachs.[21] And the sweet singing of the German *Minnesänger* had infected German poetry with allegorical images from Canticles describing the soul's relation to God in erotic terms.[22]

This revolution in religious thought was symbolized by the Lutheran battle doctrine of justification by faith,[23] a protective argument for a precious religious insight—the Pauline view that in Christ all things become new. Luther wanted no voluntary contempt of self such as classical mystics assumed, for their forced humility masked pride, the chief sin. As early as 1513 Luther had asserted that hell's torments were the despair man feels in the conflict of penitence.[24] But he did not then also claim that man's joyous love for God was possible in this world. Only after 1517, after meeting Tauler and the *Theologia Germanica,* and only after 1518 when Staupitz had taught him the meaning of *simul iustus et peccator,* did he assert future blessedness to be a present good; however, it should be confessed that in *De Libertate* he still regarded monkish cathartic as necessary for spiritual growth.[25] For Luther, faith meant resignation and repentance, a conflict of penitence in which God becomes justified *in* us. Here Luther's basic dialectical idea appears, namely, that with God's justification in us our own justification in God takes place.[26] This mystical heart of Luther's doctrine of justification implies resignation, repentance, humility here in this world, for with Luther as with Eckhart and German mysticism one act of faith unfolds itself both as man's justification by God and God's justification in man.

If God and man become justified through man's faith Christ's work is less a satisfaction and more a struggle of penitence (*Busskampf*).[27] Luther's atonement formed a whole with the remainder of his doctrine, and it was not tucked away in inaccessible works but was present in his catechisms and hymns.[28]

Christ Jesus lay in death's strong hands
For our offences given;
But now at God's right hand He stands
And brings us life from heaven . . .

It was a strange and dreadful strife,
When life and death contended;
The victory remained with life. . . .

Translating Notker's *Mitten wir im Leben sind* Luther added the new note of struggle; and during the seventeenth century this hymn was believed to have magical powers; Boehme quoted it in his *Aurora:*

In the midst of life the jaws
Of hell against us gape
Who from this peril dire as this
Openeth us escape?
'Tis thou, O Lord, alone!

These Lutheran hymns were contained in a hymnal printed in 1611 by Georg Rhambaw in Görlitz and used in Saint Peter and Saint Paul Church where Boehme worshiped: *Harmonia Ecclesiae et Scholae Gorlicensis.* For Görlitz was Lutheran, the Reformation having come quietly between 1520 and 1530 although final victory was delayed until 1550. The first Lutheran had been the industrious and temperate Pastor Martin Faber, successor to the boisterous priest, Johann Boehme, who was, as the records put it, *ein Zanker, und dem Rath viel zu schaffen machte,*[29] instigator of many beer brawls. Lutheran tracts were being circulated, sent home by the young men studying at Wittenberg and Leipzig.[30] On April 11, 1518, the Sunday after Easter, Faber announced the religious reform,[31] and after his death in 1520 came a line of Lutheran pastors who were zealous for reform: Rupertus, Rüdel, and Press.[32] Görlitz was secured for Lutheranism by the sacrifices of the pastors during the plague of 1521.[33]

Schwenkfeld's followers were probably in Görlitz as early as 1520. Small in number but influential, they consisted of three related families: Schütze, Hoffmann, and Ender.[34] Schwenkfeld was a guest of the Schützes between 1527 and 1529. Here the congregation, led by Franz Leidel, met around the year 1544. The neighboring nobility, related by marriage to these patrician families, were also associated with it.[35] In 1560 the Görlitz Lutherans refused Christian burial to Schütz's daughter Ursula, wife of Hans Hoffmann, patrician Lord of nearby Hennersdorf. The bell ringer dared not toll her passing but the municipal fathers intervened, even in the face of protests by Pastor Wirthwein. In 1565 and 1566 the Senate forbade booksellers to trade in Schwenkfelder books,[36] and the Senate ordered Schwenkfelder families to become converted or to accept banishment. Several "conversions" followed; in 1569 old Sebastian Schütze received Lutheran absolution on his deathbed.[37] In 1575 when Georg Hoffmann died, the Görlitz pastors refused to give a eulogy or to accompany his remains to the churchyard. The magistrates ordered the bells tolled and the school children to march in procession.[38] Michael von Ender von Sercha, Hoffmann's brother-in-law and later Boehme's patron, took the complaint to the Emperor who, being Catholic, sided with the Schwenkfelders.[39] The Lausatian nobility generally were sympathetic to Schwenkfelders, being loyal to their nobleman neighbor's ideas.[40] Pastor Mohr of Boehme's native village, Seidenberg, told of a Schwenkfelder in his congregation as late as 1608, ten years after Boehme had left the village, who had not taken communion for twenty-nine years.[41]

Anabaptists were in the Görlitz area in 1525 and 1529 when they were banished from Franckenstein and Schweidnitz.[42] In 1539 Johann Ender was preaching Thomas Münzer's doctrines in and about Görlitz and he gathered many followers on the Görlitz heath. They were ruthlessly suppressed. In 1549 the Senate forbade further Anabaptist controversy. Several re-baptizers were burned, others banished.[43]

In 1565 a Meister David married a tailor's daughter and then misguidedly became an Anabaptist.[44]

Görlitz became a center of Crypto-Calvinism. The first three rectors of the Gymnasium Augustum studied with Melanchthon at Wittenberg.[45] In 1563 Pastor Rauch was banished for preaching Calvinist sermons.[46] In 1591, after the Prince Elector's death, Philippists and Crypto-Calvinists were chased from Saxony[47] and Wittenberg was "cleansed."[48] In the same year both Catholics and Lutherans took the offensive against the Calvinists who were led by Nestlein.[49] The parties battled in the streets. Broadsides appeared; the authorities were perturbed; no one trusted his neighbor.[50] Görlitz sent a delegation to the Prince Elector to plead the city's orthodoxy and one of its members was Gregory Richter, later chief pastor and Boehme's persecutor. Others were Burgomaster Scultetus, Johann Weiss, Elias Dietrich, and Martin Chilius.[51] Philippism found adherents in eastern Germany: Breslau held to the *Corpus Philippicum;* Brieg and Liegnitz used these works as texts until 1601.[52] Martin Moller, Boehme's pastor and deep friend, became involved in controversy with Solomon Gessner, Lutheran champion of orthodoxy at Wittenberg.[53] At the beginning of the Bohemian war John Christian, Duke of Brieg, espoused Calvinism and Breslau adopted the Reformed worship.[54]

Görlitz was also the home of humanists, scholars, men of learning, and physicians.[55] After 1550 the sons of Görlitz had gone to Basel, Wittenberg, and Leipzig to study. Basel was then the center of northern humanism and the seat of Paracelsian studies. Chief among these young men was Bartholomäus Scultetus, who became the Burgomaster between 1592 and 1614,[56] and who with Johann Huser edited the works of Paracelsus between the years 1589 and 1590.[57] Also, there were Tobias Kober and Boehme's friend and physician, Dr. Michael Kurtz, who wrote a eulogy on Boehme.[58] In Görlitz also there was the scholarly Staudt family, especially Daniel (1566–1616), doctor of laws, who placed one thousand marks at the disposal of needy scholars and put his fine library to their use.[59]

But Martin Luther's reform had not proven final and the hatreds it had bred did not easily die. The Peasant's Revolt, although suppressed with unnecessary ruthlessness, only increased the discontent. The shoe—and Boehme was to become a master shoemaker—still was symbol of Jacquerie and Apocalypsis. Across the mountains in Bohemia the Taborites and the Adamites were holding bold social ideas which spread into Swabia and the *Oberpfalz.* Indeed, the countryside was alive with groups like the Evangelical Brethren, and the destruction of the Swabian League, May 25, 1525, had merely postponed the peasants' hope of liberation. Restless, expectant, certain of final change in their status, longing for basic religious reform, the peasants were waiting for their deliverer—perhaps even another Hans Boehme! And the nobles, faced with the disintegration of feudalism, were groping for certainty.

Long-faced Jeremiahs appeared to proclaim the coming judgment. With declining economics chiliastic dreams appeared in the Rhineland and in Silesia.[60] Landowners were hated for their grand ways, for gourmandizing, carousing, dissipating. The peasants toiled, hungered, dreamed of liberation. All the apocalyptic of the suppressed and dispossessed was molded into a dream of re-birth, culminating in an ultimately decisive day. Near the end of the sixteenth century Michael Niedermayer, a Bavarian farm hand, had predicted the world's end and in Sagan one day in 1575 he had told how the Lord was commanding him to preach repentance.[61] At Harpersdorf two prophets, Georg Rischmann and Hans Neuchel, based their prophecies on the apocalypses of Saint John and Saint Matthew.[62] Rischmann foretold famine, war, and divine judgment, all of which did follow in the Thirty Years' War.[63] In Görlitz there appeared the eccentric tanner, Christoph Kotter, who saw angels as he trudged along and who foretold the destruction of Babel, the founding of the true church, and the soon-coming Youngest Day.[64]

Luther's doctrine allowing the punitive sword to civil magistrates began to bear its logical fruit—the wars of religion. The treaties of Passau (1552) and Augsburg (1555) brought no peace because they were made by equally stubborn parties who sought only brief armistices. Creed followed creed, book answered book, dispute succeeded dispute. The Saxon Elector opposed toleration of Calvinists and united with the

Papists, whom he hated, to suppress them. The dissensions following the *Variata* and the various treaties and alliances continued the factions, and exclusion of the Reformed from religious settlements made peace almost impossible:

Deutschland soll von dreien Glauben nunmehr behalten einen;
Christus meint, wann er wird kummen, dürft er alsdann finden keinen.[65]

In Boehme's time it seemed as if pen and speech were anticipating the coming decision by sword, for like Platonic, Scholastic, and early Renaissance epochs, this time was marked by intense but unnatural intellectuality.[66] Mysticism was being rocked in the Reformation cradle but soon the cradle became too small. Rationalized dogma ended in stifling theological wrangling:

Lutherisch, päpstisch, und Calvinisch, diese Glauben alle drei
Sind vorhanden, doch ist Zweifel, wo das Christenthum denn sey.[67]

The age was indeed enamored of religious controversy. Lutheran and Calvinist both became stiff, violently opposing one another. Each became divided internally: the Lutherans between orthodox and Philippists; the Reformed regionally. Famous controversies attracted attention: Hoë von Hohenegg denounced Scultetus, the Reformed theologian.[68]

This fussing was not inconsequential and it naturally went deep at one important point—the Lord's Supper.[69] The rational change which the theologians had made was not yet popularly understood. In 1562 a broadside appeared, entitled *Von Grawlichen Misgeburten,* expressing discontent with all disputation. It said that all which Luther, the third Elias, had foretold would not come to pass because of the increase of Papists, Epicureans, Sodomites, *Schwärmgeister.* Blasphemy, cursing, vice, adultery, oppression were increasing. The trumpet call would soon be heard!

Unrest seethed. Each new star brought new fears. When a new one flashed across the heavens between 1604 and 1606,

Boehme's own pastor, Martin Moller, said that it was more tragic than a comet because it surpassed comets in magnitude.[70] The movement for calendar reform did not alleviate the unrest; Protestants suspected the Catholic insistence on reform.

Superstition, magic, witchcraft, crimes of magic were rife. The princes had delusions: Christian of Denmark ranted, Johann Friedrich of Weimar raved.[71] Personal life degenerated: intemperance in eating and drinking, extravagant dressing, exorbitant usury, sexual vice, raucous living, plundering by soldiers, barbarous manners, violent deeds,[72] became usual. Then the infidel Turk's lengthening shadow was cast over eastern Europe with grim foreboding.

And the Jesuits! Frightening legends circulated: Spanish gold from Peru and Pegu would finance his most Catholic majesty's war for world domination. The pope prayed publicly for increase in power and planned to reconvert Luther's Germany. Princes betrayed one another; government was by assassination. Holland was bleeding and the Huguenots were deserting France.[73]

With Protestant union under Frederick IV of the Palatinate at Anhausen in 1608 and with alliance of Catholic princes under Maximilian of Bavaria in 1609, Europe's unrest became crystallized into a clear Yes and No. Anxiety grew, sides were chosen, and the question of succession to the Duchies of Cleves and Jülich electrified the air. To the common man one thing was clear: his world was breaking in two. Old medieval apocalypses were being revived. Joachim of Flora had seen the third Elias coming in 1260.[74] But his reckoning was wrong for he should have begun to count from A.D. 325, from Nicea. Three twenty-five and twelve hundred and sixty gave 1585:

Wer im '85 Jahr nit wird verderben
Und im '86 nit thut sterben
Und im '87 nit wird erschlagen
Und im '88 nit wird vergraben
Der mag wohl im '89 Jahr von guten Tagen sagen.[75]

Heinrich Rätel of Sagan, following Daniel, said that 1591 was the year:

Dies Königreich, Herr Jesu Christ,
Dass dein und keinens andern ist,
Wollst du anbrechen lassen bald.
Inmittler Weil dein Reich erhalt.
Gott sei gelobt in Ewigkeit!
1591.[76]

Johannes Hilthemis said that 1606 would bring the final struggle between God and Magog, the ultimate Yes and No. Others, following the Elias calculations which allowed six thousand years, brought in Saint Matthew's "except those days be shortened. . . ."[77]

Blue prints of the new age were common. More's *Utopia,* Bacon's *New Atlantis,* the strange and wonderful visions of Christian Rosenkrantz! Here was a tense and expectant age and the people were waiting for the time when the desert should bloom like the rose, or, as Boehme said, when a lily should bloom in all the ends of the earth.

Gottfried Arnold, who was close to this time, has written of this mood of despair and of hope spawned in that bifurcating world.[78] Yes and No were clearly apparent and the schizoid threat was real, not only to individual men but to their world as well. But the solution was also apparent to some:

> The one ground . . . is that we love Christ in us, and love one another as Christ loved us. (*Gnad.* xiii, 23)

These words of Jacob Boehme point to the resolution of the polarites of his experience in a point of coincidence where Yes and No meet.

NOTES TO HISTORICAL INTRODUCTION

1. H. Ecke, *C. Schwenkfeld, Luther und die Gedanke einer apostolischen Reformation,* Berlin, 1911, p. 100.
2. *Vide:* Konrad Burdach, *Reformation, Renaissance, Humanismus–Zwei Abhandlungen über die Grundlagen moderner Bildung und Sprachkunst,* Berlin, 1926, *passim.*

3. E. Benz. *Ecclesia Spiritualis, Kirchenidee und Geschichtstheologie der Franziskanischen Reformation,* Stuttgart, 1924, *passim;* and Burdach, *op. cit.,* p. 19.
4. Windelband, *History of Philosophy,* tr. Tufts, New York, 1938, p. 353.
5. *Ibid.,* p. 367.
6. Some Paracelsian materials are found in G. Arnold, *Kirchen- und Ketzer Historei* and a sound monograph is Walterhausen, *Paracelsus am Eingang deutschen Bildungsgeschichte,* Leipzig, 1935. Also, C. G. Jung, *Paracelsica. Zwei Vorlesungen über den Arzt und Philosophen Theophrastus,* Zürich, 1942.
7. *Chronica oder Zeitbuch,* 1521.
8. Arnold, *op. cit.,* I, 778a.
9. Paracelsus was also interested in the Cabala, writing a *Theologia Cabalistica de perfecto homine in C. Jesu* which was printed in Huser's 1618 edition and so known to Boehme.
10. Arnold, *op. cit.,* I, 779a.
11. *Ibid.*
12. Paracelsus in *Paragranum,* 2, 106, in Vol. viii of the 1924 Munich edition.
13. Peuckert, *Pansophia,* Stuttgart, 1936, p. 210.
14. Paracelsus in *Prologus in die Bücher Meteorum,* 8, pp. 280ff, quoted by Peuckert, *op. cit.,* p. 202.
15. R. Seeberg, *Dogmengeschichte,* III, i, 9.
16. R. M. Jones, *The Flowering of Mysticism,* New York, 1939.
17. Augustine's earnestness, his passionate longing for redemption, and his personal faith notwithstanding.
18. Quoted by Dilthey, *Weltanschauung und Analysis des Menschen seit Renaissance und Reformation,* Berlin-Leipzig, 1923, p. 48. "God has not created us to be monks or priests, or further, that we should forsake the world."
19. *Ibid.* "Come, comrades, be prepared! Let us take courage in the Gospel! So by upright living we may win the Kingdom of God!"
20. *Vide: Das Knaben Wunderhorn,* Berlin, 1857, and *Mystische Dichtungen aus sieben Jahrhunderten,* Leipzig, 1925.
21. H. Höhn, *Deutsche Holzschnitte,* Leipzig, 1925, and Hannah Closs, *Art and Life,* Oxford, 1936. This latter work gives the relation between ideas, life, and artistic form. For a study of the relation of folk art, or peasant art, to mystical imagery, *vide* Stoudt, *Pennsylvania Folk Art,* Allentown, 1948. Boehme's imagery was much used by folk artists.
22. August Closs, *The Genius of the German Lyric,* London, 1938.

23. E. Seeberg, *Christus: Urbild und Wirklichkeit,* Stuttgart, 1937, *passim.*
24. H. Boehmer, *Luther in the Light of Modern Research,* London, 1931, p. 75.
25. E. Seeberg, *op. cit.,* p. 148.
26. G. Aulen, *Christus Victor,* London, 1940, p. 117.
27. *Ibid.,* p. 119f.
28. Cf. Johannes Meyer, *Luthers Kleiner Katechismus,* Bonn, 1913, and also *Die Deutsche Litaney* of Luther.
29. F. G. Müller, *Versuch einer Oberlausitzischer Reformazions-geschichte,* Görlitz, 1701, p. 318.
30. Neumann, *Geschichte von Görlitz,* Görlitz, 1850, p. 275.
31. Müller, *op. cit.,* p. 318.
32. *Ibid.,* pp. 324–326.
33. *Ibid.,* pp. 326–327.
34. R. Jecht, *Böhme,* p. 16.
35. *Ibid.,* p. 86.
36. *Ex memorabili Domini Eliae Metlzeri, Senat Görlitz,* Anno 1565, as quoted in Jecht, *Böhme,* p. 61.
37. Koyré, *Boehme,* p. 4.
38. *Ibid.*
39. *Ibid.*
40. The Schwenkfelder nobility consisted of Carl von Ender, Michael von Ender, Hans von Salze, David von Schweidnitz. Cf. G. Hoffmann, *Geschichte der Religionsbewegungen in Schlesien,* Breslau, 1880. Other materials in the Schwenkfelde Historical Library, Pennsburg, Pa.
41. Knauthe Ms: *Historia Crypt. in Lausitz,* in Görlitz Archives.
42. Peuckert, *Die Rosenkreutzer,* Jena 1923, p. 243.
43. *Ibid.,* p. 35.
44. *Ibid.*
45. Knauthe ms cited above.
46. Jecht, *Böhme,* p. 86.
47. Koyré, *Boehme,* p. 5.
48. *Ibid.*
49. *Ibid.*
50. *Ibid.*
51. Arnold, *op. cit.,* II, xvii, 5.
52. Moller, *History of the Christian Church,* New York, 1902, iv, p. 311.
53. Boehme was himself drawn into the Crypto-Calvinist controversy.
54. Moller, *op. cit.,* p. 331.

55. *Vide:* Neumann, *Geschichte von Görlitz,* p. 361. Scultetus was astronomer, friend of Tycho Bache and co-editor of the *Diarum Humanitatis Christi,* published at Frankfurt-Oder in 1600. Cf. M. Lipensius, *Bibliotheca Realis Theologica,* Frankfurt, 1685, I, 577b.
56. Jecht, *Böhme,* p. 60.
57. *Ibid.*
58. Material from the family records of the Staudt-Stoudt-Stout family, care of Don Ricardo W. Staudt, Buenos Aires.
59. Peuckert, *Böhme,* p. 1. Cf. also Corrodi, *Kritische Geschichte des Chiliasmus,* Frankfurt, 1781–1788.
60. Peuckert, *Böhme,* p. 3.
61. Peuckert, *Rosenkreutzer,* p. 296ff.
62. Hensel, *Beschreibung der Stadt Hirschberg,* 1799, p. 323ff.
63. Peuckert, *Schlesische Sagen,* Leipzig, 1924, p. 72ff.
64. Born, 1583; died, 1647. Cf. his *Zwey Wundertractätlein,* 1732.
65. Peuckert, *Rosenkreutzer,* p. 3. "Of three faiths Germany shall have but one. Christ intends when He returns to maintain but one."
66. T. R. Hughes, *The Philosophic Basis of Mysticism,* Edinburgh, 1931, pp. 41–42.
67. Peuckert, *Rosenkreutzer,* p. 3. "Lutheran, Papist, Calvinist—these three faiths are extant, still there is doubt where Christianity is."
68. J. G. Walch, *Einleitung in die Religions-Streitigkeiten,* Jena, 1734, *passim.*
69. Grünhagen, *Geschichte Schlesiens,* Gotha, 1886, p. 99.
70. Peuckert, *Rosenkreutzer,* p. 12.
71. *Cambridge Modern History,* IV, p. 17.
72. *Ibid.,* pp. 8–11, *et passim.*
73. Peuckert, *Rosenkreutzer,* pp. 16ff. Also, B. Duhr, *Jesuiten Fabeln,* Freiburg, 1904.
74. Peuckert, *Rosenkreutzer,* pp. 10ff.
75. *Ibid.,* p. 11. "He who does not rot in '85, and who does not die in '86, and who is not killed in '87, and who is not buried in '88, he may surely speak of good times in '89."
76. Peuckert, *Rosenkreutzer,* p. 13. "The Kingdom, Lord Jesus Christ, which is Thine and none others, do Thou permit to be established soon, since it embraces Thy Church. Let God be praised in Eternity! 1591."
77. Boehme quotes this in *Letzte Zeit,* i, 30.
78. I, pp. 609–656.

PART ONE

THE UNFOLDING OF BOEHME'S THEOLOGY

Jacob Boehme's religious knowledge began in mystical vision and realized itself in mature rational expression through living. The irrational Unconditioned became Logos through existential demands, emerging both initially as insight and finally as theology as the product and perhaps even as the reflection of his life in his Lausitz homeland. The Yes and No came from his life; their resolution, empirically as well as speculatively, however, was the result of mysticism, a final reworking of the insight he received in the quarter-of-an-hour dawning to eternity. From this he received his precious pearl which was so often cast before swine and wordlings.

Slowly, as he matured, vision and life were fused in an all-comprehending dialectical theology which was both the reflection of his environment and the projection of his mystical knowledge. He both reflected and transcended his age.

Ich lebe noch in dieser Welt
Und bin doch schon zum Himmel aufgehoben,
Ich trag ein Joch das mir gefällt,
Ich bin ein Engel, und kan Gott doch loben.

—GOTTFRIED ARNOLD

CHAPTER ONE

BOEHME'S LIFE: 1575–1600

JACOB BOEHME [1] was born in the Upper Lusatian village of Old Seidenberg, situated on a hillside south of Görlitz near the Bohemian border, on or just before April 24, 1575.[2]

He was the fourth child of Jakob Boehme who died in 1618 and of his wife Ursula whose family name is not known.[3] The parents were solid and perhaps even well-to-do [4] farmers, "of the good German stamp," [5] and in spite of the surname's foreign connotation the family was natively German, as pure Germans had lived beside Czech and Moravians in Lusatia since the thirteenth century and the Boehmes were in Seidenberg already in the fifteenth century.[6]

The theologian's great-grandfather was also Jakob, farmer in Old Seidenberg in 1558, seventeen years before the theologian's birth. His sons were Michael, Andreas, Ambrosius, and Georg.[7]

Ambrosius, the theologian's grandfather, inherited the family lands instead of the younger brother Georg, who died at an early age. Ambrosius became well-established in the community, being freed from feudal obligations. He was elder in the Seidenberg church and magistrate in the local court.[8] He had the following children: Hans, Martin, Ambrosius, Anna, Margaretha, Jakob, and Dorothea. He died in 1563 and his land passed to his youngest son, Jakob, as was the custom.

Jakob Boehme, the theologian's father, bought the land rights from his brothers and sisters for six hundred marks, on Martinmas, 1563.[9] Like his father he too was a church elder and local magistrate.[10] He married twice. His first wife bore him five children, among them the theologian; his second wife bore him three daughters.[11] His first wife died in 1611; the second in 1634. On the father's death in 1618, Michael, the youngest son, purchased the land rights from his brothers and sisters for six hundred marks.[12] An interesting but unconfirmed tradition suggests that Jakob Boehme, the father, had "enthusiastic" tendencies.[13]

Little is known of the theologian's boyhood. Farm he could not inasmuch as he was sickly, small, and underdeveloped; furthermore, having a younger brother, he was not to inherit the right to the family lands. But, as with farm boys generally, he minded the cattle and so made himself useful at home. Franckenberg, the first editor, tells a story of his boyhood:

> During the time of his being a herd-boy, he met with a curious and remarkable occurrence. Having one day, about noon, been rambling to a great distance from the other lads, and climbing up alone by himself on an adjacent mountain called *Landeskrone,* being arrived at the summit . . . he espied amongst the great red stones a kind of aperture or entrance, overgrown with bushes, and enclosed in a manner not much unlike a doorcase or passage. This in his simplicity he penetrated into, and there descried a large portable vessel . . . full of money, and he made the very best of his way out again, without taking so much as a single piece. . . . Tho' he had frequently climbed up to the same place afterwards, in company with other herd-boys, yet he could never hit upon the aperture again.

Franckenberg confessed to see in this an

> emblematic omen of his future spiritual admission to the sight of the hidden treasury of wisdom and mysteries of God in nature.[14]

Franckenberg's symbolism does not convince. The *Landeskrone* is a good eight English miles from Seidenberg and a "grotto legend" has long been associated with it. However, Lusatian herd-boys did wander long distances to graze their herds.

Next, Franckenberg says that Jacob Boehme's parents,

> having observed that the son . . . gave proof of an excellent, good, and sprightly genius, kept him to school, where together with daily prayers and good behavior, both at table and in his family, he learned to read tolerably well and a little writing.[15]

Between 1580 and 1590 the Seidenberg school was taught by Johann Leder of Schneidsburg, instruction being based on Scripture and Luther's Smaller Catechism.[16] Leder also was *Vorsinger* in the local congregation. Jacob stayed in school until his fourteenth year, learning, as has been said, to read, write, and cipher, as well as a few scraps of Latin.[17] The existence of a school in Old Seidenberg during this period has not been established.[18]

The Boehmes were prominent in the affairs of Old Seidenberg. They owned most of the village land and the theologian's father was village leader.[19] As *Kirchenvater* the father surely took his family to the Seidenberg church and sent his children to the Pastor to be catechized. This, then, was Jacob Boehme's first contact with established religion.

The Seidenberg church, like those of neighboring villages, was soundly Protestant.[20] Its first Lutheran Pastor was Johann Schneider whose ministry began in 1542[21] and continued into the lifetime of the theologian's father. In 1535 the Seidenberg estates and their municipal and ecclesiastical administration passed to Friedrich von Räder, an ardent Protestant,[22] who shared management with his brother until 1591 when he became the sole administrator. In this same year, possibly urged by the Prince Elector, he began reform of church matters, summoned his Pastors to Friedhof, his seat, and said that he wanted the remnants of superstition purged from worship and insisted that preaching be based on the Prophets, Apostles, Symbolic documents, and the Augsburg Confession. He formulated a standard form of purified worship and appointed Martin Nüssler superintendent.[23]

During these years Jakob Boehme, the father, was vestryman, his name appearing among the *tutores et nutrices ecclesiae*.[24] If more were known about von Räder and the local

Pastors, the meaning of these events for Boehme's theology might be gauged.[25] In 1624, the year the theologian died, the Seidenberg church again became Catholic.

During these years Jacob Boehme was in Seidenberg, for in 1589 when the lad was fourteen his father had taken him to the village shoemaker to learn the trade of cobbling. Apprenticeship was for three years, so Boehme began his journeyman travels in 1592. Franckenberg spins another yarn about Boehme in these trade-learning days:

> It fell out that . . . during his apprenticeship a stranger . . . comes to the shop, and asks to buy a pair of shoes; but as neither Master nor Mistress were within, he, Jacob Boehme, . . . would not venture to sell them, till the stranger . . . insisted upon his letting him have them; now, then, he, having more of a mind to put the buyer off than to sell the shoes, set a somewhat enormous price upon them. The man, however, paid down the money demanded . . . and, taking up the shoes, went away. But being arrived at some distance . . . and then stopping short, he called out with an audible and serious tone of voice: 'Jacob, come out hither to me.' An address like this from a person unknown . . . startled the boy; but . . . he got up and went into the street to meet him. The man, then, whose mien was serious and loving, with sparkling eyes, taking him by the hand, and looking him full in the face, said: 'Jacob, you are small, but you shall become great, and a man so different from the common cast, that you shall be the wonder of the world. Be therefore a good lad; fear God, and reverence His Word. Let it especially be your delight to read the Holy Scriptures, wherein you are furnished with comfort and instruction; for you shall be obliged to suffer a great deal of affliction, poverty, and persecution also; nevertheless be of good comfort, and firmly persevere, for God loves you, and He is gracious to you.' Upon which the man, after squeezing him by the hand and looking him full in the face, went his way.[26]

Such instruction, typical of Franckenberg's interest in the strange and mysterious, was aimed at keeping young Boehme from straying into heresy and nonorthodoxy; indeed, Franckenberg adds that Boehme was led to renewed seriousness and interest in his work. But the whole incident is colored by the effort to plead for Boehme's remarkable yet safe eccentricity.[27]

Boehme's journeyman travels were in a land torn by dissension, party strife, and religious unrest. Upper Lusatia was then the scene of social conflict and religious controversy, which in some instances were joined, especially between feudal barons and the rising bourgeoisie, between established and nonestablished religions; indeed, so bitter had the strife been that in 1592, the year Boehme's travels began, Rudolf of Saxony ordered a thoroughgoing religious purge.[28]

Franckenberg, to whom we are indebted for so much imaginative biography which seems to miss the truth, claims that at this time Boehme experienced his first "illumination." There is no evidence in Boehme's writings to support this statement. Indeed, Franckenberg's account is vague and indefinite in all but one point:

> Whereas now, Jacob Boehme . . . had . . . walked from his youth up in the fear of God, and had taken pleasure in attending sermons,[29] he, . . . was awakened in his own heart, and through the multiplicity of controversy and scholastic wrangling about religion . . . he set himself upon fervently and incessantly praying, seeking, and knocking, until, being at that time with his master on his travels, he . . . was . . . translated into the Holy Sabbath and glorious day of rest in the soul; and thus . . . had his rest granted him here (to use the words of his own Confession) "surrounded with the divine light for the space of seven days successively," he stood possessed of the highest beatific vision of God, and in the ecstatic joys of his Kingdom.[30]

This passage from "his . . . confession" cannot be located in Boehme's known writings, although the work in which it is said to appear may be lost. That religious wrangling gave Boehme his discontent and doubt is clear enough; the seven-day ecstasy is dubious, to say the least. Boehme never mentioned it. Surely Boehme was melancholy, serious, and even stern; and Franckenberg continues that he laid

> aside the trifling lusts of youth, and kept constantly to his church, together with reading the Holy Bible, a regular at-

tendance upon the Word preached, and participation in the Holy Sacraments, a zeal of God moved him so that he was not able to bear, or to endure, foolish conversation and least of all blasphemous expressions and curses; nay, he could not refrain from checking and rebuking them in his own master. . . . Moreover, his love of godliness and virtue made him addict himself to a modest and retired life, bidding adieu to and shaking off the wantonness and bad company, which being a turn of course drew ridicule and reproach upon him; and at length he was, by the very master he wrought with (unable to brook a family prophet like this), discharged and sent about his business elsewhere.[31]

Where Boehme served out the rest of his apprenticeship it is not clear; but as shoemakers were then scarce in Seidenberg and in Görlitz he may have gone to the larger town to finish his training.

So, around 1594 and 1595, perhaps even before his journeyman days were over, Boehme made his way to Görlitz, there to pursue his handicraft and to maintain himself "with the labor of his hands and the sweat of his brow." [32] Görlitz then was an important city in eastern Germany, one of the few German towns which had had an indigenous culture even during the medieval period.[33] Nonfeudal and bourgeois, it was typical of the new societies then arising out of the debris of medievalism and its baroque architecture externally expresses the age of its greatest prosperity. It was the home of merchant princes like Georg Emmerich and Johannes Haas who, while not as famous as the Augsburg Fuggers, were still known as the "kings" of Görlitz.[34] It was indeed a center of trade, a place where men and ideas met, a crossroads for the conflicting philosophies and religious impulses of the age.[35]

Little is known of Boehme's early years in Görlitz. If he was apprenticed at fourteen then at twenty he was free to set up his own shop. Few cobblers were able to start in business for themselves so it may be assumed that around 1595 Boehme began to work for another master shoemaker, probably for Valentin Lange. On April 24, 1599, Boehme purchased a "bench" from Lange, his future brother-in-law, for the sum of two hundred marks.[36] On May 10th he was made a citizen of the town and also became the husband of Catharina Kuntzschmann, daughter of a Görlitz butcher. For these privileges he paid three crowns.[37] Catharina's mother had been a Bartsch and one of her uncles was the influential butcher, Elias Bartsch, city alderman between 1604 and 1616. Catharina had three brothers and a sister, Sarah, wife of the Valentin Lange from whom Boehme bought the shoemaker's bench. Inasmuch as a shoemakers' guild statute of March 23, 1573, stated that when "a journeyman becomes a master he shall marry within half a year" it may be assumed that Boehme had become master shoemaker just before his marriage.[38] Catharina probably brought Jacob a substantial dowry, for on August 29, 1599, he bought a house in the Rabengasse from Paul Adam for three hundred marks.[39] Jacob and Catharina had the following children: Jacob, baptized, January 27, 1600[40]; Michael, baptized, January 8, 1602[41]; Tobias, baptized September 11, 1603[42]; and "little Elias," baptized September 14, 1611.[43] The two girls with the surname Boehme baptized during this period were children of another Jacob Boehme in Görlitz, by trade a tanner.[44]

Christopher Knauthe (died, 1784), pastor at Friedhof, seat of the von Raders during the eighteenth century, has left an important reference about Boehme's early days in Görlitz.[45] He wrote that Martin Moller became chief pastor in 1600, that many conversions followed, that among these was Jacob Boehme who because of his awakened condition associated with like-minded persons in the conventicles Moller had organized.[46] Glusing, editor of the 1715 edition of Boehme's writings, also said that Moller was the instrument which awakened Boehme's spirit.[47]

This was indeed a fateful year. Even the weather was erratic. On Easter a great snow came down and the cold lingered long into the spring. It was only a week before Whitsunday that the cattle could be taken from their stalls into the open fields and the trees still had no leaves. The cherry trees were not in bloom until Trinity Sunday.[48] In this remarkable setting the shoemaker had his "second illumination," as Franckenberg called it, for his spirit

was . . . enraptured with the astral spirit of the soul by

means of an instantaneous glance . . . cast upon a bright pewter dish . . . introduced into the innermost ground or center of the . . . hidden nature.[49]

The pewter dish is psychologically suggestive and may have been the immediate stimulus, but it is more likely that the ultimate origin was Martin Moller's bright and shining spirit.

Martin Moller had been born at Liessnitz, son of a mason. He had attended school at Wittenberg and at the Görlitz gymnasium, but poverty prevented him from hearing lectures in the university. Nonetheless he was appointed cantor at Löwenberg, and in April, 1572, he was ordained to the ministry in Kesseldorf. In the autumn he became deacon at Löwenberg and in 1575 the pastor at Sprottau. In July, 1600, he became the chief pastor in Görlitz where he organized the "Conventicle of God's Real Servants," a group in the true German mystical tradition to which Jacob Boehme belonged.[50]

Moller wrote much. Already in 1584, 1590, and 1591 he had published volumes of religious poetry. The first, *Meditationes sanctorum patrum durch Martin Mollerum,* appeared in Görlitz.[51] It consisted of prose and poetry from Augustine, Tauler, and other devotional and mystical writers. In it Moller's translation of Bernard of Clairvaux' *Jesus dulcia memoria* appeared, later a favorite of the Pietists and included by Johann Arndt in his *Paradiesgärtlein,* his book of prayers. The first stanza is still precious:

> *O Jesu süss, wer dein gedenkt,*
> *Dess Hertz mit Freud wird überschwemmt,*
> *Noch süsser aber alles ist,*
> *Wo du, O Jesu, selber bist.*[52]

The second part of this work shows Moller's chiliastic ideas [53] as the hymn which begins, *Der letzte Tag nu kommen wird.* In 1595, while still at Sprottau, he had published a little mystical work [54] in which union was seen in erotic imagery as union of the believer with the inner church, saying that the individual's life should be a pattern for congregational living.[55] In 1601, having been chief pastor in Görlitz for a year,

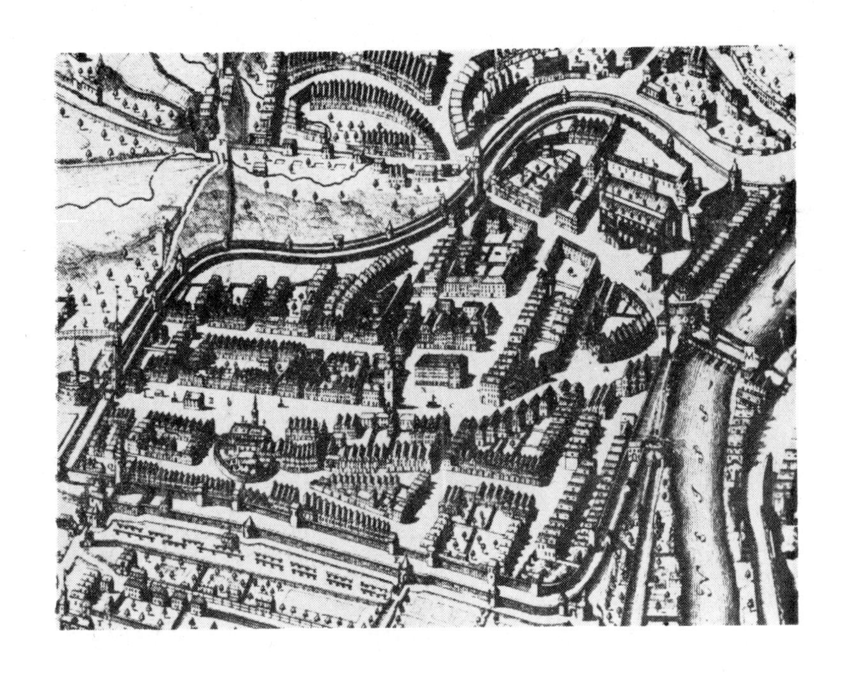

GÖRLITZ IN BOEHME'S TIME

Jacob Boehme lived, as his last place of dwelling, just outside the bridge-gate at the place marked "M" on the map.

he published his sermons on the pericopes, *Praxis Evangeliorum,*[56] sermons doubtlessly preached with Boehme in the pew. Dr. Peuckert, who has investigated these materials in detail, has found numerous verbal passages of parallel character between this work and Boehme's first work, the *Aurora,*[57] passages which not only prove Moller's spiritual influence on Boehme but his literary dominance during these years. This work of Moller was challenged by the orthodox Solomon Gessner of Wittenberg.[58] Moller's devotional tracts continued to appear: *Manuale Mortis* which went through many editions; *Schedia Regia,* 1605, et cetera. Even after Moller's death on March 2, 1606, his writings were in demand.[59]

When Martin Moller had come to Görlitz in 1600 Boehme had been a young, pious shoemaker of twenty-five with enthusiastic tendencies. Newly married, beginning his career as a prospering workman, with restless mind, and moved in his heart by the tensions of the age, he had attended Moller's conventicles where he met similarly minded people: noblemen, physicians, peasants, burghers, fellow craftsmen.[60] Surely it was this spirit which Martin Moller communicated, rather than the pewter dish or other fanciful objects, which brought to the young Boehme a deep interest in the devotional life. For Boehme was not yet a philosopher.[61] His interests were in the deepest that Christianity had to offer, for Moller was surely a lover of Apostolic Christianity, a "pure" witness, the translator of the martyred Ignatius' letters, of Theodoretus' dialogues, and of other patristic literature.[62] Moller also knew Tauler, and he culled excerpts from Augustine, Bernard of Clairvaux, the Victorines, Ruysbroeck, Suso, and Thomas à Kempis.[63] Here Boehme was brought face to face with Christian mysticism at its medieval best and Dr. Peuckert's comparison of the parallel passages in Moller and Boehme's *Aurora* establishes that Moller's spirit worked on Boehme much as that of Thomas à Kempis and Arndt.[64] Ritschl, no friend of Pietism, said that Moller's soteriology had stressed regeneration instead of justification.[65] For Moller and for Boehme it was Christ *in* us rather than Christ for us. So Martin Moller was the first and perhaps the continuingly deepest influence on Boehme, bringing to the shoemaker the rich imagery of bride mysticism, a tempered chiliasm, and an ideal of a pure Christianity.

One of Moller's prayers [66] has survived within German devotional literature, a sacramental prayer of the indwelling spirit: [67]

Thou dost unite Thyself so deeply within me that Thou dost abide in me all of the time, quickening me through Thy Spirit, never wanting to depart therefrom again. . . .[68]

Four of Moller's hymns have become part of German hymnody,[69] and they show the depth of his spirit:

Ach Gott! Wie manches Herzeleid
Begegnet mir zu dieser Zeit . . .

Both Boehme and Moller designate man as a worm, Boehme in *Busse* i, 6, and Moller thus:

Hier lieg ich armes Würmelein,
Kan regen weder Arm noch Bein
Für Angst mein Hertz in Leib zerspringt,
Mein Leben mit den Tode ringt,
Vernunfft und alle Sinn sind matt. . . .

Here Moller, dead and blind, poured out his suffering soul: life was at war with death, reason was inadequate and vitality much too weak.

So, Martin Moller was the first and perhaps the dominant influence on Jacob Boehme. Boehme's silence about him is surprising and perhaps even logical—surprising in that Moller meant so much to him, logical because Boehme cherished the memory of Moller preciously during the days of his persecution by Moller's successor, Gregory Richter. Only once does Boehme even mention the name and that is in 1624 when he sends his greetings to the pastor's son from Dresden (*Epist.* lxiii, 12), showing that the friendship endured to the end.

NOTES TO CHAPTER ONE

1. The name is variously spelled even in the old records. German scholars use Jakob Böhme; the British Museum uses Jacob Boehme.

2. The date is gotten: a) the year, from Franckenberg's *De Vita et Scriptis*, #1, and by calculating back from Boehme's death; b) the day and month, from the implication in the *Görlitzer Bürgerbuch,* 24 April, 1592.
3. Jecht, *Böhme,* p. 15.
4. *Ibid.*, p. 16, where property holdings of the Boehmes in Old Seidenberg are given.
5. Franckenberg, *De Vita* . . . #32.
6. Oldest reference to a Boehme in Seidenberg is October 23, 1416, when Hans buys land. Cf. Jecht, *Böhme,* p. 19.
7. *Ibid.*
8. Cf. Fechner, *Sketch of the Life of Jacob Boehme,* trans. in Earl's *De Electione Gratiae,* London, 1930, pp. xivff.
9. Jecht, *Böhme,* p. xiv.
10. Fechner, *op. cit.*, p. xiv.
11. Elizabeth, Dorothea, Maria.
12. Fechner, *op. cit.*, p. xiv.
13. Fechner suggests the father's evangelical leanings.
14. Franckenberg, *De Vita* . . . , #6. Legends about the holy grotto are common in European folklore.
15. Franckenberg, *op. cit.*, #6.
16. Fechner, *op. cit.*, p. xiv.
17. Neumann, *Geschichte von Görlitz,* p. 365.
18. Jecht, *Böhme,* p. 20.
19. Neumann, *op. cit.*, p. 367.
20. The Reformation *Graf* was Matthias von Bieberstein whose two sons were at Wittenberg when Luther nailed his theses to the door. Cf. Müller, *Versuch einer Oberlausitzischen Reformazionsgeschichte,* pp. 353ff.
21. Müller, *op. cit.*, p. 562.
22. *Ibid.*
23. *Ibid.*, p. 563.
24. Jecht, *Böhme,* pp. 20–21.
25. Müller, *op. cit.*, p. 563.
26. Franckenberg, *De Vita* . . . #5, #9.
27. *Ibid.*, #7.
28. Peuckert, *Böhme,* p. 14.
29. Franckenberg takes pains to protest Boehme's orthodoxy, seeking to vindicate Boehme from the suspicion of heresy.
30. Franckenberg, *op. cit.*, #7.
31. *Ibid.*, #10.
32. *Ibid.*
33. Jecht, *Böhme,* p. 84.

34. For a list of chronicles and other sources of Görlitz history, *vide* Jecht, *Quellen zur Geschichte der Stadt Görlitz,* Görlitz, 1909.
35. Müller, *Oberlautzischen Reformazionsgeschichte,* p. 318.
36. *Görlitzer Kaufbuch,* 1598ff., Bl. 77, Cf. Jecht, *Böhme,* p. 10.
37. *Görlitzer Traubuch,* 10 May 1599, Cf. Jecht, *Böhme,* p. 10.
38. Koyré, *Boehme,* p. 11. Peuckert, *Böhme,* p. 12.
39. *Görlitzer Kaufbuch,* 1598ff., Bl. 77. Cf. Jecht, *Böhme,* p. 10.
40. *Görlitzer Kirchenbuch,* #29, 1600.
41. *Ibid.*
42. *Ibid.,* 11 September, 1603.
43. *Ibid.,* 9 September, 1611.
44. Jecht, *Böhme,* p. 18.
45. *Historia Cryptocalvinismi in Lausat., suc.,* in Görlitz Archives, Annales, 255ff.
46. *Neues Lausitzischen Magazin,* Vol. 94, 1918, pp. 48ff.
47. *Mehrere Merckwürdigkeiten,* #8 (in the biographical materials in Volume X of the 1730 edition).
48. Max Kwiecinski, *Das Wichtigste aus der Stadt Görlitz,* 1902, p. 170.
49. Franckenberg, *De Vita . . .* #11.
50. Jecht, *Böhme,* p. 27 and Koch, *Geschichte des Deutschen Kirchenlieds,* Stuttgart, 1852, I, pp. 178–180.
51. Wackernagel, *Das Deutsche Kirchenlied,* Leipzig, 1877, II, p. 34ff.
52. This hymn became quite popular.
53. Wackernagel, *op. cit.,* #55.
54. The title, *Mysterium Magnum,* was later adopted by Boehme as the title of his main work.
55. Ritschl, *Geschichte des Pietismus,* II, 27.
56. Peuckert, *Böhme,* p. 24.
57. There are at least four major parallel passages.
58. The controversy lasted several years. Moller was being accused of Calvinism.
59. The posthumous works were reprints.
60. Heckel, *Geschichte der deutschen Literatur in Schlesien,* Breslau, 1929, I, p. 164.
61. Bornkamm, *Luther und Böhme,* p. 75.
62. *Mehrere Merckwürdigkeiten,* #8.
63. Ritschl, *Pietismus,* II, p. 57.
64. Peuckert, *Die Rosenkreutzer,* pp. 259–260.
65. Ritschl was incapable of understanding Moller's theology.
66. *Vide:* F. Heiler, *Das Gebet,* München, 1923, pp. 284–386.

67. *Vide: Versuch eines allgemeinen evangelischen Gesang- und Gebetsbuch zum Kirchen und Hausgebrauche,* Hamburg, 1833, pp. 722ff.
68. Koch, *op. cit.*, I, p. 179.
69. *Geistliches Gesangbuch,* Gotha, 1738, p. 350, p. 620, p. 727, and p. 1756.

Sponsae cultum aemulantes,
Sponsae vultum speculantes,
Sponsae cultu sociemur,
Sponsae vultu satiemur.
—DE BEATA MARIA SEQUENTIA

CHAPTER TWO

SUNRISE TO ETERNITY: 1600

SOMETIME in the spring of the year 1600 Jacob Boehme, the young Görlitz shoemaker who was under the spiritual influence of Martin Moller, had a shattering mystical experience which became the vital center of his life and thought, the stimulus to a remarkable literary and theological career, and the dawn of a new life of the spirit—a true sunrise to eternal life.

This experience has been much misunderstood and it needs to be reconstructed from the three accounts which Boehme has left in which he tries to piece together what happened with tolerable precision: the famous nineteenth chapter of the *Aurora,* which was written in 1612; portions of the preface to *I Apol. Tilke* which were written towards the beginning of 1621; and an Epistle to Caspar Linder, written on May 10, 1622. Speaking of this watershed experience, Boehme said,

It unfolded itself within me from time to time. . . . I went around pregnant with it for twelve years, and a hefty impulse arose in me before I could bring it to external form. (*Epist.* xii, 10)

As his first writing was probably in 1612 the experience then took place in that year when the cold lingered so long and just after the pious and devout Martin Moller had come to Görlitz as chief pastor. So these three accounts record a mellowing but still vital memory of an astonishing conflict of ideas and of the still more astonishing resolution which followed. They are not, like Pascal's directly snatched record, the cryptic accounts of a vision caught in passing but the lingering tones of a melody once played but remembered with fervency of spirit.

Franckenberg, with his penchant for the occult and strange, claimed that the reflected light from a pewter dish set Boehme's spirit to moving in the deep subconsciousness, but Boehme himself is much more precise and sensible:

> The right heaven . . . has until now been tightly concealed from human children and there have been many explanations of it.
>
> The learned also have scratched around it with many queer writings, and fallen into each others' hair with calumny and disgrace . . .
>
> People have always believed that heaven is many hundreds or thousands of miles from this earth, and that God only lives in that heaven; some physicists have even tried to measure this height and have brought forth quite strange things.
>
> Indeed, before this my knowledge and revelation, I myself believed this to be the right heaven which extends above the stars in a round light-blue sphere. . . .

This was indeed the usual medieval view which was then being questioned by the worldly immanentism of the Renaissance.

> When this had given me many a hard blow . . . I finally fell into deep melancholy and sadness when I contemplated the great deep of this world . . . and considered in my spirit all the world's creation.
>
> Then I found evil and good, love and wrath in all things, in irrational creatures, in wood, stones, earth, and elements as well as in men and beasts. (*Aurora* xix, 1–6)

Here Boehme had felt the confusion of his times and he rebelled against the upward surging of medieval thought, against the soaring gothic which was the goal of medievalism. Renaissance natural philosophy and man's new interest in this world had dimmed high heaven's light for him and brought good into the world. He continues,

But after I found a strong contradiction within me . . . I put myself so hard against the serpent's seed that I thought I should overcome and destroy the in-born evil will and propensity and join myself to God's Love in Christ . . . so that God's spirit might rule, drive, and lead me. (*I Apol. Tilke,* preface, 21)

In addition I contemplated man's little spark (*Füncklein*), what it should be valued before God along side of this great work of heaven and earth.

As I found that evil and good were in all things . . . and that it went as well in this world with the impious as with the pious, also that the barbarous people possessed the best lands and that they had more good fortune than the pious . . .

I therefore became very melancholy and highly troubled. No Scripture could comfort me, though I was quite well versed in it . . .

. . . When in such sadness I earnestly elevated my spirit into God and locked my whole heart and mind, along with all my thoughts and will, therein, ceaselessly pressing in with God's Love and Mercy, and not to cease until He blessed me . . . , then after some hard storms my spirit broke through hell's gates into the inmost birth of the Godhead, and there I was embraced with Love as a bridegroom embraces his dear bride. (*Aurora,* xix, 7–11)

A strange break-through—through the gates of hell!

What kind of spiritual triumph it was I can neither write nor speak; it can only be compared with that where life is born in the midst of death, and is like the resurrection of the dead. (*Aurora,* xix, 12)

"Like the resurrection of the dead"! How could Boehme know what this was like? In *I Apol. Tilke* he uses other images:

I proposed to keep myself . . . dead until God's Spirit got a form in me, and I comprehended Him so that through Him and in Him I might direct my life . . .

Also I proposed to will nothing but what I knew in His Light and Will . . .

And what thereupon took place only God and my soul may know . . .

So I wrestled in God's presence a considerable time for the knightly crown . . . which later with the breaking of the gate in the deep center of nature I attained with much joy, whereupon a remarkable light arose in my soul (Preface, 22–25)

which was, indeed, a sunrise to eternity. His wrestling had been for a considerable time and was not, as Franckenberg claimed, instantaneous. Moreover, Boehme broke through the "gate in the deep center of nature" and so the mystery of the Godhead was not profaned.

In this light my spirit directly saw through all things, and knew God in and by all creatures, even in herbs and grass. . . . In this light my will grew in great desire to describe the being of God. . . . (*Aurora,* xix, 13)

Now from this light I have my knowledge, as well as my will and drive; and I will write this knowledge according to my gifts . . . and let God work His Will; . . . I will attend and wait what the Lord intends. (*Aurora,* xix, 17)

I shall not hide from you the simple, childlike way I go in Christ. For of myself I can write nothing, as a child who knows nothing and understands nothing . . . I never wanted to know anything about the divine mystery, much less understood I how I should seek it or find it . . . I sought only Jesus Christ's heart, to hide myself therein before God's grim wrath and the devil's violent assaults; . . . I yielded myself wholly to Him that I might not live to my will but to His, that He only might guide me, that I might be His child in His Son Jesus Christ. In such earnest seeking and desiring . . . the gate was opened for me that I saw and knew more in a quarter of an hour than if I had been many years in the universities. . . . (*Epist.* xii, 5–7)

Here was no ecstasy, no *nirvana,* no bridal chamber mishmash of subject and object, of creator and creature. Here was no loss of individuality, no melting of the subject into the formless abyss of being. Here was no rending of the veil of divine mystery, no merging with the Godhead, no *unio mystica* in the classical sense! Boehme's mystical experience was gnostic in the sense that from it he gained what was for him new knowledge.

> Therein I first knew what God and man were and what God had to do with men . . .
>
> Previously I understood little about the high articles of faith . . . much less about nature . . . For the Spirit shot through me like a bolt of lightning . . . I began to write like a school-boy, and so I wrote continuously, but only for myself. (*I Apol. Tilke,* preface, 26–28)

Boehme outlines the knowledge which he had received in this remarkable quarter of an hour and his outline sounds much like the topics of an orderly theological system:

> For I saw and knew the Being of all beings, the ground and the unground (*Ungrund*); the birth of the holy trinity; the source and origin of this world and all creatures in divine Wisdom (Sophia) . . . I saw all three worlds in myself, (1) the divine, angelical, or paradisaical; . . . (2) the dark world . . . ; (3) the external, visible world . . . ; and I saw and knew the whole Being in evil and in good, how one originates in the other . . . so that I not only greatly wondered but also rejoiced. (*Epist.,* xii, 8)
>
> Moreover, I wrote only my own mind as I understood it in the Deep; and I made no commentary on it as I did not intend that it should be read; I wanted to keep it for myself; had I known that it would be read I would have written more clearly . . . Also my spirit's labor in it and with it was continuous . . . For the Light's spirit moved my soul very much . . . repeating many things very often, ever deeper and clearer, from one step to another—it was the real Jacob's ladder. . . . (*I Apol. Tilke,* preface, 31–37)

Several points are significant in this piecing together of the three extant accounts of Boehme's mystical experience. He sought to resolve the disunities of his experience as he could not accept the medieval cosmology with its sharp separation of heaven and hell and with its transcendence. Moreover, Boehme was asking again the old, old question of religious philosophy, the question of evil. Why does the all-good, omnipotent God appear indifferent to good and evil? Here the young shoemaker's heart, tutored by the pious pastor Moller, became the collision-ground where two Renaissance trends met head on: mystical devotion and nature philosophy.

Secondly, Boehme's mystical experience does not contain the classical element of union with the Godhead in substantial terms. He did not climb a ladder into the Bosom; he did not follow to Dante's Golden Rose there to be lost in contemplation; he was not melted into an abyss of being. What then? Hear his revolutionary words:

> I did not climb up into the Godhead, neither can so mean a man as I am do it; but the Godhead climbed up in me, and revealed such to me out of his Love, which otherwise I would have had to leave it quite alone in my half-dead fleshly birth. (*Aurora,* viii, 7)

This was in full rebellion against the soaring gothic transcendence of medieval thought; this was the mystical heart of Lutheranism, the notion which Staupitz had taught to Martin Luther which was that God's love is in men even before they search for Him. Boehme did use the ladder image, but with him it was merely the repetition of a Scriptural phrase and had no organic relation to his thought:

> Jacob's ladder was shown to me upon which I climbed up . . .

but this ladder was not the old mystical hierarchy of states of being; it was rather the struggling path:

> Therefore if anyone will climb . . . after me, let him be careful that he be not drunk . . . For he must climb through a gruesome deep . . . and . . . hell, and he will have to endure scoffing and mocking . . . In this struggle I had often had to experience it with sad heart; the sun was often eclipsed . . . but it rose again and the more it was eclipsed the brighter and clearer it rose again. (*Aurora,* xiii, 20–22)

Like other mystics Boehme used sensory images to describe this break-through:

> When the Light arises . . . one tastes the other; . . . then the spirits become alive and life's vitality presses through all. In that vitality the one smells the other . . , feels the other. So there is only a heartily loving and friendly seeing, fragrancing, relishing, and loving . . . ; here is love, joy, and delight; here is light and brilliance; here is fragrance; here is pleasant and sweet taste . . . eternally, without end! (*Aurora,* ix, 38ff)

He added:

> But now I have climbed too high and I dare not look back again or else I shall get giddy . . . When I ascend I have no giddiness; but when I look back and want to return, I get dizzy and fear I may fall. (*Aurora,* xiv, 41)

Boehme's moving experience which lighted a new dawn for him was not all joy and exaltation; he never left this world of sin and evil and the consciousness of it was ever present:

> Do you believe that my spirit has sucked this out of the corrupt earth, or out of a felt hat? Truly no . . . for at the time I am describing my spirit . . . did . . . unite with the deepest birth of God. From that I got my knowledge, and from that it is sucked. . . . What I thereafter had to suffer from the Devil . . . who rules my outer man . . . you cannot understand . . . unless you dance in his round. (*Aurora,* xviii, 78ff)

From the passionate character of the latter half of the *Aurora,* Boehme's first book, it is clear that Boehme's initial speculative urge had two sources of confusion. The first was his inability to find answers in the writings of the "high masters" (*Aurora,* x, 27). The fruitless disputes, the endless theological bickering, the bitter confessional controversies of the post-Reformation age, had not resolved man's religious doubt. The second source, related to the first, was Boehme's prophetic discontent with the evil of his time. For Boehme's mysticism was bipolar; to want to seek unity is to already know both the disunity that exists and the possibility of its resolution; to seek resolution is to know evil's stubbornness. Boehme's mysticism embraced both joy and misery, both the mystical elevation and the mystical death. In him these two poles cannot be separated and his full mystical experience embraces both. This is clear from the following lyrical passage in the eighth chapter of the *Aurora*:

O gracious and great Love, how sweet you are! How friendly you are! How lovely is your relish, who can express it? . . . Or what do I write—I who stammer like a child who has just learned to speak! To what shall I liken it? If I liken it to the world's love it is only a dark vale—and that large . . . O noble guest! why have you departed from us? . . . O you wrathful Devil, what have you done? . . . Why do I complain? you stinking goat! O you cursed stinking Devil, how you have contaminated us . . . O you lying Devil! stay a little while and the Spirit will uncover your shame . . . O woe, you poor blind man, why do you let the Devil make your body and soul so darksome! . . . O security, the Devil awaits yours; O pride, you are hell's fire; O beauty, you are a dark valley; O power . . . O ego-centric will, you are God's grim wrath! O man! Why is the world become too narrow for you? Would you have it alone? And if you did have it you would not have enough! . . . O man, man! Why do you dance with the Devil who is your enemy? . . . You have but a narrow stage on which you dance; beneath the stage is hell! . . . O blind man! Is not heaven and earth yours, and thereto God Himself? . . . O you poor man, turn around; the Heavenly Father stretches out both arms and calls to you; come, He wants to fold you in His Love; you are His child and He loves you! If He hated you He would be at odds with Himself! . . . O you watchmen of Israel, why sleep you? Wake up from the sleep of whoredom, and trim your lamps; the bridegroom comes, your trumpets sound! O you stiff-necks and drunkards, how you go a-whoring with the greedy Devil! Thus speaks the Lord! Will you not feed my people whom I have entrusted to you? See, I have put you on Moses' chair, and trusted you with my flock; but you mind only after the wool and not to the sheep; thereby you erect great palaces; but I shall set you on the pestilential stool and my Shepherd shall tend my sheep . . . O blessed Love and clear Light! Remain with us for the evening comes . . . O! why do I write of the world's evil—I must do it and the world gives me the devil's thanks for it. O! Amen! (*Aurora*, viii, 96–109)

The reference is obvious. Martin Moller, the good pastor, had died in 1606, blind and deaf, yet with the welfare of his flock at heart. As Boehme's experience had "opened" from time to time he saw the untended sheep and the haughty rational theology of Moller's successor, Gregory Richter. This passage, probably written just after 1606, most likely in 1608, puts Boehme among the prophets and divine ambassadors. He was another in the line of farmers' sons who predicted the victory of God's righteousness over an evil world. In 1675 Quirinius Kuhlmann, the Silesian *Schwärmer*, wrote to the then chief pastor in Görlitz: *tres tibi proponam Dei nuncios nostri seculi, unum Prophetum, alterum Sophum, tertium Literarum!* [1] The first was Christoph Kotter mentioned above, the second was Boehme, and the third was Johann Arndt. Thus Boehme found his place in the prophetic succession; he railed against the world's sin; he fought with a very personal devil. Apocalyptic urgency is an important and in some ways exciting aspect of Boehme's growing mystical experience inasmuch as it emerged from the contemporary situation:

The tribulation and collapse of Babel fast approaches; the thunderstorm arises in all places; it will rage violently; vain hope deceives for the tree's destruction is near . . . Babel's tower has become without foundation; one hopes to keep it up with props, but a wind from the Lord will collapse it. Men's hearts and thoughts shall become manifest . . . Many shall betray themselves . . . Hypocrites and mouth-Christians shall wail when the false foundation becomes manifest . . . An eagle [the German emperor] has hatched out young lions [the Electors] in his nest, bringing them prey so long that they have grown great, thinking that they should also bring their prey to him again . . . They take the eagle in his nest, pluck out his feathers, bite his claws off . . . so that he cannot fetch prey for them any more . . . If the rich and powerful knew whereupon their foundations rested they would look to themselves and see to their end . . . At that time . . . Grace shall flow . . . and the afflicted and oppressed shall be refreshed. (*Epist.* xli, ps. 1ff.)

Boehme did not work out a dated apocalypse like many of his chiliast contemporaries:

To me is given to know that the time is now and even now at hand, but the year and day I know not; . . . I leave it to God's counsel, and to those to whom God shall reveal it. (*Letzte Zeit,* I, 59ff.)

Boehme, however, was a prophet in more than a metaphorical sense because he created a philosophy of history more profound than the dated apocalypses of his contemporaries. He saw a new world emerging from a new man, a new level of religious living begetting a new social order, and, so intense had his sunrise to eternity been for him, he gave himself a place in creating this new world. He felt that he was himself a new Luther to a profounder reformation, a reformation of the spirit when Christ's children would not be called shoemaker's blacking (*Epist.* lxiii, 9).

You shall still hear remarkable things as the time of the reformation is born of which it was told me. (*Ibid.*)

Indeed, this time already was born,

the time already appears, and soon will come; he who wakes sees it. . . . First there must come a great tribulation before it be fully manifest. The cause is the great contention of the learned. . . . Let no honest man defile himself with such contention. (*Epist.,* xlvi)

This new age was one of certainty, knowledge, truth, righteousness, and peace.

Boehme's apocalyptic was part of his basic mystical experience and he believed, and it appears with sincerity, that his experience of 1600 was a sunrise to eternity, heralding the coming of a new age (*Princ.,* xx, 15). Moreover, he believed, and it appears with sincerity, that God had chosen him to reveal that which had remained hidden to the rest of mankind. He held his revelation to be unique (*Aurora,* xiv,

38) and he said that his life mission was to make the great lily manifest (*Dreyfach* iii, 5). Only his lowly station in the world seemed to bother him:

> Because I here write of . . . divine things . . . the reader doubtless will wonder at the simplicity of the author . . . What was Abel? A shepherd. What were Enoch and Noah? Plain . . . men. What were Abraham, Isaac, and Jacob? Herdsmen. What was David when . . . the Lord called him? A shepherd . . . How came . . . Jesus Christ into this world? Poor, in trouble and misery, and had nowhere to lay his head. What were the Apostles? Poor . . . illiterate fishermen. And what were they who believed their preaching? The poorer and meaner people. . . . What were they who in all ages of the Church . . . have stood by it most loyally and constantly? The poor . . . people who shed their blood . . . But who were they that falsified . . . pure doctrine? . . . Even the learned Doctors . . . popes, cardinals, bishops, professors. . . . Who was it purged out of the German churches the Pope's greediness for money, his idolatry, bribery, deceit, and cheating? A poor depised monk! By what power and might? By the power of God the Father . . . and God the Holy Spirit. (*Aurora,* ix, 1ff.)

Boehme believed himself to be Luther's heir and successor, a prophet possessed of the Spirit, dedicated to the cleansing of a church once again corrupted. Reason and rational theology could not regenerate man. Only an experience born of suffering availed:

> The world . . . supposes that one must see God with the earthly . . . eyes; it knows not that God dwells not in the outer life, but in the inner. It sees nothing strange in God's children, it says: O! he is a fool, he was born foolish, he is melancholy . . . Listen, Master Hans! I well know what melancholy is. I also know what is of God. I know both of these and also you in your blindness. But such knowledge requires no state of melancholy, but a knightly wrestling. (*Menschw.* II, vii, 11)

Boehme knew that rationally discovered creeds could not save man or make him whole. Faith was deeper than reason. Experience of the living Spirit in this world was necessary to overcome its evil. Boehme was not seeking to "go" to heaven any more than he was trying to avoid "going" to hell; he had done with the upward striving of medieval religion; his God had climbed up into him. He believed that the pregnant quarter of an hour had brought the invasion of the Spirit into his heart. This fired his soul.

> If all trees were scribes and all branches pens, and if all hills were books and all waters ink, they could not give a sufficient description of the sorrow which Lucifer has brought into this place. (*Aurora* xvi, 26)

Hell was here and now; paradise's lily could grow in the world. Boehme's problem was to regenerate the world.

Conceived in its broadest aspect, Boehme's experience was the sunrise to an eternity within the world, something undreamed of in medieval thought.

NOTE TO CHAPTER TWO

1. Gottfried Arnold, *Kirchen- und Ketzer- Historei,* II, 199ff.

Ich muss die Creaturen fliehen
Und suchen Hertzens Innigkeit,
Soll ich den Geist zu Gotte ziehen
Auf das er bleib in Reineheit.
—ASCRIBED TO TAULER

CHAPTER THREE

BOEHME'S LIFE: 1600–1612

THE YEAR 1600, then, brought Jacob Boehme the sunrise but a long prosaic day of work lay ahead, for man cannot live by "illuminations" alone. He was just twenty-five years of age; he was not yet established as a substantial burgher; he was in reality a young dreamer who thought he had been given special, divinely inspired knowledge.

Outwardly he began to prosper. Obviously a careful and serious workman at his last he soon became established in his trade and a leader in his guild. During this period the tanners and the shoemakers were at loggerheads and Boehme was right in the middle of this controversy. So zealous had he been for success that he had been tanning more hides than he needed himself, selling the surplus to other shoemakers, thus competing with the tanners. On July 24, 1604, he was released from prison on the condition that he would not tan hides for other shoemakers and upon payment of six shillings fine within two weeks.[1] The jealousy of the guilds further appeared in an ambiguous reference in the *Ratsprotokol* for April, 1606, when a Jacob Boehme and Jacob Kissling were imprisoned for calling Max Röhricht a swindler. The trial disclosed that Röhricht had swindled Boehme and Kissling, so he was packed into jail. On May 2 they were all released, bond having been posted by Hans Löwe, Paul Hillebrand, and Hans Seidel.[2] The ambiguity arises from the possibility that the Jacob Boehme mentioned may have been the tanner of that name, although the probability is that it was the shoemaker-theologian as Paul Hillebrand was the man from whom the shoemaker bought his house. Jacob Boehme, the shoemaker, was an active member of his guild.[3]

On July 2, 1607, the theologian's father, whose first wife had died, divided his property among the children of his first marriage, and Boehme was in Old Seidenberg to receive his share of almost two hundred marks. So, in March, 1608, when Boehme's sons took part in the *Gregoriusfeste* they were listed among the *locupletiores* (affluent) and not among either the *pauperes* or the *equites* (nobility).[4]

On July 28, 1608, Boehme sold his house in the Rabengasse next to Paul Hillebrand, mentioned above, to Zacharias Kiesslingen for the sum of three hundred and thirty marks, a profit of thirty marks.[5] Two years passed before he again became a householder; [6] this is why his name does not appear in the list of master-shoemaker property-holders for the period.[7] The fact of the matter is that he had probably already moved into the house he was soon to buy, which was owned by his brother-in-law, Valentin Lange. In 1610 he was made trustee for his unmarried sister-in-law, Rosine, daughter of Hans Kuntzschmann, an act suggesting the death of Boehme's father-in-law [8] and implying Boehme's prosperity. On June 22, 1610, Boehme bought Lange's house in the Neiss gate just outside of the city and on the road to Liegnitz and Hirschberg, one of the busiest highways in eastern Germany. To finance this he borrowed, on November 10, 1610, the sum of fifty marks and contracted for periodic payments.[9] He made them as follows: November 13, 1610, two hundred marks; February 28, 1612, twenty-five marks; February 9, 1613, twenty-five marks; 1614, twenty-five marks; 1616, twenty-five marks; and 1618, twenty-five marks.[10] This sequence seems to suggest the slow settling of Boehme's father-in-law's estate jointly by Lange and Boehme.

Sometime around the year 1610 Franckenberg claims that Boehme experienced his "third illumination." About this Boehme himself is silent and does not hint at anything more than continuing understanding. However, Franckenberg says according to God's holy counsel . . . about ten years after . . . he was a third time stirred up and renewed by God. Whereupon . . . he could not put it out of mind, nor strive against God. Therefore [he] did . . . write secretly for himself.[11]

In 1612 the strife between the tanners and the shoemakers again broke out and again Boehme was involved, for Boehme and Hans Bürger had been sent to Lemberg by the shoemakers to buy leathers. They returned with three hundred and thirty-two pieces which they had bought at two thalers apiece. Protesting this invasion of their rights, the tanners went to court. The *Protokoll* vindicated the shoemakers and the record in their guild book is in the handwriting of Jacob Boehme and therefore is the first bit of writing from his pen. Inasmuch as it is not in his works the German text is given below in the notes.[12] His authorship, however, has been questioned [13] but not with convincing argument.

On May 25, 1612, Boehme served as security for Lorentz Nüssler, a Lauterbach farmer who, as tenant, had allowed a farm to become vacant and waste.[14]

These few scattered surviving facts present us with a bit of the outward man—a sometimes boisterous young shoemaker, prosperous, energetic, and immersed in the active mercantile life of his town. He was no idle dreamer. The world's turmoil was mirrored in his life. And it was a turbulent age. In 1608 the union of Protestant princes under Frederick of the Palatinate had taken place, and on July 11, 1609, Emperor Rudolf's *Majestätsbrief* had allowed freedom of conscience to his Bohemian and Silesian subjects. But Rudolf's long years of misrule had only intensified religious hatreds; the Thirty Years' War became inevitable. Imperial authority was collapsing; the eastern frontier had been saved only when Rudolf effaced his guardianship, the western frontier only by the assassin's dagger.[15] Boehme saw his world composed of

greedy stiff-necks . . . you who . . . seek pride, honor, praise, power, money, and goods, who sweat and bleed the poor, oppressed, and distressed, spending their labor on your vanities, holding yourselves better than simple laymen. . . . (*Aurora*, xii, 19)

His reference was to the clergy, particularly to Gregory Richter who had followed Martin Moller as chief pastor.

So in 1612, driven by inner compulsion and by outer pressure, Boehme began to write. On New Year's day he set pen to paper (perhaps, though, he had already written eight chapters before 1608) and put down in bold German characters: *Morgen Röthe im Aufgang. . . . Die Würtzel oder Mutter der Philosophie.*[16] A new day was dawning; the old beaten world was not yet done; a new ground had been revealed to Boehme and he would declare it abroad! The shoemaker's ambition was confident; he knew that the sun had risen for him; now he was going to reveal the true basis of all philosophy, astrology,[17] and theology. For he believed that he wrote not

from the instruction . . . received from men, nor from . . . books, but I have written out of my own book which was opened in me . . . the book of the noble . . . image. (*Epist.* xii, 14)

And the *Aurora*, he says so many times, was not written for the public but as a memorial to himself and such caution was prudent in an intolerant age: Giordiano Bruno had been burned in Rome in 1600; Valentin Weigel refused to allow his writings to be published; Kepler and Galileo were in difficulties; and Johann Arndt, whose works appeared between 1606 and 1612, paid heavily for his indiscretions.[18] And then the *Rosenkreutzer* books, however they may have come to be written, were anonymous and they also advocated thoroughgoing reform. Boehme's *Aurora* suggests that he knew these last works and in the twelfth chapter he foretells the time of wonder, with 1604 hinted at as the year when Elias, the artist, was to have removed man's misery. Paracelsian prophecies also were suggesting the time between 1599 and 1603 as that age of new reformation which was to have come with "singing, ringing forth, dancing, rejoicing, and jubilating" as Boehme himself said (xii, 22). And in 1604 that new star standing in the serpent and crown had appeared and men searched for its meaning.[19] Boehme, who was no master in courage, knowing the fate of foolish publication,

> intended to keep . . . my writing by me all . . . my life . . . ; but it fell out . . . that I entrusted a certain person with it; by means whereof it was published without my knowledge or consent, and the first book was taken from me. (*Epist.* xii, 12)

This "certain person" was the Schwenkfelder, Carl von Ender von Sercha,[20] who had been associated with Boehme in Martin Moller's conventicle. Of an old family, widely traveled, student at the Görlitz gymnasium between 1586 and 1595, graduate of Frankfurt, von Ender was a man with searching mind and heart.[21]

Now when Carl von Ender discovered that Boehme had written a book, a curious book of promise and prophecy, he had some copies made, unknown to the author, which he circulated. One of these fell into the hands of the churlish successor to Martin Moller, Gregory Richter,[22] chief pastor in Görlitz since 1606. From Boehme's writings Richter appears as a zealous watchdog of orthodoxy, an opponent of enthusiasm in all forms, rational, proud, and eager to persecute. This may be exaggeration. Born on February 1, 1560, probably at Ostritz, son of the monastery smith, he had turned from the anvil to the pulpit where he hammered out stringent Lutheran sermons, becoming orthodoxy's champion in Lusatia.[23] He had helped to protest Görlitz's orthodoxy at court during the crypto-Calvinist troubles.[24] Unpopular as a preacher, his sermons were long and poorly spoken, and not of Martin Moller's spirituality.[25] The Görlitz council reproved him for his reforming zeal and during the plague of 1612, after he had reviled a busy physician for not minding his business and then had himself fled to Sprottau, the council admonished him and ordered him to remain within the parsonage.[26] The burghers had little respect for him and wrote:

> *Quaeritur inclusus cur sit Richterus in aedes?*
> *Me Samaritani calce petavit equus.*[27]

Morgen Röte im auffgang.
Das ist
Die wurtzel. oder mutter der PHILO=
SOPHIA. ASTROLOGIA. und THE=
OLOGIA. aus rechtem Grunde.
oder,
Beschreibung der natur / wie alles gewesen
und im anfang worden ist, wie die Natur
und Elementa Creatürlich worden sind, auch
von beiden qualiteten / Bösen und guten, wo=
here alle ding seinen Ursprung hat, und
wie es ietzt stehet und wircket, und wie
es am Ende dieser Zeit werden wird:
Auch wie Gottes / und der hellen Reich
beschaffen ist, und wie die Menschen in
iedes Creatürlich wircken. alles aus
rechtem grunde, in erkendnis des Geistes
im wallen Gottes, mit fleiss
gestellet
Durch Jacob Böhmen in Görlitz Im Jahr 1612
ETATIS SVE 37 Annor. In Die [illegible]
[illegible] Anno 1612

TITLE-PAGE OF THE *AURORA* MANUSCRIPT

When, then, Richter learned that the shoemaker whose face he saw near the pillar in Saint Peter's and Saint Paul's Church every Sunday had written a book, when he knew that the already suspected Carl von Ender was quietly passing the word around of a new prophet, he was enraged. He wangled a copy of the book. And his attitude surely was not helped when he read passages like this:

> You teach others the way and you are always seeking it yourselves; you grope in the dark and see it not . . . O you blind men! Leave off contention and shed no innocent blood; lay waste no country or city to fill the devil's will; but put on the helmet of peace, gird yourselves with love to each other, and practise meekness. Leave off pride and greed, grudge not one another different forms . . . but live in meekness, chastity, friendliness, and purity. (*Aurora* xxii, 4ff)

Richter, it seems, was not the man that Moller, his predecessor, had been, and his words did not speak to the condition of his flock.

But there appears to have been more reason than a *Ketzerbuch* to turn Richter's wrath, for Cornelius Weisner in his *Wahrhaftige Relation,* one of the early biographical materials, records an incident which gives plausibility to Richter's dislike of Boehme. Richter

> did lend to one of Jacob Boehme's nephews, a young baker, . . . one dollar . . . to buy wheat to make white bread at Christmas for which he presented him in thankfulness a good white loaf; soon after the holidays he brought the dollar . . . to him again; in hope that the preacher would . . . accept his former present in full satisfaction, as he used it only a fortnight. The preacher, unsatisfied, pronounced God's anger . . . against him and so . . . terrified the young baker . . . that he fell into . . . deep perplexity . . . and despair of his salvation . . . so that for . . . several days he spoke to no being . . . but went up and down sighing . . . Till . . . on the . . . entreaty of his wife, her uncle Jacob Boehme took the matter in hand . . . till he found what lay upon him . . . and spoke peace to him . . . and . . . went to the en-

raged preacher and . . . entreated him no longer to be angry with the young man, that he himself would satisfy the enraged preacher . . . yet thought that the poor man had paid enough . . .

Whereupon the preacher . . . broke forth saying what had that rascal [Boehme] to do with him to . . . molest and disturb him?

But he continued . . . and entreated his favor, promising to make satisfaction . . . Ashamed of his injustice . . . [the minister] would not acknowledge it . . . but showed him the outer door out of which he was to go.

The *Primate* sat on his chair and had his slippers on and when [Boehme] . . . went away, as he was going out of the door, he gave the angry *Primate* a Christian valediction, saying, God preserve your worship. The *Primate* was angry . . . , took off his slipper, and threw it . . . at the honest man saying, what have you to do, you wicked rogue, to bid me . . . a good night? . . .

Sunday morning following the preacher . . . vehemently inveyed against [Boehme] . . . and thundered abominably . . . against him by name, . . . threatening the destruction of the whole city. . . .

He admonished the magistrates . . . to be avenged against such tumultuous opposers of the holy office . . . of preaching who disturb the preacher . . . and write heretical books. . . .

Upon which the . . . falsely accused man, who sat . . . at the pillar . . . against the pulpit . . . held his peace until all the people were gone . . . staying in his seat until the preacher with his chaplain . . . went out of the vestry through the church.

He then followed and . . . in the church-yard spoke to the preacher . . . and asked what harm he had done. . . .

The preacher answered nothing but looked . . . as if he would kill him with his looks and in a rage . . . began to curse . . . , saying, Get thee from me, Satan . . . Do you not see that I am a clergyman? . . .

But the troubled . . . man gave . . . this answer: Yes, reverend Sir, I well see you are a . . . clergyman . . . and [I] esteem you . . . and I come to entreat you as a clergyman what hurt I have done you.

And turning . . . to the . . . Chaplain entreated him, saying, Reverend . . . Sir, help me in my entreaty to the preacher that he will tell . . . what I have spoken or done against him. . . .

The preacher was still more enraged. . . . He would have sent . . . a servant . . . for a city bailey to take him away and put him in prison . . . which the chaplain spoke against. . . .

Monday morning following . . . the magistrates met . . . and sent for [Boehme]; they examined him, perceived no evil in him . . . asked . . . what harm he had done the preacher? He answered he knew not, neither could he know from the preacher himself, and . . . entreated . . . that they . . . would send for the preacher and cause him to say what he had done. . . .

The Council concluded that it was just that the preacher . . . be . . . entreated to come to . . . the council house . . . to relate those grievances . . .

Whereupon he was enraged and sent . . . word [asking] what had he to do with the council house . . . he would speak . . . from the pulpit . . . they should banish the vain, wicked heretic from the city . . .

The Lords consulted and could not find how they should justly help the master, fearing the vehemence of the preacher in his pulpit, and concluded to banish . . . Boehme . . . , in which conclusion some . . . would not consent, but rose and went their way . . . The executioner . . . caused the uncondemned, faithful citizen . . . to be instantly banished out of the gates.

. . . The patient man . . . answered . . . 'My lords, I will do as you command and depart . . . but may I not go to my house first and take mine along with me . . . ?' But they forbade it . . . , saying they could not alter the sentence . . . Then he said, 'Dear sirs, let it be done, seeing it cannot be otherwise. I am content.' So he was banished and gone away at night . . .

The following morning, when the council were met, and had reconciled their disagreement they made another conclusion: to hunt the . . . man, and sent up and down . . . and at length found him and brought him solemnly with honor into the city again.[28]

This account, here stripped of its unnecessary verbiage, may represent the melting together of three different episodes in Boehme's life: 1) the episode of the young baker nephew and Richter; 2) Richter's denunciation of Boehme from the pulpit; 3) Boehme's banishment. There are, fortunately, other sources for the second and third episodes, for July 28, 1613, Burgomaster Scultetus wrote in his *Diarum* that Jacob Boehme, the shoemaker, who lived between the gates behind the hostel, had been brought to the *Rathaus* for examination, that he was questioned about his beliefs, that he was thereupon put in the stocks, and that as soon as Oswald [Krause] had fetched the quarto book from Boehme's house he was released and advised to leave off such things.[29] This was Friday. Sunday, which happened to be the eighth Sunday after Trinity when the Gospel lesson deals with false prophets who come garbed as sheep, Richter preached a sharp sermon against Boehme. Tuesday, July 30, Scultetus records that Boehme was brought to the manse, vigorously questioned about his beliefs, and warned not to continue writing.[30] In *Epist.* xii, 12, Boehme says that in 1613, when he was called before the Görlitz Senate, he wrote an answer to Richter's attacks. This answer has been lost.

This seems to have been the sequence of events. Inasmuch as Boehme was banished in 1624, Weisner's account may be confused, although he may have been banished twice.

In any event Gregory Richter's sharp attack on Boehme was a decisive factor in his development, one which gave him an increasing dissatisfaction with institutional religion. Also his writing brought him trouble; the manuscript of the *Aurora* was confiscated and it circulated only in copies which were not accurate. Boehme said that he

> saw this first book no more in three years: I supposed that it was . . . gone until a certain learned man sent me some copies . . . who exhorted me to proceed and manifest my talent, to which the outward reason would by no means agree, because it had suffered so much already . . . ; moreover the spirit was . . . weak and timorous . . . ; my light was for a good while withdrawn from me and it did glow in me as a hidden fire so that I felt nothing but anguish and perplexity within me, and outwardly I found nothing but contempt; and inwardly a fiery instigation. (*Epist.* xii, 13)

NOTES TO CHAPTER THREE

1. *Ratsprotokol,* July 24, 1604. Cf. Jecht, *Böhme,* p. 23.
2. *Ibid.,* April 29, 1606, May 2, 1606. Cf. Jecht, *Böhme,* pp. 23, 24.
3. Jecht, *Böhme,* p. 23.
4. *Ibid.,* p. 27.
5. *Görlitzer Kaufbuch,* 1605ff. Bl. 186a. Cf. Jecht, *Böhme,* p. 10.
6. *Ibid.,* Bl. 45b. Cf. Jecht, *Böhme,* p. 12.
7. *Ibid.,* p. 10.
8. *Ibid.,* p. 24.
9. *Görlitzer Kaufbuch,* 1605ff., Bl. 45b. Cf. Jecht, *Böhme,* p. 12.
10. Neumann, *Geschichte von Görlitz,* p. 367.
11. Franckenberg, *De Vita . . . ,* #12.
12. The text is as follows: LAUS DEO! LAUS DEO! LAUS DEO! Den 25 August half Gott der Herr, der rechte Augustus, dass die Rottgerber mit Schanden ihren hochweisen, übernatürlichen samt ihren Helfershelfern geschmiedeten, unauflöslichen, wie sie condeten, Abschied wieder ein antworten mussten und den erkaufte Rauleder aus den Häusern in ihr Gerbehaus mussten folgen lassen; deren waren 332, so wir, die Schuhmacher, zu Lemberg bei einem Kauf- und Handelsmann kaufften das Stück pro 2 Thaler und 2 Argent. Wurde getheilet und gezahlet. Gott sei ewig Lob! Hans Bürger und Jakob Bem kaufften solche Leder zu Lemberg, waren trefflichen Leder, also dass wir, Gott Lob, den Schaden und Jammer vergessen cunnten, den uns die Gerber gemacht hatten. Wurden gegerbet schön und gut hernach getheilet, dafür wir Gott danken! Cf. Jecht, *Böhme,* p. 23.
13. Jecht, *Böhme,* pp. 23, 24, 28.
14. B. Scultetus, *Kirchenwesen,* Varia 98, Ratsarchiv 238. Quoted by Jecht, *Böhme,* p. 24.
15. *Cambridge Modern History,* III, p. 735.
16. The Ms differs in title from the printed versions. Imperfect versions based on Ender's copy have been printed. The text of the 1730 edition follows the autograph, and Barker's English translation and reprint does not.
17. In Boehme's day astrology meant science generally.
18. Johann Arndt dabbled in astrology. See the fourth book of his *True Christianity, Mysterium Incarnationis.*
19. This star was still being discussed in 1641. Cf. Peuckert, *Die Rosenkreutzer,* p. 55ff.
20. Franckenberg, *De Vita . . . ,* #3.

21. Heckel, *Geschichte der deutschen Literatur in Schlesien,* p. 164.
22. Richter may have been roughly handled by the Boehmdists. Jecht believes that Richter was a competent, good, and kindly man. Cf. *Böhme,* p. 32ff.
23. Jecht, *Böhme,* p. 61.
24. *Ibid.,* pp. 32–33.
25. Scultetus wrote that Richter had been examined on August 1, 1604, about the quality of his sermons.
26. Jecht, *Böhme,* p. 33.
27. Jechner, *Leben . . .* pp. xlivff.
28. Weisner, *Wahrhaftiger Relation,* #28. Translation modernized from the *Remainder of the Books,* London, 1662. Koyrè holds the episode apocryphal. Cf. *Boehme,* p. 17, note 1.
29. Jecht, *Böhme,* p. 36.
30. Cf. G. Köhler, Görlitzer Wegweiser, 1635, #45. Also Neumann, *Geschichte von Görlitz,* p. 392.

Nur hoffe, wart, und beit,
Es ist noch eine kleine Zeit,
Bis Teufels Reich darnieder leit.
—QUOTED BY BOEHME, *Aurora*, xiv, 107

CHAPTER FOUR

THE *AURORA:* 1612

WHAT SORT of book was it that made such a stir, bringing down on Boehme's head this storm of condemnation? Was it, as Carl von Ender thought, a work of promise and exciting anticipation which the thirty-six-year-old shoemaker had written? Was it really an aurora, a sunrise to eternity?

The *Aurora* is a primitive, profound, chaotic, exasperating, prophetic work of cant and rant as well as of insight and of revelation. It clings to antiquated ideas and yet shows knowledge of Copernican theories and of the circulation of the blood. Brilliant and dull, a hodgepodge of promise and of fulfillment, it shows the Renaissance search for modernity alongside of a valuation of antiquity.

Boehme later called it a work of his "spiritual childhood" (*Epist.* xii, 56), written without full reason by some sort of "magical" consciousness, and the book's structure supports this. It is ungainly, unorganized, incomplete, and revolving around two focal points which rarely meet. It consists of twenty-six chapters, the first eight of which clearly show that they were to have formed a complete work by themselves, and which may have been written before 1612. The Preface was added much later because it mentions the second and third books.

Although the scope and organization of this book may be primitive, the problems which Boehme's mystical intuition proposed were not; they were among the most perplexing of religious philosophy. Koyré suggests that the problem was that of evil and of God's relationship to the world. Boehme formulated this in three questions: 1) that of freedom being manifested in being; 2) that of spirit expressing itself in body; and 3) that of the double necessity of dialectic[1] both in being and in thought. This resulted in a living God of whom nature and man's soul are emanations, in a living world containing the hidden God. Both posit the same problem: how, if God is good, is He the source of all; and if evil is so visibly present in man's soul, how can God also dwell therein.[2]

Boehme also got knowledge from his experience of 1600—the insight that good and evil are in all things. This insight both posited his problems and pointed towards their solution. The *Aurora's* solution was more pantheistic than mystical unless one concedes that mysticism may be a speculative metaphysics which changes outer into inner, historical into eternal, and natural and historical processes into the generation of the gods.[3] Thus conceived, Boehme's pantheizing in the *Aurora* constitutes his first effort at metaphysics, showing his kinship with Renaissance nature-philosophy whose chief idea was the divine unity of the living all.[4] Boehme discloses no cleft between thought and life: evil is not the absence of good. In the *Aurora* it is physical and moral, essentially necessary but existentially irrational. To probe the source, the *Quell,* of nature's dualism he could have become a Manichean; his evil was earth-bound. If he thought of this solution his piety rejected it; the God that he had met in Martin Moller's conventicle could not thus be retained. In the *Aurora* two tendencies collided, creating an empirical dialectic: the one was the piety of resignation and selflessness traditional to German mysticism; the other was Neoplatonic naturalism. The former came to Boehme by way of Moller from Eckhart,[5] Tauler, Suso, Mechthild,[6] the Ebners, Nicolas of Strassburg, the *Theologia Germanica,* Luther, and Schwenkfeld.[7] One form of mysticism was absent—the Dionysian search for the names of God. The other tendency came to Boehme from Platonism, Neo-Platonism, and from Renaissance philosophy by way of the humanists of Silesia. In the *Aurora* the primary problem was the reconciliation of the pantheizing tendencies of the one with the supranaturalistic dualism of the other; Luther's devil, the target of a loaded inkwell, was not at home in a Plotinian world:

> The learned have had many disputations, questions, and opinions about grim evil in all this world's creatures, in the sun as well as the stars; moreover there are some very poisonous beasts, serpents, and growths in this world. Therefore rationalists have preemptorily concluded . . . that God has also willed evil because he has made so much evil. (*Aurora,* xvi, 28)

This is Boehme's problem, the old problem of theodicy,—the impetus of his thought in the *Aurora* where he seeks but never finds a solution. Though he believed that he had the true answer, none here was presented. He emphatically denied that God had made evil; was it not the devil who

> taught men sorcery and witchcraft . . . Come on, ye jugglers . . . you who go a-wooing and a-whoring after the devil. Come to my school. I will show you how . . . you are carried into hell . . . Poor man did not fall because of a resolved . . . will but through the poisonous infection of the devil. . . . (*Aurora,* xvi, 1, 3; xvii, 38)

The *Aurora* then was not theology for its author sought to know the world, its being and becoming, its divine birth. He wanted to know how in a divinely created world, evil, wrathful nature came to be. Here he was not yet focused on redemption, on the removal of that evil; but he looked, searched, probed, inspected; he was, in short, a metaphysician. However, as the *Aurora* was unfinished, such matters may have been reserved for the end of the book; no solution was even broached and so the fragment is a pansophic book which seeks the wisdom of the all within nature:

> What still remains hidden? Christ's true teaching? No; but the philosophy and God's deep ground, the heavenly joy, the revelation of angelic creation, the revelation of the devil's gruesome fall from which evil comes, the creation of this world, the deep ground and mystery of man and all the creatures in this world, the youngest judgment and the transmu-

tation of this world, the mystery of the resurrection of the dead, and eternal life. (*Aurora,* ix, 8)

These Boehme sought to disclose because he believed that a new vision of eternal nature had been given him. Nature was a book containing the "great mystery" (*Epist.* x, 36) and to reveal this hidden God was his aim. To do this the arrogant, self-centered nature was not adequate; the Holy Spirit was wanted (*Aurora* ii, 13) as the same divine Spirit is both in God and within eternal nature which is His "body."

. . . in nature all qualities are in one another as one quality in the way and manner that God is all and how all comes from and proceeds from Him; God is the heart or source of nature; from Him all comes. (*Aurora* i, 6)

Those who propose to search God's being in nature must be enlightened by the Holy Spirit for this Spirit is in God, in nature, and in man (*Aurora* i, 16–18). Though good and evil are in all things, in God there is only good (*Aurora* ii, 63); so evil cannot come from God. It

has in God no substance . . . He is a spirit in whom all powers are (*Aurora,* ii, 69) . . . If God should be angry with Himself then all nature would be afire. (ii, 64)

God was here the coincidence of contraries where contrasts are reconciled—the One. He was unity, an idea, the consequences of which were theodicy and "negative theology." How the harmony and joy of God's inner being became the divided natural world is Boehme's problem.

The *Aurora* was an original work in that it raised questions without bringing answers and in that Boehme did not accept the false identification of evil with nonbeing. For him evil was in positive and powerful struggle with good, a struggle which begat life. Resolution is victory but victory was less satisfying than struggle—*in der Ueberwindung ist Freude!* (*Myst. Mag.,* xvi, 6) And perhaps Boehme's *Aurora* was more struggle than victory, more an effort to overcome the irrationalities of his vision than final delineation of his own matured philosophy.

Boehme was held by an ancient antimony: God and the world should both be united and apart. God, however, can be put so far beyond the world as to be out of it, or so much in it as to be one with it. At first Boehme struggled with deistic transcendence in the earlier years, and this struggle bore him his "illumination." Later he struggled with immanence in *Bedenk. Stief.* and *Irrth. Stief.* He made two solutions: from the world to God during his alchemical period, and from the soul to God during the period of his maturity. Neither of these solutions is present in the *Aurora.*

Boehme saw good and evil struggling in all qualities, a struggle of contraries which was nonexistent in God (*Aurora* ii, 35), angels, or demons. These had but one quality. Man stood between good and evil, able to choose.

Here Boehme's characteristic idea of quality appears: the Holy Spirit "qualifies" the good while Lucifer "qualifies" evil. This struggle assumed special meaning for Boehme for the conflict is endured within nature too, for good and evil stand there in contradiction; he conceived of *Qualität* as *ein quellende Kraft,* a surging vitality.

Here man must consider what the word quality means . . . A quality is the mobility, surging, or drive of a thing. (*Aurora* i, 3)

It is an egressive energy, an inherent libido—to use a modern term—an urge much like Bergson's *élan vital,*[8] a "power of life" (*Aurora* i, 6). In the *Aurora* Boehme adopted the four qualities of Galen and medieval medicine: heat and cold, bitter and sweet. To these he added sour and salt. Heat burns and also illuminates, thus combining fierceness and light in an internal dialectic, operating within nature to warm all reality (*Aurora* i). Light opposes heat's fierce rage, allaying it; it is likewise made of two activities: the power to reduce heat and the power to freeze to immobility. From heat and light come two elements, air and water, the former chiefly from heat and the latter from cold. Between them life is created. The bitter attracts the air's water and makes the earth's vegetables, dissipating evil and producing a joy (*Aurora,* i, 30) wherein the Holy Spirit works; yet, at the same time, if it be too preponderant, it contains a house of death (*Aurora* i). Sweet opposes the bitter, tempers all creatures, makes them pleasant, causes vegetables to be fragrant, tasty, yellow, ruddy, is a source of divine meekness; although when it dominates it breeds disease, plagues, pestilence, corruption, and fermentation (*Aurora* i). Sour opposes both bitter and sweet and it is the flowing vitality in all things in which spirit dwells (*Aurora* i, 38); also, however, when it predominates it begets melancholy, putridness, and sadness. Salt is the bitter's good temper which opposes bitterness and makes things pleasant as a pleasant life-source; but it makes for hardness, producing scabs, sores, pox, and a "mourning house of death."

Boehme, possessing a smattering of medical knowledge, here was seeking adequate psychological terms to describe the inner life; also, he was convinced of the relationship between physical and psychological states. These qualities[9] were really spiritual modes and, writing before modern subjective language had been created, he was searching for terms to describe the substantial as well as spiritual character of reality. This suggests one of the dominant motives of Boehme's thought: the effort to find correspondence between God, nature, and human nature. This "great analogy," as Schleiermacher called it,[10] was conceived substantially:

> If you will not believe that in this world all descends . . . from the stars, I will demonstrate it to you, if you are not a blockhead . . . (*Aurora* ii, 52) If not, it will be . . . with you as with the wise heathen, who gazed . . . at creation, and would . . . sift it with their ego-centric reason; and though with their fictions . . . (*Dichten*) they came before God's countenance, yet they were not able to see it, but were stark blind. . . . (*Aurora* ii, 21)

Nature was for him God's body; He was the all in All; reading nature's mystery gave knowledge of God. And man, chief of created beings, was made in God's image and anatomical allegorization revealed all nature: the abdomen signified the deep between the stars and the earth while the whole body signified the entire heaven and earth. Flesh was earth, blood water, breath air, the heart fire. The head, seat of the mind, signifies heaven and contains the "astral principle" as well as the five senses (*Aurora* ii, 19ff). Boehme enjoins the reader to open here the "eyes of the spirit" and see the Creator. His interest in this great analogy was to the minutest detail. Each created form was an analogy to the divine world. As all things existed in fire, air, and water they had a threefold meaning.

> Everything in the world has become a similitude of the trinity . . . Thus you find three fountain-heads in man: first the vitality in your whole mind which signifies God the Father; then the light in your whole mind which enlightens the mind and which signifies the Son. And thirdly there goes forth from all your vitalities, and out of your light too, an understanding Spirit. (*Aurora* iii, 36, 41–42)

Boehme saw this ternary in all created things (*Aurora* iii, 101) but man is made of nature's pith while beasts are made of nature's wilder nature. This threefoldness dwells in (*einwohnt*) all nature (*Aurora* xiv, 91) and Boehme believed that natural insight was therefore also divine insight, the vision he himself had attained in his illumination. He felt compelled to communicate this analogy between nature and God:

> When one considers all nature and its properties he then sees the Father; when one beholds heaven and the stars then he sees His eternal energy and wisdom . . . All the vitalities in nature come from God the Father; all light, heat, cold, air, water; and all earth's vitalities, bitter, sour, sweet, astringent, hard, soft, and more . . . all begin from the Father. (*Aurora* iii, 8–9)

God does not dwell in a transcendent heaven nor is he shut off from His creation. He is the generator, begetter, creator, the beginning beyond whom and before whom there is nothing. The Son is the source of joy (*Aurora* iii, 23). God is symbolized in nature, but more than symbolized for he is nature and yet He is more than nature.

> Now I will show you a similitude. Look at heaven which is a round sphere having neither beginning nor end but is everywhere beginning and end; so also is God in and above the heaven having neither beginning nor end . . . The stars denote the Father's various energies and wisdom . . . Now the whole deep between the stars along with the earth signify the Father . . . The seven planets signify the seven spirits of God . . . The sun goes around in the deep between the stars in a round curve; it is the heart of the stars, giving light and energy to all the stars . . . Even so is God's Son . . . the Father's heart. (*Aurora* iii, 18–21)

In the *Aurora* this kind of symbolism does not yet go beyond the pantheist's identification of God and the world and as the initial urge to Boehme's speculation had been dissatisfaction with deist separation of heaven and earth, so here in the *Aurora* he expresses this in an image which is close to pantheism, an image which links God and the world by symbolic conjunction and union.

This "great analogy" either is tomfoolery or else it has meaning in a metaphysical sense in the same fashion that Thomas Aquinas, opposing Maimonides,[11] taught knowledge of God by analogy. Boehme, however, asserted that God dwelt beyond analogy[12] because he was not the aethereal deep: He is *like* the heavens but He is not the heavens. His Christ was *like* the sun, but He was not the sun. This analogy interpenetrates all reality.

> In wood, stone, and herbs are three things and nothing can be born or grow if one of the three be left out. First there is the vitality from which a body comes, be it wood, stone, or herbs; then there is juice in the same which is its heart; thirdly, there is therein an up-surging energy, smell, or taste which is the thing's spirit and by which it increases and grows . . . So you find the similitude of the Trinity in the Divine Being and in all things, look wherever you will. . . . (*Aurora* iii, 47–48)

The trinitarian image therefore inhabits all reality and this is the key to God's power over the world. The Father, moreover, is the organic as well as the psychic vitality of all reality and the pattern of its essential structure. The Son is consciousness, life, rational being. The Spirit is the living essence, life's support. Not only has the world been generated by God, not only has He borne it, but it also expresses His inner nature and all creatures are patterns of His threefold being. Yet in some passages Boehme seems to suggest that only the Father is God and that a cleft has appeared between Him and the other forms of life. This, however, presages a profounder solution yet to come, his idea of the *Ungrund.*

The order of creation is thus explained in a passage which, like so many in Boehme, is hard to put into English.[13]

> From God's vitalities the heavens came; from the heavens came the stars; from the stars the elements, from the elements the earth and the creatures. So everything had its beginning. . . . (*Aurora* ii, 44)

The difficult word is vitality.

So Boehme's general point of view is clear from the *Aurora's* opening chapters: God is in the natural world. Having reacted against barren deism in his basic experience, he was pitched into deeper difficulties; in one sense God was both nature and the cosmos but in another sense he was neither because He was "beyond nature and creature." Yet this transcendent God has manifested his threefold structure within nature which he also inhabits (*einwohnt*), thus becoming both source and synthesis. The world has come from Him, exhibits His inner nature, and returns to Him again. At each step God has expressed himself by intermediaries. These sensible symbols, material or spiritual, are expressions of God, admittedly spatial symbols the final overtones of which are noumenal.[14]

The *Aurora's* first eight chapters form a complete book, even to a final Amen! The ninth chapter begins in a new mood, speaking of the dawn of the day when man no longer may sleep, when the proud shall be humbled and the lowly exalted! A new note has been added—the prophetic—and Boehme's style becomes repetitious, wandering, and centered in two foci: explanation of his nature philosophy and deep-grounded Christian piety. Here the basic "rift" in his consciousness appears, one that separated his metaphysics from his devotion, the tension between reason and passion. He starts, stops, starts again, following no orderly road as in the first eight chapters. He begins one theme only to break into another. Like the psychoanalyst's patient there comes a point where his mind jumps and the flow of his ideas is broken off. All his works from the *Aurora's* eighth chapter to *Sig. Rer.* reveal this schizoid character.[15]

The cause of this rift is clear. It was the harsh treatment he had gotten from Gregory Richter, pastor of the Görlitz church. Boehme's prophetic denunciations, his holy discontent with institutional religion, produced a divided heart: he could not forget his vision nor could he forgo the piety he had learned from Martin Moller. So the *Aurora* was perhaps not meant to be finished, remaining an incomplete, preliminary, provisional statement. No higher synthesis could yet appear: repetitions occur, the story of the three realms being told three times (xii, 17ff, xv, 26ff, xxii, 11ff). One new idea does creep in, one which later becomes important, that of the seven qualities of the divine nature. Here the influence of the Jewish Cabala is apparent [16] and so his connection with Jewish traditions is already evident.[17]

But the *Aurora* remains a hodgepodge reworking of one central theme, the manifestation of God within the world, showing deep insight into nature philosophy on the one hand and breathing living religious spirit on the other, promise of a twice-born man struggling towards solution of one of man's profoundest problems.

NOTES TO CHAPTER FOUR

1. Dialectic is used in meaning E in André Lalande, *Vocabulaire Technique et Critique de la Philosophie*, Paris, 1951, p. 227.
2. Koyré, Boehme, p. 72. I am heavily indebted to Koyré's brilliant analysis of the *Aurora.*
3. Cf. Windelband, *A History of Philosophy*, p. 366. This definition agrees with Schleiermacher in the *Reden:* "It does not arise from being sated and overladen by external influences, but, on every occasion, some secret power ever drives the man

back upon himself, and he finds himself to be the plan and key of the whole. Convinced by a great analogy and a daring faith that it is not necessary to forsake himself, but that the spirit has enough in itself to be conscious of all that could be given from without, by a free resolve, he shuts his eyes forever against all that is not himself." (Oman's translation, London, 1893, pp. 133–134). Here the Peripatetic-Stoic doctrine of analogy between macrocosm and microcosm is the "great analogy." In the Renaissance this doctrine was revived by Weigel and Paracelsus.

4. Windelband, *op. cit.*, p. 367.
5. Eckhart was not yet known as a name although his ideas were in Tauler and others.
6. Cf. A. M. Heiler, *Mystik Deutscher Frauen im Mittelalter*, Berlin 1929.
7. Some of Tauler's prayers were in Moller's *Meditationes sanctorum patrum, Vide: Bornkamm, Luther und Böhme,* p. 77.
8. *Vide:* Jacques Chevalier, *Bergson*, Paris, 1926, pp. 192, 193, 221.
9. Boehme's use of quality bears no relation to the word's usual philosophical use. *Vide:* "Qualité" in Lalande, *Vocabulaire* . . .
10. See note number 3.
11. Cf. R. L. Patterson, *The Conception of God in the Philosophy of Aquinas.* London, 1933, pp. 227ff.
12. This idea of analogy was found in Babylon and India. Cf. H. Olderberg, *Die Weltanschauung der Brahmantexte*, Göttingen, 1919; also, Conger, *Microcosmos und Macrocosmos*, New York, 1923; E. Cassirer, *Das Erkenntnisproblem in der Philosophie und Wissenschaft der neueren Zeit*, Berlin, 1911, pp. 200-244.
13. The difficulty is not with the words but with their meaning. Here the only difficult word is *Kräften*, but what does it really mean? Energy, vitality, power? Is it to be translated in vitalistic terms?
14. See part two for discussion of the symbols.
15. The books become increasingly coherent as he matured and a solution is finally achieved.
16. Koyré, *Boehme*, p. 126.
17. During this period knowledge of the Cabala was not unusual. Reuchlin's works were available for those unable to read the Hebrew, and it was not hard to find someone who had read him. Agrippa von Nettesheim and Paracelsus were also well known. In his later works Boehme even used the word Cabala twice (*Theos. Frag.* iii, 34, vi, 11).

But is not solitude, too, a gate? Is there not at times discovered, in stillest loneliness, an unsuspected perception? Can concern with oneself not mysteriously be transformed into concern with the mystery?

—MARTIN BUBER, *I and Thou*

CHAPTER FIVE

PERIOD OF SILENCE: 1612–1619

THE YEAR 1612 was, then, the turning point. Boehme had become an author. But other events were taking place, too. In 1611 his mother had died, and on March 12, 1613, he sold his shoemaker's bench to Georg Süssenbachen for four hundred seventy marks,[1] the value of his business having doubled since 1599. In spite of the two recorded borrowings of thirty-six marks, November 19, 1605, and of fifty marks, November 16, 1610, his business seems to have been well-managed.[2] Upon selling his shoemaker's bench he was engaged in the linen and wool business in the interests of which he made yearly journeys to Prague and perhaps to the Leipzig Fair.[3] He is known to have bought woolen gloves from the farmers and sold them at retail.[4] But times were worsening. In 1566 the *Thaler* had been worth sixty-eight crowns; in 1614 it was worth ninety-two; and in 1618, one hundred eighty-six.[5] War inflation and paper currency became prevalent; the rulers sought funds by any means: Emperor Matthias tried to boil gold and was searching his destiny in the stars.[6] This economic instability was mirrored in an incident of October 10, 1616, when Catharina Boehme, with seventeen other women, was prohibited from trading cotton yarn in the Görlitz streets. Fourteen days later Boehme was himself punished for the same offense.[7] He was not forbidden to trade in yarn, but only to peddle it from house to house as the free and open selling of yarn was a privilege of free merchants.[8]

As long as times were good and trade was moving freely Boehme was prosperous; but crop failures, inflation, devaluation of monies, and the miserable plague undermined business. Carl von Ender became Boehme's patron and began to send him provisions.[9] Rudolf von Gersdorf and Augustin Cöppin sent him food.[10] Near the end of 1618 Boehme's father passed away and he shared the inheritance.[11] In 1620, probably in return for permission to copy manuscripts, Boehme received money from Christian Bernhard, but as early as 1613 times of scarcity had arrived (*Epist.* xxxiv, 6) and Boehme could read the signs, for he knew that wars, uproars, calamities, and death were to come. The systematic deterioration of currency by the kippers and wippers, as they were called, almost brought an insurrection among the lower classes.[12]

For Boehme, however, economic considerations were no longer basic. He was established well enough as a substantial burgher with a widening literary fame. Frankenberg relates:

One day there came a stranger to his door, . . . little in stature, cunning in look, and quick in . . . understanding. After an overture of civilities he began by acquainting Jacob Boehme that, whereas he had been informed of his being endued with a singular spirit, such as is not to be met with in common, and it was incumbent . . . to let his neighbors share in the good which had been communicated to himself; he, . . . Jacob Boehme, should do him the favor of bestowing the same singular spirit upon him, . . . making it over to him . . . for a sum of money. Upon which . . . Jacob Boehme . . . gave the man to understand that he . . . esteemed himself . . . unworthy of the supposed extraordinary gifts and arts . . . that he could lay claim to nothing more than a life and conversation grounded upon . . . faith in God and brotherly love to his neighbor . . . that he was as little acquainted as he was fond of any singular . . . spirit. But that, if he would needs be possessed of a spirit, he must take the . . . same course . . . , repent of his sins, fervently imploring the heavenly Spirit of grace . . . in which case He would surely give it to him. Which advice the poor . . . creature was so far from taking, that without much ado . . . he wanted to exhort the . . . familiar spirit out of . . . Boehme till he . . . , chagrined, caught hold of him full in the face . . . Upon which the conjurer, trembling and astonished, begged pardon, which made . . . Boehme remit his zeal. . . .[13]

Boehme's increasing fame began to break in upon his inner life; no longer was he the solitary and lonely man of single vision; his *Aurora* was quietly circulating and his name was being admiringly whispered.

After the confiscation of this first book and the Town Council's ban on further writing he endured a "full sabbath of years" (*Apol. Richt.* 69) in silence. This was indeed that significant period of dryness characteristic of mysticism, that dismal desert before the oasis of splendor which was to follow. He felt that he could not work because the breath of the Most High (*Epist.* xii, 13) had been withdrawn. Moreover

After the persecution I proposed to do nothing further but to keep myself still in God and let the devil roar . . . But it went with me as with a grain sown in the earth which grows unreasonably in all storm and tempest . . . My outward man did not want to write more, for it was quite timorous . . . And even then the Great Mystery appeared: then I understood God's counsel and cast myself upon His Will, wanting neither to think or dream according to reason . . . placing my will in God's will so that my will would be dead. . . . (*Epist.* x, 6ff)

A "fiery instigation" was leading him.

During these years of silence Boehme probably wrote the strange preface to the *Aurora*, perhaps in 1615, possibly later. This was an allegory of history and Boehme gave himself a place in the spirit's descent. The Pope had been a merchant who had been opposed not because he sold holy wares but because his wares were not holy:

Now the merchant, seeing . . . that his false wares were discovered, grew very angry . . . and bent his bow against the holy people . . . and destroyed many, and blasphemed the green twig that was grown out of the tree of life. But then the great Prince Michael . . . came and fought for the holy people, and overcame. (*Aurora, Preface,* 59)

Luther's reformation had succeeded.

The Boehme who had written the *Aurora* was no unlettered peasant and shoemaker who had spun his conceits out of vision-stuff; there was, indeed, somewhat of the Faust in him; and he claims to have read contemporary science. In fact, already in 1612 he knew of the circulation of the blood (*Aurora* ii, 7), and was conversant with Copernican ideas (*Aurora* xxv, 43), but he was searching for other treasures. Moreover, he was a humble man who underplayed his learning.

I can neither say anything of myself, nor boast . . . ; I am a simple man . . . a poor sinner, and have need to pray daily, Lord, forgive our sins. . . . (*Aurora,* preface)

Nevertheless, he was well and perhaps even deeply read in contemporary scientific and theological literature according to his own testimony:

I have read the writings of the high masters . . . but I have found nothing but a half dead spirit. (*Aurora* x, 27)

Further:

I understand the . . . meanings . . . and I have perused their writings also, and taken notice how they describe the course of the sun and stars, neither do I despise it, but . . . hold that . . . good and right . . . I do not have my knowledge from study . . . I have read the order and position of the seven planets . . . and find them to be very right. (*Aurora* xxv, 43ff)

The novelty of their science did not disturb his calm confidence in his mystical experience of 1600 and he was not deterred in searching for the key of all knowledge, a *religious* key:

I do not know how to measure their circles: I take no great care about that. . . .

(He here rejects the mathematical analysis of reality)

> However, they will have so much to learn that many will not comprehend the ground . . . all the days of their lives. I have no use for their tables, formulae, schemes, rules . . . I have another teacher . . . total nature. From . . . nature . . . have I learned my philosophy . . . and theology. For . . . in the most part they stand upon the right ground, and I will diligently endeavor to go according to their rules and formulae . . . Their scheme of formulation is my master; from it I have the first elements of my knowledge, and it is not my purpose to controvert or amend . . . but rather to leave them where they are. I will not . . . build upon their ground, but . . . I will dig away the earth from the root, that . . . men may see the whole tree with its root, stock, branches, twigs, and fruits, and . . . that their philosophy and my philosophy are one body, one tree, bearing one and the same fruit. (*Aurora* xxii, 10–15)

So Boehme was already writing in 1612, and this statement must surely be qualified by consideration of his later writings. Examining them, however, we learn that during this sabbath of years he learned more than "first principles" from contemporary science; he learned also to hate arrogant, self-sufficient, impious learning and to distrust the capacity of human reason:

> I bring in no complaints against them . . . , condemn them for anything, except for their wickedness and abominations, as pride, covetousness, envy, and wrath, against which the spirit of nature complains . . . and not I. . . . They walk up and down in their drunkenness, seeking the key, when they have it about them and they know it not, . . . like the country man looking for his horse who all the while he was looking for him was riding on the back of that very horse. . . . What could I . . . poor . . . layman, write of their high art if it were not given me by the spirit of nature in whom I live and am? (*Aurora* xii, 16ff)

Boehme was then not a vision-snatching shoemaker illuminated by a quick gleam from a pewter dish—this is indeed the Boehme myth! Already in 1612, in the same work in which he first described his experience, he affirms his understanding of contemporary science. But he rejected its mathematical basis, asserting that insight was more germane. This is an astonishing claim.

In any event, how did Boehme come to such knowledge? And the answer appears plain: he received from his Silesian neighbors, as Silesia and especially Görlitz itself became, after 1580, a center of "alchemy," especially among physicians whose affinities were Schwenkfeldian.[14] In 1589 Elias Schadeus had brought together the Silesian Schwenkfelders and the Paracelsians.[15] The following were leaders: Balthasar Flöter and Francis Kretschmeyer in Sagan; Johann Huser and Paul Linck in Glogau; Marcius Ambrosius in Neisse.[16] Görlitz was the center of a larger group: Christopher Manlius, Johann Rothe, Balthasar Walter, Tobias Kober, Michael Kurtz, and the burgomaster Scultetus.[17] Alchemists in a metaphysical sense only, these men were philosophers whose "first principles" were from Renaissance Neoplatonism as proclaimed by Reuchlin and Paracelsus.[18]

The man who mediated Paracelsus to Boehme was his friend and physician, Tobias Kober of Görlitz. Of an old family, Kober had attended the Görlitz gymnasium and then the university in Basel.[19] Later he wrote *Observationes Castrenses.*[20] The intimacy of the letters Boehme wrote to Kober from Dresden in 1624 show the close personal friendship which existed between them; indeed, while Boehme was in Dresden, Kober cared for his family, and when Boehme died Kober was executor of his will and took care of Boehme's widow and the children.[21]

Another *sonderbare alchemist und adeptus* was Johann Rothe, Boehme's close friend, a student of Tauler, medieval mysticism, and Johann Arndt.[22] Michael Kurtz, *medicinae canditatus et practicus,* and Dr. Kober's assistant, composed a eulogy on Boehme.[23] These physicians were within the immediate circle of Boehme's friends. Burgomaster Scultetus was a Paracelsian who, with Johann Huser of Glogau, edited an edition of Paracelsus; and Huser's son Johann was the addressee of Boehme's *Epist.* xlvii.

So in close association with Boehme were these people who were well-acquainted with contemporary scholarship.

And in this galaxy, one star shines brightly: Balthasar Walther.[24] He had been in Görlitz as early as 1587 and several entries in burgomaster Scultetus' *Diarium* prove Walther's close association with the Görlitz Paracelsians.[25] Between 1592 and 1599 he had traveled into Poland, Wallachia, Greece, Syria, and Egypt, and upon his return publishing an account of his journey which he dedicated to Scultetus and to Sebastian Hoffmann, the Schwenkfeldian lord of nearby Hennersdorf.[26] Walther became acquainted with Boehme in 1617, spending three months in Boehme's house the following year,[27] having been introduced to Boehme probably by Carl von Ender, Hoffmann's nephew.[28] In 1620 he became director of the chemical laboratory in Dresden and personal physician to the Prince of Anhalt.[29] In 1622 he was in Lüneburg where he got to know the north German "lovers of wisdom." [30] In 1624, in association with Morsius, he published a book in Lübeck along with other works.[31] He was Boehme's most learned intimate friend, entirely typical of the times, dabbling in the occult arts and somewhat of a theologian.

What did Walther teach Boehme during these three months? In the 1652 edition of some of Boehme's works which is said to have been edited by Gregory Richter's son Gregory there is a reference to the subjects discussed. It is there said that Boehme's philosophical globe, a part of *Seel. Frag.*, came from these conversations and that Walther had gotten it from Reuchlin.[32] And surely in Reuchlin's *De Arta Cabalistica* there is such a globe. So Boehme learned the Cabala from Walther, for the *Aurora* shows little if any allusion to Jewish mysticism; moreover, Boehme knew merely the contents of the Cabala, the name came later. And Walther gave Boehme the androgynous Adam Cadmon of the Cabala and the *En-sof* or *Ungrund*,[33] neither of which ideas is in the *Aurora*. Walther may also have brought occult materials to Boehme, for in *Gnad.* xi, 21, Boehme mentions the *Fourth Book of Ezra*, a popular Cabalist work.[34]

C. G. Jung's *Psychologie und Alchemie* [35] brings significant psychological insight to bear on the meaning of Boehme's interest in alchemy and Hermetic philosophy. When the Church, he says, by formalism of rite and dogma, separated itself from the roots of doctrine in the unconscious, alchemy sought to bridge the gap to nature again, to the unconscious. The old planetary gods became fate-components of the *spiritus mettalorum.*[36] Hermetic philosophy and alchemy led consciousness back to knowledge of the *Heimarmene,*[37] that is, back to temporal natural forces, giving place for the projection of psychical archetypes which do not appear in more rational Christian processes. This is why alchemy has stood on the border line of heresy; this is why Gregory Richter was enraged when he suspected Boehme of writing alchemical books. Dr. Jung concludes that alchemy represents the projection of the unconsciousness and that the naive *opus* in the laboratories, which Boehme disclaimed, was not the alchemists' goal and that, as Boehme wrote, goldmakers are deceiving themselves. So, *aurum nostrum non est aurum vulgi,* and the serious business was psychical, the process of individuation and the uncovering of Christ within nature.[38] Alchemical symbols stirred both the consciousness and the unconscious, and the usual method of explaining the obscure by the obscure accentuated just those processes which churchly tradition sought to eradicate. The deep-buried traditions of the heresies, especially Gnosticism, re-emerged in alchemy, establishing a fateful dialectic between alchemy and dogma—a conflict evident in Boehme's works between 1619 and 1623.

Alchemy's significance for Boehme lies in Dr. Jung's assertion that for seventeen hundred years it had existed as a dialectical undercurrent to dominant rational theology. There was alternation between the even numbers of dogma and the odd numbers of alchemy.[39] Rational dogma made the Father-Son important; in the unconsciousness this is symbolized by the mother-daughter myth; in Boehme's later works this "male" Trinity stands "opposite" the Virgin Sophia, and that Sophia plays so important a role in Boehme's mature system shows that the unconscious is not only complementary but is consciousness' helper and aid.[40] That the Son-type calls forth as fulfillment image from the chthonic unconscious not a daughter but a son is significant for an idea of God within human nature, an idea made suggestive by the image of the Holy Spirit within the *Beata Virgo.* And the *filius philosophorum* is a manifested androgynous man with masculine names and feminine unconsciousness. The answer from the female-mother world shows that the cleft can be bridged as the unconscious has a kernel of each. The essence of consciousness is distinction, conditioned being. For self-knowableness the *Ungrund's* chaos must be broken and the opposites separated. In manifested being the opposites seek one another, then tending back again to rest.

Dr. Jung's explanation solves the problem cleanly for it tells us why, when Gregory Richter, proponent of rational (square) doctrine, persecuted him for writing a book of natural philosophy, Boehme turned with interest to the alchemical symbolism being urged upon him by his friends. His alchemy then became but the projection of his own inner conflicts and of the outer difficulties emerging from his church life. In 1613 when Boehme had promised the Council that he would refrain from writing, similar silence had been asked of Richter. But the Pastor continued his attacks on Boehme, making Boehme out a fool (*Epist.* liv, 6) and circulating the *Aurora* in strange places where it was sometimes viewed with "other eyes" than Richter's (7); thus it circulated from *einer Stadt zur andern* among the learned, physicians, and nobility who transcribed it, wrote Boehme, pestered him at his house, and begged him to continue "his talents" as he had no right, they said, to hide them in continuing silence (*Epist.* liv, 8). Generously Boehme answered these requests, not meaning to write for general circulation (*Epist.* liv, 9). When he wrote again he was no longer fully Martin Moller's spiritual son; the Richter persecution had driven him deep within himself, and so at his friends' requests, his "external man" became eager again.

When this was done, then the internal man was armed, and got a faithful guide, and to him I wholly yielded my reason, and did not study nor invent anything, neither did I give reason leave to dictate what I should write, save only that which the Spirit did show me in a great mystery. (*Epist.* x, 8)

So during the sabbath of silence Boehme was brought to alchemy both by outer pressure and inner need. He came to

Paracelsus who had been neither interested in the tomfoolery of the laboratories nor allured by gold-cooking quackery,[41] thus becoming an enemy of the endless prescriptions, the daubing and greasing of the apothecary shops. The *Aurora* already betrayed some alchemical knowledge but he denied empirical knowledge:

> Do not take me for an alchemist . . . I write only in . . . the spirit. . . . Though I could here show . . . in how many days and hours these things might be prepared, for gold cannot be made in one day, but a whole month is needed for it . . . I know not how to manage the fire. . . . (*Aurora* xxii, 104)

This "sabbath," however, brought Boehme face to face with a study which dealt with *living* things. For the alchemist's problem was not simple: if God is hidden within living substance then when matter burns does God burn? When a tree grows does the hidden God also grow? Look at burning wood! What is happening? The alchemist said that burning wood was sulphur-like, smoke was mercury-like, and ashes salt-like. These three *Grundsubstanzen* were in all things and to transmute baser into higher these elements have to be known essentially.[42] Alchemy also held that the lower was image of the higher: thus sulphur, mercury, and salt corresponded to God's trinitarian life as well as to man.[43] The process of transmuting lead into the tincture was like the process of changing an impious heart into a pious one.[44] The word "process" came to have soteriological significance. And when the alchemical process or hope of transmutation is understood then God's birth and man's spiritual rebirth become clearer.[45]

The alchemist needed to prepare himself spiritually for the work. To make other things into one he first had to make himself one.[46] Unity was the condition *sine qua non,* for after the *projectio* came *cogitatio,* the identity of the alchemist with his work.[47] Boehme made the seven stages of the alchemical work the later basis of his theogony, cosmology, and regeneration, altering however their psychological implications by saying that regeneration of man was like the process of resolving the contradiction in the elements.[48] He understood that the philosopher's stone which produced natural change was also the corner stone which the builders had rejected.[49] Already in the *Aurora* the seven alchemical steps [50] were different than Boehme's seven stages of creation.[51] Thus the inner decay of alchemy began, not with the Enlightenment, but with Jacob Boehme.[52]

Boehme had already said in the *Aurora* that "their scheme of formulation" was his master and from them he had had the first elements of his knowledge. (xxii, 11ff) What were these first elements? In an important passage of his *Liber de nymphus* . . . Paracelsus had presented Boehme with an important key to nature. Parcelsus had written:

> There is more than that which is comprehended by the light of nature . . . It is grounded in the light of man which is above nature. For nature produces a light by which she may be known in her own character; but in humanity there is also a light beyond the light which by nature is within man—a light by which man experiences, learns, and understands supernatural things. Those who search in the light of nature speak about the natural light; those who search in the light of humanity seek beyond nature. For man is more than nature; he *is* nature; but he is also spirit; he is an angel, having all three properties.[53]

Alchemy's field was the light of nature, but the other realm was not natural, although it did have the same goal. For the light of Grace sought union by the mystical process. Paracelsian Neoplatonism allowed older Germanic elements to enter the mystical stream,[54] like that of Hermes Trismegisthos [55] and that of pseudo Albertus Magnus [56]—elements directed towards union with the God hidden in nature.[57] So Paracelsus' teachings were confirmed in Boehme's folk soul.

Finally, nearly a century before, Paracelsus too had seen that in all things there was good and evil.[58] Neither Paracelsus nor Schwenkfeld nor Weigel, who also had seen this duality, saw what Boehme saw—that the goal of this duality was resolution in man and in nature. Between Paracelsus and Boehme there stood the towering figure of Martin Luther with his doctrine of original sin. And Boehme was heir of both, and his natural man had to be born again;[59] for the difference between Paracelsus and Boehme was simply Luther.

It has been proven that Boehme read an anonymous little work, *De Secretis Creationis,* part three of Huser's Paracelsus edition. Dr. Peuckert had found parallel passages between this work and Boehme's *Sig. Rer.*[60]: in this work the three alchemical substances were associated with the medieval mystical methodology of purgation, illumination, and union,[61] a suggestive idea.

These, then, are the things that Boehme learned in the sabbath of silent years after the *Aurora's* confiscation. But his inner spirit grew active too and he hints at further "illuminations":

> I was not able to comprehend that light till the breath of the Most High did help me again, and awakened a new light in me, and then I obtained a better style of writing, also a deeper and more grounded knowledge; I could bring everything better into outward expression . . . I have written out of my own book which was opened in me. . . . (*Epist.* xii, 13ff)

This illumination probably took place in 1619 and it produced a strong inner drive to say what his vision gave him.

> It behooves the Doctor . . . to study the whole process . . . then he may find the universal, provided he be born again of God; but the selfish pleasure, worldly glory, covetousness, and pride lie in the way. Dear Doctor . . . the coals are too black, you defile your white hands therewith. (*Sig. Rer.* x, 10ff)

Boehme had come again to inward certainty, even when it was opposed to institutional religion, and achievement of intellectual courage which was remarkable for his time. The theologians

> wrangle and contend about the church, yet none will take care of the poor, forsaken mother of Christ. They are mad . . . they are wolves and lions . . . foxes and hares. . . . They continually contend, wrangle, grin, and bite one an-

other for the letter. . . . Let these wolves, bears, and lions go. . . . Take John, the Disciple, . . who teaches love and humility. (*Sig. Rer.* xi, 61ff)

Historical faith was sterile and believers were welcome in the churches. Preachers only tickle consciousness and do not lead to living religion (*Gelassen.* ii, 51); the churches are full of books about the new birth composed by research but are empty of those who have been reborn (*Princ.* v, 12). The churches cannot live by meanings.

Boehme's prophetic spirit in the *Aurora* now was turned against institutional religion as well as against formal theology. His seven-year silence brought him courageous assurance that the gifts he had were enough. So why should he remain silent?

Seeing I know experimentally in power . . . that it is a . . . gift of God . . . I must write what I know and see. Therefore I will obey God rather than man, lest my office . . . be taken from me again. (*Epist.* iii, 8)

These gifts, though dormant, were not quite dead

and gone, albeit they were hid . . ; yet now they often appear and show themselves more deep and wonderful. (*Epist.* iii, 17)

Nowhere did Boehme describe his illumination of 1619 though he hinted at it several times. The nearest he comes to full description is in the tenth chapter of *Princ.*

I followed the words of Christ when He said, 'You must be born anew . . .' which at first stopped my heart, and I supposed such . . . could not be done in this world. And then my soul was in anguish to the birth, and would have tasted the Pearl; and gave itself up more vigorously to the birth until finally it obtained a jewel. According to which I will write, for a memorial to myself, and for a light to them that seek . . . When I found the Pearl, then I looked Moses in the face. (x, 142)

His timidity vanished. Requested by noble and learned friends to continue writing, driven by an inner urge to share his knowledge, he was finally led to produce during the next five years some twenty books and eighty or more letters, writings that belong to the most profound which man has produced.

NOTES TO CHAPTER FIVE

1. *Görlitzer Kaufbuch,* 1605ff. Bl. 383. *Vide:* Jecht, Böhme, p. 25.
2. Jecht, *Böhme,* p. 25.
3. See the 1715 edition of Boehme's works, Appendix, pp. 62ff.
4. *Ibid.*
5. Peuckert, *Die Rosenkreutzer,* p. 108.
6. *Ibid.,* p. 6.
7. Ratsprotokoll, 22 October, 1616, *vide,* Jecht, *Böhme,* p. 24.
8. G. Aubin, *Die Leinwandsachen in Zittau, Bautzen u. Görlitz,* n.p., 1915, p. 596.
9. *Epist.* v, 2; vi, 1. At the end of 1618 and in May, 1620, Boehme received wheat from Ender.
10. *Epist.* xxxii, 2; xxxiii, 6; xxxvii; lxv; lxvi, 10.
11. *Schöpenbuch, Alt Seidenberg,* Bd. I. Cf. Jecht, *Böhme,* p. 1.
12. *Cambridge Modern History,* IV, p. 7.
13. Franckenberg, *De Vita* . . . , #22.
14. Hans Heckel, *Geschichte der deutschen Literatur in Schlesien,* p. 164.
15. Peuckert, *Die Rosenkreutzer,* p. 225.
16. Peuckert, *Pansophia,* pp. 524–525, also, Peuckert, *Böhme,* pp. 50ff.
17. Heckel, *op. cit.,* p. 164.
18. Hahnemann, founder of homeopathy, was a Boehme student.
19. Jecht, *Böhme,* pp. 57–58.
20. Peuckert, *Böhme,* p. 60.
21. Jecht, *Böhme,* pp. 57–58.
22. *Ibid.,* p. 58.
23. *Ibid.,* p. 59.
24. Three entries in Scultetus *Diarum* mention Walther as from Liegnitz; Franckenberg says that he came from Grossglogau. The *Diarum* is probably correct.
25. Jecht, *Böhme,* p. 63.
26. *Balthazari Walthari vera Descriptio Rerum ab Dno. Jon Michaele Mold. Transalp. S. Walachiae Duce et Platina Gestarum.*

27. Koyré, *Boehme,* p. 48, note 1.
28. *Mehrere Merckwürdigkeiten,* #48.
29. Peuckert, *Böhme,* p. 100.
30. *Ibid.*
31. *Ibid.*, p. 63.
32. This Richter reference is from *Mehrere Merckwürdigkeiten,* 1715 edition, *Vide:* Peuckert, *Böhme,* p. 101.
33. Peuckert, *Böhme,* p. 101, quoting from Don Georg Morhof, *Polyhistor,* 1732, III, v, #6–11, 111, p. 55. Peuckert lists the passages which Boehme wrote which recall the Cabala. *Vide: Böhme,* p. 177.
34. Walther was the praeceptor of the children of Lord Schweidnitz, Balthasar Tilke. This is how Tilke came to read Boehme.
35. Zurich, 1944.
36. Jung, *op. cit.*, p. 57.
37. The doctrine of individual and cosmic faith was significant for Gnosticism, especially *Pistis Sophia. Vide:* Leisegang, *Die Gnosis,* pp. 363, 367.
38. Jung, *op. cit.*, p. 39.
39. *Ibid.*, p. 42.
40. *Ibid.*, p. 43.
41. *Vide:* Franz Hartman, *Paracelsus,* London, 1887.
42. Paracelsus wrote: "All things (man included) are composed of three substances . . . These three . . . are . . . sulphur, mercury, and salt, and they are acted upon by a fourth principle which is life. These . . . are not seen with the physical eye . . . [but] are held together in forms by the power of *life.* If you take these three invisible substances and add . . . the power of life, you will have three invisible substances in visible form . . ." Cf. Hartmann, *op. cit.*, p. 165.
43. The poet Angelus Silesius wrote in *Cherubinischer Wandersmann,* I, 251:
    Dass Gott dreieinig ist, zeigt mir ein jedes Kraut;
    Da Schwefel, Salz, Merkur in einem wird geschaut.
44. Cf. Angelus Silesius, *op. cit.*, I, 104:
    So bald durch Gottes Feuer ich mag geschmeltzet sein,
    So drückt mir Gott alsbald sein eigen Wesen ein.
45. Cf. Angelus Silesius, *op. cit.*, I, 246:
    Der Heilige Geist der schmeltzt, der Vater der verzehrt,
    Der Sohn ist die Tinktur, die Gold macht und verklärt.
46. Quoted by Jung, *Psychologie und Alchemie,* p. 349, from Dorsius, *Theatr. Chem.*, 1602, I, p. 472.
47. Jung, *op. cit.*, p. 366.

48. Peuckert, *Böhme,* p. 56.
49. Cf. Angelus Silesius, *Cherubinischer Wandersmann,* I, 280:
    Dein Stein, Chymist, ist nichts; der Eckstein, den ich mein,
    Ist meine Goldtinktur und aller Weisen Stein.
50. The stages were: distillatio, solutio, putrefacto, nigredo, albedo, rubedo, projectio. *Vide:* Peuckert, *Böhme,* pp. 166ff; Peuckert, *Rosenkreutzer,* pp. 81ff, 85ff, 112, 117ff, 155ff.
51. Cf. *Myst. Mag.* ilviii. *Vide:* Brinton, *The Mystic Will.*
52. *Vide:* Jung, *The Integration of the Personality,* New York, 1939, pp. 205ff.
53. Quoted by Peuckert, *Pansophia,* p. 209. Colberg in *Platonisch-hermetisch Christenthum,* I, 314, says that Erasmus Francisci in *Gegenstrahl der Morgenröthe,* found more than thirty passages where Boehme directly quoted Paracelsus.
54. Peuckert, *Pansophia,* p. 227.
55. Gunholf, *Paracelsus,* Berlin, 1927, pp. 69–70.
56. *Vide:* Albertus' widely read folk books on "sympathetic" medicine.
57. Cf. Walterhausen, *Paracelsus am Eingang der deutschen Bildungs-Geschichte,* Leipzig, 1936, p. 1.
58. Cf. Peuckert, *Böhme,* p. 54.
59. *Ibid.,* p. 55.
60. *Ibid.,* p. 56.
61. *Ibid.,* p. 164.

Here Christ, the Serpent-bruiser,
stands in Man,
Storming the Devil's hellish,
self-built Plan;
And hence the Strife within the
human Soul,–
Satan's to kill, and Christ's to
make it whole;
As by Experience, in so great De-
gree,
God in His Goodness causes you
to see.

—JOHN BYROM: *A Poetical Version of a Letter from Jacob Behmen*

CHAPTER SIX

ALCHEMICAL SEARCH: JANUARY, 1619–MARCH, 1620

HAVING THUS spent seven years obeying the Görlitz Council's order not to write, Boehme again took pen to expound what he believed were his God-given intuitions. But when in January, 1619, he resumed his writing he was no longer the naive young shoemaker who had dreamed of unlocking the secrets of all reality. He had now met the intellectual forces of his age. And, stretched by these contacts, he nevertheless remained convinced of the importance of his inner convictions:

I have no controversy with God's children because of the diversity of gifts. I can reconcile them all in myself . . . I only bring them to the center . . . There I have the proof and touchstone of all things . . . If you will . . . follow me, then you shall find it so by experience, and later perhaps bitter experience what I have written. (*Epist.* xii, 38)

His new purpose was evangelical: to communicate to and if possible to reproduce his experience in other people. It was not to dogmatize. Even though his theology was gained as *gnosis* in mystical experience, what Boehme sought to share was not the knowledge but the experience which had produced it.

What good does knowledge . . . if I live not . . . according to the same. The knowing and . . . will . . . and performance . . . must be within me . . . Not only to contend . . . about knowledge . . . , but you must become a new man . . . Then what need I then contend . . . about that which I myself am—which I have essentially within me, and of which no man can deprive me? (*Epist.*, xii, 62ff)

By refusing to make his experience a new law Boehme's purpose thus gained a new focus after 1619.

I have . . . a fair garden of roses; which I do not want my brothers to partake of, but I desire . . . that the golden roses might . . . bloom in them . . . When I go to the center . . . I find the whole ground . . . for I find . . . understanding both of good and evil, of God's Love and anger . . . These I set . . . in Christ's humanity . . . I write not as one dumb and blind, without knowledge; I have myself found it by experience. I have been as deep in your opinion as yourself . . . I wish . . . that you might have the insight into my seeing and that you might see out of my seeing. (*Epist.* xliii, *passim.*)

Before 1619 his sources had been Moller, Paracelsus, Luther, and Christian mysticism. Now these became peripheral. Eclectic, synthesizing, he learned only what suited him, retracing in each book the old ground. His theme, like Bach's in the *B Minor Mass*, was repeated, growing, never the same.

Boehme was himself aware of his growth. In 1621, writing to Caspar Linder, he grouped his writings: 1) the *Aurora;* 2) *Princ., Dreyfach, Seel. Frag.;* 3) *Menschw., Sig. Rer., Theos. Punkt.* (*Epist.* xii, 66–70) This classification was made before the apologetic works and before those of 1621 and following.

The earliest surviving *Epist.* sets the tone for Boehme's alchemical search. Writing in answer to a query from Christian Bernhard, a stranger, Boehme did not admit authorship of other works beyond the *Aurora;* he did, however, suggest that Bernhard might find out what they were by asking Dr. Balthasar Walther. Boehme then suggested that the noble stone was an acquisition of great joy and once possessed it was more valuable than silver. (*Epist.* xxvi, 1–4)

> It is more beautiful than the sun, more costly than the heavens, and he who finds it is richer than any prince . . . He has the entire art and understanding of the earth. (*Epist.* xxvi, 3)

While not admitting authorship, Boehme asserts that his writings will show Bernhard

> many beautiful and noble things, which . . . have remained hidden . . , around which the learned have searched and danced, thinking that they had discovered the noble stone. (*Epist.* xxvi, 4)

Because a wonderful time was coming when the sun would shine at midnight (*Princ.*, Pref, 21) he felt that the time was short. So, with uncharacteristic courage, he screwed up his determination and wrote: *Beschreibung der Drey Principien Göttliches Wesens.*[1] It was a book of twenty-seven chapters and in manuscript it came to a hundred sheets. He finished it in October, 1619. He says that it is

> a key and alphabet for all those who desire to understand my writings. It treats of creation, of the Deity's eternal birth, of repentance, of the justification of man, of his Paradisaical life; also the Fall, and then the new birth, and of Christ's Testaments, and man's total salvation. Very profitable to be read, for it is an eye to know the wonders of the mystery of God. (*Epist.*, xii, 67)

But nothing about the world's generation!

This book's essential problem was the same as the *Aurora's:* justification of God.[2] The *Aurora's* simple solution was forsaken and Boehme now was convinced of the world's necessity because Christ's Incarnation had been willed eternally, thus making the world eternally necessary.

The *Aurora's* three realms of angels became the dialectical idea of the three principles (*Aurora* xii, 37ff). Where Paracelsus, Schwenkfeld, and Weigel had seen good and evil, Boehme understood that good and evil between them generated substantial being, a body.[3] Like the trinity, these principles were then in all things—in God, the world, and man.

These principles are not the Trinity's persons, Plotinus' three modes, nor Hegel's logical stages. They are rather psychological types: wrath, love, and movement—or in the language of science, plus, minus, and creative power. Life, like the power in an electric appliance, is produced only when the opposites agitate each other.

For Boehme principle was a birth, a mode of divine activity, a life-source, a mode of divine revelation. Each principle bore and ruled a world: wrath gave hell, love gave paradise, and life the sensible world. The first, symbolized by sulphur, was an ardent life-source like libidinous pride; the second, symbolized by salt, was meek, self-yielding love. The first was fire, the second light. These two are necessary to each other and between them they set up a dialectical tension. The wrath [4] is demonic but not wholly evil; self-will is evil as long as it remains untinctured by self-giving, for as Boehme says, and in this instance his German is quoted to show his newly found style,

So wir nun von Gott wollen reden, was Er und wo Er sey, so müssen wir ja sagen, dass Gott selber das Wesen aller Wesen sey: Denn von Ihme ist alles erboren, geschaffen, und herkommen, und nimt alles Ding seinen ersten Anfang aus Gott . . . Dass aber nun ein Unterschied sey, dass das Böse nicht Gott heisse und sey, das wird in dem ersten *Principio* verstanden: dass da ist der ernstliche Quell der Grimmigkeit, nach welcher sich Gott einen zornigen, grimmigen, eiferigen Gott nennet. Denn in der Grimmigkeit stehet des Lebens und aller Beweglichkeit Urkund: so aber derselbe . . . mit dem Lichte Gottes wird angezündet, so ist nicht mehr Grimmigkeit; sondern die ernstliche Grimmigkeit wird in Freude verwandelt. (*Princ.* i, 1–2)[5]

God is the source of being, not of evil. Potentially this will-to-be is good or evil, depending on how the second principle "tinctures" it. When no tincturing by love takes place eternal stillness results. Life is then the result of the interplay of forces.

Boehme's ideas on the generation of being in *Princ.* have advanced far beyond those of the *Aurora.* A new range of ideas also appears—redemption, a theme lacking in the first work. The chastened Boehme who wrote *Princ.* was no longer the chesty pantheist of the *Aurora;* he tackled those disruptive ideas which upset the earlier smooth-flowing pantheism. *Princ.* alternates around two poles: emanation of all from God and man's need of the new birth. There is as yet no connection between them and they are merely analogic.

In *Princ.* the way of redemption is from the world to God; however, this doctrine was not yet fully spun. Boehme here conceived of it as regeneration and for this Christ's work was symbolic: He had brought new life out of the darksome earth (*Princ.* viii, 9) and Boehme interpreted Logos substantially (viii, 9); this was here vaguely expressed. His chief problem was to tell how Jesus got a body without *Grimmigkeit* in it. This drove him, as it has driven the Roman Church, into Mariology; this, however, only pushes the Incarnation back to Mary's lap. In *Princ.* Boehme still held that Mary bore the new man's heavenly image and that Christ got His perfection from her, receiving from her the "pure element" which He incorporated in a body free from wrath. (*Princ.* xxii, 48) In this body He brought the pure element also to death, separating the natural soul from this world, from death, and from hell, thus opening a gate for us all (*Princ.* xxii, 49). This "pure" flesh is appropriated in the Holy Supper by the believer who thus gets a "pure" body. Before this, man must walk the road from Jerusalem to Jericho. In a beautiful passage, Boehme said:

When I was at Jericho, there my beloved Companion opened my eyes for me, that I saw and beheld a great generation of men and multitudes of peoples and nations were together, one part were like beasts, and one part like men, and there was strife between them. And beneath there was the abyss of hell, and the beasts saw that not, but the men were afraid and were gone; to which the Devil would not consent, because his garden had no gates; but they broke open his garden so he had to watch at the door so that they would not run away from him; but the beasts . . . did eat of his food, and drank his drink, and he did nothing to them, because he fattened them for the slaughter. . . . Do you suppose that this is not true? . . . Then come with me to Jerusalem, we will go together along the way to Jericho, and see it well enough. (*Princ.* xxiv, 10–11)

But in *Princ.* this lonesome road to Jericho, however much trodden, escapes clear definition and there is as yet no understanding of how "grim nature" is to be renewed.

In November, 1619, immediately upon finishing *Princ.*, Boehme plunged into another work, designed perhaps as a sequel, entitled: *Vom Dreyfachen Leben des Menschen nach dem Geheimniss der Dreyen Principia Göttliche Offenbarung.*[6] Writing to Carl von Ender on November 29, 1619, Boehme said that soon he would be able to send something which clearly "opened" what man is, what man must be, and what he must do to attain the highest good (*Epist.* v, 9). Sixty sheets in length, it was probably completed by August, 1620 (*Epist.* x, 11). Boehme said that it showed

the whole ground of the three principles. It serves everyone . . . He may sound the depth and resolve all questions. . . . (*Epist.* xii, 68)

The problem of *Dreyfach* is like that of *Princ.* and the *Aurora;* however, Boehme now no longer asks why is evil? If God is good then how did an evil world come to be? A good God cannot be responsible either for a fall which He has not willed nor for sin which He has not decreed. So Boehme came to freedom, fall, and restitution; his focus now was narrowed to creation. Two ideas here were in conflict: God's goodness and the worth of His creation. Boehme's solution in *Dreyfach* tried to safeguard freedom while maintaining creation's worth and man's freedom.[7]

Why was the world created? Because God wanted to manifest Himself.[8] The God who is the will-to-be is also the will-to-be-manifested, an *ens manifestativum sui* (*Aurora* xiv, 9–10). By creating a world He expressed Himself in nature and creature. As the eternal no-thing, beyond nature and creature, He cannot be conscious of Himself, as no being can be conscious of nothing. To be conscious He needs something to be conscious of; this is His *Gegenwurf* or *Wiederwille;* in *Dreyfach* this is the created world. Although this will not be Boehme's final position it is nevertheless a step from the *Aurora's* frank pantheism: God no longer brims over in self-manifested creativity; here the world is the counter-image of God's self-consciousness, the dialectical precondition of self-knowledge. To be conscious of self God first must create the image which He may contemplate.

Boehme's mystical *gnosis* that good and evil were in all things was here enlarged so that these tendencies to self-projection and to self-knowledge govern all life-forms. Opposed to the creative urge is a self-negating denial; the one is anxious, defiant, self-assertive; the other is calm, silent, free.

Each principle has a mother from which it springs. To change the principle must return to the mother and be "born again." The source of the selfish desiring will is the *centrum naturae* (*Dreyfach* iii, 56; vi, 44; viii, 5, 61); however, this is not ultimate for behind this is the inmost center's *centrum.*

The image of this change is borrowed from alchemical transmutation–fire, and this image dominates the works of Boehme's alchemical period; indeed, the use of this image determines the nature of this period. In alchemy fire was the agent of change. In Boehme's mind fire was the purgative which brought the new birth. In a remarkable simile Boehme described this idea of mystical union:

> Behold a bright flaming piece of iron which of itself is dark and black, and the fire so penetrates through the iron that it gives light. Now, the iron does not cease to be; it is iron still; and the source of the iron retains its own property; it [the fire] does not take the iron into it but it penetrates through the iron; and it is iron then as well as before, free in

itself; and so also is the source of the fire; in such a manner is the soul set in the Deity; the Deity penetrates through the soul, and dwells in the soul, yet the soul does not comprehend the Deity, but the Deity comprehends the soul. (*Dreyfach* vi, 84ff)

He continues:

if the flaming iron be cast . . . into the water then the property of the fire and the . . . heat which proceeds from it are all quenched together. (*Dreyfach,* vi, 87)

This image, which appears also in other writers,[9] reveals the relationship between Boehme's mystical regeneration and transmutation.[10]

Boehme's fire, however, like that of Pythagoras, was not merely the peripatetic element or even the mysterious event on the hearth in Balthasar Walther's laboratory. His fire was spiritual calcination, a power capable of making hard metals pliable, changing them; it was an "ardent source" which begot being and conscious life—the burning, self-consuming life-heart (*Dreyfach* viii, 18). Fire was life, the passionate *libido* at the center of conscious, willing reality. Holy Fire was the source of regeneration and of the new life's center in God (*Dreyfach* ix, 71–72).

Alchemy's goal was not laboratory work; ever since Hermetic philosophy[11] an eclectic Platonism had continued in Neopythagorean and Neoplatonic guise those Gnostic speculations which had been basically mystical,[12] the central axiom of which was expressed by Maria Prophetissa: the One becomes two, the two three, and out of the third the One becomes a fourth.[13] Here creation also becomes the process by which consciousness is achieved; here too is what Schelling called "theogony."

Balthasar Walther, who had been Boehme's guest for several months, was responsible for the form of Boehme's next work, *Seel. Frag.,*[14] or forty questions concerning the soul. The English translator of 1665 wrote in his introduction,

Boehme wrote [answers to] these questions . . . chiefly for the benefit of all such as love the knowledge of mysteries.

This friend . . . was Dr. Balthasar Walther, who, travelling for learning and hidden wisdom, and on his return home, happened to hear of this author in the city of Görlitz; and when he had obtained acquaintance with him, he rejoiced that at last he had found at home, in a cottage, that which he had travelled for so far, and not received satisfaction; then he went to several universities in Germany, and did there collect such questions of the soul as were thought and accounted impossible to be resolved . . . , which he made this catalogue of, and sent to the author, from which he received these answers to his desire.[15]

Boehme probably had Walther's questions on January 18, 1619 (*Epist.* i, 47); the manuscript was done August 3, 1620,[16] consisting of twenty-eight sheets. (*Epist.* xii, 69) The supplement, entitled *Das Umgewandte Auge,* an appendix to the first question's answer, was probably written in 1622. Naively Boehme says that this work

treats of all things which are necesssary for man to know. (*Epist.* xii, 69)

Seel. Frag., being answers to set questions, lacks structural unity, but it marks a significant step ahead. Two important ideas appear: *Ungrund*[17] and Wisdom. Both poles of Boehme's mystical theology—God as *Nichts* and God as *Alles*—are more evident. *Ungrund* is his word for the absolute devoid of determination and as Schopenhauer suggested it probably came to Boehme from his environment, perhaps from Walther who had spent some time in the East and was probably familiar with the Hindu Brahman.[18] The idea of the divine all—Wisdom—is also an Eastern idea.

When Boehme achieved his ideas of the Unconditioned and of Sophia, as Wisdom became known, his thought achieved a new center because his problem had found a new focus: how can God exist in determination? This embraces the question of God's self-manifestation in two clearly distinguishable creative acts. *Seel. Frag.* posits but it does not solve this problem: his next work, *Menschw.*, which is a logical sequel, attempts solution (*Menschw.* I, 1, 15).

This change appears in Boehme's use of the fire image. In

Seel. Frag. fire dominates his thought, appearing as sufficient manifestation of the essence of all essences (*Seel. Frag.* i, 11). It is life's first principle, the soul's first root. God, who called Himself a consuming fire, becomes reality's burning center; *Seel. Frag.* uses fire, however, more than metaphorically for here is broached a metaphysics of light (*Lichtmetaphysik*) for when Boehme wrote fire he had luminosity in mind too, the *Feur-blitz.*[19] Fire is both light and heat

the light-life has its source and drive, and the fire-life its source and drive, each in itself; but the fire-life is the light-life's cause, and the light-life rules the fire-life. (*Seel. Frag.* i, 62)

He thinks of this in psychological terms:

. . . look at glowing fire . . . First there is matter from which it burns . . . Fire has a wrathful, harsh, strong, bitter, desiring source, a devouring and consuming . . . which has all essences of life in it and is the vitality . . . That makes a . . . seeking for freedom, and in the fire it attains freedom . . . thereby we know that one spirit separates into two principles, two spirits . . . Now fire in itself is first a seeking to draw into itself (Die Sucht, in sich zu ziehen). (*Seel. Frag.* i, 63–66)

Fire bifurcates into concupiscent passion and freedom (*Seel. Frag.* i, 72).

Boehme here transforms the alchemical image of fire[20] into an interesting analogy of the vital urge at the center of conscious being. His fire, however, is not artificial like the fire of Heracleitus[21]; it was "depth psychology," a pantheistic image because the same divine fire which kindled life sustains it too. From fire came freedom; out of life's central passion came fulfilled stillness. He pictured this idea graphically in the Philosophic Globe which he borrowed from Reuchlin, a fanciful picture of the world-soul's generation which he based on his theory of the "natural language," an idea adapted from the Cabala.[22]

The ideas of *Ungrund* and Sophia, along with the change in the fire image, brought Boehme new confusion,[23] and his philosophy was still more confused by the new tension between God as the no-thing and as the All. He was not to resolve this easily.

Transformation of the fire image also transformed alchemy. Fire was no longer the tool or an element; it was life, an *élan vital,* a drive, an energetic source.

Man's place in this fire-flaming world is not yet clear to Boehme. He was writing about the soul's flaming center because he wanted to change men—even the old fire-consuming Adamic man.[24] His vision of regeneration did not yet embrace the way to Christ, for it still arose from reality's burning heart.

Sometime before the middle of August, 1620, and probably as early as May,[25] Boehme completed *Of the Incarnation of Jesus Christ* (*Menschw.*), the most lucid of his alchemical works and showing his growing mastery of the German language. Of it he said:

> The fifth book has three parts: the first is concerning the Incarnation of Jesus Christ; the second part is very deep and profound, treating of Christ's passion, suffering, and death, and how we must enter into Christ's death, and both die and rise again in and with Him, and why Christ was to die, wholly brought forth, enlarged, and confirmed out of the center through the three principles, very deep. The third part is the Tree of Christian Faith, also demonstrated through the three principles, very profitable to be read. (*Epist.* xii, 70)

He no longer believed that God had to manifest Himself; incarnation was voluntary. Here he achieved new focus:

> If we would write of the Incarnation . . . we must reflect upon the cause, and consider what moved God to become man, seeing He was not in need of this for the realization of His being. (*Menschw.* I, i, 5)

Evil is no longer his central problem; now it was Christ in the world. God was both fire and light; Christ united both in equivalence.

> For there have been from eternity only two principles, one

in itself, the fiery world, and the other similarly in itself, the light-flaming world; although they were not separated, the light dwelling in the fire, without being laid hold of by it. We are thus to understand two kinds of spirits united into one another. (*Menschw.* I, i, 7–8)

The adjustment here implied brought Boehme further clarification of his doctrine of principles. In *Princ.* he had identified them with the alchemical *Grundsubstanzen.* His changing fire image projected these into Christ.

[the] nothing has in the nature of fire and light advanced into a ground, and yet issues from nothing but the spirit of the source which gives birth to itself in itself in two properties, and likewise separates into two principles. . . . For the Father's *proprium* stands in fire and light. He is Himself the Being of all beings. He is the unground and ground, and in the eternal birth divides into three properties, or into three persons, or into three principles, although in eternity there are but two in being, and a third is the mirror of the first two, from which this world has been created a palpable existence in a beginning and an end. (*Menschw.* I, xi, 11ff)

Boehme could not yet forget his fire image; His God was light only (*Menschw.* I, iii, 3) whose light-majesty could not be laid hold of by consuming fire. Light became freedom

because we were gone from the freedom of the angelic world into the dark source, with fire as its abyss, there was no necessity for us unless the power and Word of the light . . . became a man and brought us out of the darkness through the torment of fire, through death in fire, again into the freedom of the divine life. . . . (*Menschw.* I, iii, 5–7)

Into darkness beyond the fire-world was the Devil cast because, despising the light, he remained consuming fire; other angels became light, receiving love (*Menschw.* I, iii, 10–11). This light was Christ and in the Incarnation He took on the dark consuming anguish of the fire to change man:

And let this be plain . . . : if you would find the *lapis*

philosophorum set yourselves to attain the new birth in Christ. (*Menschw.* I, iv, 10)

This tolls the doom of speculative alchemy, transforming it into Christian mysticism. Hear these words and then consider whether Boehme was a gold-cook:

> Man was created to be lord of the tincture, and it was subject to him; but he became its servant . . . He seeks only for gold and finds earth . . . As the tincture of the earth is shut up in the wrath, till the judgment of God, so also is the spirit of man shut up in the wrath, unless he go out and be born in God . . . Man . . . had power to disclose the tincture and bring forth the noble pearl . . . if he had remained in innocency. (*Menschw.* I, iv, 10–11)

Boehme's alchemy, if such it was, here led to religious regeneration.

In *Menschw.* Boehme continued to play with the fire image, ringing the changes on it, conceiving of the religious change in similar fashion. This is the period when he had worked through alchemical imagery, found it lacking, and was nearing the later solutions of Christ-mysticism. For the early Boehme, then, alchemy afforded analogy of regeneration:

> Lying in view is a rough stone, and in some we find the best gold . . . This stone is inert, and knows not that it contains . . . noble gold. This holds also of us: we are an earthly sulphur, but have a heavenly sulphur in the earthly, where each is its own possession . . . The rough stone is not the gold, but only the receptacle of it. . . . So it is also with man: the earthly man is indicated by the rough stone, and the Word that became man is indicated by the sun, which makes the corrupt man pregnant. . . . The new man is not mere spirit; he lives in flesh and blood; just as the gold in the stone is not merely spirit. . . . So is it also with the old earthly man; when he receives the Word of Life . . . he receives it in . . . his flesh and blood, in the . . . center that is shut up in death, and there the rough earth covered his gold . . . so that the heavenly nature had to remain in death. . . . In the same center the Word of life, which in Mary be-

came man, moved itself; there the essence that was shut up in death obtained a living tincture. (*Menschw.* I, xiv, 4–7 *passim*)

In various alchemical images Boehme here speculated about problems which were widely discussed during the sixteenth and seventeenth centuries—the problems of *communicatio idiomatum, communio naturarum,* and *propositiones personales.*[26] All these have to do with the relation of Christ's two natures; how were they joined? how were they united in one being?

So, during this period which can be called the alchemical, fire was for Boehme the root of life (*Menschw.* II, i, 5) and Christ is the flame of love in the light-world (II, iii, 14) who begets a soul purified by fire (I, xiv, 3). Even this new life is conceived of in terms of fire:

> Dear children, let us discourse together deeply . . . Our true life . . . is a choked fire; in some even as the fire shut up in a stone; we must kindle it by right and earnest turning to God . . . so that [we] . . . may become capable of the divine fire. . . . Historical faith is tinder which glimmers as a small spark; it must be enkindled. (*Menschw.* II, viii, 1)

So the man who wrote *Menschw.* was basically religious, one who thought of the religious transformation in unusual terms; surely he was not an alchemist who seriously sought the tincture of transformation.

Following *Menschw.* Boehme wrote *The Six Theosophical Points* (*Theos. Punkt*) which were a lucid step forward in his fast-maturing thought. This was late in 1620.[27] Of it he said,

> The sixth book . . . is the six points, treating . . . how the three principles do mutually beget, bring forth, and bear each other . . . it is a key to all. (*Epist.* xii, 71)

Truly it is a philosophical work of strength which deals with the idea of the *Ungrund* and like all works of this period also with the fire image. For all sense . . . must have fire. Nothing springs from the earth without fire's essence. (*Theos. Punkt*, iii, 13)

Here he treats the problem with more objectivity and he is beginning to understand that knowledge is not enough:

> It is not merely a question of taking comfort (in knowing) but of keeping down the impostor lest he become master in the house. (*Theos. Punkt*, vi, 22)

His mystical salvation by knowledge was starting to break down and a new interest was emerging:

> There must be doing . . . a striving against the Devil's will. . . . Man must here be at war with himself, if he wishes to become a heavenly citizen. He must not be a lazy sleeper. . . . Fighting must be his watchword, and not with tongue and sword, but with mind and spirit, and not give over. . . . (*Theos. Punkt*, vi, 22ff)

Boehme has traveled a long and roundabout way from nature philosophy to the struggle for penitence, or, in Kierkegaard's phrase, to the place where he again became subjective,[28] thus achieving that inwardness which has been the continuing treasured heritage of German mysticism.

Sometime during 1620 [29] Boehme wrote *The Six Mystical Points* (*Myst. Punkt*), another short, clear discussion of six ideas. Of it he wrote in the preface:

> The precious knowledge is not found unless the soul has once conquered . . , so that it obtains the knight's garland . . . Then a wonderful knowledge arises, but with no perfection.

Here he was beginning to probe the relationship between faith and knowledge.

On May 8, 1620,[30] Boehme wrote nine short texts, *Of The Earthly and Heavenly Mystery* (*Ird. u. himl. Myst.*), short, succinct, clear recapitulations of his main ideas. The third text records a major change, and here Boehme supplants the central fire image with will; his voluntarism finally emerges from his alchemical search. Originally fire had been the central ἀρχή of being; now however

> We recognize . . . the eternal will-spirit as God . . . there is nothing prior . . . [it] is an eternal knowing of the unground. (iii, 3)

Along with these works of the alchemical period Boehme also wrote eight letters to friends who were beginning to form a Boehme "circle."

NOTES TO CHAPTER SIX

1. The autograph ms is lost. The printed text comes from the corrected copy of Michael von Ender which Prunius found in Görlitz with Hans Rothe. The Appendix was written later, either on December 27, 1623, or in February, 1624. The first English version of 1648 varies from the standard German version.
2. Koyré, *Boehme,* p. 179.
3. Underhill, *Mysticism,* London, 1930, pp. 144–145.
4. The demonic is described in Book Twenty of Goethe's *Dichtung und Wahrheit.*
5. Translation: Seeing we are not to speak of God, what He is, and where He is, we must say, that God Himself is the essence of all essences; for all is generated, or born, created, and proceeded from Him, and all things take their beginning out of God . . . But there is yet this difference: that evil neither is, nor is called God; this is understood in the first principle, where it is the earnest fountain of the wrathfulness, according to which God calls Himself an angry, wrathful, jealous God. For the original of life, and of all mobility, consists in the wrathfulness; yet if the same . . . be kindled with the light in God, it is then no more tartness, but the severe wrathfulness is changed into great joy.—Comparison will show how the English words do not convey the spirit of Boehme's words.
6. The autograph ms is lost. Six early copies, each with a slightly different title, survive. Michael von Ender's was the basis of the printed text.
7. Koyré, *Boehme,* pp. 240–241.
8. This is good scholasticism: *deus non destruit, sed perficet eam!*

9. Fire's cleansing power is an Eastern idea. St. Macarius the Egyptian wrote: "As iron, or lead, or gold, or silver, being cast into the fire, are melted from the hardness which belongs to them by nature, and are changed into softness, and so long as they are in the fire, their natural hardness continues to melt and be altered on account of the vigorous heat of the fire, in like manner also the soul which, having renounced the world, is possessed by the desire for God alone, in great searching and pains and conflict of soul, maintains an increasing watch for Him in hope and faith, and having received the Celestial fire in the Godhead and of the Love of the Spirit, it is then, in truth, freed from all the love of the world and is set at liberty from all evil affections and casts all things out of itself and is changed from its own natural habit and hardness of sin and sets aside all other things for the sake of the heavenly Bridegroom alone, whom it receives, as rest in this fervent and ineffable Love." (Margaret Smith, *Studies in Mysticism in the Near and Middle East,* London, 1931, p. 64) Here the fire image is only metaphor, but in the following from John of Lycopolis it is more: "As when iron is placed in the fire, and the fire passes into it and becomes one substance with it, the iron partakes of the fire, and assumes its likeness and colour, and no longer appears as it formerly did, but takes on the aspect of fire, because it has become absorbed in it, and so they have become one, so when the Love of Christ comes into the soul, it becomes one substance with Him and He with it. That which was old has become new, and that which was dead is now alive." (Smith, *op. cit.,* p. 192.) *Vide:* Bernard of Clairvaux' use of this image in T. L. Connolly, *Saint Bernard on the Love of God,* New York, 1937, p. 45.
10. Cf. Underhill, *Mysticism,* p. 143. ". . . the proper art of the Spiritual alchemist . . . was the production of the spiritual and only valid tincture or philosopher's stone, the mystic seed of transcendental life which should invade, tinge, and wholly transmute the imperfect self into spiritual gold."
11. *Vide:* E. Zeller, *Philosophie der Griechen,* Leipzig, 1903, III, ii, pp. 242–254; E. Reitzenstein, *Poimandres,* Leipzig, 1904; J. M. Creed, "The Hermetic Writings," in *The Journal of Theological Studies,* Oxford, 1914, xv, pp. 513–538.
12. Willoughby, *Pagan Regeneration,* Chicago, 1929, p. 223.
13. C. G. Jung, *Psychologie und Alchemie,* p. 41.
14. Also known as *Psychologia Vera.*
15. In Barker's 1911 London reprint, p. xxi.

16. Cf. W. Buddecke, *Verzeichniss*, p. xx.
17. "We have already explained what we assume in the first respect: that there must be a being *before* all basis and before all existence, that is, before any duality at all; how can we designate it except as 'primal ground,' or rather, as the 'groundless.'" Schelling, *Of Human Freedom*, tr. Gutmann, Chicago, 1936, p. 87. *Werke*, vii, p. 406ff.
18. *Ueber die Vierfache Wurtzel des Satzes vom zureichen Grunde*, Ch. ii, #8, in Werke, *Inselverlag*, III, p. 31.
19. Koyré, *Boehme*, p. 284.
20. "God made the body of the All of fire and earth—joining them by the natural property of proportion," Plato, *Timaeus*, 310.
21. "This ordered universe, which is the same for all, was not created by any one of the gods or of mankind, but it was ever and is and shall be ever-living fire, kindled in measure and quenched in measure." Fragment 22. *Vide:* Freeman, *Ancilla to the Pre-Socratic Philosophers*, Oxford, 1948, p. 26.
22. *Vide:* C. Dornsieff, *Das Alphabet in Mystik u. Magie*, Leipzig, 1925, *passim.*
23. It is significant that the world soul arises in the book where Boehme tries to expound the human soul.
24. *Seel. Frag.* presents the strange distinction between the Son of God and the heart of God. The latter is reality's divine center but not its Redeemer! Cf. Koyré, *Boehme*, p. 300.
25. Buddecke, *Verzeichniss*, p. xxi.
26. Luthardt, *Kompendium der Dogmatik*, Leipzig, 1937, pp. 253ff.
27. Buddecke, *op. cit.*, p. xx.
28. Cf. Kierkegaard's *Concluding Unscientific Postscript*, tr. Swenson, Princeton, 1941, pp. 115ff.
29. Buddecke, *op cit.*, pp. xx.
30. *Ibid.*

Still live in me this loving strife
Of living Death and dying Life,
For while Thou sweetly slayest
me
Dead to my selfe, I live in Thee
—RICHARD CRAWSHAW

CHAPTER SEVEN

RELIGIOUS APOLOGETICS: AUGUST, 1620–JUNE, 1622

AFTER A BURST of creativity, stemming from his sunrise to eternity, had thus produced an astonishing group of works which sought to interpret Christian regeneration in the imagery of alchemy, Boehme's spirit, pushed from within by mystical drive, grew weary. Having driven his initial insight to its speculative limits he again met life and found existential demands again decisive. The conclusions to which his thought was tending became clear and he recoiled from distortion in a series of apologetic works which were written at a more leisurely pace, without the pressing intensity of the earlier works of the alchemical period.

First, his insistence on urgency in religious decision tended towards chiliasm and, as the region in and about Görlitz was full of precise apocalypses, Boehme's two letters to Paul Kaym sought to reject this millenarianism. Secondly, his pantheistic tendencies were challenged by Crypto-Calvinist predestinarianism and his two apologies against Balthasar Tilke protected him in this direction. Thirdly, his emanationism tended towards the deification of the world and of man and Boehme had to dissociate himself from the messianism of Stiefel and Meth. So Boehme's spirit rejected the three distortions: chiliasm, predestinarianism, and Methism.

But Boehme was no housebound prophet. Business took

him abroad. Traveling over eastern Germany and Bohemia, the theater of the Thirty Years' War, Boehme probed the spirit of those exciting times. Beginning November 1, 1619, he spent a week in Prague just when the new king, Frederick of the Palatinate, was there:

> I was present at the coming of the new king. . . . He came in at the fort upon Retskin of Shlan, and was received of all the three orders with great solemnity. . . . I exhort you well . . . whether the time of the great expedition be not at hand upon the mountains of Israel in Babel . . . especially with respect to the *Siebenbürger* (Bethlem Gabor) who should get help from the Turk, and very easily come to the river Rhine, where the great slaughter of the children of God then will come to pass.[1] We know for certain the ruin of Babel to be nigh. (*Epist.* iv, 38ff)

For war had come! Before going to Prague Boehme had known that Upper Lusatia had become more closely bound to Bohemia, Silesia, and Lower Lusatia.[2] After the Union of 1619 Upper Lusatia had become an ally. With the death of doddering old Emperor Matthias, March 20, 1619, the boom was lowered and the hordes came on.[3] The Royal Brief accorded in 1609 by Rudolf II to Hussites and other Protestants in Bohemia, Moravia, and Silesia, securing religious freedom, was withdrawn. The Emperor's regents suppressed popular liberties. An election of August 22, 1619, found Upper Lusatia outvoted by the other provinces.[4] Bohemia, Moravia, and Silesia declared themselves independent from the successor, Ferdinand II, and attached themselves to the Palatine Elector, Frederick V, champion of the Protestants. Revolt was general. Villagers sided against burghers, evangelicals against Romans, Lutherans against Calvinists. The divisions were not just between prince and prince, creed and creed, but it was between neighbor and neighbor and the whole world seemed to be divided into a Yes and No. Boehme shared in this revolt: he disobeyed the Görlitz Council's order not to write.

The war came to Boehme's doorstep. On March 10, 1620, Ferdinand came from Breslau to Görlitz with an entourage of 329 people and over 400 horsemen.[5] On April 25 the citizens were put under arms,[6] the mild Boehme among them. Soldiers were recruited and mercenaries enlisted.[7] When in August a detachment of British and Scottish troops passed through the city they brought along the fever [8] and for six weeks Boehme was ill with what he called *der bösen Soldaten zugefügten Kranckheit.*[9] The Congress of Lesser Nobility met in Görlitz on September 4 and when the Saxon Elector took Bautzen, Görlitz pledged him allegiance.[10] Ferdinand maneuvered Saxony, a Protestant prince, over to the Catholic side, thus enabling Saxon soldiers to be quartered in and around Görlitz.[11] In September General von Jägerdorf made Görlitz his headquarters and trenches were dug.[12] The burghers were commanded to win God's Grace by "earnest prayers, faithful attendance at services, and repentant living." [13] Houses and bridges were destroyed, soldiers went about plundering, Calvinist services were allowed.[14] Meanwhile Frederick had been defeated in Bohemia and had fled to Britain. The Saxon Elector occupied Löbau and Bautzen.[15] The Silesians begged for mercy and, as the Elector passed through Görlitz on his way to Silesia, passing right by Boehme's house, the citizens asked for mercy and love. Boehme subscribed his ninth letter, written during these days: The Lord's name is a mighty fortress; the righteous flee to it and are lifted up.

Boehme's mind, long concerned with its own thoughts, now was drawn out into the external course of events. In a letter to Christian Bernhard, November 11, 1620, he asked for news about the war's progress in Sagan and Lower Lusatia. He told Bernhard that on Martinmas the Elector and his entourage had entered Görlitz, that houses were full, and that the festival of allegiance—the reason for Ferdinand's visit—had been shortened by skirmishing near Lübe in Bohemia where the Elector had been camping. The previous summer there had been skirmishing around Görlitz; half the land was ravished and plundered. Boehme felt that the countryside was done for. The encampments near Rackenwitz were so close to one another that skirmishing was almost continuous, spreading even as far as Raudnitz. Nearly all areas both in Leutenmeritz and Sals, as well as parts of Schlau, had been burned out. Boehme reported that the battle of Prague had had enormous casualties. (*Epist.* lxvii, 1–4)

No wonder chiliastic dreams arose! Boehme himself felt that God's ruin was at hand, that the time of "the great expedition" could not be long delayed. But he could not go along with those who dated the end. On July 20, 1620, Paul Kaym, tax collector at nearby Liegnitz, had written Boehme asking for his ideas about the "end of time" and sending along two tracts. Boehme answered Kaym in two letters dated August 14 and November 18, the eighth and eleventh *Epistles.*[16]

Kaym was no ordinary chiliast, frightened into believing that the world was soon going to end; Gottfried Arnold called him a learned man,[17] author of some important works including *Biblische Rechnung, wie lange die Welt gestanden und noch zu stehen habe* which probably was read by Boehme and may even have been one of the tracts which Kaym sent him. Kaym also wrote commentaries on the Song of Songs and Revelation,[18] and he displayed his ecumenical ideas in his *Bekänntniss eines unpartheyischen Christen wegen des seligmachenden Glaubens unter allen religionen und völckern auf Erden,* which was an early plea for the union of Christendom appearing in 1646 and sought to reunite Orthodox and Roman Churches too.[19] Kaym argued that the Logos which illuminates all men was also present among the Jews and the heathen as "natural law"; [20] he also asserted that inward illumination was the only basis for spiritual growth. Gottfried Arnold says that Kaym's writings were Quaker in tone,[21] for he spoke of internal absolution, inward baptism, inner union, stressing inwardness at the expense of the external church.[22] These anti-ecclesiastical ideas brought Kaym into conflict with one "P.C.," a pastor who accused him of being a follower of Weigel.

Kaym seems to have had greater spiritual maturity than one gathers from Boehme's epistles, although Boehme was friendly, making a sympathetic effort to explain his eschatological views. Boehme suggested that

> the manifestation of the thousand years sabbath is not of much importance or concern to the world, seeing we have

not sufficient ground of the same, it should of right rest in the divine omnipotence. (63)

Boehme confessed to have found earnest purpose and diligent labor in Kaym's book, even though he could not agree to the dating of the end. Boehme denied that the world's state was unusual, as evil was, but insisted that it was coming to fruit so that man could recognize it. He repudiated the popular *Fourth Book of Esdras* and denied knowledge of computed dates,[23]

but whether they shall be a thousand solar years, or how it may be referred . . . , I leave to God. (36)

Concerning the end . . . (viz. that Babel should be wholly destroyed about the year 1630, according to your computation, and . . . many more be of the same mind), the same likewise is not . . . manifest to me. To me indeed is known that the time is night and even now at hand, but the year and the day I know not. (73–75)

Boehme's second letter to Kaym,[24] a reply to a second query from him, is a short and at times brilliant exposition of the still more excellent way of Christian love.

When we attain the new man in Christ then we are . . . already in the Sabbath. . . . For we are with Christ in God, we are together with Him planted into His Death, we are buried in Him, and arise with the new man out of the grave . . . and live eternally in our own essence. . . . We are with and in Christ in God, and God in us. Where should we then keep the sabbath? (ii, 48)

Here Boehme inwardizes the thousand years of peace, rejecting outward ages. His final answer is that apocalypse is spiritual,

it requires a high illuminated mind and understanding which has power to enter into the mystery of God. (ii, 57)

Here Boehme recognizes a divine knowledge which is the highest form of knowing. (58)

Towards the end of 1621 Boehme wrote the *First Apology Against Balthasar Tilke.*[25] Tilke, a Silesian nobleman, had written a refutation of Boehme's *Aurora* on April 13, 1619.[26]

Sometime during 1620 Boehme got hold of this and, at the request of Abraham von Sommerfeld, proceeded to answer it. Tilke, a strict Crypto-Calvinist, contended that nature was the hidden God's manifestation as were also other acts and that Boehme was a false prophet because he argued that Christ was natural (*I Apol. Tilk.*, 108, 126) and that he was seeking to

> make Christ . . . pure humanity, natural; and thereby prepare an entrance . . . for His seduction from God. (220)

Tilke, in good Calvinist tradition, argued that by nature man is a child of wrath and that natural man perceives no spiritual things. (221)

> Is Christ a man in the wild nature? Then He was by nature vain or corruptible as other men. And how then has He revealed the mystery of God? . . . Could He pay our debts, and offer an acceptable sacrifice . . . and reconcile us to the Father? (221ff)

Tilke here raised orthodox Calvinist objections to Boehme's nature philosophy, especially at its most vulnerable point, soteriology.

At Luther's death Protestantism had been torn apart by deep-rooted party and doctrinal antagonisms.[27] The enmity of the Schmalkaldic War had been expanded into tension with Frederick of the Palatinate.[28] Part of these difficulties arose from Melanchthon's affinities to Calvinism. Three points of controversy had appeared: synergism, the necessity of good works, and the Lord's Supper. Gottfried Arnold lists [29] these marks of the Crypto-Calvinists: they denied that the sacramental elements were blood and body, they suspected the union of Christ's two natures was impossible, and they disputed the *communicatio idiomatum.*[30]

During the latter half of the sixteenth century Crypto-Calvinist troubles increased, especially in eastern Germany where Lutheranism dominated. In Eilenberg some yokels had waylaid Pastor Kempf and almost killed him.[31] In Zwickau Pastor Held was driven from his pulpit. In Freiburg so many broadsides were being published each day against Pastor

Riedel that the authorities intervened.[32] In Wittenberg the students called Pastor Pierum *Bier-Urben.* In 1591 matters came to a head when Friedrich Wilhelm became Saxon Prince Elector, for he ordered all secret Calvinists purged and appointed a Committee of Visitation [33] to examine pastors in the various creedal tests,[34] on the Lord's Supper, Christology, Baptism, and Election.[35] Uproars continued; two Dresden court preachers, Salmuth and Steinbach, were attacked [36]; indeed, not only Saxony but all Silesia was aroused.

Tilke forced Boehme to clarify his views on Christ, one of the controversial points. Boehme did this, discussing Christ's human nature (226ff), the incarnation (229ff), election (360ff), and the divine within nature. Boehme knew the significance of the controversy. He was dealing with

> Criers at Babel, the Grace Electioners, the cripple electioners at Babel (613). . . . He [Tilke] need not contend with me; I have written for myself, and not for the Grace-Electioners; much less for the new Babel. . . . It is now high time to prepare for the gossip's gift.[37] (67)

In controversy like this Boehme could take care of himself in robust seventeenth-century fashion; and he did not spare personal attack, for the "libeller"

> is a false . . . judge . . . an advocate of God's anger (563) . . . but hearken libeller, why should I talk long with you about it; you are wholly blind as to my writings; you bring everywhere other meanings thereinto (417). . . . He thinks he has caught a mouse and sees not that he himself sticks in the trap. (110)

After spirited defence Boehme wrote "instructions in time of temptation for a continuing sad heart and soul"—texts of comfort for the afflicted. This was his next tract, *On the Four Complexions* (*Complex.*), written in March, 1621.[38] In the Preface to the English version, translator Sparrow says that *Complex.* was compiled by Boehme who had been asked to write a work for one who was afflicted and tempted by Satan.

It is a curious and dated work wherein Boehme accepts the four peripatetic elements (earth, air, fire, water) as bases of the four humors (melancholic, sanguine, phlegmatic, choleric)—a formal scheme useless in a modern sense. The essential idea is that as the basic elemental character is changed the humor, or complexion which is dependent upon it, also changes.

On April 18 [39] of this same year Boehme completed *Considerations on Esaiah Stiefel's Book* (*Bedenk. Stief.*) which owed its origin to Boehme's friends. On February 24, 1614, the Saxon Elector had signed a mandate directed against Ezechiel Meth and Esaias Stiefel,[40] fanatics who believed themselves to be new Christs. Boehme's friends wanted him to dissociate himself from such harebrained fanaticism and *Bedenk. Stief.* is his refutation of Stiefel's work, *Unterschiedliche Erklärung* . . . which had appeared in 1610,[41] written because an unknown nobleman correspondent wanted Boehme's opinion about the book. The references to "dear brethren" and to "dear Sirs and Brethren" suggest that the work was intended for a group.

> You have sent . . . a little book for me, together with your other friends, to peruse; and you desire me to discover to you my knowledge thereupon. (11)

Boehme says that Stiefel, whom he did not know, might have been an honest, virtuous, newborn man (18) but he seemed to want philosophical understanding of the three principles which brought him gross error. Stiefel had claimed to have been transported to Paradise. To this Boehme replied,

> If the author . . . has put on Paradise, then he is taken up . . . I can say no such thing of myself at present, yet I have with earnestness sought the Pearl and have . . . also attained a jewel; also it is given to me to know the first man in Paradise, how he was before the Fall and how after the Fall, and have also seen the paradisaical property, but not in the outward man. (57)

Stiefel's perfectionism was abhorrent to Boehme:

> also the author mentions: he is thus through Christ transmuted into death; he can sin no more; and for that cause

leaves the outward name . . . that needs very much clearer description. . . . For the holiest men or greatest saints have acknowledged themselves sinners, (61) . . . The author says: it is not possible for the regenerate to sin, whereby it may be understood that he does not . . . understand the mystery of the soul. (66)

Boehme here recoiled against arrogation of righteousness because he understood evil's reality:

> If we put on Christ . . . we are rightly called Christians. . . . The new man lives in Christ; but we should not say [as Stiefel did]: I am Christ. (75)
>
> When the author says . . . : I the living Word of God in this my holy flesh and bones say this or do this; then is God's dear name . . . abused. . . . He is not in flesh and bones the Lord; but in the life of Christ, a fruitful humble little sprout. (84ff)

Boehme agreed with Stiefel that the time was clearly born (104) when the beginning shall find the end and the middle be manifest and revealed. Boehme's epilogue was kind and mild, remarkable in an age of bitter polemic and revelatory of his spirit:

> This . . . I was not to hide from you . . . for my conscience requires it of me in the Lord, not with intent to suppress or reject the author's book . . . ; but in love towards him. I would give him my gifts and understanding . . . as one member to another. . . .
>
> For I know the author's spirit very well, and I would fain speak with him, seeing he has suffered much for the sake of Christ's name . . . and has willingly brought his life into Christ's foot-steps; therefore I acknowledge him as a right true Christian.
>
> But he should not be ashamed of this: to learn better to know himself, and to learn more of the spirit of Christ.
>
> I say nothing of my self but that I first am become an ABC scholar . . .
>
> I do not ascribe to myself any perfect knowledge yet; for what is any way perfect, that is not from my understanding, but manifested or revealed in the Spirit of Christ in my brethren . . . I myself am nothing.

Therefore I exhort you to understand this . . . Christianly. . . . For I am not a master of your spirit and knowledge but your helper in the Lord; that the author's course might not be in vain; and the name of Christ in His members may not be reproached, as Babel has done. (158–163)

Boehme here protected himself against the charge, so often leveled against the mystics, that they arrogate spiritual perfection to themselves.

On July 3, 1621, Boehme completed the *Second Apology to Balthasar Tilke* (*II. Apol. Tilke*) which he sent to Johann Daniel Koschowitz,[42] Striegau physician, to whom the Preface is addressed. This work resulted from a discussion between Tilke and Boehme at a meeting in the castle of von Tschesch, later one of the editors of Boehme's works under the pen name of H. Prunius. Balthasar Walther had gathered a group, including Carl von Ender and Christian Bernhard, which met secretly at various neighboring landed estates. One such meeting took place in the summer of 1621 at von Tschesch's castle.[43] A letter dated July 3, 1621, has this to say about the discussion with Tilke:

In our late meeting I was ill disposed to . . . disputation, for wine and sumptuous fare hide the Pearl's ground, especially because I am not accustomed thereunto, and do at home fare very meanly and soberly, and Mr. [Tilke] was not sufficiently answered; but I offer to answer him, and all others that mean Christianly, let them but give me their questions in writing . . . I will give them a fundamental . . . expositive answer, and not defend myself with . . . any sectarian name . . . not a Flaccinian, as Tilke supposes . . . I teach no self-ability without Christ to attain the Adoption as D. Staritius thinks, only I am not satisfied with his opinion, much less with Mr. . . . Tilke's, which wholly clashes with Scripture; for I am dead to all opinions in me . . . what have I as a lay, illiterate, unexercised man . . . to do with you who are bred in the high schools. . . . (*Epist.* xv, 7–8)

Boehme now was meeting intellectuals; but this meeting was not merely a gathering for philosophy and theology. Here there was some sort of secret order, a brotherhood, as the context of this letter shows:

Concerning our secret discourse [44]. . . you must be patient to go on in that known process a good while; and in the beginning no other will be admitted; it may well, in the seventh year, be accomplished in this process; for it must be opened through all the six properties of the spiritual ground; albeit it is already opened through the sun, yet the key is scarce come into the first or second degree. . . . (*Epist.* xv, 10)

Next Boehme outlines a seven-stage process which clearly is some guarded teaching. He concludes that the long dramatized teaching is well known to him for

I have lately seen it . . . Therein much is revealed to me . . . If I come to you I may entrust you with something which I have lately seen and received; yet I shall go as far as I dare . . . I come to Breslau about Shrovetide; and so may visit you in my return. Mr. Doctor, become seeing, read . . . with inward deliberation . . . Be faithful in the mysteries . . . ; what you cannot understand parabolically, there questions are requisite; somewhat more shall be revealed to you, yet, in order to do that, I am prohibited by the Prince of the Heavens. (*Epist.*, xv, 17ff)

This is not the confused language of a muddle-headed alchemist; rather, here is man concealing knowledge from the unworthy and the uninitiated. Boehme, then, was in a secret society where philosophical and theological problems were discussed. Dr. Peuckert, erudite in these matters, is convinced that a secret circle grew up around Boehme.[45] It is known that Schwenkfeld's teachings were preserved in secret associations of Silesian nobles and physicians. Carl von Ender was a member of such a group in 1618 [46]; von Sommerfeld had been denounced as a Schwenkfeldian, as had also von Schweinichen and von Tschesch; and finally von Franckenberg belonged.[47] (Franckenberg was Sommerfeld's nephew.) Peuckert believes that these men studied Saint Paul, the *Theologia Germanica,* Tauler, á Kempis, Weigel, Johann Arndt, and the Schwenkfelders.[48] Inasmuch as Schwenkfeld's followers were not allowed to meet in public, mystical groups had to meet secretly.

What kind of meeting took place at von Tschesch's in the summer of 1621? What philosophy was dramatized in secret ritual? Why did Boehme return from a dispute with Tilke to write an apology? Boehme wrote a letter to Koschowitz as preface to the book telling exactly what the subject was: predestination.

> I have . . . presented it before him and other readers . . . to consider . . . ; since I see that not only my opposer but also others . . . are thus perplexed . . . about the predestination of God. (7)

Boehme also felt that Tilke

> lamentably goes astray concerning Christ's humanity, and concerning . . . Mary; which opinion is quite contrary to our Christian faith. (5)

Boehme had little respect for Tilke who dragged "Scripture by the hair of the head" (14) and exchanged words with words; nor did Tilke understand the light of nature. Boehme here achieved the same respect for Scripture as had energized Luther and Calvin—the "ground and corner stone of faith." Such faith, however, was not

> an historical conceit but a right life; the spirit of God must be generated in the Center . . . and spring up in the mystery of the mind; and therein rule and shine; it must be man's will and deed, yes, it must be his inward life and understanding, and man must be resigned to it. (16)

Boehme next recounted the philosophy on which his views rested, showing, although not as clearly as in his later works, the ontological basis of freedom. He spoke of the generating Virgin, but in the tract his perplexity appeared and he resorted to proof-texts to show man's moral freedom.

The second part of *II Apol. Tilke* dealt with the Incarnation, another point in the Crypto-Calvinist controversy.[49] The Calvinists said that the

> children of God must be generated out of the woman's seed,

as the dew of the morning redness, and reject Adam and Eve's seed, and make a strange seed. (230)

Here again the union of Christ's two natures (*communicatio idomatum*) was again central and Boehme was strictly orthodox. Mary was Eve's daughter. He concluded the tract with a plea for the end of theological wrangling:

What now are the Christians so-called better than Turks and heathens if they live Turkishly, and more than Turkishly or heathenishly? Where is the Christian and Evangelical Truth? (319)

About the same time that he was writing his second Apology to Tilke he also wrote his *Reply to Stiefel's Exposition* (*Irrth. Stief.*). It was completed either on the sixth or twenty-sixth of April.[50] The origin of this book is clear from its preface:

There has lately come into my hands a treatise, sent from good friends, concerning some points. . . . Thereupon I have been entreated . . . to give my . . . understanding and explanation upon these points. Seeing, therefore I observe that some . . . opinions . . . run contrary to the Holy Scriptures and true understanding . . . therefore I would take the labor and express it in a more rectified language. (1–3)

Stiefel was seeking to explain Genesis i, 27, I Timothy iii, 16, Isaiah liv, 5, and I Corinthians ix, 2. Stiefel, whose confused mind did not escape Boehme, sought to prove these points: 1) that when God created man in His image He made man visible in Christ who was the first-begotten image; 2) that God manifested Himself in Adam and Christ was the second Adam; 3) that God was related to Christ in various ways; and 4) that Christ's androgynous nature transcended asexuality.

All this Stiefel expressed with dull confusion and Boehme was performing an onerous duty to which he had no mind, for he confessed that Stiefel's writing is altogether contradictory and runs counter to itself (426). Nothing new is added to Boehme's thought by this tract.

During this period, then, Boehme moved out to challenge contradictory ideas in the world around him. No longer the visionary shoemaker set only on the exposition of his own vision, now he was the dynamic center of a group of men whose interest in intellectual discussion was strong. Thus meeting the turbulent, seething welter of ideas in the world outside, Boehme was forced to adjust his own thought, thus disciplining his growing, maturing mind.

NOTES TO CHAPTER SEVEN

1. This slaughter took place, but not quite as Boehme had anticipated.
2. H. Knothe, "Der Anteil der Oberlausitz an den Anfängen des 30 jährigen Krieges" in *Neues Lausitzisches Magazin,* lvi, 1890, pp. 19ff.
3. Arnold, *Weingartens Zeittaflen und Ueberblicke zur Kirchengeschichte,* Leipzig, 1906, p. 190.
4. Knothe, *op. cit.,* p. 23.
5. *Epist.* lxvii, 2.
6. Knothe, *op. cit.,* p. 44.
7. *Ibid.*
8. *Ibid.,* p. 47.
9. *Epist.* xvii, 1.
10. Knothe, *op. cit.,* p. 66.
11. *Ibid.,* p. 48.
12. *Ibid.*
13. *Ibid.*
14. Phrases and cadences of the Palatinate liturgy, basis of Calvinist worship, were evident in Boehme's work for this period.
15. Knothe, *op. cit.,* p. 68.
16. Buddecke, *Verzeichnis,* p. 3.
17. G. Arnold, *Kirchen- und Ketzer Historei,* II, pp. 21–23.
18. *Ibid.,* II, pp. 1095–1096.
19. Arnold asserts that Kaym wrote the popular devotional tract, *Helleuchtender Hertzenspiel* (*Op. cit.,* II, pp. 21–22), a work based on Tauler.
20. Ritschl, *Geschichte des Pietismus,* II, p. 304.
21. *Op. cit.,* II, p. 236.
22. *Ibid.,* II, p. 236.

23. Peuckert holds that Boehme's chiliast works are lost. *Böhme,* p. 82.
24. Buddecke, *Verzeichnis,* p. xx.
25. The autograph ms has been rediscovered.
26. The first work on Boehme was by this Silesian nobleman. No copy has been found.
27. Heussi, *Kompendium der Kirchengeschichte,* Tübingen, 1933, pp. 316ff.
28. *Vide:* J. G. Walch, *Historische und Theologische Einleitung in die Religions-Streitigkeiten,* Jena, 1734.
29. *Op. cit.,* I, 865a.
30. *Vide:* Luthardt, *Kompendium der Dogmatik,* Leipzig, 1937, pp. 253–259. Also, J. A. Dorner, *Entwicklungsgeschichte der Lehre von der Person Christi,* Berlin, 1853, pp. 613ff.
31. Arnold, *op. cit.,* I, 865a.
32. *Ibid.,* I, 965b.
33. Selneccer, Mirus, Mylius, Hunnius, Horbart.
34. Arnold, *op. cit.,* I, 866b.
35. *Ibid.,* I, 866b.
36. *Ibid.,* I, 868a.
37. The "gossip's gift" was doubt about parenthood.
38. Buddecke, *Verzeichnis,* p. xx.
39. *Ibid.,* p. xx.
40. *Ausführlicher Bericht,* #39.
41. Herzog-Hauck, PRE3, "Stiefel."
42. Buddecke, *Verzeichnis,* p. xx.
43. Peuckert suggests the date as 1623 (*Böhme,* p. 98). This presumes incorrect dating of five letters and of *II Apol. Tilke.* If this meeting was at Christmas it must have been either in 1621 or 1623 for Boehme was at Seifersdorf in 1622 (*Epist.* xv). The probability is that it was a summer meeting.
44. This discussion must have been heated and personal (*Epist.,* xviii, 1).
45. Peuckert, *Die Rosenkreutzer,* pp. 254ff.
46. *Ibid.,* p. 258. Peuckert believes that the Conventicle around Moller had been a secret one too.
47. *Ibid.,* pp. 258–263.
48. *Ibid.,* p. 261.
49. Sparrow in the preface to the 1661 English edition.
50. Buddecke, *Verzeichnis,* p. xx.

Dein Stein Chymist, ist nichts;
der Eckstein, den ich mein,
Ist meiner Gold-Tinktur, und al-
ler Weisen Stein.

—ANGELUS SILESIUS

CHAPTER EIGHT

THE FUTILITY OF ALCHEMY: 1622

BOEHME came to grips with alchemy. In February, 1622, while busy with his apologetic writings, he began what should have become his greatest work, that is if his alchemical presuppositions had endured.[1] *The Signature of All Things* (*Sig. Rer.*), however, became instead the book which marks the failure of his alchemical quest. Though alchemical works continued to appear in European literature, Boehme's *Sig. Rer.* marks the end of serious Faustian search for the philosopher's stone and perhaps even the end of alchemy itself. Boehme says that *Sig. Rer.* is

a very deep book . . . of the signification of the . . . forms and shapes of creation. . . . It shows what the beginning, ruin, and cure of everything is. . . . (*Epist.* xii, 73)

Sparrow, early English translator, said that it

sets forth . . . the birth, sympathy, and antipathy of all beings; how all beings originally rise out of one eternal mystery, and how the same mystery begets itself from eternity to eternity; and likewise how all things, which take their original out of this Eternal Mystery, may be changed into evil, and again out of evil into good.

Sig. Rer. is a deep, powerful, profound book, conceived in wide terms, yet missing greatness because of the falsity of its presuppositions. While likening regeneration to alchemical transmutation, Boehme adopted the old idea of the sympathetic signature. Sympathy was the influence that one thing was thought to be able to exercise on another. This was accomplished through the core, or what may perhaps be termed the idea, of the thing. Thus, bloodstones cured hemorrhages, yellow flowers cured jaundice, because their signatures were sympathetic. Boehme elevates this medical idea into an epistemological process; transmutation proceeds from the knowing of a thing's signature.

> Whatever is spoken, written, or taught of God, without the knowledge of the signature is dumb and void of understanding; for it proceeds only from an historical conjecture, from the mouth of another, wherein the spirit without knowledge is dumb; but if the spirit opens to him the signature, then he understands the speech of another; and further, he understands how the spirit has manifested and revealed itself. . . . For though I see one to speak, teach, preach, and write of God, . . yet this is not sufficient for me to understand him; but if his . . . spirit enter into my own similitude . . . then I may understand him . . . be it either spoken or written, if he has the hammer that can strike my bell. (i, 1–2)

Sympathy, an affinity between similar things, is here a principle of knowing as well as of therapeutic. To change, to heal, and to know one must exert sympathetic power on the signature, which is perhaps but a popular version of the Platonic form, as it is

> no spirit, but the receptacle, container, or cabinet of the spirit, wherein it lies; for the signature stands in the essence and is as a lute that lies still; and it is indeed a dumb thing that is neither heard nor understood; but if it be played upon [by sympathy] then its form is understood, in what form and tune it stands, and according to what note it is set. Thus likewise the signature of nature in its form is a dumb essence; it is a prepared instrument of music, upon which the will's spirit plays. . . . (1, 5)

In the human mind this signature must remain passive until the "wise master" comes to strike his instrument.[2] Each person's instrument was tuned at his conception (6) and his knowledge comes from how it then was tuned. All things, including men, are known by their signatures, and by external manifestations in sound, form, voice, and speech a thing's hidden spirit is expressed. The signature is the expressed form of an individuated being's inner essence.

Boehme's world of signatures was the "language of nature." Here he comes close to Plato's theory of language in the *Cratylus*. But with Plato names never were immediate intimations of things; for him language was imitation of imitations, copies of copies.[3] But for Boehme language conveyed inward essence by suggesting the signatures.[4]

Boehme's signature is an epistemological and an ontological key at the same time: a man's face shows his inward self, and by it the self can be known. As a principle of knowledge it is neither inductive nor deductive but productive, the necessary basis of created being. The doctrine of signatures is antagonistic to reason: the scientist who describes, measures, classifies things is interested in repeatable similarities and separating distinctions. Boehme sought to understand nature from within without mathematics or logic because he held that meaning rested on the concordance of inner *κερκίς* and external form. His symbol was the blooming lily. Evil, disease, and pain were a contradiction between inner will and outer form. When once this conflict is understood cure becomes possible; thus the old principle that "like cures like" here attains a religious meaning, for then there comes

> the satisfaction of the will, viz., its highest joy; for each thing desires a will of its likeness, and by the contrary will it is discomfited; but if it obtains a will of its likeness it rejoices in the assimulate, and therein falls into rest, and the eternity is turned into joy. (ii, 3)

Here at the close of the alchemical period Boehme saw evil as disharmony between signature and outer form.

Alchemy attached significance to qualities. If a metal looked like gold it was gold—all that glittered was gold! The external quality was meaningful. Metals as well as heavenly bodies were given spiritual qualities. Gold was the sun's earthly image, silver the moon's. Copper signified Venus, iron Mars, tin Jupiter, and lead Saturn. To this heavenly hierarchy of elements there was added the idea that the lower always seeks to become transmuted into higher.

In this early period Boehme's thought was dominated by the notion that Christian regeneration takes place like the supposed alchemical transmutation:

> You must eat of God's Bread if you will transmute your body out of the earthly property into the heavenly. Christ said, 'He that eateth not the flesh of the Son of Man hath no part in Him'; and He says further, 'He that shall drink of the water that I shall give, it shall spring up in him to a fountain of eternal life.' Here lies the pearl of the new birth. It is not enough to play the sophister; the grain of wheat brings forth no fruit unless it falls into the earth; whatever will bring forth fruit must enter into its mother from whence it first came to be. (x, 49ff)

Boehme's alchemical language, however, described merely the archetypes of the psyche. It was projection.[5] Reason, formulated in dogma, found difficulty in combining spiritual and psychical; alchemy made this junction. The laboratory "artist" worked with physical stuff, yet gold-making was not the goal. Nor was it bluff. The secrecy came from the fact that the "work," done in substances, was symbolical projections of inner states. Projection, therefore, is not studied; it happens. What Boehme says in his speculative alchemy was the inner needs; what the alchemist experienced was his inner self.

Spiritual "preparation" was needed. "You will never make One out of other things if you do not become one yourself," said Dorneus.[6] After *projectio,* the casting of the tincture on the lead, came *cogitatio.* Boehme used the word *imagination* to describe this process by which the soul's lost image is restored (*I Apol. Tilke,* 82), for Adam fell through imagination and so through it we are again restored (*Letzte Zeit* II, 7, 8). Imagination was the voice of the "other," the Unconscious, and its development is basic.[7] In a remarkably apt phrase Boehme writes that imagination is the projection (*Aushauchen*). (*Test.* I, i, 6)

Boehme said that he wrote only "in the spirit of contemplation" (*Sig. Rer.* xiv, 1), and the fifteenth chapter of *Sig. Rer.* finally brings junction between alchemical symbolism and Christian thought. The significance of this final integration is that the threatened schizoid separation of Boehme's experience, which was also the focus of his age and time, was avoided. He no longer felt that his own inner struggles were foreign to the language of Christianity. Burdened by a powerful Yes and No, alchemy served to project his schizoid psyche, but it could not, and did not, bring regeneration.

All during his alchemical period, up to this fateful fifteenth chapter of *Sig. Rer.*, Boehme had been playing with alchemical images: fire, transmutation, process, work, and all the quackery of Faust's laboratory. Now it changed. He read his Bible, the Gospel of John, and with Nicodemus asked the old, old question:

> 'How can one being old enter his mother's womb, and be born again?' . . . 'Except ye be converted, and become as children, you cannot see the Kingdom of Heaven.' (x, 51)

Here is Boehme's newly found answer:

> Hear, O man! understand what you are to do: behold yourself in yourself, what you are, whether or no you stand in the resignation of your mother (out of which you were generated and created in the beginning), whether you are inclined with the same will; if not, then know that you are a rebellious, stubborn, disobedient child, and have made yourself your own enemy. . . . For your will is entered into selfhood; and all that does vex, plague, and annoy you, is only your own selfhood; you make yourself your own enemy, and bring yourself into self-destructive death. (xv, 8ff)

Here the old Christian way of German mysticism—regeneration, resignation, repentance, disinterestedness—is put into the alchemist's imagination, and it becomes the key to all transmutation. All this is foreshadowed in a beautiful use of a beloved Christian metaphor:

> Christ said, "Seek and you shall find; knock and it shall be opened to you": You know that Christ signifies in a parable

concerning the wounded traveler, that he fell among murderers, who beat him and wounded him, and pulled off his clothes, and went away, and left him half dead, till the Samaritan came, and took pity on him, and poured oil into his wounds, and brought him to an inn: This is a manifest and lively representation of the corruption of man in Paradise, and also of the corruption of the earth in the curse of God, when Paradise departed from it. Now, would you be a magus? Then you must become a Samaritan, otherwise you cannot heal the wounded and decayed; for the body you must heal is half dead, and sorely wounded; also its right garment is torn off, so that it is very hard for you to know the man whom you will heal, unless you have the eyes and will of the Samaritan. (vii, 39, 40)

By thus discovering again the inwardness of Tauler and the German mystics, Boehme finally achieved his place as a mystic of stature and depth. He had learned that the "artist" must be first transformed before he can change wrath into love and evil into good (viii, 53; xi, 86). This he can learn only from Christ's "process":

Both have wholly one process. Christ overcame the wrath of death in the human property, and changed the Father's anger into love in the human property; the philosophers likewise had even such a will. He wills to turn the wrathful earth to heaven. (xi, 6)

And the more Boehme pondered this process the greater his discontent became. Knowing was not being changed. There must be earnest striving too.

A true Christian is a continual champion, and walks wholly in the will and desire in Christ's person. . . . He desires to die to the iniquity of death and wrath, and gives himself up to obedience, and to arise and live in Christ's obedience in God. Therefore . . . take heed of putting on Christ's purple mantle without a resigned will; the poor sinner without sorrow for his sins, and conversion of the will, does only take it in scorn to Christ; keep you from that doctrine which teaches selfful abilities and works of justification. (xv, 35)

Here Boehme entered upon his mature synthesis. He was

now no longer the naive natural philosopher. Before *Sig. Rer.* he had sought knowledge symbolized by the philosopher's white stone. Now, however, he sought the rejected corner stone as keystone to his mystical theological arch. But the development of his mind needed one more step, the deepening of his own inward struggle, before he could find his way to Jesus Christ.

NOTES TO CHAPTER EIGHT

1. Buddecke, *Verzeichnis*, p. xx.
2. Cf. Plato's theory of the technician who discovers the instrument naturally fitted for each purpose. *Cratylus* 389c.
3. Cf. *Thaetetus* 206D. *Vide:* Demos, *The Philosophy of Plato*, New York, 1930, p. 263; Taylor, *Plato, the Man and His Work*, New York, 1936. Taylor does not believe that Plato's language theory was seriously intended. But the κερκίs imposed on a piece of wood by the carpenter is not far different from Boehme's passive receptacle or even from the κλίνη of the *Republic*, X.
4. Boehme, though, is not too far from the ideas of Pseudo-Dionysius.
5. Jung, *Psychologie u. Alchemie*, p. 333.
6. Quoted by Jung, *op. cit.*, p. 349, from Dorneus, *Theatr. Chem.*, 1602, I, p. 472.
7. Underhill, *Mysticism*, pp. 144, 146.

I know what is expedient for me; now I am beginning to be a disciple. May nothing of things seen or unseen envy me my attaining Jesus Christ. Let there come on me fire, and cross, and struggle with wild beasts, cutting, and tearing asunder, racking of bones, mangling of limbs, crushing of my whole body, cruel tortures of the Devil, may I but attain to Jesus Christ.

—ST. IGNATIUS TO THE ROMANS, V, 3

CHAPTER NINE

THE WAY TO CHRIST: JUNE TO DECEMBER, 1622

JACOB BOEHME came from his alchemical search to the search for Jesus Christ, thus confirming the ancient subjectivity of German mysticism in his own experience. He had been looking for the Logos incarnate within natural reality but he came to the knowledge that nature's wrath could not be changed into harmony without first changing himself. This momentous experience, which has been confirmed over and over again in the inner life of Teutonic mystics, was the watershed dividing the pansophist of the first period from the Christian of the last. At the end of *Sig. Rer.* he had written:

The election is set upon him who departs from sin; he is elected who dies to sin in Christ's death, and rises to Christ's resurrection, who receives God in Christ . . . in the will and new birth . . ; knowledge apprehends it not, only the earnest desire and breaking of the sinful will. . . . (xvi, 43)

Here his age's second impulse asserted itself and conquered his gnostic search for the philosopher's stone.

This second mood had, of course, not been absent from his earlier writings. It had been a second theme. The *Aurora* had shown knowledge of older mystical traditions and he had already learned the best of this tradition in his association with Martin Moller. Sometime around 1620, however, he came into serious contact with Schwenkfeld, Franck, Tauler, Weigel.[1] Thus he combined the two streams from which Protestant mysticism derives: the first is that which stems from Paracelsus and the hermetical-alchemical tradition and which dominated Boehme's first years of productivity; and the second is that which comes from Tauler, the *Theologia Germanica,* Luther, and the Spiritual Reformers.[2] Boehme is their full union.

But Boehme also hints of new "illuminations," unrecorded by Franckenberg. He said:

> For the time is born of which it was told me three years since by a vision, namely of reformation. (*Epist.* lviii, 13)

Having written this in 1624, the passage hints of a vision sometime around 1621.

Boehme, however, was born, bred, and buried a Lutheran. This was the most significant fact about him.[3] He may have strained its strict orthodoxy; he may even have strayed in a few details; but even throughout his alchemical period he did not wander far from the *Smaller Catechism* of Luther. And even his rebellion against self-appointed guardians of orthodoxy was shared by Luther.

As a child of the reformer, Boehme was a Bible-reading Protestant. He knew the great, good book. The booming cadences of Luther's version echo themselves in Boehme's clear German. Hear now the rhythm of the Lutheran psalms:

> Freuet euch ihr Himmel mit uns, und die Erde jauchtze, denn des Herrn Lob gehet über alle Berge und Hügel: Er thut uns auf die Thüre zu Mutter, dass wir eingehen; lasset uns freuen und fröhlich seyn, denn wir waren blind gebohren, und sind nun sehend worden. Thut auf die Thoren des Herrn ihr Knechte Gottes, dass die Jungfrauen mit ihrem

Spiel einhergehen; denn es ist ein Reihen, da wir und sollen mit den Jungfrauen . . . fröhlich seyn, saget der Geist des Herrn. (*Dreyfach* xii, 10)

This strongly rhythmed language was from a mind filled with the cadences of Luther's mighty Bible.

The Saxon reformer—and, it will be recalled, the Lutheran jubilee had been celebrated in 1617—gave Boehme the insight that God approaches man in love and wrath. The *Smaller Catechism,* basis of study in schools like the one in Seidenberg which Boehme had attended, repeatedly admonishes, *wir sollen Gott lieben und fürchten.* Lutheran phrases occur in Boehme's writings: in *Busse* and *Gebet* Boehme repeats the familiar Lutheran prayer formula: *Ich armer unwürdiger, sündiger Mensch;* [4] in *Busse* baptism is called a *Bund* (11); in *Apol. Richt.* 57 and *Aurora* xiv, 133, he quotes Lutheran hymns. Indeed, the Lutheran hymnal like the one used in worship in the Görlitz church was a thesaurus of Lutheran faith and, as with German churches generally,[5] was used as a book of devotion.

Now Luther's hymns explained his views on atonement, ideas which had significant bearing on Boehme's mystical conversion. Neither Luther nor Boehme accepted Anselm's Latin view but insisted that Christ fought death and overcame.

Boehme recorded his estimate of Luther in the *Aurora's* Preface. The great merchant Pope had sold divine knowledge, saying,

> I have power in heaven and earth. Come to me and buy for money the fruit of life. Whereupon all nations flocked to him, and did buy and eat, even until they fainted. All the kings of the south, the west, and towards the north, did eat of the fruits, and lived under a great impotence . . . and there was a miserable time. . . . But in the evening God in His mercy took pity on man's misery and blindness. . . .

People flocked to eat; but true religion was being revealed in a new twig [John Huss] growing from the great tree's root. Men heard and were mightily rejoiced, and did eat of the tree of life with great joy and refreshing, and so got new strength from the tree of life, and sang a new song concerning the true real tree of life. . . .

The Pope again seduced man, tempting him with false wares, hawking about the fruit of life . . .

But then the great prince Michael [Luther] . . . came and fought for the holy people, and overcame. . . . But the Prince of darkness, perceiving that his merchant had a fall, and that his deceit was discovered, raised a tempest from the north . . . and the merchant of the south made assault upon him.

But the reform's glory soon faded too

when the . . . holy tree was revealed to all nations, so that they saw how it moved even them and spread its fragrancy over all peoples, and that any one that pleased might eat of it, then the people grew weary of eating its fruit. . . . They forgot to eat of the fruit of the sweet tree, by reason of the controversy about the root of the tree.

Boehme thought that he was living in a time of controversy about the root of the tree, a search for definitive creeds which circumscribed the nature of the tree's life and which neglected the tree's fruit.

For Boehme, Luther was Prince Michael who had fought the southern merchant and brought good fruit again to all people. However, having seen good fruit, people again became blind and the post-Reformation controversies spoiled the fruit.

Luther's influence on Boehme's mature thought was large for Boehme came from nature mysticism to Lutheranism; the opposition of love and wrath, of law and Gospel, the problem of justification, man the lord of creation, freedom of the will, and interpretation of stories of creation [6]—these were Lutheran. Moreover, Boehme's idea of divine omnipotence, his dualism, his clear voluntarism were also Lutheran, and on the main points of his Christology Boehme followed the Saxon reformer.[7]

The tracts of 1622, gathered together under the title of *The Way to Christ,* united the better elements of Paracelsian nature philosophy with traditional German mysticism, thus creating a new area which covered the fields least cultivated by the reformers: the doctrine of God, of Trinity, of creation, of man's relation to God, and of knowledge and revelation.[8] Classical mysticism, true to its Dionysian and Neoplatonic affinities, had aimed at self-annihilation in God. Medieval mysticism had become somewhat more subjective, seeking forgetting of sin and individuality in the next life. The Reformation, proclaiming pardon now, anticipated Protestant mysticism by emphasizing nature within the divine order, thus discussing nature's relationship to the soul.[9]

Boehme's search to define his soul's relationship to the natural world was furthered by his contact with both Schwenkfeld and Weigel. Boehme mentions Schwenkfeld twice only to say that he "stumbled" at some points. In a note on the cover of a Schwenkfeld manuscript there is this note:

C.S. was born Ao. 1490, came to Lutheranism in 1519, and came to a true knowledge of Jesus Christ in 1527.[10]

In the Wolffenbüttel catalogue of Boehme's writings there is a parallel reference:

J.B. was born Ao. 1575, reborn Ao. 1600, and newly enlightened 1610.[11]

Schwenkfeld and Boehme both had been grasped by gracious visitation: the nobleman had been "baptized by the Holy Spirit"; the shoemaker had seen more than the universities could teach. The experiences were not alike: Schwenkfeld's spirit was theological, Boehme's philosophical.[12] Dr. Peuckert has found many parallel passages between Schwenkfeld and Boehme, some so similar that Boehme must have copied them.[13] The shoemaker took the title of one of Schwenkfeld's tracts: the nobleman had written *Von dem dreyerley Leben des Menschen;* Boehme wrote, *Von dem Dreyfachen Leben des Menschen.* Both men were dualists in the same sense.[14] In *Test.* II, iii, 11, Boehme used the same

Biblical references for the Lord's Supper as Schwenkfeld; also, Boehme's doctrine of regeneration was a copy of Schwenkfeld's. Sometimes, however, Boehme's words seem to be in direct contradiction of Schwenkfeld (*Dreyfach*, 12, 39a). Boehme also changed Schwenkfeld's repudiation of Tauler's idea of resignation, accepting medieval disinterestedness. Boehme knew Schwenkfeld less than he knew Paracelsus.

The *Aurora* betrays no knowledge of Schwenkfeld but *Dreyfach* was different, for the book's theme was the new birth although not in the exact Schwenkfeldian sense; Boehme called it *ewige Geburt.*[15] In the works that followed, especially those in *The Way to Christ,* there was a growing stress upon the eternal birth until in *Test.* we come to a fully Schwenkfeldian work.

Who brought Boehme to Schwenkfeld? Carl von Ender, Boehme's patron. Erasmus Francisci, in his *Gegenstrahl der Morgenröthe,* suggests this to be so.[16] Others were Abraham von Sommerfeld, Abraham von Franckenberg, Hans Sigmund von Schweinichen,[17] David von Schweidnitz, and Hans Dietrich von Tschesch, all loosely known as Schwenkfelders, for ever since Valentin Krautwald's death the Schwenkfeldian church had embraced more than the reformer's strict followers,[18] and the denomination's official history suggests that the churches had secret congregations of Schwenkfeld's adherents.[19] After Boehme's death Boehmists continued to exist among Schwenkfelders, although most leaders went to Amsterdam; [20] upon migration to Pennsylvania in the eighteenth century the church still had a Boehmist party,[21] showing his continuing influence upon them.[22]

Boehme also may have come to Schwenkfeld's writings through Valentin Weigel for he said that Weigel wrote about the eternal birth as well as Schwenkfeld (*Epist.* xii, 59ff). Valentin Weigel, meek pastor at Zschopau, continued German mystical impulses and united Paracelsian and Schwenkfeldian traditions. After his death in 1588 his writings circulated in manuscript and beginning in 1609 they were being printed.[23] Although banned they continued to appear just during Boehme's period of silence.

Weigel, having seen good and evil in all things, likewise

asserted that their opposition could be removed by a new birth. This, good German mysticism, revived Eckhart, Tauler, and the German Theology. Weigel, however, was basically a Neoplatonist, as his *Dialogus de Christianismo* suggests.[24] From Weigel Boehme received Tauler's deep spirit, as Prunius says.[25] Weigel's pantheism gave Boehme [26] words like *Ichheit, Gelassenheit,* and *eigene* which he also shared with Tauler.[27] New problems were added to the traditional ones of German mysticism: Christology and the *communicatio idiomatum,*[28] the Lord's Supper, and freedom.

Schwenkfeld had two kinds of ubiquity: natural ubiquity, *presentia potentia,* pantheistic in implication; and ubiquity of faith, resulting from participation in the Eternal Word.[29] This doctrine realized Luther's two divine modes, the hidden God and the revealed God, becoming the hook where the Paracelsian "light of nature" was jointly hung with the "light of Grace." In Schwenkfeld's doctrine of ubiquity, then, Boehme found place for the theogonic ideas of his doctrine of God, and Neoplatonism, working in the area of God's relationship to creatures, needed Schwenkfeld's doctrine of the Lord's Supper for logical integration. This joining was Boehme's rôle.

In Schwenkfeld's and Weigel's writings Boehme thus found confirmation of his own insight and the clue to his inward apprehension of Christ. As with Osiander this indwelling Christ—*iustitia essentialis*—implied substantial regeneration through acquiring Christ's mystical body, an idea which opposed the reformer's *iustitia forensis.* These doctrines were what alchemist Boehme had been searching for and when he found them he gave them their finest expression.

There are veiled intimations that new visions were appearing but nowhere did Boehme describe them. (*Busse* i, 11)

On June 1, 1622,[30] Boehme began to write *Of True Repentance* (*Busse* I). Writing to Christian Bernhard on June 21, 1622, Boehme said

By exhortation and request I have written a fine tract, *Of Penitence and True Repentance,* along with a Prayer Formulary . . . which on request I send to Herr Rudolf von Gersdorf zu Weicha. . . . As this tract will lead you to the *Praxis*, you will experience its good since it was born through the fire of an anguishable twig, and it was and still is my own process through which I have attained the Pearl of divine knowledge. (*Epist.* xiv, 3, 4)

This process was not transmutation of elements but the conflict of penitence and the psychological steps by which this might be obtained.

On June 24, 1622,[31] Boehme completed *Of Regeneration*, or *Of the New Birth*, (*Wiedergeburt*). Here he did not profess to write psychologically but wrote

for a service to the simple children of Christ and at the request of good friends, a short summary of regeneration . . . for the hearts that hunger and thirst after God's fountain. . . . For scorners I have not written. (*Preface* 1, 3)

In his own words, here is his newly achieved inwardness:

For the righteousness of a Christian is in Christ; [in His Righteousness] he cannot sin. For Saint Paul says: For our conversation is in heaven, from whence we look for our Saviour Jesus Christ. (*Phil.* 3:20) If our conversation is in heaven, then heaven must be in us. Christ lives in heaven, and if we are His Temple, then that same Heaven must be within us. But sin nevertheless attacks our being, by which the Devil has access to us, then hell also must be within us, because the Devil lives in hell. (i, 7–8)

Boehme here saw the world's Yes and No within his own being, and resolution of his conflict was the beginning of the way to Christ.

Of True Resignation (*Gelassen.*) was written in 1622, whether before or after *Wiedergeburt* is not clear.[32] Weigel also had written a tract entitled *Von der Gelassenheit* which contained little of Boehme's depth and his solid distrust of reason. Boehme here showed the same "learned ignorance" as found in Nicolas of Cusa, an attack upon the elevated human will, selfhood's rational life (i, 2), by which man conceives great and wonderful things (14).

From out of this sort of reason false Babel in the Christian

Church on earth arose, wherein men rule and teach by rational conclusions and have enthroned as a fair virgin that child which is intoxicated with selfhood and ego-centric passions. (16)

Resignation supplants transmutation as the way out of man's misery:

The creaturely will . . . must . . . descend into itself, becoming like an unworthy child which is not worthy of so high a Grace. It must not arrogate to itself any knowledge nor understanding, nor should it, in creaturely selfhood, request or desire any knowledge from God. But, simply, and plainly, it must resign itself to the Grace and Love of God in Christ Jesus, becoming dead to its desires, yielding itself freely to the life of God so that He may do what and how He wishes with His own instrument. (i, 23)

Here was Boehme's way, that of absurd ignorance, allowing the Devil no prideful place where he might take hold. Here was no fire and flame and tincture and substantial transmutation! Here was German mysticism's traditional inwardness.

During the time that Boehme was writing these tracts he achieved a good, plastic German style. His writing was no longer barbaric and, buoyed by confidence in his literary abilities, he wrote his next tract, *Of the Supersensual Life* (*Uebersinn. Leb.*), as a dialogue between a master and a disciple. It was completed late in 1622.[33] It traces the course of the conflict in the soul, for its theme is the psychology rather than the mechanics of penitence: "How will it happen that I shall love that which despises me?" (25) "How can man hate and love himself at the same time?" (24) "Why must love and suffering, friends and foe, live together?" "Would it not be better if Love were alone?"

Near the end of 1622 Boehme began *Of Divine Contemplation* (*Beschau.*) but he never finished it.[34] It was the rejected beginning of a new philosophical work, a new synthesis. Its central problem was stated in its first paragraph:

Reason says: I hear many say of God that there is a God who has made all things, who also sustains and supports them; but I have not yet seen anyone, nor heard tell of anyone, who has seen this God, or could tell me where or how He is. For when they look at the world's essence, and consider that it goes as well with the pious as with the impious, that all things are mortal and fragile, also that the pious can find no redeemer to free them from the anguish and perversity of evil . . ; then they think that all happens capriciously, that there is no God who accepts the sorrowing since He rejects those who hope in Him and allows them to stew in their miseries; and no one has ever been heard to return from corruption and claim that he has been with God. (1)

Thus did Boehme begin again to try to solve his ever-changing yet inwardly consistent problem. *Beschau.* was broken off at the end of the fourth chapter as he was coming to clarity of style and expression.

On February 9, 1623, in the middle of important other matters, Boehme wrote *On Penitence* (*Busse* ii)[35] which usually appears as the second book of *Busse* i.

Considered together these tracts of the latter half of 1622 present a new Boehme, one who was no longer the pansophist of the *Aurora* but a man who was now seeking the marriage of the Lamb (*Busse* ii, 1). He has forsaken alchemical imagery and symbolism, although a few words, phrases, and conceptions continue to appear; now he has worked through to the traditional inwardness of the German mystics.

This change was accomplished sometime during the year 1622. The bizarre and occult speculations with their outmoded ideas, however significant for his development, were rejected because they had brought him to a *cul de sac.* Two facts support this: the scope and kind of the books he wrote after his mystical conversion, and the change in the nature of his central imagery. But even more important was the change from *gnosis,* or saving knowledge, to regeneration. Now he knew that reason was a false way to a false God; only by overcoming Yes and No within his soul was evil to be overcome.

What led Boehme to this conflict of penitence? The writings for the period are silent. The Boehme of *The Way to Christ* was still seeking knowledge, but only in a superficial sense; now "knowledge" was metaphor:

> Therefore it is necessary for God's children to know what they are to do with themselves if they want to learn God's way. As they destroy and cast off even their thoughts and desire nothing and want to learn nothing, they will then experience true resignation. They will discover that God's Spirit leads, teaches, and instructs the human spirit, and that the human egotistical will towards ego-centric passion must be completely broken and resigned to the Lord. All speculation about the mysteries of God is a very dangerous thing by which the will-spirit may be captured soon enough.

–And all this from a man who had sought to probe the whole of philosophy!

> I do not say that man should not investigate and learn from the natural arts and sciences. No, this is useful for him. But ego-centric reason should not be the energizing of it. Man is to rule his life, not through the external light of reason–this is all very good–but he should sink himself down into the deepest humility before God and employ the Spirit and Will of God at the beginning of his investigations so that the light of reason can see through God's light. (*Gelassen.* i, 33ff)

The most striking change was Boehme's doctrine of sin. In the *Aurora* sin had been dark, mysterious, formless vitality capable of being subjugated by knowledge. Now sin was a separated will that wanted to be like God. He said:

> God hardens no one. On the contrary, the ego-centric will, which persists within the sinful flesh, hardens the mind, for it brings the vanity of this world into the mind by which the mind remains closed. God, in so far as He is and is called God, can will no evil; for in God there is only one single will, and that is eternal Love–a desire for similar things, as for vital energy, beauty, and virtue. God desires nothing but what is like His own desire; His Desire appropriates nothing except that which it itself is. (*Gelassen.* ii, 25ff) [36]

Life's end was not knowing, but unknowing. A pure branch was to grow–Aaron's rod shall bloom again. Boehme pictured the total restitution of substantial existence in eschatological symbols which command respect from imaginative minds: this is the blossoming of the noble lily-twig, the finding of the pearl, the joyous love-play of God. The old imagery of Solomon's Song pictured union not of God and the soul but of Sophia and man. For the transcendent Abyss of undifferentiated Being remains inviolate!

New birth was substantial; the earth too was renewed with man's renewal. This was the celebrated restitution-of-all-things doctrine which contrasts so sharply with Eastern *Nirvana* and reincarnation. The true wedding of the lamb was the "passing from history to substance" (*Wiedergeburt,* 97).

For his growth in spirit a second major experience is needed. Boehme hints at it, but nowhere does he describe it. Perhaps, in his pilgrimage, the transcendent had become passingly familiar.

The year 1622 was, then, the second watershed, dividing the pansophist from the Christian.

NOTES TO CHAPTER NINE

1. He mentions the following books: *Der Wasserstein der Weisen* (*Epist.* xviii, 14), the third part of the pseudo-Weigelian work, *Gnothi Seauton* (*Epist.* ix, 14), the *Fourth Book of Ezra* (*Letzte Zeit* i, 27). He also mentions Luther, Calvin, Schwenkfeld (*Aurora* xx, 51ff), Hans Weyrauch, Weigel (*Epist.,* xii, 51ff), and Paracelsus (*Letzte Zeit,* i, 6, 8, 9).
2. *Vide:* R. M. Jones, *Spiritual Reformers in the Sixteenth and Seventeenth Centuries,* New York, 1928. Cf. also, C. G. Jung, *Paracelsica,* Zürich, 1942.
3. Erich Seeberg returned from Boehme to a renewed interest in Luther. "Mein Weg zu Luther setzte bei Jakob Böhme ein; ich spürte unmystischen Züge in seinen Denken und fand den Grund dafür in seinen Beeinflüssen durch Luther." *Luthers Theologie, Motive u. Grundformen, I. Gottesanschauung,* Göttingen, 1929, p. 5.
4. *Vide:* Taufe, I, 4, iv, 15.
5. Anabaptist hymnals for this period are of much interest.
6. Bornkamm, *Luther u. Böhme,* p. 103.
7. *Vide:* Erich Seeberg, *Christus Wirklichkeit und Urbild,* Stuttgart, 1937, *passim.*
8. Dorner, *History of Protestant Theology,* Edinburgh, 1871, p. 178.

9. *Ibid.*, II, p. 179.
10. Peuckert, *Böhme,* p. 69.
11. *Ibid.*
12. *Ibid.*
13. *Ibid.*, pp. 171–173. The parallels are with these Schwenkfeld works: *Caspar Schwenkfelds Schriften, Der Erste Theil der Christlichen Orthodoxischen Bücher und Schriften,* n.p., 1564; *Epistolar I,* 1566; *Epistolar, Ander Theil,* 1570; *Das 2. Buch des andern Theils des Epistola,* 1570.
14. Schwenkfeld taught that God's plan did not rest with one person but on Adam and Christ, created one and begotten one.
15. *Vide* especially the last part of Ch. xiv. Cf. also *Dreyfach,* iii, 49; *Menschw.*, I, 8, xii, 17; *Princ.* iv, xxii, 23; *Epist.*, xxviii, 6; *Gnad.*, viii, 97ff.; *Myst. Mag.* v, 19; *Irrth. Stief.*, 66.
16. Quoted by Peuckert, *Böhme,* p. 73.
17. Peuckert, *Rosenkreutzer,* pp. 244, 245. Cf. *Das Geschlecht derer von Schweinichen,* Breslau, 1906, I, p. 42.
18. Peuckert, *Rosenkreutzer,* pp. 244, 245.
19. *Erläuterung für Caspar Schwenkfeld,* Sumneytaun, Penna., 1834. The Enders (now Anders), Johns, and Schweidnitz's are still Schwenkfelders in Pennsylvania.
20. Gichtel, *Theoscopia Practica,* Amsterdam, 1722.
21. H. W. Kriebel, *The Schwenkfelders in Pennsylvania,* Lancaster, Pa., 1904, p. 57.
22. Schwenkfeld also thought of redemption in medical images. *Vide: Von der Himmlischen Arzeney,* Allentown, Pa., 1820.
23. Peuckert, *Böhme,* p. 78. *Vide:* Opel, *Valentin Weigel,* Leipzig, 1864; A. Israel, *M. Valentin Weigels Leben und Schriften,* Zschopau, 1688.
24. Peuckert, *Pansophia, passim.*
25. *Einleitung in den Edlen Lilien Zweig,* Amsterdam, p. 44.
26. Bornkamm, *Luther u. Böhme,* p. 170. (*I Apol. Tilke,* p. 174.)
27. Boehme did not accept Tauler's self-negating mysticism.
28. Weigel stressed Christ's double identity.
29. Bornkamm, *op. cit.*, p. 169.
30. Buddecke, *Verzeichnis,* p. xx.
31. *Ibid.*
32. *Ibid.*
33. *Ibid.*
34. *Ibid.*
35. *Ibid.*
36. This is an old German mystical idea. *Vide: Theologia Germanica,* ii.

All men are led to heaven by their own loves; but these must first be sacrificed.

—COVENTRY PATMORE

CHAPTER TEN

THEOLOGICAL RECONSTRUCTION: 1623

AFTER Boehme's interest had thus centered in the problems of the soul he became a kerygmatic apostle of regeneration and redemption in Christ. In an Epistle to Christian Bernhard, October 13, 1623, he recounted the results of his unordained ministry.

God has opened his door of Grace to me more and more, and not only to me, but many others, who get these writings to read, whose hearts God has touched so that they entered into repentance and conversion, and come to the divine vision within themselves. . . . Indeed, several days ago, such a stirring up of two persons . . . was presented . . . ; in whom I saw the new birth take place with great power . . . I never saw the like since my childhood, except that which God worked in my own person . . . One of whom despised himself with regard to his earthly world-affairs, and disesteemed his former mode of living; and did sink down into resignation and repentance . . . considering himself . . . dead and wholly unworthy . . . Thereupon the divine Sun shone upon him. And for three hours he spoke nothing else . . . than: 'God-Dung, God-Dung, God-Dung,' . . . Whereupon he, together with another man in like condition, came to me. After I had seen that awakening in him, they greatly rejoiced with me in that through my tract *Of Repentance* they were drawn to it. As indeed in a short while many more also were seen in like condition. . . . (*Epist.* xlv, 1–6)

Boehme's new evangelical role brought Pharisees to God's Light in converted "renovation of the Spirit of Christ," those who teach

> that all disputation is dung, and an unprofitable frivolous thing . . . [and who are directed] to the Life of Christ. (*Ibid.*, 10)

So Boehme got a new focus for his theology which necessitated that he recast it. This produced three major works, the writings which contain his nature thought: *On the Election of Grace* (*Gnad.*), the answer to the theological problem of election; *On the Great Mystery* (*Myst. Mag.*), the answer to the cosmological problem; and *On Christ's Testaments* (*Test.*), the answer to the Christological problem, a work not of the stature of the other two.

Gnad. was completed February 8, 1623.[1] It was written at the request of learned, well-placed gentlemen (*Epist.* xxiii, 3) among whom was Balthasar Tilke (*Epist.* xl, 2, 4), now one of Boehme's most ardent admirers. Boehme himself thought it to be his greatest work (*Clavis,* 147) and many would agree with him, as Franz von Baader did. Writing to Friedrich Krause, Boehme said:

> I have written a pretty large book concerning Election . . . I hope that the same shall put an end to many contentions and controversies, especially of some points between Lutherans and Calvinists, and other controversial sects. . . . (*Epist.*, xxxix, 5)

In another letter to Krause he wrote:

> Upon the advice of yourself . . . and Tilke I have considered those sayings of Scripture which . . . Tilke set down in his letter . . . wherein I was exhorted to expound the same in Christian Love, according to my gift and understanding but especially the ninth and eleventh chapters of . . . Romans. . . . (*Epist.* xl, 2ff)

This ground was more fully explained in a letter to Abraham von Franckenberg:

The work is so deeply grounded that not only the ground of the question concerning God's will may be understood; but likewise the hidden God may be known in his manifestation in all visible things, with a clear explanation how the ground of the mystery has brought itself through the expression . . . , through the Word of God . . . , into a severation . . . and how the original of good and evil is to be understood . . . and then a clear explanation of the phrases of Scripture. . . . Yet not in a logical way as 'tis treated of in the schools. . . . (*Epist.*, xli, 5ff)

Indeed, Boehme's treatment of this great theme was antirational and a far cry from the way it is treated in the schools and in Jonathan Edwards' *Careful and Strict Enquiry into the . . . Freedom of the Will,* and he emphasized to a remarkable degree the nonrational element in freedom. *Gnad.* was mainly directed against false reason and Boehme's writing often took the form: "reason says . . . answer." Sometimes he simply addressed himself to reason:

Hearken, you blind Babylon. . . . What is the election and the Grace with which you comfort yourself, and spread the mantle of Grace over yourself, over your whoredom and vices? . . . Where does it stand in Scriptures that a harlot can become a virgin by royal warrant . . . Can that indeed be? (x, 28–29)

The key to Boehme's solution of the problem of freedom is the simple proposition: no externally imputed Grace avails. This rejects any legalistic view of Christ's work. Grace is an uncovering, unveiling, and unmasking of the God hidden within man by the revealing power of Christ, for

it is not the individual born of man and woman from the corrupted nature that attains to the Grace of filiation, so that he can comfort himself and say, 'Christ has done it! He has freed me from sin! I need only believe that it is done!' No! The Devil knows this. . . . Now, what is the will which they must do to attain this filiation? . . . For Christ's will is the will of God, and they who would do this will must be new born from Christ's flesh and blood, from the Word which became man. . . . (x, 29–31)

The unveiling of the divine spark in man, the fanning into flame of the fire of divinity until the creature becomes new—this is freedom. All men were created with this divine spark; there was no election at creation! The rekindling of freedom's fire is an inward experience.

Not by comfortings from an adopted external shine or luster, but an essential way, as self-subsisting children of Christ, in whom the inspoken covenant of Grace is fulfilled substantially, in whom the soul eats of Christ's flesh and blood, has life, and that not from without, but in itself, in whom Christ continually says . . . Take, eat my flesh and drink my blood, so abidest Thou in me and I in Thee. *John* vi, 36 (x, 32)

This rich mystical indwelling, a precious Protestant form of sacramentalism, became possible only when the Mass had been rejected as a "cursed idolatry," as the Heidelberg Catechism called it, and in the tradition of Calvin (whose mystical doctrine of the Supper is frequently misunderstood), along with Schwenkfeld and Osiander. Historical faith must be followed by regeneration, and Boehme was aware that this was but partly achieved in this life and he awaited the resurrection at the end of time.[2]

. . . it is not a question of external knowledge, as that I know I have in Christ a gracious God who has cancelled sin . . ; but rather . . ; 1) that such take place likewise in me; namely that Christ . . . rise up also in me, and rule over sin in me; 2) that He kill sin, viz. nature in its evil will, in me; 3) that a new will proceeding from nature in Christ's Spirit, Life, and Will arise in me, which has God for its object. . . . This will fulfills the law . . . gives itself up in obedience to the law and fulfills it with the divine love-will. (x, 34)

The "freedom" of regenerate man unfolds itself from within out of the primal freedom which was in him at creation. The end comes to the beginning again.

The renewed Boehme who had known victory was now readjusting the focus of his interest. The devotional piety of his earlier years, molded by Martin Moller, and which had been overclouded by his alchemical speculation, now reasserted itself in a deeper form which was enriched by nature mysticism. Indeed, Boehme's mature works reconciled medieval piety with Renaissance nature-mysticism, creating a philosophical theology of depth and devotion. The God who created man became the God who redeemed man.

> Faith is not an outward thing, that any should say: 'With this is the Election of Grace, for Christ has taught and acknowledged; he has chosen us before other peoples, that we may hear His voice. And though we are wicked, yet he has forgiven us our sins, in His Purpose . . . We need only appropriate this and comfort ourselves therewith; it is imputed to us from without and bestowed on us as a Grace.' No! No! This is of no effect. Christ Himself is the imputed Grace, the gift along with the merit. He who has Christ in him, and in whose inward ground Christ Himself is, and is crucified and dead with Christ, lives in His Resurrection. . . . It is not a question merely of knowing and taking comfort, for Christ dwells not in the body of iniquity. (*Gnad.* x, 35–38)

This final heart of Boehme's theology portrays his resolution of the disunities of his experience. Here is the completion of the inward process of regeneration:

> If Christ is to arise in you, then must the will of death . . . die in you. For Christ has broken death . . . and become Lord over death and hell. When he makes his entry in a man, there must death and hell in the inward ground of the soul break and give way. He destroys the Devil's kingdom in the soul . . , makes the soul into God's child . . . gives it His will . . , slays the will of the corrupt nature. (*Gnad.* x, 38ff)

This was the final end of Boehme's groping. Now he had his "Pearl"; God was still distant, and the God-man dualism remained; but now he knew where to look for the ever-lingering Love.

> O God! the time of Thy Visitation has come, but who recognized Thy Arm before the great vanity of Anti-Christ. . . Destroy him, Lord, and break down his power that . . . Jesus may be revealed to all languages and peoples . . . Hallelujah! From the east and north the Lord roars with His

Power and Might; who shall prevent it? Hallelujah! His Eye of Love sees into all lands, and His Truth remains eternally. Hallelujah! We are delivered from the yoke of the oppressor, no one shall build it up any more; for the Lord has shut it up in His wonders. Hallelujah! (*Gnad.* x, 49)

Towards the end of 1622, even before *Gnad.* was finished, Boehme had begun the second great work of his maturity, *The Great Mystery* (*Myst. Mag.*), which he finished on September 11, 1623,[3] but already as early as February, 1623, forty-eight signatures had been completed (*Epist.* xxiii, 6). Completed, it contains seventy-eight chapters.

Its theme is breath-taking. Boehme had nothing to do with allegorical, tropological, and analogical meanings. His doctrine of the three principles gave him, he believed, his key to unlock creation's story in Genesis. Boehme's book is a *tour de force* because each character, incident, figure, or event in Genesis became part of his scheme of three principles. Each fact had three meanings in each of Boehme's three worlds. Yet this is not all! Here is allegory on a grand scale. Here nature philosophy became also a philosophy of history; the order of creation became also the order of salvation. The whole scheme is so astounding that, as Schopenhauer remarked, one can withhold neither admiration nor tears.

The central insight supporting this work was not original with Boehme but came, however indirectly, from the Calabrian Abbot, Joachim of Flora,[4] who had divided history into three ages: of the Old Testament, of the New Testament, and of the Spirit. Boehme's scheme was not chronological but dialectical. Reality was threefold, and Genesis, the record of creation, had therefore a threefold meaning. In the preface Boehme wrote:

And we will enlarge this exposition through all the Chapters . . . and signify how the Old Testament is a figure of the New; what is to be understood by the deeds of the holy patriarchs; wherefore the Spirit of God did give them to be set down in Moses, and at what the figures in these written histories do look and aim; and how the Spirit of God in His children . . . did allude with them . . . concerning the Kingdom of Christ. . . . And how the whole time of this world is portrayed and modelized, as in a watch-work; how afterwards it shall go in time; and what the inward spiritual world, and also the outward material world is; also what the inward spiritual man of the essence of this world is; how time and eternity are in one another, and how a man may understand this. (12, 13)

Each figure of Genesis had meaning for each of these three principles, and from the account time and history could be deduced. Nature-philosophy was also Bible history and a Protestant like Boehme saw all of reality within the ideas of the Bible. One has to understand, he says, that God's vitality is

hidden to visible elements, and yet dwells through and in the elements; and works through the sensible life and essence, as the mind in the body. For visible sensible things are an essence of the invisible; from the invisible and comprehensible the visible and comprehensible proceeded. (Preface 4)

So from the Biblical account of creation Boehme proceeded to deduce the inner spiritual world.

Genesis, then, comprehends Boehme's system. The seven days of creation are prototypes of God's seven spirits and of the seven natural principles. His philosophical-theology here is reoriented to the Biblical structure and it is hard to see how the writer of the chaotic *Aurora* achieved the self-discipline to write also on the great mystery. His style has become mature.[5]

A few alchemical terms survive, but on the whole he has forged a new and adequate vocabulary.

Myst. Mag. is bold and thorough. Here he explains how God operates within nature and history. Here is a philosophy of history far more profound than Augustine's parallelism because it is Biblically grounded and does not make God transcendent. The book's third part, sometimes printed with the title *Iosephus Redivivus,* describes the prototype of the New Being in the figure of Joseph who was the "cleerest figure of the new man regenerated out of the earthly Adam," as the 1654 London edition calls him. Joseph was the prototype of the true Christian.

Boehme's method is clear from the following sample passage wherein he seeks to explain several Scriptural passages:

He will wash away his garment in wine, and his mantle in the blood of the grape. That is, Christ will wash our humanity, viz. the garment of the soul, in the wine of His Love, and with the Love wash away from the defiled Adamical flesh the earthly dross and spawn of the Serpent that Adam had received with his desire and lust, from which the earthly man became a beast; and leave the spawn of the serpent to the earth, and in the end burn it up with the fire of God.

And His mantle in the Blood of the Grape. The mantle is the cover which covers the washed garment, and is even the precious purple mantle of Christ, viz. the scorn, affliction, torment, and suffering; when he thereby washed our sins in His Blood, that is, the right blood of the grape, wherein He washed His mantle, which now he casts over our garment and covers it, viz. over our humanity; that God's anger and the Devil may not touch it. (*Myst. Mag.* lxxvi, 59, 60)

Scriptural figures point forward towards Christ's work and the restoration of man by reunion of opposites within history. For Boehme the reunion of opposites remained for the end of time. Individual men could not be saved alone, apart from the race. When Adam fell the race fell; so, when the new man comes, the race will rise again. His mystical idea of restitution was a social idea because no one could be renewed unless nature itself was restored to her original purity. A universal fall means a universal redemption. This presages the true unsectarian—*unpartheyisch*—religion when Babel and Fabel will disappear, when good and evil will be supplanted by a harmony in which the conflicting wills have become one.[6] History stands under dialectical tension; eternity is beyond desire.

Boehme traced the line of the covenant with skill and originality and Joseph prefigures the new Adam to come.

As the next book, *Of Christ's Testaments* (*Test.*), now stands it contains a preface, two versions of a tract on Baptism, one on the Supper. Boehme partially re-wrote the one on Baptism "for the simple-minded," which follows as Book Two in most editions. The first composition was November and December, 1623,[7] and the revision was begun on April 1, 1624.[8]

Boehme's sacramentarian views form a central point in his thought, expressing the idea of the indwelling Christ. Just as the medieval Mass rested on Anselm's legal atonement, so Boehme's views rest on the Protestant view that Christ conquered death and brought new life to man as it was expressed by Luther, by Schwenkfelder, and by Osiander (however they may have differed in detail). Boehme's *Test.* is really a thoroughgoing Schwenkfeldian work, confirming that trend in his thought which began with his nature-philosophy and moved towards the more specifically religious inwardness of traditional German mysticism. Though Boehme employed words like *Bund,* his idea of substantial indwelling and his conception of substance mark his views as his own. Then he also used the old fire image again, an image which Luther shared.[9] Baptism was by fire as well as by water.

> For when the Logos and life-force of the Holy Fire became man, revealing itself in Christ, the holy Logos in the Holy Fire spoke through this assumed humanity into its fellow-members of the Covenant. (I, ii, 29)

Through the fire-sacrifice Israel was redeemed, and the new birth was conceived as sacrifice through fire (I, ii, 12). Fire baptism was baptism of the primitive human libido; water baptism was renewal of the image, the prototype of which was circumcision. The Supper was communion first with Christ's vitality and secondly with fellow believers. But man should not cling to the medium, for

> faith, when it hungers for God's Love and Grace, always eats and drinks Christ's flesh and blood, through the medium of the hallowed food, or without the medium of the food. (ii, iii, 42)

Now, after vicissitude and devious search, Boehme gained stature as a front-ranking philosophical theologian. He had met the stressing viewpoints of his time and, contrary to his own claims to ignorance which were born of his humility, he was a moderately learned man. He did not spring up unheralded and unsung, an untutored peasant's son who stood in the direct beam of divine illumination. He won his way through struggle to victory.

NOTES TO CHAPTER TEN

1. Buddecke, *Verzeichnis,* p. xx.
2. This point needs emphasis. Union was anticipated, not experienced, forming the irreducible core of his thought.
3. Buddecke, *Verzeichnis,* p. xx.
4. D. 1202. Joachim wrote a harmony and other works. *Vide:* Peuckert, *Rosenkreutzer,* pp. 41ff.
5. Example of this maturity of style is the first paragraph: Wenn wir wollen die neue Wiedergeburt verstehen: was sie ist, und wie es geschehe; so müssen wir erstlich wissen, was der Mensch ist, und wie er Gottes Bilde ist, und wie die Göttliche Inwohne sey; Auch was der geoffenbarte Gott sey, dessen der Mensch ein Bilde ist (i, 1).
6. Erich Seeberg, *Gottfried Arnold, Die Wissenschaft und Mystik seiner Zeit,* Meerane, 1922.
7. The date of this tract depends upon the correct date of *Epist.* xliv, which is given as May 7, 1623, but which was more logically dated May 7, 1624. Here he mentions a printed version of *Test.* Where? We here accept Buddecke's order, *op. cit.,* pp. xxii ff.
8. Buddecke, *Verzeichnis,* pp. xx, xxi.
9. "Why could Christ not confine His Body within the substance of bread, just as in the accidents? Fire and iron are two substances; yet they are so mingled in red-hot iron that any part is at once iron and fire. What prevents the glorious body of Christ from being in every part of the substance of bread?" Luther, *The Babylonish Captivity. Vide:* also Plato, *Timaeus,* 52D.

La agonía es, pues, lucha. Y el Cristo vino a traernos agonía, lucha y no paz.
—UNAMUNO: *La Agonía del Christianismo*

CHAPTER ELEVEN

BOEHME'S LIFE: 1619–1624

THE Boehme who had written the *Aurora* had been an obscure young shoemaker, but the Boehme who emerged from enforced silence to continue one of the most creative periods in modern philosophical theology was a sensation. For a book-writing "illuminated" shoemaker was as much of a curiosity as the bears, camels, and five-legged calves at the Leipzig Fair.

Boehme's fellow burghers mistrusted the strange, high-browed little man who lugged fat books to his shop, who had intercourse with nobility and learned people, who made mysterious journeys to visit the landed gentry, and who entertained visitors from far-off places in his house for lengthy periods. Unlike the Nürnbergers of the previous century, who had held shoemaker *Meistersinger* Hans Sachs in esteem, the Görlitz citizens suspected their cobbler neighbor whose fame then was spreading over all Silesia. Tension between landed gentry and the middle classes was rising; Boehme, the merchant, was a *protegé* of the nobility; his class resented it and rejected him. But a band of disciples in aristocratic, medical, and official classes arose who hung on his every word, who copied out his books even before they were finished, who paid him for the right to transcribe, and who wined and dined him in their manors.

Balthasar Walther had won the first Boehme converts, among them Christian Bernhard, as early as 1618 (*Epist.* xxvi, 3). Along with Carl von Ender, Bernhard proved to be a devoted friend. In 1619 he had further intercourse with "high persons" who urged him

to write what I saw in an effectual manner, and knew in spirit. (*Epist.* i, 2)

The "good and known" Doctor Walther already had given the forty questions to answer, but Boehme wrote

I am much busied with worldly affairs and employments, else a part might have been finished. (*Epist.* i, 17)

Boehme now was a prosperous man although there is no suggestion about the kind of business he pursued after selling his shoemaker's bench; most likely he was a linen merchant and draper.

Business, however, no longer was primary; he was an author—an "illuminated" man. He had a large correspondence with noblemen, officials, and physicians. Among the nobility were Carl von Ender and Michael von Ender, Abraham von Sommerfeld auf Falchenheim und Wartha, Rudolf von Gersdorf, Abraham von Franckenberg. Among the officials were the tax collector at Sagan, Christian Bernhard, the Electoral Superintendent at Lissa, Augustin Cöppin, the tax collector at Beuthen, Casper Linder, the mintmaster at Glogau, Johann Jakob Huser, and the Imperial Tax collector at Liegnitz, Paul Kaym. The physicians were Balthasar Walther, Christian Steinberg, Friedrich Krause of Goldberg, Gottfried Freudenhamer von Freudenheim of Gross-Glogau, Johann Daniel Koschowitz of Striega, and Tobias Kober of Görlitz. Other correspondents whose professions are not known were Johann Butowski, Martin Moser, and Valentin Thirnes. Balthasar Nitsch was a cloth-maker. Moreover, Boehme had close friends among some of his neighbors in Görlitz, mostly the professional people with whom he was in close rapport.

Boehme, although flattered by the attentions of the learned, seems to have kept his head. But when they asked him to continue his writing he dared not refuse. Although his literary activity was secret, his fame was spreading. He admitted that he knew that "haughty" people were reading his works and he cautioned against careless exposure. (*Epist.* ii, 11) In

October, 1619, writing to Carl von Ender, he said that he had gotten his writings back from Zieger. Late in September or early in October he spent several days journeying "to another country where . . . my outward man was not at home"; he also mentions his impending journey to Prague (*Epist.* iii, 3). On November 14th he wrote to Christian Bernhard,

> I have been so busied with travelling . . . and other affairs, that I could not pleasure you therein . . . for I have yet so much to do by reason of my brother's daughter (who [the brother] is lately dead) that I must run every week into the country. . . . So do worldly affairs hinder God's Kingdom. Yet I know at present no other remedy or means to maintain the earthly body, with wife and children. (*Epist.*, iv, 28–31)

He went on to say that the transcribing of his writings should not be done by anyone; not everyone could keep peace. Near the end of November he spent a longish time at Carl von Ender's; he finished *Princ.* there (*Epist.* ii, 11). This work was also sent to a Mr. Fabian (*Epist.* v, 14). Boehme and his friends were circulating the manuscripts and printed works:

> As for the other two books, viz. the New Testament and the third part of *Gnothi Seauton* [a pseudo-Weigel work], have a little patience, for they are not yet in my hands, till the Leipzig Fair, but I am confident, then they shall be sent you. (*Epist.* ix, 4)

The most interesting of Boehme's *Epistles* was addressed to Abraham von Sommerfeld und Falckenstein auf Wartha, scion of a well-known house, answering an inquiry about the *Aurora.* Boehme wrote in fawning, flattering style, admitting authorship of the work, describing his experiences, saying that he was going to send some later writings including a copy of *Seel. Frag.* Apparently Boehme had sufficient copies to lend them out.

Not only books but food as well was shared during these trying times when the Thirty Years' War was beginning. On November 10, 1619, Boehme asked Christian Bernhard to send a letter through Michael Specht to Balthasar Walther and to have three sacks filled with wheat at Mr. Weigel's, and then returned. He asked for war news, saying that the Saxon Margrave had come to Görlitz after a skirmish at Lübe, and that other skirmishes had resulted in damage which Boehme had seen on his visit to Prague (*Epist.* lxvii).

Boehme's relationship to these friends is not fully known; but their effect upon his spirit is clear. That Boehme was impressed by the coterie of important people who hung on every word that he wrote, is evident from a letter to his patron, Carl von Ender, wherein he acknowledged the urgent pleas to continue writing as coming from God (*Epist.* xi, 2). Writing to Abraham von Franckenberg he said,

> Seeing, Sir, that you together with your brother, Mr. H. S., and likewise the deep learned doctors, J. S., and J. D. K., are very much respected friends; and in the life-tree of Christ my eternal fellow-members . . . I . . . do rejoice with them . . . I have taken order that they should get a copy of this treatise . . . and communicate it to each other for the transcribing. . . . (*Epist.* xl, 11)

Franckenberg was a serious student of German mysticism; Boehme, whom he learned to know in 1623, introduced him to it and he went on to read Tauler, Kempis, the *Theologia Germanica,* Schwenkfeld, Weigel, and Arndt. Franckenberg became the first editor of Boehme's works, collected the biographical materials in *De Vita et Scriptis* and forged the popular but not quite accurate picture of Boehme.

In May, 1621, Boehme asked Christian Bernhard for a secret conference, requesting that Boehme's name be not mentioned (*Epist.* lxviii). On June 6, 1621, Boehme said that after the conference he had gone to Rudolf von Gersdorf's [1] manor where he found in von Gersdorf a "hearty desire for our talent." He asked Bernhard to get certain papers and send them to von Gersdorf who was on the right way, piously adding that "our angelical Kingdom is increasing." [2] In another letter of the same date he said,

> I acquaint you that this writing . . . The *Aurora,* is sought and read by many learned . . . noble persons. . . .

Immanuel L. 67.

Mein lieber Herr Stephan Uhlen wündsche ich alle wolfarth. weil ihr anitzo gesonnen
nach Breslau zu reisen, so bitte ich, wollet mir doch diesen pack schreiben
an Herr Doctor Müllern von Troppau, welcher nach Breslau [illegible],
Er hat zu Breslau eine [illegible] gedinget, da er seine gelegenheit hat, so er
zu Breslau ist: bey Sanct Catharin ausser der Catharin gassen in Ludwig
[illegible] hause. daselbst wollet doch anfragen ob er in Breslau sey,
wo nicht, so hat er seine bestallung mit mir verlassen, das ich es ihme
sol bey Herrn Andreas Hannibal Zobel ferber auf dem graben lassen, und
[illegible] der solle ihme nach Troppau schicken, so bringet nur diesem Zobel
[illegible] und saget ihme, das der [illegible] ausser Troppa H. Doctor [illegible] schreiben, er wird
wol wissen damitte zu thun, denn also ist es bestellet: daran thut ihr mir
einen angenehmen dienst. Ich habe noch gar nie kein büchlein von der neuen
widergeburth und zur Penitentz gehöret, welche kurtz [illegible] gut ist. wie
[illegible] wenn ihr wieder werdet zu hause kommen auch schicken. [illegible]
[illegible] dem Corrector [illegible]. [illegible] mir [illegible] das ihr H. [illegible]
das Büchlein von der Busse für einem [illegible]
[illegible] nicht vergessen, [illegible] verschulden. [illegible] in liebe. den 9 Julius 1622
[illegible]

Jacob Böhme

[illegible] 70. Brief. 14.

THE SEVENTIETH EPISTLE

Men very much, in all Silesia as also in many places in the Mark, Meissen, and Saxony, as letters come to my hand that are sent . . ; also eminent people entreat that they be put into print; which to me at present, while Babel burns, is not acceptable or convenient. (*Epist.* xiii, 1)

Having been forbidden to write, Boehme was torn between two desires: to obey the Council or to expose his talent:

I thought that I wrote only for myself, and intended to have kept it by me . . .; yet now it is manifest, and come into men's hands without my knowledge and endeavor. (*Epist.* xvi, 9ff)

Boehme, with pardonable curiosity, was also interested in how his literary efforts were being received. Writing to Christian Bernhard, October 29, 1621, he said:

How goes it with your brother at Beuthen, to whom you have lent these writings, and what judgment does he make of them were very acceptable for me to know, for there are some more people at Beuthen . . . who also have some of them, and exceedingly desire the other; and you would show a service to your brother and others if you would lend them what they desire. . . . These writings are spread far and wide in many Countries; among high and low . . . I send you with directions three sacks for the corn, which Herr Rudolf [von Gersdorf] will send. . . . (*Epist.* xxi, 2ff)

Boehme was sending copies of his own works:

I send you the magical Globe, with the explanation thereof. . . . Send it back again as soon as you can, I will shortly send you something else . . . I thank you for sending the corn. I will . . . pay you for it. . . . If Herr M. Weigel would send my sack again, I should rest content, but I perceive . . . well how his heart is. I have discovered to him the Babylonish whore; and still friendly write to him, to try if he will be seeing. (*Epist.* xxx, 111)

Solicitous letters continued to come to Boehme. Dr. Adam Brux, of Strottau, wrote him for the third time asking for friendship and asking permission to borrow some of his writings. Since none were immediately available he copied something out for him (*Epist.* xxv, 5). But when Dr. Christian Steinberg requested further explanation of some terms in the *Aurora* Boehme refused, saying

> I give you to understand that at present it is not convenient to write . . . in letters seeing the time is dangerous, and the enemy of Christ horribly rages and raves; till a little time be past. (*Epist.*, xxviii, 7)

On July 9, 1622, Boehme sent a package by way of Christian Bernhard to Dr. Göllner of Troppau then in Breslau (*Epist.* lxx, 1). Dr. Friedrich Krause of Goldberg wrote Boehme for more explanations; Krause had been led to Boehme by Balthasar Walther (*Epist.* xxx, 6). Boehme thanked Krause for the "present I have received," (9) evidence that he was being remunerated by his friends for copies of his writings. That his industry was not without reward is clear from this letter to Christian Bernhard on November 12, 1622:

> I send you . . . two sacks, and pray you to take pains to fill them with corn, and take notice and seal it a little. In the sack there is a packet to Herr Rudolf von Gersdorf and to Herr Friedrich von Kregwitz; which should only be sent to Herr Gersdorf, he will send Herr Kregwitz's part . . . but pray take the pains to convey it to Herr Gersdorf. If you cannot light upon a messenger to your mind, then send it by a messenger on purpose. He will be well paid by Gersdorf, else I will pay him myself if he does not. Pray make the whole pack again, for I have left it unsealed for you. There is with each letter a treatise annexed, which is useful for you. You should do well to copy them out with the soonest conveniency, and then speedily without further delay, send it to the forementioned place. But pray pack each treatise with its proper . . . letter, and seal that by itself. . . . By Herr Kregwitz's letter you should only write out the bound or stitched sheets, the other two sheets that are loose, or unsewed, you may leave to Herr Gersdorf. Kregwitz has the beginning fair. Concerning the list of books from Herr Linder at Beuthen, I answer, that those mentioned books are mine, which were all made half a year ago, and part of them this summer. That which you have now received from Gers-

dorf is the one against the Methists, and here in Kregwitz's writing you may find also one of true Resignation. The others are partly great ones, especially the book *De Signatura Rerum,* the signature or impress of all things . . . Doctor Bruz also has one, and Doctor Gyller of Troppen. . . .

The expedient of smuggling out his writings in grain sacks was used to circumvent the ban on his works. He continued:

Concerning the Cossacks . . . they lie in Leutenmeritz in Bohemia, even to Lippe, and very much lay waste the country. It is said that they are to draw by us, and go towards Poland. But we have nothing certain . . . I suppose they will remain in Bohemia or Lusatia, and not see Poland, for we shall shortly have new times. The present peace is not firm, for the sickness is to death. (*Epist.* xxxii)

Balthasar Walther was, however, winning more admirers; Boehme mentioned a Mr. Nagel and a Mr. Teikmann (*Epist.,* xxxiv, 20). Also Boehme said that

I am continually exercised in writing; and therefore I have laid aside my trade to serve God and my brother in this calling, to receive my reward in heaven; albeit, I shall incur displeasure, and an ungrateful odium at the hands of Babel and the Anti-Christ. (19)

Times were bad. Boehme said to Ender that money could buy nothing. He also said that he had passed one of Ender's fields and seen the beets with which God had blessed him, and Boehme asked for three sacks of them (*Epist.* lxxiii, 3), adding greetings to Ender's sister and wife, and paying him for wheat and other foodstuffs. Ender sent Boehme fish and grain (*Epist.* lxxiv) which was duly acknowledged. Meanwhile, Boehme's writings were being copied; one copyist wrote three signatures a day (*Epist.* xxiii, 4). Ender was employing several copyists.

Thus did Boehme find religious fellowship outside of the institutional church, and his conviction deepened that the churches were incapable of building faith. He asked one of his correspondents, a Silesian nobleman, not to regard the loud cry, and pratings, where they promise to us the golden mantle of grace, and put them about us, and comfort, tickle, and flatter us with a strange pretence . . . All which will avail nothing. . . . There is great heed to be taken in respect of accepting and joining any of the supposed religions, for which men contend and fight; and not to assent with the conscience of faith to one party that gets the victory. . . .

Without the heretic's arrogated individualism, Boehme trusted his inward experience, believing that it was universally valid:

I pray . . . God . . . that He would . . . open His heart that his soul may see into the ground of my gifts; for truly I am a simple man, and I never either studied or learned this high mystery, neither sought I after it . . . I sought only the heart of Love . . . and when I had obtained that . . . then this treasure of divine and natural knowledge was opened and given unto me, wherewith I have not hitherto vaunted but . . . begged God whether the time were yet come that this knowledge might be revealed in the hearts of many. (*Epist.* xl, 14ff)

This claim was misunderstood; his "precious pearl" was despised by others and he hoped that his further writing would not scandalize his good name (*Epist.* xl, 19). Writing to Gottfried Freudenhamer he reasserted his claim:

I write not as one blind or dumb, without knowledge; I have myself found it by experience. I have been as deep in your opinions as yourself . . . I wish . . . that you might have an insight into my seeing, and that you might see with me out of my seeing. . . . I may come to see you myself if my affairs will permit, provided that it may conduce to God's honor and man's salvation; for I know many thirsty souls . . . with whom I might refresh myself, and they in me. (*Epist.* xlii, *passim*)

This circle, whether secret lodge of initiates or cautious group of half-heretics, was growing around Boehme, and he had an evangelical zeal to communicate, not a creed, but a religious experience.

This was enough to inflame Boehme's old antagonist, Gregory Richter. Boehme's fame, his association with nobility and physicians, his secret meetings with persons of quality, aroused the pastor's suspicions. Rumors spread. Yet since the *Aurora's* confiscation Boehme had to all appearances refrained from further writing; only his friends knew of the works after 1619.

So it must have come as a shock to Richter when on New Year's Day in 1624 several of Boehme's high-placed friends had the boldness to publish several of his tracts in a work entitled *Der Weg zu Christo.* Sponsored by von Schweinich, this work contained *Busse, Gelassen.,* and *Wiedergeburt.* Boehme had taken pains to maintain correct ecclesiastical relations; he had partaken of the communion regularly; he had worshiped with his family every Sunday; his sons had been baptized, catechized, and confirmed. Richter had no ecclesiastical grounds for complaint. What, then, was behind his anger? He seems to have been much annoyed by the secret meetings.

Richter stirred up trouble. He incited mobs to attack Boehme's house. Windows were smashed; Boehme was called vile names; Richter denounced him from the pulpit. Writing to Martin Moser on March 5, 1624,[3] Boehme said:

> The Devil is terrified . . . and . . . has raised up a great tempest. . . . The report . . . which came to you was nothing else but a pharisaical revilement . . . by means of a scandalous . . . lying pamphlet of one sheet of paper in . . . Latin . . . wherein Satan has plainly set forth . . . the pharisaical heart . . . And I confidently believe that the grossest Devil did dictate the pamphlet. (*Epist.* 1, *passim*)

Richter's broadside pamphlet, bearing the printed date of March 7, 1624, said that Boehme's work had as many errors as pages, that the work smelled of wax and shoe-blacking, that it was full of blasphemies, that God did not want His honor proclaimed by heretical shoemakers, tanners, tailors, wives, spiritualists, and doctors, that the old Arian heresy was not as bad as this new one, that Boehme denied God's infinity and taught quaternity instead of trinity.[4] Richter also charged that Boehme was an arrogant, presumptuous man pretending to a knowledge that he did not own,[5] and asserted that he was every day befuddled with brandy, beer, and "*Schnapps*," "all which," Boehme replied, "is untrue and he himself is a drunken man." (*Epist.* lii, 1) Richter wrote Pastor Fries in Liegnitz asking him to denounce Boehme from the pulpit and to the Görlitz Council, which he did.[6] Boehme probably was visiting at von Schweinich's near Liegnitz. Meanwhile Richter was demanding that the Görlitz Council[7] clap Boehme in jail.

The Görlitz Councillors had read Boehme's book and could find nothing offensive or heretical in it. The citizens liked it. They even said that Boehme's teachings were on the same ground as the Fathers (*Epist.* liii, 9). But the Council could not resist Richter's pressure and Boehme was clearly guilty of disobeying the order of 1613 forbidding him to write. So he was arraigned. The decree in the Minute Book reads:

> Anno 1624, the 23rd of March. As regards the shoemaker of this city, named Jacob Boehme, it is decreed that, on account of manifold complaint respecting his alleged pernicious doctrine, he be summoned before the Council and enjoined to seek fortune elsewhere.[8]

On the 26th Richter's second *Judicum* appeared in which he called Boehme the Anti-Christ and vituperatively lampooned Boehme's claim to high knowledge.[9] On the same day Boehme was again arraigned. The Minutes again say:

> Jacob Boehme, the shoemaker, and confused enthusiast or visionary, says that he composed the book, *The Eternal Life* [sic], though he did not have it printed, but that one of the nobility, Hans Sigmund von Schweinichen, had it printed. He was warned by the Council to seek fortune elsewhere, or in default of fair means this must be reported to the illustrious Prince Elector. Thereupon he declared that he would take his departure as soon as possible.[10]

(Boehme already had received summons to the Electoral Court and he was waiting for the Leipzig Fair before leaving.) Dr. Weisner's *Relation* gives the following fuller account of the examination:

When the magistrates were met . . . and sent for the falsely accused . . . they examined him, perceived no evil in him, they found no anger nor dislike in words or in deeds or behavior, to proceed from him; nor did they observe anything that was blamable; they asked him what hurt he had done the preacher? and therefore he intreated most submissively and earnestly: that their wisdoms would send for the complainant or preacher and cause him to say what he had done him.

Upon which the whole Council concluded that it was just that the preacher should be required to signify the . . . grievances, and thereupon sent two men . . . to the preacher, and intreat him to come to them . . . or . . . to relate those grievances. . . .

Whereupon he was enraged, and sent them word what had he to do with their judgment house . . ; what he had to say, that he shall speak in the place of God, from the pulpit . . ; what he had there said, they should follow that, and banish the vain, wicked reprobate heretic from the city. . . .

Accordingly the lords consulted, and could not find how they should justly help the master [shoemaker]; fearing the vehemency of their preacher . . ; and concluded to banish the innocent J.B. out of the city, in which conclusion some men of the Council would not consent, but rose and went their way, but the rest executed it, and . . . caused the uncondemned . . . citizen to be instantly banished out of the gates.

Which the patient blessed man disliked not; but answered in the name of God, my lords, I will do; but may I not go to my house first, and take mine along with me, or at least tell them my necessity? But they forbade it and he instantly was to be led . . . out of the city, with derision and scorn; then he said, Dear Sirs, let it be done seeing it cannot be otherwise. I am contented. So he was banished and gone away all night long.[10]

Next day, the twenty-seventh of March, Richter's third *Judicum* was published, in which he rejoiced that the city was rid of Boehme. He asked Boehme to leave quickly and to move far away so that no curse should descend upon Görlitz. The dirt which the shoemaker had spewed forth, he said, had contaminated the whole town, adding significantly, You have ignited all Silesia with your teachings! Weisner continued, saying,

But the next morning, when the Council were met together again, and had somewhat reconciled their disagreements, they made another conclusion, to hunt after the persecuted innocent man, and sent up and down about the country to seek him, and at length found him, and brought him solemnly and with honor into the city again, which was a wonder from God. . . .

Boehme returned home on the third of April and composed his answer to the Council. In this letter he defended himself against Richter's accusations in reasoned and temperate manner. Inasmuch as this letter is so revealing of his character and is otherwise unavailable in English it is here quoted in full:

Noble, Most Worthy, Esteemed, Very Learned, Most Kind, and Most Wise Gentlemen! I presently appear before my lords as a Christian and I am prepared to give account of my talents and knowledge which I have singly received from God's Grace only, as a gift.

As to my person, I know of nothing else to say except that I am a lay and simple man, and as a Christian [I] have become enamoured with my Savior's Love, and He has loved and betrothed Himself to my soul's inwardness, of which, since it is requested of me, I shall give account.

I have my knowledge and science out of such gifts, and certainly not from the Devil, as I am unjustly accused, to which a serious reckoning before Christ's judgment belongs, as is written: whosoever mocks the Holy Spirit eternally has no forgiveness, yet on my part I wish him God's heartfelt-compassion.

I wrote my first book in such knowledge, and only as a memorial for myself with intention to keep it only by myself and to show it to no person; but this, through divine intervention, was taken from me, and given to the *Primarius*, as the worthy Council well knows.

In this same book a philosophical and theosophical ground is described in such words as I at the time of my simplicity could understand by myself and I did not intend that anyone else should read it. The *Primarius* has advertised this same book for me with a wholly strange understanding contrary to my meaning and so scolded this whole time which for the sake of Christ's Glory I have thus borne with patience.

When I defended myself against him before the *Ministerium* [11] and proved my ground I was then obligated by the *Primarius* not to write more which I readily conceded. But at that time I did not understand God's way, what He would do with me. On the other hand the Lord *Primarius* as well as the other preachers promised me to be silent in the pulpit which has not taken place. But [he] has insultingly slandered me the whole time and often ascribed things to me which I am not guilty of, thus slandering and deceiving the entire city so that I as well as my wife and children had to be a spectacle, jest, and fool among them. Further at his command I left all my writing and speaking about such high knowledge of divine things alone for many years, and hoped that there would be an end to the slandering, which did not happen, but became worse.

But the lord *Primarius* did not let it rest here, but loaned out my book and answer to strange places, towns, and villages, and himself spread the same without my knowledge and desire, where it has been copied out and viewed with other eyes than he viewed it; through which it has gone from one city to another, to many of the educated, both priests and doctors, and many noble persons, also to the Duke of Liegnitz, who wanted it, but wholly without my knowledge, unknown to me.

Afterwards many educated persons or priests, doctors, also noble and ducal as well as princely persons united themselves in writing and also a part in person, asking for more of my gifts, knowledge, and confession; to whom I said in the beginning that I dared not do it, it was forbidden of me by the *Primarius*. But they produced Scripture with serious threats of divine punishment, and demonstrated that each one shall be prepared to give an accounting for his gifts and faith, as well as his hope, and that God would take the pound away from me and give it to him who accepts it; also that one must obey God more than men, which I considered and implored God that whatever such as did not redound to honor His Name He would take it from me, and [I] gave myself fully and completely to His Will, with prayer to Him and with petitioning day and night, until the divine noble gift was renewed for me and became enkindled with great heavenly light.

So in divine knowledge I began to answer the gentlemen's questions and upon request and desire to write some little books, among which also is this *Of True Repentance,* which now has been published.

For in this book my own process is shown through which I have gotten my gifts from God, which was written at the request of high and educated people and fell so deeply into the hearts of some that one of the nobility had it printed.

But since the Lord *Primarius* thunders so violently against it, condemning the same to the fire, also citing my person so insultingly, and setting the whole congregation on [my] neck, also proclaiming that I have poisoned the whole city of Görlitz as well as the principality of Liegnitz with it, and spread the same, and because of this the great clamor of the priests of Liegnitz arose about me, also that because of it the Honorable Council as well as the city of Görlitz stood in danger.

Therefore do I give answer, that such count for nothing and that such things are ascribed to me out of evil bias only by a few and perhaps even the aggravation of the Lord *Primarius* himself, since he observes that my innocence shall come to [the light of] day.

For in the first place I myself did not let the book be published. Secondly I did not circulate it in the principality of Liegnitz. Thirdly I know that his fears regarding such danger that the Duke of Liegnitz and the whole clergy would be annoyed do not hold up for I know this much that the Duke as well as some Counselors, also many of the clergy themselves, read [the book], who along with some of the high schools who are highly learned men love it; also it is beloved by some distinguished gentlemen in the Electoral courts in Dresden and Saxony, as also by some Prince Electors and gentlemen of Electoral cities, as I could demonstrate by many letters.

And [I] therefore fully consider that this is both from the Devil, directed for his kingdom, since he sees that his kingdom is revealed through it, and man is directed to repentance and Christian living.

Since the Lord *Primarius* condemns my books to the fire I

then ask and request that the Honorable Council, for God's will, shall command him that he show me my errors in this book item by item, allowing me to come to an answer or to a verbal conference in the presence of some gentlemen of the Council. Were he then to show me an error, I should gladly allow myself to be instructed and to follow him. But if not, since it is in print, he may also write against it, if it please the Honorable Council. There are surely learned people who will take my [cause] and answer him.

Finally he denounced me before the whole congregation, saying that I despised the church and the Holy Sacraments, often scolding me as a heretic, *Schwärmer,* and knave, and attacked me with regard to my honorably begotten good, honorable name [which has always been maintained] in good repute, and ascribed to me such things as are not true, saying that I continually drink myself full of brandy and other wines and beers like a hog, which is ascribed to me against God, honor, righteousness, and truth, out of bad feeling to make me hated by the congregation.

First, I do not despise the church because I myself go into it, much less the Holy Sacraments which I myself partake of. On the contrary I profess the temple of Christ Jesus in us, that we should hearken to Christ teaching us in our hearts according to Saint Stephen and the Apostles' teaching. Also I have written more clearly about the Holy Sacraments than I have ever heard from him in the pulpit, how they were to be explained.

So I am also no teacher nor preacher, and I do not preach nor teach, but I only give account of my gifts and knowledge, how I came thereto. And as far as I am concerned I dare not fear disciples for with my talent I do not associate with common people but with doctors, priests, and noblemen who are educated.

On this account [I] ask the one most worthy and wise Council to take me into proper protection against such slanders, insults, and untrue accusations for with such accusations, violence, and injustice are done me, and [I] live wholly soberly with prayer and mediation on God's gifts. I appeal to the whole city and know that there is no man who can show me to be so. But with the Herr *Primarius* one can often discover a drunken man! Yet I hardly go to one person's house, much less to beer-parlors or wine-cellars. But I dwell alone and quietly, as is well-known to the Council.

Boehme next wrote his answer to Richter himself which he completed on the tenth of April. It is known as *Apol. Richt.*[12]

Gregory Richter's attack had spread Boehme's fame and had called civil and ecclesiastical attention to him. For orthodoxy then was zealously guarded by ecclesiastical watchdogs like Richter and by civil magistrates who under the provisions of the various treaties managed such affairs.

After the second brush with the Görlitz Council, Boehme prepared to go to Dresden, viewing the summons he had received before the Council's action as a chance to vindicate himself. On May 9 he started for Dresden by way of Löbau and Bautzen, arriving sometime before the fifteenth.

Dresden was in jubilee. The Saxons had news from Hungary that peace had been arranged between the Emperor and Bethlem Gabor. It was, of course, temporary. English and Scottish soldiers were around and the lull was prior to the storm.[13]

Boehme was not unknown there. Balthasar Walther, who had been director of the Elector's laboratory, had spread the word to his successor, Benedict Hinckelmann, with whom Boehme stayed. Here he was offered all Christian love and friendship, and his arrival was announced to courtiers and Boehme wrote that they read his little book and used it daily.[14]

Boehme wrote four letters home to Dr. Kober which describe his welcome and treatment. Courtiers sought him out for long talks. Joachim von Loss invited him to his castle for a visit, and Major Stahlmeister, the Elector's chief master of the horse, furthered his suit with the Elector. Some of his new friends gave him money. In Dresden he heard nothing of the tumults and uproars which had been his daily diet in Görlitz.

My printed book is already come into the hands of many officers and learned men, all of whom count it to be good, and a gift from God, and they labor and contrive how such things may be published. (*Epist.* lxi, 1)

And the *Primarius'* . . . libel is very wonderfully looked upon. . . . Some suppose that the . . . spiteful spirit has dictated it . . . He is despised by the priests . . . Herr Hincklemann has shown it to the Council and to the learned who wonder at the man's folly, that he dare vomit out his evil affections in public against a Christian book, some of the . . . councilors have signified . . . that . . . they will cause me to be invited to them for a Christian converse . . . with me. . . . My writings are copied out. . . .

This conference took place at Hincklemann's where Dr. Aegius Strauch and others talked about some misunderstood points in his book. Strauch commended Boehme's writings. Boehme nowhere mentioned an examination before the Elector himself, and the seventeenth-century writers (Calov, Spener, and Arnold) assumed that it took place for two reasons: Hegenicht asserted that it did, and Weisner gave an account of it. Others denied that Boehme had received Electoral vindication. Weisner's account, here given, is generally trustworthy. Boehme was

cited to Dresden and was examined in the presence of the illustrious prince Elector, by the chief doctors assembled together . . : Dr. Hoë, Dr. Meisner, Dr. Baldwine, Dr. Geryod, Dr. Leisler, and one Doctor more which I cannot name . . . and two professors . . . of mathematics . . . appointed to discourse about his writings; also in several ways to set about with all sorts of . . . questions but not overcome by any of them, but . . . rapidly and distinctly answered . . .

The illustrious prince Elector highly wondered at it and desired to know the final verdict; but they . . . excused themselves and entreated that . . . he would have patience until the spirit of the man should be more plainly clear to them . . .

Then the deeply-grounded . . . man asked them several questions . . . The simple man held forth . . . the truth plainly . . . and discoursed friendly with them. . . .

To the astrologers he said . . : Dear Sirs, thus far is the spirit of your mathematics right, exact, and grounded upon the mysteries of nature . . .

So they left him quietly . . . The illustrious prince Elector had great satisfaction in the answers. He required him to come apart by himself, and spoke with him . . . and admitted him to all favors, and gave him liberty to go to his house in Görlitz. . . .

The four letters which Boehme wrote to his good friend, Dr. Kober, back home in Görlitz, show his concern for his family. He asked Kober to

> treat with my wife, and tell her she shall get patience, and give herself to quiet, and not be so fearful and dismayed at it, as I perceive she is, for it is very well with me and I am preserved with honor and love . . . I intend, God willing, to take care of her and my children. . . . There is a time coming wherein it will not be dishonorable to her; none know how to speak disgraceful things of us, but only one wicked man, who belies us. . . . Concerning my son Jacob, that he is come home, I rejoice, and desire . . . that he would stay in Görlitz till my coming, and not . . . dispute . . . with any. . . . Comfort my wife, that she may let go her fruitless care; there is no danger about me. I am at present well and better than in Görlitz. (*Epist.* xli.)

In the second of these letters he asked Kober to tell

> my wife that she should not perplex herself by reason of me, but diligently pray that God would order it for the best, and if she wants anything, she knows very well where she may have it, she should only keep herself within, and a little submit herself; this stormy tempest will soon blow over. (*Epist.* lxii)

In the third of these letters Boehme asked Kober to

> salute my wife and son, and let them read this, and exhort them to patience and prayer. I hope all will be well; they should have patience a little, who knows how the current may run? This persecution may serve for the best. I will within three weeks, if it may be, come home. . . . And exhort my son Jacob to wait, and that he should go often to Hans Berger and see what Elias learns, and that he behave himself with his schoolmaster in love, to whom he shall present my salutation, and not conceal my purpose, that he should look upon it, as if there were any cause to flee from [Richter], and for that cause Elias might be abused and evilly treated by the schoolmaster.[15] (*Epist.* lxiii)

In the fourth of these letters he said,

My wife need not cause any window shutters to be made; if they will break them they will, and then the fruits of the high priest will be seen; let her have a little patience. If she cannot get a place in Görlitz, I will get a place for her somewhere else, where she will have quiet enough; but let her stay at home and not go out except upon necessity, and let the enemy rage, but he will not eat her up. . . . By the bearer I send two reich-dollars to my wife for her occasions, if she want anything she knows well where she may have it; the key of the drawer lies in the parlor by the warming-pan on the shelf. . . . Salute my wife and two sons for me and exhort them to Christian patience and prayer, and to purpose no self-revenge. . . . My Jacob shall stay at Görlitz that his mother may have some comfort there until I can dispose it otherwise.

Boehme left Dresden only partly vindicated, neither justified legally nor branded an illuminated heretic. In comfort he went to his noble friends—to von Schweinichen, von Gersdorf, and von Franckenberg. From June to October he was at von Schweinichen's. Tales of his "hidden sight" were still being told [16] and he was still a sideshow freak to his Görlitz neighbors. The burghers said that he

frequented the company of the foremost enthusiasts, he often had his *raptus* and quakings, so that he sat in his corner writing, even though previously he could neither read nor write. He brought great books home . . . [and wrote some] that the theologians and professors could not contradict.[17]

Surely the sight of the short, high-browed, bent shoemaker lugging big books home, and his continuous writing, were enough for stories to grow on. During the last half-year he had been writing several things: two philosophical tracts, two mystical tracts, and one large but unfinished speculative work which might have become his greatest work.

In February, 1624 he wrote the *Table of the Three Principles* (*Taf.*),[18] showing that his final orientation towards the doctrine of God was still tinged with alchemical imagery although his nature philosophy had changed from the cruder ideas in the *Aurora.*

In March or April he wrote the *Clavis* [19] which was the

key to his works so much requested by his friends, a simplified glossary of the unusual terms which had appeared in his earlier writings. It does not represent a progressive step in his thought.

On March 25 he completed a lovely little work, *Dialogue Between an Enlightened and Unenlightened Soul,* (*Gespräch 2er Seel*),[20] the zenith of his mysticism, describing the psychological order of salvation as a dialogue between a regenerate and an unregenerate man.

Before the middle of June, while at Hinckelmann's in Dresden, he began *Of Divine Prayer* (*Gebet*), one of the towering monuments in the literature of devotion, an incomplete prayer book[21] which was to have had prayers for the week, at waking, rising, dressing, eating, working, et cetera—prayers for the Ten Commandments, and prayers on the Catechism. It remained unfinished.

In October he began *The Theosophical Questions* (*Theos. Frag.*),[22] a work which, had it been completed, would have become his deepest, clearest work. Who formulated these questions is not known, but there are hints that his Silesian friends propounded them. The work was planned to set forth a view of revelation, God, nature, creature, heaven, hell, and the world. But the same old problems, and the same mystical insight, here persist.

The reader is to know that in Yes and No all things consist. (iii, 2)

Abraham von Franckenberg recorded his last meeting with Boehme:

Having in the year 1624 been several weeks with us in Silesia . . . he was seized with a burning fever, and much swelled and bloated by an immoderate drinking of water, so that, at last by his own desire, he was brought in such condition to his own house in Görlitz.[23]

This was November 7, 1624.[24] Catharina was not at home, but Dr. Kober, his good friend, cared for him. But the end was near. Kober wrote

As we could find no satisfactory cure, I, along with Christoph Kütter of Sprottau, concluded that he should be buried without scandal.[25]

In the evening Kober asked Master Elias Dietrich to question Boehme on his faith, preparatory to final celebration of the Lord's Supper. Dietrich made the official reply. On the fifteenth of November, at eight in the morning, Boehme, growing weaker, was examined regarding his beliefs.[26]

Primarius Thomas, successor to Richter who had just died, granted Dietrich permission to administer the Supper, provided satisfactory answers were obtained. Dietrich's report [27] to the church authorities listed some of the questions put to Boehme.

Dietrich asked whether he believed that God was in essence and substance one and in person threefold. Boehme answered yes.

Dietrich asked whether he believed that in the beginning God had made man in His image, that man of his own self-will and beguiled by the Devil, had turned away from God and so fallen into temporal and eternal death and sin, that because of sin man must be punished eternally unless God took pity on him. Boehme answered yes.

Dietrich asked whether he believed that in the mediatorial person of Christ there were two distinct natures, that by divine nature He existed from eternity, equal in essence, honor, and glory to the Father and Holy Spirit. Boehme answered yes.

Dietrich asked whether he believed that the only mediator and the only way to salvation was Christ who must be seized through real faith which is a divine gift. Boehme answered yes.

Dietrich asked whether he believed a Christian ought to lead a holy, blameless life, according to God's command, as far as possible in this corrupt nature; yet with God he can gain nothing by this, but is saved by pure unmerited Grace. Boehme answered yes.

Dietrich now asked whether, if God prolonged his life, he would keep to Lutheranism. Boehme answered yes.

Dietrich reminded Boehme that he was to be content with

the revealed Word and not to dabble in revelations and visions. Boehme answered that he had read the New Testament and that diligently.

Dietrich exhorted him to combine Old and New as the Old referred to the New and the New to the Old. Further he was to write no more books. Boehme replied with an account of *occasionem scribendi* upon which Dietrich did not comment.

Dietrich asked whether he had partaken of the Supper lately. Boehme replied that the last time had been about three-quarters of a year before, with his wife and two sons in public church assembly. Catharina added that her husband had been several times absolved in Herr Andrea.

Dietrich asked whether his repentance and desire for the Supper was earnest. Boehme said yes.

Dietrich exhorted Boehme to watch what he was doing, for though he might deceive men, he could not deceive God, and he prepared to administer the Supper. But with a view to further defence against calumniators he proceeded further to ask whether Boehme felt that he was a sinner. Boehme answered yes.

Dietrich asked whether he sorrowed with all his heart for his sins. Boehme answered yes, and added, "*Manibus complicatis, oculis elevatis.*"

Dietrich asked whether he believed that Christ had died and shed His blood for his sake. Boehme answered, "Yes, for He Himself says, 'Come unto me all ye that are weary and heavy laden and I will give you rest.'"

Dietrich then asked whether he believed that God, for Christ's sake, would pardon and forgive all sins and be gracious and merciful, Boehme said, "Yes," firmly.

Dietrich asked whether with God's help he would mend his life and guard against sin. Boehme said, "Yes."

Dietrich asked whether he was ready to pardon and forgive everyone by whom he had been injured. Boehme said, "Yes, with my whole heart I forgive and desire of them like forgiveness."

Dietrich absolved Boehme in Christ's name, blessed the elements, and partook with Boehme of the Lord's last supper.

Boehme grew weaker. Saturday, the sixteenth,[28] he told

Hans Rothe and Michael Kurtz that in three days he would enter another world. Sunday, at two in the morning, he asked his son Tobias whether he also heard the sweet music. Tobias said that he did not. Then Jacob Boehme said, "Let the door be opened so as to hear the singing better." Later he asked, "What time is it?"

"Three o'clock."

"My time is not yet. O Thou strong God of Sabaoth, deliver me according to Thy Will! O Thou crucified Lord Jesus Christ, be merciful to me and take me into Thy Kingdom!"

At six in the morning, before the city gates were open,[29] he bade farewell to his wife and sons, murmured, and gasped, "Now I go hence to Paradise." [30]

The sun was rising on eternity.

NOTES TO CHAPTER ELEVEN

1. Zinzendorf's mother was a von Gersdorf.
2. Gichtel, editor of the 1682 edition, founded an "angelical brotherhood."
3. This letter's contents show that it was written after the *Judicum.* The letter's date is March 7. Probably the letter is incorrectly dated.
4. Cf. Jecht, *Böhme,* pp. 70–71.
5. Fechner, *Leben,* liii.
6. *Ibid.*
7. The Council consisted of Wolfgang Stolberger, Burgomaster; *Consules:* Fr. Schwettig, Barth. Jakobi, M. C. Staudt; *Scabini:* C. Cunrad, B. Hagendorn, Fr. Beyer, Nath. Scultetus, W. M. von Mollerstein; *Senatores:* F. Föster, Tob. Grautzke, S. Schnitler; *Syndikus:* N. Seb. Krebs. Of these M. C. Staudt (1580–1639) was patron of the arts and sciences, whose brother Daniel gave 100 marks to scholars and placed his fine library at their disposal. Materials from the archives of the Staude-Staudt-Stoudt family, c/o Don Ricardo W. Staudt, Buenos Aires.
8. Jecht, *Böhme,* p. 43. Was he still a shoemaker?
9. *Ibid.*
10. Weisner's *Wahrhaftiger Relation,* both passages.
11. No account of this meeting survives.

12. This survives in the autograph ms. Cf. Buddecke, *Verzeichnis.*
13. Peuckert, *Böhme,* p. 132.
14. *Ibid.*, pp. 136ff.
15. Elias, thirteen, was scholar in a church-controlled school.
16. Franckenberg, *De Vita,* #23. *Vide:* Freytag, *Bilder aus der deutschen Vergangenheit,* II, pp. 426ff.
17. *Ibid.*
18. Buddecke, *Verzeichnis,* p. xxi.
19. *Ibid.*
20. *Ibid.*
21. W. R. Garrison in a review of a translation of *Gebet* in *The Christian Century.*
22. Buddecke, *Verzeichnis,* p. xxi.
23. *De Vita,* #23.
24. Peuckert, *Böhme,* p. 140.
25. Kober, *Umständiger Bericht.*
26. Peuckert, *Böhme,* pp. 140–141.
27. Okeley, *Memoirs,* pp. 81–86.
28. The Knauthe ms dates it September 25, following references in Hans Emmerich's diary.
29. Boehme lived just outside the gates.
30. This account of the catechization and death is from Dr. Kober, #6. Kober, his physician, was with him when he died.

PART TWO

THE SCOPE OF BOEHME'S THEOLOGY

Although Jacob Boehme's thought, beginning in mystical experience, emerged out of the tensions of his age and region, it grew to become a mature organism as his day-star continued to rise. His theological metabolism was rapid and he quickly replaced old cells with new ones. He was ever rewriting, recasting, reformulating and his mature theology emerged as a body of positive thought only after he had firmly joined vision and life.

He struggled with the Yes and No in his own self. As long as he had only anticipated union he was schizoid, a divided self. His mature theology, result of final triumph over the bipolarity of his experience, united the two apparently contradictory sides of his personality. He struggled to join Renaissance nature philosophy with the usual subjectivity of Christian mysticism. In his earlier works connection was only sought, never found. Only in the works after 1623 did integration appear.

Our cross-section of Boehme's theology, then, is an attempted exposition of what we consider to be his integrated thought.

Theogonies described the origin and development of the world from obscure primordial impulses to the clear and distinct variety-in-unity of the organized kosmos.
—ERWIN ROHDE: *Psyche*

CHAPTER TWELVE

GOD BEYOND NATURE AND CREATURE: THEOGONY

BOEHME'S basic insight, gotten in the sunrise to eternity and realized in life, was that in Yes and No all things consist (*Theos. Frag.* iii, 2). To realize this he had to present solution to the problem of being which explained the world's generation, its "birth" and development. He had to postulate a source which was both unthinkable and contradictory, the origin of bifurcation and lying beyond necessity as the coincidence of contraries from which all finite realities proceed.

Like the Gnostics he had to give theogonic explanation of how Yes and No arose from a basically indifferent dynamic One. How did the one God become Yes and No, love and wrath? How did the dialectical [1] world arise?

Boehme separates theogony from emanation. The former explains how a trinitarian God arises, the latter how the manifold things of the world come to be. He proposed two schemes for solving these two problems: the "seven spirits of God" and the seven natural principles. Many Boehme students, including Hegel, have mistakenly identified these two schemes, with confusing results.

The doctrine of the seven spirits of God had already appeared in the *Aurora* and persisted through his mature thought.

The whole or total God stands in seven species or kinds, or

in a sevenfold form or generating; and if these births . . . were not, then there would be neither God, nor life, nor angel, nor any creature. And these births . . . have no beginning, but have generated themselves from eternity. . . . These seven generations are none of them the first, the second, or the third, or the last, but they all are seven. . . . Yet I must set them down one after another, according to a creaturely way . . , otherwise you could not understand it. (*Aurora,* xxiii, 15ff)

To write otherwise would be to give the Deity imagined form (*Aurora* xxiii, 46ff). These seven spirits were seven ways of talking about a God and God was not to be restricted to these forms. Each of Boehme's major works repeats this warning: the Deity's immeasurable extent cannot be described (*Aurora* x, 26); external nature generates itself without beginning (*Princ.* iii, 3); the Deity has no beginning (*Sig. Rer.* iii, 1) but is an eternally generating series (*Princ.* vii, 14).

Boehme did not bother himself about the relationship of this theogonic "myth" to reality: when God is mythologized, is the mystery profaned? Schleiermacher held all mythologies vain and ruinous mysticism [2] because in his view the complex divine genealogies, long emanations and procreations, were not religious, as they aimed at breaking the highest unity, the idea that all that moves us is One.[3] The impulse behind theogony is the desire to solve the problem of evil: "it is not easy to avoid the appearance of making God susceptible of evil." [4] Here did Boehme's problem begin because he tried to show God's self-manifestation without making him the source of evil.

Coleridge suggested that Boehme mistook the peculiarities of his overwrought mind for realities and modes of thought common to all minds.[5] He asked whether Boehme's speculations were based on experience or upon fancy, suggesting that a second error is implied in that he confused active natural powers with God.[6] This is really the question of the validity of Boehme's symbolism.[7]

When Boehme wrote, modern subjective language had not yet been created. And when he looked within he saw forces and powers which he could not name, so his words bear meanings which they do not now bear, meanings which were forged in the process of personal integration.[8]

From the time of pseudo-Dionysius the Areopagite the problem of the "names" of God has been more than the semantics of symbolism. In his theogony Boehme tried to describe how three persons came from One; in his doctrine of seven natural principles he tried to describe how the manifold world came from One. Here an antinomy appeared: the Source is no-thing, yet all, accessible to thought and yet irrational. Two roads present themselves: a positive way and a negative way. Two theologies result: apophatic and cataphatic. The former subordinates affirmation to negation; the latter subordinates negation to affirmation. If the Source is all then by affirming creation's multiplicity it may be reached; if the Source is no-thing then by denying created reality it may be reached. Boehme's significance was his combining of both theologies in one comprehending system of thought.

Boehme's final statement of his theogonic stages was presented in the *Tabula* appended to *Epist.* xlvii, addressed to Johann Huser. These stages are: 1) God as *Ungrund* with related descriptions; 2) God as primordial will, or God the Father as no-thing and all; 3) God as subjectivation of the will or Christ; 4) God as objectivation of the will, or Spirit, movement, life; 5) God as trinity; 6) God as Logos; 7) God as Wisdom.[9] However, Boehme cautions:

> I exhort the reader not to understand in an earthly manner the high supernatural meaning. (*Gnad.* iii, 10)

The seven spirits of God also have psychological, or logical, connotations because they do describe according to a creaturely way and manner, that is, they reveal the logic of God-consciousness within man. They show also how man comes to a knowledge of God. Outer and objective parallel inner and subjective.

Boehme's God is no abstract, formal idea to be toyed with, reasoned, and seized outwardly "by selfish will and reason," but He is known only by him who achieves inward unity of will (*Myst. Mag.* xl, 54). Man finds himself seized by

God when he yields to God and becomes a willing instrument of God's desire (*Sig. Rer.* xv, 85).

Boehme's theogonic explanation was demanded by his taking St. John's Logos doctrine seriously. This is clear from the following:

For it is said (*John* i, 1–3): 'In the beginning was the Word, and the Word was with God, and the Word was God. The same was in the beginning with God. All things were made by Him and without Him was not anything made that was made.' In this brief statement we have the whole ground of the divine and natural revelation in the Being of all beings. For 'in the beginning' means the eternal beginning in the will of the Unground for a ground, that is, for the divine apprehension, since the will apprehends itself in the center for a foundation. . . . For the one will apprehends itself in the one power, wherein lies all hiddenness, and breathes itself forth through the power into an intuition, and this wisdom, or intuition, is the beginning of the eternal mind as the conspection of itself. This amounts to saying, the Word was in the beginning *with* God, and was God himself. The will is the beginning and is called God the Father, and He apprehends Himself in power, and is called the Son. . . . And in this connection it is said: The Word (i.e., the formed power) was in the beginning *with* God. For here two things are to be understood: namely, the unformed power, i.e., the *In;* and the formed power which is the *with,* for it has come into something and so into motion. The *In* is still, but the *with* is formed and compacted, and from this compaction and motion arise nature and creature, together with all being. (*Gnad.* ii, 7–11)

Here Boehme shows his dependence upon Christian theology.

Boehme's basic designation of God—the first of his seven theogonic spirits—is God the *Ungrund,* the no-thing and the all (*Epist.* xlvii, 37). He is first "hidden, unrevealed" (*Gnad.* ii, 20), or the hidden and the invisible (*Myst. Mag.* preface, 6).

God's transcendent unknowability has for him a twofold significance: first, it means God's transcendence, unknowability, irrationality. In Him all human antitheses are united, all irrational disunities resolved. So God is the dwelling of the unity (*Theos. Frag.* i, 1), unapprehended of anything (*Myst. Mag.* xxix, 1), on the other side of good and evil, of Yes and No, of freedom and desire. Meonic, he is without inclination and properties, deeper than thought.

But this unknowableness has another, profounder meaning. God is unknown to Himself as He has not yet won form and knowable, comprehensible being for Himself; He is not yet self-conscious. Already in the *Aurora*,

> God in Himself knows not what He is; for He knows no beginning of Himself, also He knows not anything that is like Himself, as also He knows no end of Himself. (*Aurora* xxiii, 17b)

So God is a nothing even to Himself (*Myst. Mag.* xxix).

God is unknown to creature for there is as yet no creature to know Him; He is also unknown to Himself because He has not yet won the formed image of His own self-consiousness.

The first word to describe this "spirit" comes from traditional Neoplatonic mysticism: God is the no-thing (*Nichts*).[10] This stands in dialectical relation to creation but it is not the negation of being.

> God is called the seeing and the finding of the nothing. And it is therefore called a nothing (though it is God Himself) because it is inconceivable and inexpressible. (*Theos. Frag.* ii, 13)

The no-thing, Lord Sabaoth, is beyond nature and creature (*Sig. Rer.* iii, 2) as the eternal one God (*Irrth. Stief.* 245).

The second word to describe this "spirit" is Boehme's own: the *Ungrund*, Unground. Meister Eckhart had spoken of the *Abgrund*, the Hindus have Brahman, but Boehme selects *Ungrund* as conscious antithesis to *Grund*. The *Nichts* seeks to become an *Ich*, the *Ungrund* a *Grund*.

> In Eternity . . . there is nothing but a stillness without being; there is nothing either that can give anything; it is an eternal rest . . , a groundlessness without beginning and end. (*Menschw.* II, i, 8)

A dark craving lives in it which drives it towards a ground, towards nature and creature, towards revelation and self-knowledge.

> The nothing hungers after the something, and this hunger is the desire . . . For the desire has nothing that it is able to conceive. It conceives only itself, and draws itself to itself . . . and brings itself from Abyss to Byss (*vom Ungrunde in Grund*) . . . and yet remains a nothing. (*Myst. Mag.* iii, 5)

All visible and invisible things originate in the speaking of the Word, the finding of the ground (*Taufe* I, i, 1–7).

The third description has no clear origin: God in his transcendent unknowability is an eye that sees in a mrror:

> . . . we recognize it to be like a mirror, wherein one sees his own image: like a life, and yet it is no life, but a figure of life and of the image belonging to life. Thus we recognize the eternal unground out of nature to be like a mirror. For it is like an eye which sees and yet conducts nothing in the seeing wherewith it sees: for the seeing is without essence. . . . It is like . . . a mirror, and yet there is nothing which the eye or the mirror sees; but its seeing is in itself, for there is nothing before it that was deeper there. . . .(*Theos. Punkt.*, i, 7ff)

The fourth description is that God is the "all in unity" (*Alles*). This word came into prominence as his pantheism began to wane. Thus in his last major work he wrote:

> God is the eternal unity . . . which has nothing after nor before Him that can give Him or bring Him anything, or that can move Him; and He is devoid of all tendencies and properties. He is without origin in time and in Himself one only, as a mere purity without attingence. He has nowhere a place or position, nor requires such for His dwelling; but He is at the same time out of the world and in the world, and deeper than any thought can plunge. If the numbers of His greatness and depth should be uttered for a hundred thousand years together, his depth would not have begun to be expressed; for He is infinitude . . ; but the unity of God cannot be expressed, for it is through everything at the same time. (*Theos. Frag.* i, 1)

The fifth description is that God is the Mystery. This comes from alchemy.

> The *mysterium magnum* is the . . . hiddenness of the Deity, together with the Being of all beings, from which one *mysterium* proceeds after another, and each *mysterium* is the model of the other. . . . But you must understand this according to the properties of the mirror, according to all the forms of nature. . . . (*Myst. Punkt.* vi, 2–3)

The *Ungrund* is also the mystery hidden in all things, thus closely approximating the Hindu Atman.

The sixth description is that God is eternal mind, *das ewige Gemüth*, of the heart of God. This is unabashed idealism.

> As we men . . . rule over all things, that is the whole sphere of intelligibility, through the distinction of words, so does God, as the eternal mind of the one power, also work and rule through such image-like words. (*Theos. Frag.* xi, 1)

This description appeared in his earlier writings and gradually disappeared.

In this first spirit of God, described by these words, two cadences were aroused, one which led to self-consciousness and the other which led to self-revelation. For God is unknown to creature and to Himself. The dark Abyss's first movement is dual: a tendency to self-subjectivation which leads to self-knowledge and self-consciousness, and a tendency towards self-objectivation which leads to emanation and manifestation.[11] This is strange! An eternal no-thing desires to become a thing! It cannot remain eternal and become a something. The *Urwille* struggles to project itself into actuality. Freedom and desire, each negate the other. This is what Boehme means by the eternal love-play in God where the Abyss wrestles, sports, and plays with itself (*Myst. Mag.* v, 3). Thus begins Boehme's dialectical theology, a view *ex idea vitae deducta.*

Now a great step takes place. God the unknown—natureless, passionless, groundless, with no tendency to anything, but with a dark, unfathomable will towards a something—

strives to introduce Himself into a something so that He can find, feel, know, and behold Himself. (*Sig. Rer.* ii, 8)

For in the nothing the will would not be manifest to itself, wherefore we know that the will seeks itself, and its seeking is a desire (*Begierde*) and its finding is the essence of the desire, wherein the will finds itself. (*Sig. Rer.* ii, 8)

The *Ungrund's* dark craving is unfathomable, without essence, directed towards being where it can feel, will, know, love and be felt, willed, known, and loved.

Here we remind the reader that God in Himself . . . has no more than one desire, which is to give and bring forth Himself. (*Gnad.* i, 18)

This understanding is a free will, without source or cause, unapprehended and a nothing to itself (*Myst. Mag.* xxix, 1), a desire for a something (*Seel. Frag.* i, 13). The process of God's becoming self-conscious is described:

In this Chaos the eternal nothing comprehends itself in an eye or eternal power of seeing, for the beholding, feeling, and finding of itself. In such case it cannot be said that God has two wills, one to evil, and the other to good. For in the unnatural, uncreaturely deity there is nothing more than a single will, which is called also the one God; and He wills in Himself nothing more than just to seize and find Himself, go out from Himself, and with the outgoing bring Himself into intuition. . . . There is no cause of the divine power . . . save the one will, that is to say, the one God who brings Himself into a threefoldness as into an apprehensibility of Himself. This apprehensibility is the center . . . and is called the heart or seat of the eternal will of God, in which the *Ungrund* possesses itself in a ground. This heart . . . of the *Ungrund* is the eternal mind of the will, and yet has nothing before it that it can will, save only this one place of its self-discovery. The first will is therefore the father of its heart or the place of its discovery. . . . The unfathomable will . . . generates itself within itself into a place of apprehensibility. And the place is a ground and beginning of all beings, and possesses in turn the unfathomable will, which is God the Father. . . .(*Gnad.* i, 8ff)

All effort to probe beyond this will which gets a ground for itself produces confusion (*Menschw.* II, vii, 1ff).

> The first, unoriginated, single will . . . generates within itself the one eternal good as an apprehensible will. . . . The second will is the first will's eternal feeling and finding, for the nothing finds itself as a something. And the unfathomable will . . . goes forth, and brings itself into an eternal intuition of itself. (*Gnad.* i, 5)

> In the depths of not-yet-being potential dialectic exists for the desire to self-subjectivation and self-knowledge contradicts the will towards self-objectivation, or emanation. These are fire and light. Fire consumes, light illuminates. In not-yet-being no will has yet arisen and so distinctions like that between good and evil are not yet (*Gnad.* ii, 37).

> For it cannot be said of God that He is this or that, evil or good, or that He has distinctions in Himself. For He is in Himself natureless, passionless, and creatureless. He has no tendency to anything, for there is nothing before Him to which He could tend, neither evil nor good. . . . There is no quality or pain in Him . . . [He] is a single will in which the world and the whole creation lies. . . . He is neither light nor darkness, neither love nor wrath, but the Eternal One. (*Gnad.* i, 3)

Knowledge comes after emanation, after the will has brought comprehensibility and form to itself. Previous to this act a gentle, harmonious "love" exists, but no essential tension. In *Ird. u. himl. Myst.* Boehme contrasted the formed will with the *Ungrund's* dark desire:

> The *Ungrund* . . . makes an eternal beginning as a craving (*Sucht*). For the nothing is a craving after something. But as there is nothing that can give anything . . . the craving itself is the giving of it, which yet also is a nothing . . . which makes within itself where there is nothing . . . though this craving is also a nothing, and there is nothing that can give it anything: neither has it any place where it can find or repose itself. (i)

This craving is self-centered and desirous; the eternal will is free (ii, 2) for it is

> free from the craving, but the craving is not free from the will. . . . The craving is indeed a movement of attraction or desire, but without understanding; it has a life but without knowledge. (iii, 1)

Desire, by realizing itself in and through the will, becomes an entity in the will's life, knowing what it is and does (iii, 2).

This process of making a formed will is pictured as the eternal speaking of the Word. The Logos, or spoken-forth Word, is the formed and found essence; the act of speaking is not that which has been spoken. The speaking has as yet no essence, for essentiality means for Boehme comprehensibility. The will is not yet the known Word. In the *Ungrund* then is the center of eternal nature where

> the eternal speaking word brings itself into a generation and also makes itself . . . a speaking Word. (*Myst. Mag.* ii, 7)

God was the Word which He spoke Himself. The act of speaking, *Verbum Fiat,* is also the spoken, *Verbum Domini,* the Word which creates where nothing was (*Myst. Mag.,* iii, 8). The formed Word is Christ; the speaking is the Father; and Boehme contrasts God's heavenly words with the halting momentary verbosity of man. Only prophets understand God's language (*Bedenk. Stief.* 84) and self-will prevents full understanding in ordinary men.

This eternal will is also designated as freedom, a drive to introduce the nothing into something so that the will may find, feel, and behold itself (*Sig. Rer.* ii, 6). The craving is not the freedom.

> The eternal divine understanding is a free will, not arisen from anything or by anything; it is its own peculiar seat, and dwells only and alone in itself, unapprehended of anything; for beyond and without it is the nothing, and that same nothing is only One; and yet it is also a nothing to itself. It is the one only will of the Abyss, and it is neither near nor far off, neither high nor low; but it is an all, and yet is nothing. (*Myst. Mag.* xxix, 1)

The eternal will is the first of two dialectical forces inherent in the *Ungrund*, the will-to-be, the *sich-in-sich-selbst-fassen.*

The second tendency latent in the *Ungrund* constitutes the third spirit of God—the tendency of the will to draw in upon itself in self-subjectivation, the yielding, propitiating, loving will which "tinctures" the harsh assertive Father will.[12] If the all were one then it could not be revealed for there would not be anything to which it might be revealed. (*Myst. Mag.* iv, 29)

The One, as the Yes, is pure power and life, and is the truth of God, or God Himself. He would in Himself be unknowable, and in Him would be no joy of elevation, nor feeling, without the No. The No is the counterstroke of the Yes, or the Truth, in order that the Truth may be manifest and a something, in which there may be a *contrarium*, in which the eternal love may be loving, feeling, willing, and such as can be loved. (*Theos. Frag.* iii, 2)

The process of begetting, imagining, seeing, speaking, mirroring (or however the Incomprehensible's self-discovery be named) results in the discovery of comprehensible forms; it is the discovery of consciousness.

The unfathomable will, i.e. the indiscoverable One, by its eternal discovery goes forth, and brings itself into an internal intuition of itself. Thus the unfathomable will is called Eternal Father, and the will that is found, grasped, and brought forth by the *Ungrund* is called His begotten or only Son, for it is the *Ens* of the *Ungrund*, whereby the *Ungrund* apprehends itself in a ground. (*Gnad.* i, 5–6)

This begetting is described by several images: mirroring, and eternal speaking:

It is the Father that speaks it, and the Word which is spoken out of the center of the Father is the Son thereof; and seeing the Father in His center calls Himself a consuming fire, and yet the Son (His Word) is a light of Love, Humility, Meekness, Purity, and Holiness. (*Dreyfach.* i, 40)

Three basic figures of speech are used: father-son, speaker-word, fire-light. These are not ultimate, however; Boehme is looking behind the images.

> The Father . . . generates out of Himself a second will, which in the first eternal will . . . opens the principle of light, in which the Father . . . becomes amiable, friendly, mild, pure, and gentle; and so the Father is not the source of darkness; for the recomprehended will which goes forth out of the center, and dispels the darkness, is His Heart, and dwells in itself, and enkindles the Father . . . and is rightly another person; for He dwells in the Father's essences in Himself, and is the Light of the Father; and His Word (or will) has created all things. (*Dreyfach.* i, 53)

The metaphor is immaterial. The Son has an illuminating function with regard to the Father's darkness.

Boehme's knowledge seems to go beyond the limits of language and his faltering use of metaphors attests to the failure of language to express his thought rather than to the paucity of his vision. He found words inadequate, especially the traditional terms of theology, and he forged new words to describe divine action:

> The Son is the first will's humility, and in His turn desires powerfully the Father's will, for without the Father He would be a nothing. And He is rightly called the Father's longing, or desire, for the manifestation of powers, viz. of the Father's taste, smell, feeling, and seeing. (*Gnad.* i, 23)

Here dialectic holds Father and Son together: a paternal will to be and a filial will to submit. (Cf. the fifth and sixth spirits of God, *infra*) The *Ungrund,* God unknown both to Himself and to creature, begets a will to be which begets the Son where the outgoing will turns back upon the Father. This is a picture of the divine self-consciousness. After this outgoing will finds itself in the Son it returns into the *Ungrund* of mysterious incomprehensibility to propitiate the wrath.

> The Son is a person other than the Father, for He is the Light-world, yet dwells in the Father, and the Father begets Him in His will. He is truly the Father's Love, as well as wonder, counsel, and power (*Kraft*), for the Father begets

Him in His imagination, in Himself, and leads Him forth through His own fire, through the principle, through death, so that the Son makes and is in the Father another world or another principle than the fire-world in the darkness. (*Menschw.* II, iii, 11)

Here at the depths where the Trinity is generated the two embryonic forces of the *Ungrund* have divided into two forces leading to God's self-consciousness on the one hand and to His self-manifestation on the other. The Son as the instrument of divine self-consciousness returns to the Father's hidden depths, bringing light therein; as the instrument of self-manifestation, the center of being, He goes out to creation:

Accordingly, this outgoing is a ray of the power of God, as a moving life of the Deity, in which the unfathomable will has brought itself into a ground. (*Gnad.* i, 13)

The dialectic of Yes and No has thus produced a God of wrath and love, but the God who seeks to be known has not yet come to be. Nor is there a creature to know Him. He has become what we would call a personal God because He is now conscious of Himself, but to manifest His Power he has to go beyond self-consciousness. So the fourth spirit of God, or the third person in the usual Trinity, appears as the instrument of God's efflux (as Boehme says) or emanation. Already in the *Aurora* he had said:

The third diversity, or the third person in . . . God, is the moving Spirit, which exists for the rising of the terror or crack when life is generated, which now moves in all powers, and is the spirit of life. (xxiii, 25)

This was written before he had found the *Ungrund.*

Boehme's God, then, brims over into creativity for the *Ungrund's* driving will for a ground creates the instrumentality of its creativity, the Holy Spirit.

He is the Spirit . . . of God, and has not its original in nature, but is the first will to nature; yet he gets his sharpness in nature; and therefore He is the former and framer in nature . . . He is the bringer forth, the conductor, and the director; also the destroyer of malice and wickedness, and the opener of the hidden mysteries; he existed in the Father from eternity, without beginning: for the Father, without Him, would only be an eternal stillness, without essence. He is the essence of the will . . . out of which air rises. (*Dreyfach* iv, 77)

(This too was written before he had discovered the *Ungrund.*) Air is the first analogy of primitive minds.

God needs to become Spirit to manifest and realize Himself. So the Holy Spirit is the instrument but not the substance of creation, the tool that moves out into the void, creating, sustaining, fashioning, and forming. Spirit likens known with unknown, Source and End, Alpha and Omega. He is the work-master of the world's birth (*Aurora* xiii, 77), the creator of the all (*Dreyfach* viii, 72), the fashioner and former of all nature (*Dreyfach* iv, 77), the opener of nature's divinity (*Dreyfach* iv, 84). He dwells in man's soul (*Aurora,* preface 88) where He is born of will (*Menschw.* II, x, 11) and is responsible for the original, essential spirit of man. The Holy Spirit is also the creative force which drives man by anxiety to a new birth (*Menschw.* I, x, 1), leading to repentance (*Busse* i, 21), creating the courage to be humble and meek (*Complex.*). And at the end of time the Holy Spirit will move to fill the world, bringing it into conformity with God's will (*Seel. Frag.* xx, 11). All these figures are functions of God related to something beyond His self-conscious life.

The Father is the power . . . and the Son is the Light and the splendor of the Father and the Holy Spirit is the moving or exit (*Ausgang*) out of the powers of the Father, and of the Son, and forms, figures, and images all . . . and moves or acts, forms of frames, and images all that is in this world. (*Aurora,* vii, 42, 43)

This is the *Aurora.* In a mature work Boehme wrote:

The Holy Spirit is therefore called Holy and a flame of

Love, because He is the emanating power from the Father and the Son, viz., the moving life in the first will of the Father, and in the second will of the Son, in His Power; and because He is a shaper, worker, and leader in the emanated joy of the Father, and the Son in Wisdom. (*Gnad.* i, 24)

The Holy Spirit completes Boehme's trinity but three other "spirits" of God emerge in the process of generating the self-conscious, manifested God. His fifth spirit is the theogonic hypostatization of the tendency of the many to be encompassed within the One (*Taf. to Epist.* xlvii, 5). This is God's self-conscious transcendence and generally corresponds to the centripetal force of Plotinus,[13] the ἐπιστροφή, and it is the dialectical counterpart of the sixth spirit of God.

The *Ungrund* is the all and the no-thing. This is an antinomy, giving rise to dialectic. The *Ungrund* is "nothing and yet is everything" (*Gnad.* i, x). Now, the fifth spirit is the negating, self-appropriating, ingoing to the center which results in a God who from the creature's point of view acts in His own interests or as a "wrathful" God. This return is the Nay-saying, the wrath emerging from a self-conscious God, the darkness with Him.

And yet it cannot be said that Yes is separated from the No, and that they are two things. . . . Without these two, which are in perpetual conflict, all things would stand still without movement. This same is to be understood regarding the eternal unity of the divine power. . . . If receivability is to arise, there must be a special will to receivability which is not identical with nor wills with the one will. For the one will wills only the one good, which it . . . itself is; it wills only itself in similarity. But the emanated will wills dissimilarity, in order that it may be distinguished from similarity and be its own something, in order that there may be something in which the eternal seeing may see and feel. And from the special individual will arises the No, for it brings itself into ownness, that is, into receptivity of self. It desires to be a something, and does not make itself one with the unity. For the unity is an emanating Yes . . . being insentient; for it has nothing in which it can feel itself save in the receptivity of the differing will, as in the No which is a counterstroke of the Yes, in which the Yes is revealed, and in which it has a something that it can will. (*Theos. Frag.* iii, 3–5)

The Yes and No are not wills, that is persons, but tendencies and drives:

And the No is therefore called No, because it is a desire turned inwards, as shutting into negativity. And the Yes is therefore called Yes, because it is an eternal efflux or outgoing and the ground of all beings, that is, truth only. For it has no No before it; but the No first arises in the emanated will of receivability. (*Theos. Frag.* iii, 10)

This abiding-in-self, as Schleiermacher called it, is God's self-consciousness and is

Intrahent, and comprehends itself in itself, and from it come forms and properties. The first property is the sharpness, from which comes hardness, coldness, dryness, and darkness. . . . The second property is true feeling, as between the hardness and the motion, in which the will feels itself. . . . And in accordance therewith God is called an angry jealous God and a consuming fire; not according to what He is in Himself independent of all receivability, but in accordance with the eternal principle of fire. And in the darkness is understood the foundation of hell, as an oblivion of the Good; which darkness is entirely concealed in the Light, like night in the day, as may be read in John i, 58. (*Theos. Frag.* iii, 11)

The wrath is the No that returns from the found, discovered, and comprehended Son into the unknown hiddenness of the transcendent Father; it is God's self-consciousness, to draw His Self in again and contemplate in His mysterious self-interest. In *Beschau.* Boehme suggests Scriptural basis for this In and Out within God, his fifth and sixth spirits of God:

In John i, 11–13 it stands written: 'He [Jesus Christ] came to his own and his own received him not. But as many as received him, to them he gave power to become children of God, even to them that believe on his name; which were born, not of blood, nor of the will of the flesh, nor of the will of man, but of God.' The valuable ground of divine manifestation lies in these words—the eternal In and Out. For they speak of how the hidden, divine eternal Word—the divine mighty in unity—receded to its ownness out of the manifested, natural, creaturely Word. (iv, 1)

This "In" is the tendency to unity in the Godhead for in spite of his threeness He still is One:

When you are told about three persons in the Deity, and about the divine will, know that the Lord our God is one God only. (*Gnad.* i, 25)

One will therefore subsumes three persons and three functions, and the *Drang* to unity is Boehme's fifth spirit of God.

The sixth spirit of God, as already mentioned, is the movement of the unity towards manifoldness. Generally it corresponds to the Plotinian centrifugal force, *πρόοδος*,[14] and is the affirming, "loving" outgoing of the one will.

This outgoing is a ray of the power of God, as a moving life of the Deity, in which the unfathomable will has brought itself into a ground. (*Gnad.* i, 13)

This basic determination of the no-thing to become things, of a will to be, becomes the basis of creative activity.

From this holy fire has emanated the Yes, as a ray of the perceptible unity. This ray is the precious name *Jesus,* which had to redeem the poor soul from the wrath; and in assuming humanity, introduced itself into the soul, into the dissident central fire-wrath of God's anger, and kindled the soul again with the fire of love and united it with God. . . . In God there is no anger, there is pure Love alone. But the foundation, through which Love becomes mobile, is the fire of anger, though in God it is only a cause of joy and power. On the other hand, in the center of the wrath-fire it is the greatest and most terrible darkness, pain and torment. These two (the Yes and the No) are in one another like day and night, where neither can take hold of the other, but one dwells in the other. And they make two eternal beginnings. The first beginning is called the kingdom of God's wrath, or the foundation of hell wherein dwell the expelled spirits. The foundation of the Kingdom of God is pure Yes, as powers of the separable Word. And the foundation of the wrath of God is pure No, whence lies have their origin. . . . This emanated holy fire, when it was yet operative throughout the earth, was Paradise. And it is Paradise still, but man has been expelled from it. (*Theos. Frag.* iii, 6–7)

Yes is the movement out to manifestation in creation. This leads to Boehme's seventh spirit of God, which in many ways is his most characteristic idea—that of Wisdom, or as he called it, the Virgin Sophia.

When Boehme discovered his *Ungrund* as a dark deep of indeterminate Being he also came to understand that such a deep stood in dialectical contrast to the rich fullness on which all created things are mirrored.

Wisdom is the receptacle in which God's eternal will seeks, sees, and finds itself.

A one has nothing in itself that it can will, unless it double itself that it may be a two; neither can it feel itself in oneness, but in twoness it feels itself. (*Theos. Frag.* iii, 6–7)

One must become two before comprehensibility and consciousness are possible. The eye sees its image in the mirror —the mirror being the reflecting receptacle. Instead of having the One and nonbeing as the poles of his emanation, like Plotinus, Boehme's God had the *Ungrund* and Sophia, or Wisdom, co-operating to generate the world of things. The *Ungrund* makes a counterstroke so that the related dialectical processes of self-knowledge and self-projection may take place.

Boehme found the idea of Wisdom in the Wisdom literature of Scripture, in the Wisdom of Solomon [15] and Proverbs, and in the Cabala, although the ultimate source of the world-soul is Plato's *Timaeus* and the Plotinian world-soul.

Sophia is the image of God (*Seel. Frag.* i, 205) by which and in which the *Ungrund* can know itself; she is the body of God, the perceptibility of God in which the world's manifold differentiated powers are contained, the essential power of God's Love from which things get existence, the core of God's active Love, God's throne of Grace in man, the mediation between God and creature, the mirror in which the eternal will has seen a preview of all creation, the mother of all things (of Christ and of reborn souls), and the bride of man's soul. With Sophia man can enter into erotic union.

Sophia is the likeness of the Trinity (*Dreyfach.* v, 41), the likeness of God (*Ibid.*), a likeness according to the Deity and Eternity (*Menschw.* I, ix, 7), the image's framing of itself (*Gnad.* i, 16), the pattern of God's spirit (*I Apol. Tilk.*, 64), a figure in the mirror of God's Wisdom (*Menschw.* I, ix, 6).

Wisdom, as God's mirror, possesses the means by which He can come to self-consciousness. He sees His self projected against Himself. Seer, mirror, and image are God. The act of self-contemplation is also the act of self-revelation and differentiation, and He creates an antithetical counterstroke of His undifferentiated Deep to see Himself.

> The eternal wisdom . . . resembles the eternal eye without essence. . . . It is not essential, as in a mirror the brightness is not essential . . . for no seeing is without spirit; neither any spirit is without seeing. . . . Seeing shines forth from the spirit, and is its eye or mirror, wherein the will is revealed. . . . Seeing makes a will, as the *Ungrund* of the Deep without number knows to find no ground nor limit; hence its mirror goes into itself and makes a ground in itself. (*Theos. Punkt.* i, 11–12)

Again, the Father

> reveals the Word in the mirror of Wisdom, so that the threefold nature of the Deity becomes manifest in Wisdom. (*Menschw.* II, ii, 12)

Secondly, wisdom is *Gegenwurf,* counterstroke (*Beschau.* iii, 6). Here Boehme's theory of knowledge is implied. God's image, created by His self-consciousness and self-projection, is the image of all things in which creatures know, revealing the fullness of His being, an instrument by which He unveils His inward depths and myriad forms to the world and to man.

Thirdly, Wisdom is the discovered (*das Gefundene*), that which is intuited. If the begetting of the Son is the comprehension of His being, then Wisdom is the comprehension of this veiled form in visible image.

Eternal Wisdom is the begotten being, as a mirror and ornament of the Holy Trinity, in which the powers, colors, and virtues of God become revealed, and in which the Spirit of God has seen all things from eternity. (*Bedenk. Stief.*, ii, 30)

Discovering His own dark nature God is born as a living image—that which has been born from within.

Wisdom is the emanated (*das Ausgeflossene*) which makes the hidden life visible, a matrix in which the Word has become formed.

Wisdom is the egressed (*das Ausgegangene*), the form in which the inner trinitarian life comprehends itself and then projects itself.

What has gone forth from the will, love, and life is the wisdom of God, that is the divine intuition and joy of the unity of God, whereby the love eternally introduces itself into powers, colors, wonders, and virtues. (*Theos. Frag.* ii, 1ff)

Wisdom is the exhaled (*das Ausgehauchte*), the breathed forth.

as an out-breathing or manifestation; and this egress from the will in the speaking or breathing is the spirit of the Deity, or the third person, as the ancients have called it. And that which is outbreathed is wisdom . . . which it . . . conceives to a life's center or heart, for its habitation. (*Myst. Mag.* vii, 8, 9)

Allied to this description is that of Wisdom as the articulated (*das Ausgesprochene*). The mute God strives to frame Himself as Word, the framed, spoken Word is the Son, the Word's articulation is the Spirit, and the articulated in which the hidden God comes from silence to hearable form is Wisdom.

The egress from the generation is the spirit of the formed Word and that which is spoken forth is the power, colors, and virtue of the Deity, viz. the Wisdom. (*Myst. Mag.* vii, 10)

Wisdom as the articulated is one of the commonest expressions in Boehme (*Princ.* xxii, 25; *Dreyfach* v, 40, 41)

Now how does the traditional trinity fit this scheme? Does Boehme have four "persons" as his critics claimed? His three-in-one God has a secretive life in Himself; but He also has a knowable life in which He steps out to form the world after His image and by which He may be known, for Wisdom is God's body (*II Apol. Tilke,* 57), the chest or container of God (*Kasten Gottes*) (*II Apol. Tilke,* 67), the receptacle (*Menschw.* II, i, 10). Wisdom

> is not a genetrix, neither itself reveals anything. . . . It is the house of the Holy Trinity, the ornament of the divine angelic world. (*Theos. Punkt.* I, i, 10)

Clavis presents an excellent picture of Wisdom:

> The Holy Scripture says . . . Wisdom is the breathing of the divine power . . ; it also says, God made all things by His Wisdom, which we understand as follows: the Wisdom is the outflown Word of the divine power, virtue, knowledge, and holiness; a subject and resemblance of the infinite and unsearchable unity; a substance wherein the Holy Ghost works, forms, and models; I mean, He forms and models the divine understanding in the Wisdom; for the Wisdom is . . . passive and the spirit of God is . . . active. . . . In her the powers, colors, and virtues are made manifest; in her is the variation of the power and the virtue. . . . She is the divine vision wherein the unity is manifest. She is the true divine chaos wherein all things lie, . . a divine imagination. (19ff)[15]

Wisdom is the passive principle in the Godhead and so is feminine. But she is also "virgin" because she contains but does not beget (*Theos. Punkt.* I, i, 62). As the world of ideas she is far more vital than the Plotinian static νοῦς. The Plotinian emanation was not dialectical and the One was not a person, thus safeguarding theism at the price of a self-conscious, personal God. Boehme's Wisdom was needed to make God in Trinity self-conscious. Surely, some equivalent of Wisdom, or world-soul, is still today, as it was with Plato and Plotinus, the alternative to materialism.

Thus did Boehme think about God, seeking to maintain the active, personal considerate God of his experience. His idea of the seven spirits of God is Biblical, coming from Revelation i, 4 and commanding as much interest as Tertullian's legal conception of *persona.* Boehme elevates Plato's world-soul to the mystical theogony and it becomes the dialectical counterpart of Eckhart's *Abgrund* and of the Hindu Brahman. And Boehme maintains the overtones of Luther's distinction between the God of Revelation and the God of mystery.

Several problems emerge. First, the problem of the divine Being as such involving generation of a triune God from unity—theogony. Secondly, the relation of the triune God to creation—theodicy. Thirdly, the problem of life conceived as interplay of Yes and No—dialectic. By elevation of these problems to one plane in his seven spirits of God Boehme suggests a relationship.

On the trinitarian problem Boehme adds depth in that the *Ungrund* becomes separated from the Father; this saves him from pantheism. The problem of creation is that of the archetypes of finite beings, the world of forms. Boehme here is a full-blown Platonist. The problem of dialectics emerged from his sunrise to eternity and was the core of all his thought. By combining these in one comprehensive system Boehme achieved his greatness.

The doctrine of the Trinity has really two postulates: that within unity is trinity and within trinity is unity—one substance, three persons. Sophia is the "one substance," the consubstantiality within the Trinity and so must be distinct from the three persons although unable to exist apart from them. Sophia belongs in hypostatic being and is related to each of the persons. A curious prejudice associated Sophia only with the Son, but this is untrinitarian. Sophia's relation to the Father is that of revelation. She lets Him come to self-knowledge and self-consciousness, disclosing His depths. Her relation to the Logos is that she cannot exist apart from her connection with the Logos. Logos is in-going, a return and a propitiation; Sophia is outgoing to creation and to man. Sophia is the ὀυσία with which the Spirit works and out of which He makes the created world.

Boehme's whole idea of God is construed with a view towards maintaining two precious divine attributes: his personality and his tender concern for the world. The antinomies that result are due to his stubborn desire to hold on to both. A dialectical God results, a God of two modes, a God of love and a God of wrath.

Here begins to appear Boehme's solution to the problem of evil. Evil is related to self-consciousness, to nay-saying, to mystery. He distinguishes between the God in self-contemplation and the God in action. Two cadences, passive and active, give a God of these two modes. And for Boehme evil is the rebellion of self-centered activity against the passive, unyielding, mysterious power of the self-contemplating God.

NOTES TO CHAPTER TWELVE

1. On meaning of dialectic in this special sense, Cf. André Lalande, *Vocabulaire technique et critique de la Philosophie,* Paris 1951, p. 227, sense f.
2. *Speeches on Religion,* London, 1893, p. 49.
3. *Ibid.,* p. 134.
4. *Ibid.*
5. *Aids to Reflection,* London, n.d. p. 294.
6. Coleridge held this to be definitive for mysticism as a whole, for a man elevates his own experiences as typical of all mankind. Cf. *op. cit.* Cf. further: I. A. Richards, *Coleridge on Imagination,* New York, 1935, p. 71.
7. *Aids to Reflection,* p. 293.
8. Cf. C. G. Jung, *The Integration of the Personality,* and *Psychology and the Unconscious.*
9. Seven has a long history in folklore and other areas. *Vide:* W. H. Rascher, *Die Sieben- und Neunzehn in Kultus und Mythus der Griechen,* Leipzig, 1904.
10. The distinction between the divine nothing and the nothingness from which all has been made and of which nothing proceeds must be maintained. The latter is nonbeing, the former beyond being. Nonbeing is rational; superior being irrational.
11. Cf. Schleiermacher, *The Christian Faith,* p. 8: "Life is to be conceived as an alternation between an abiding-in-self (*In-*

sichbleiben) and a passing-beyond-self (*aussichheraustreten*) on the part of the subject."

12. Boehme's Christology has three modes: the eternal birth, the birth of the natural Logos, and the birth of Jesus from Mary. Only the first belongs to theogony. Boehme asserts that the first birth is unknowable (*Aurora* xviii, 23).
13. *Vide:* E. Zeller, *Die Philosophie der Griechen*, III, 2, Leipzig, 1881, p. 47ff.
14. *Ibid.*, p. 300ff.
15. The Scriptural passage is the seventh chapter of the Wisdom of Solomon which was included in the Lutheran Bible: "For she is a breath of the power of God, and a clear effluence of the glory of the Almighty; therefore can nothing defiled find entrance into her. For she is an effulgence from everlasting light, and an unspotted mirror of the working of God, and an image of His goodness. And she, being one, has power to do all things; and remaining in herself, renews all things; and from generation to generation passing into men's souls she makes men friends of God and prophets. For nothing does God love save that which dwells in wisdom. For she is fairer than the sun, and above all the constellations of the stars; being compared with light, she is found to be before it; for the light of day succeeds night, but against wisdom does not prevail."

Flower in the crannied wall,
I pluck you out of the crannies;—
Hold you here, root and all, in my hand.
Little Flower—but if I could understand
What you are, root and all, and all in all,
I should know what God and man is.

—TENNYSON

CHAPTER THIRTEEN

ETERNAL NATURE

WISDOM is the central aspect of God's self-manifestation in a threefold sense: first, theogonically, as His revelation of His self to Himself; secondly, theodocially, as His revelation of His self in creation; thirdly, regeneratively, as His revelation of His Self as Grace.

The second is Wisdom's creative function as a living being with a body having organic life. To escape pantheism, which holds that the world is God's body (thus implying the eternity of the world and making God responsible for the evil within it) one must give God His own body. Only with this idealism can materialism be avoided. A God having a life and body apart from the world transcends it. Here the opposite danger of deism appears and it is possible to shut Him up in impenetrable transcendence. Only an organic, creating, sustaining God with separate consciousness will be theistic, a πᾶν ἐν θεῷ.

Wisdom conceived as the instrumentality of God's self-manifestation is Boehme's solution to the problem of the relationship of God to the world. Wisdom is the revealeress (*die Offenbarin*) (*Menschw.* I, i, 12), the revelation of God's unity (*Taf.* 19), the revelation of life (*Menschw.* II, 1, 10), the unknown God's desire for revelation (*Gnad.* i, 9), and for self-manifestation (*Myst. Mag.*, vii, 6). She makes the triune God clear (*Menschw.* II, ii, 3), opening up the divine wonders (*Princ.* iv, 88), revealing the wonders of the divine element (*Princ.* xxii, 26), lighting up the Godhead's dark depths (*Dreyfach* xi, 15), becoming the figure in which God's wonders are known (*Dreyfach.* xi, 137), revealing the heavens and the divine wonders (*Princ.* xxii, 71).

These functions express Wisdom's functions; and, as Boehme conceived Sophia as feminine, his doctrine of God was therefore androgynous. Sophia, female divine principle, passively bears what the fatherly will seeks. This relationship is boldly expressed erotically in the old terms of bride mysticism:

> Wisdom is the bride and the children of Christ are in Wisdom also God's brides. (*II Apol. Tilke* 73)

(In German soul is feminine; hence no difficulty arises.) He further says:

> The Virgin is visible like a pure Spirit, and the Element is her body . . . the holy earth . . . and into this the invisible deity is entered . . . that the deity is in the pure element and the element is in the deity; for God and the element . . . are become one thing, not in spirit, but in substance. (*Princ.* xxii, 72ff)

The Father's love for Wisdom, for Himself, is His desire which brings self-realization, comprehensibility, and the ultimate embracing of the form thus revealed (*Gnad.* i, 9). Wisdom is the suffering, female, maternal, generating aspect in which the representation, revelation, and procreation of the Deity is perfected.

> All things spring out of the eternal mother; and as she is in her own birth, so she has generated this world, and so every living creature is generated. (*Princ.* v, i, 2)

In this matrix God moves himself to creation (*Princ.* vi, 24).

In this first act of self-realization there is as yet no breaking of the unity. Opposition has not yet come, only self-knowledge. There is neither strife nor tension, only what Boehme called "love-play," harmony. So Wisdom is "virgin," a term often repeated. Virginity means that tension between God's active and passive principles has not yet produced creatures. There is dialectic, yes, but no procreation. Wisdom still mirrors God's image:

> She is a virgin and never generates anything, neither takes anything into her; her inclination stands in the Holy Spirit, which goes forth from God, and attracts nothing to Him, but moves before God. (*Princ.* xiv, 87)

The image is born without separation; she is God's image in which He glimpses Himself as spirit, seeing into the unfathomable deep (*Theos. Punkt.* I, i, 24).

Boehme was, of course, a vitalist and all creatures partook of a single vital center (*vis vitalis*) which alone accounts for their existence. An agent of separation is needed by which things were carved out. This is the Platonic demiourgos or, as Boehme called it, Archaeus (*Beschau.* ii, 11), or Separator (*Test.* II, 3, 19). When life's irreducible nature is granted and a vital center posited, this vital center can become identified with God. To avoid such pantheism the vital center is separated from divine being. God is spiritual, the world is partly material. Nor can the world simply be the object (*Gegenwurf*) of God. Boehme makes Wisdom the object both of God and of the world, thus avoiding pantheism in its true sense.

This is suggested from Boehme's anthropomorphic symbolism, the notion of macrocosm and microcosm. An androgynous God prefigures an androgynous man. The creative process is described in an important passage in *Menschw.*

> The nothing causalizes the will so that it becomes desireful, and the process of desire is a mode of imagination, as the will beholds itself in the mirror of Wisdom. . . . The mirror remains eternally a virgin without bringing forth, but the will becomes impregnate with the aspect of the mirror. . . . The will is Father, and the impregnation . . . is heart or Son . . . and proceeds from the will in the ground into the Virgin Wisdom. Thus the will's imagination, viz. the Father, draws the mirror's vision or form . . . into itself, and thus becomes pregnant with the splendor of wisdom . . .

This arises in the will and seizes itself in the center of the heart. . . . For the will . . . with the movement of the Spirit speaks forth power into the mirror of wisdom. . . . And with the speaking forth the spirit proceeds from the will, from the word . . . of God . . , into what is spoken forth, viz. into the mirror, and reveals the word of life in the mirror of wisdom, so that the threefold nature of the Deity becomes manifest in Wisdom. Thus, we recognize an eternal, unfathomable divine essence, and in its nature three persons, whereof one is not the other. (II, ii, 1–4)

These words partly describe Wisdom's revealing function. Revelation perfects itself not in the One's self-sufficiency in self-contemplation but in that the One leads itself into separate opposition to itself. First, Wisdom creates a fruitful self-realization of God's inner life; life's unity realizes itself in multiplicity; unity of knowing in multiplicity of knowing; voluntaristic unity in plurality of wills. As counterstroke Wisdom is beginning of separation, making fruitful manifestation of individual forms possible in God; she is the first principle of differentiation in which God glimpses potential variations of being.

This image makes the will of the Eternal One separable; it is the separability of the will from which powers and qualities arise. (*Beschau.* iii, 5)

Further unfoldings lead the One into ever new separations:

These powers are an efflux of themselves, each power bringing itself into individual wills. . . . From thence arises the multiplicity of wills, and from this also the creaturely life of eternity has taken its origin. . . . And yet it cannot be said that by this . . . a creation is understood, but the eternal imaged existence of the divine word and will . . . has . . . sported with himself in the formation of similitude. . . . The outgoing of the one will of God has . . . introduced itself into separability, and the separation has introduced itself into receptibility . . . passing out of the unity into plurality. Desire is the ground and beginning of the nature of the perceptibility of the particular will. For therein is the separability of the unity brought into the separability of self-hood. . . . For the will of the eternal One is imperceptible, without tendency towards anything; for it has nothing towards which it could tend, save only towards itself. Therefore it brings itself out of itself, and carries the efflux out of its unity into plurality, and into assumption of self-hood . . . from which qualities take their rise. For every quality has its own separator and maker within it, and is in itself entire, according to the quality of the eternal unity. Thus the separator of each will develops in turn qualities from itself, from which the infinite plurality arises, through which the eternal One makes itself perceptible, not according to the unity, but according to the efflux of the unity. (*Beschau.* iii, 7–11)

This first separation is not yet the beginning of dialectic but only God's discovery of His plurality. Structural dialectic appears only when free spiritual man has rebelled against God. The original separation comes through Wisdom and is the point of departure for the creation of separated representations of God's inner plurality in visible forms. The first Fall—Satan's altercation—disturbs the will's unity by self-hood. Only by this act in which a creature made in God's image seeks to put himself at being's center does dialectic arise.

Boehme's world is neither creature nor God's body nor the object of God. Nor is it cut off from life's center. Boehme avoided both pantheism and gnosticism. Life is a mystery, a paradoxical reality, the source of which is God.

God's self-knowledge and self-revelation perfect themselves in a *Blick*, a lightning-flash of divine imagination. This *Blick* is the central creative act unlocking the inner secrets of the great mystery.

The point of departure is the view that the *Ungrund* is an eye that "sees" itself in a mirror (*Theos. Punkt.* I, i, 7). The nonseeing divine darkness becomes seeing in a flashing glance of self-contemplation in which God sees himself. He simultaneously achieves self-consciousness and manifestation.

From such a revelation of powers, in which the will of the eternal One contemplates itself, flows the understanding and the knowledge of the something (*Ichts*), as the eternal contemplates itself in the something and in wisdom introduces itself into . . . a likeness and image. (*Beschau.* iii, 4)

Boehme's *Realdialektik* now begins to emerge, and one of his most startling ideographs appears, the view of the divine separation in fire which came to him from alchemy.

In the enkindling of the fire lies the entire ground of all mystery. . . . [In it] the spirit of God becomes moving, in the manner that air rises from fire.

Light is an old symbol which plays a large role in ancient metaphysics, especially Philo. God was light, and this separation was visualized as a breaking of the light into many rays. But Boehme's God is light only as far as He is spirit. Light demands fire, for fire is light's root (*Myst. Mag.* xxvi, 28). Light stands for the Son and the Son's begetter must be fire; indeed Scripture calls Him a consuming fire, a fire that never consumes itself nor exhausts itself. Like life fire synthesizes opposites:

Thus the two genetrixes, that of the wrath in fire and that of love in light, have brought their form into wisdom, where then the heart of God longed in the love to make this mirrored form into an angelic image, composed of the divine essence, so that they should be a likeness and an image of the Deity. (*Menschw.* I, ii, 4)

Fire produces light only when it is burning; to burn there must be matter, stuff. This primitive figure is Boehme's way of describing the burning, driving source at life's center comparable to the modern *libido*. Yet fire is not in itself ultimate.

Fire is the life of all principles—understand, the cause of life, not the life itself. (*Theos. Punkt.* ii, 10–12)

To burn fire needs fuel, something to consume.

Fire . . . cannot subsist without substance; therefore its hunger is after substance. (*Theos. Punkt.*, i, 27)

Wrathful fire engenders amiable light and destroys matter by changing it into spirit. This is the mystery. For Boehme fire was life.

> When we consider what life is, we find that it consists mainly in three elements, viz. desire, the disposition, and the thinking. If we investigate further . . . we find the center of the essential wheel, which contains within it the fire-smith himself. (*Menschw.* II, iii, 7)

The results of this metaphor-symbol are many. If God has a burning center then He has matter which burns; fire needs fuel. Now where does God's fuel come from?

> The principle of fire is the root, and it grows in the root. It has in its *proprium* sour, bitter, fierceness, and anguish, and these grow in the *proprium* in poison and death into the anguishable stern life, which in itself gives darkness, owing to the drawing in of the harshness. (*Theos. Punkt.* ii, 38)

Its properties are sulphur, mercury, and salt, symbols of alchemy's three principles. The dark matter, root, or *proprium,* is diaphanous and luminous in so far as it is penetrated by and "vanquished" by light. The burning matter is God's dark inchoate body; but the fire is filled by light.

> In the eternal nature there are not more than two principles: . . the eternal burning fire, which is filled with light. . . . The fire takes to itself the fire's property, viz. life and self-discovery. And the second principle is understood in the light; but the essential substantiality from which the fire burns remains eternally a darkness and a source of wrath. . . . We see that fire is a thing other than that from which the fire burns. (*Menschw.* II, iii, 179)

Fire or burning the dark matter makes wrath and the wrath's propitiation. Here is destruction and birth, death and procreation.

So fire has a destructive calcinating force, a poisonous life (*das böse Leben, das giftige Leben*) opposed to pure being, to the amiable light before God. Like light the poisonous life is produced by fire sharing the source which is a *coinci-*

dentia oppositorum, a source which bifurcates into two principles.

In the end, however, fire is only an "illuminating" symbol of life's source, of the deepest mystery. Boehme was no fire-worshiper and the role he gave to fire went beyond anything that the alchemists held.

The dark world and the light world, wrath and love, the self-in-self-contemplation and the self-in-self-projection form the Yes and No which become the bases of manifold forms. The self-conscious God begets a hunger; the self-acting God begets being in all its manifold variety. Here then are two centers: a center of desire which makes a natural center and a center of the will which produces God's trinity. In the will there is a "birth" to desire and a "birth" to freedom.

So when Wisdom begins to manifest God's inner richness the distinction between freedom and desire emerges. The being of the Absolute (if such a formal word may be applied to Boehme's God) forms itself into two contradictory centers, that of freedom and that of desire. Desire opposes will in two ways. First, will in essence is movement and expansion, a wanting to give itself. The will is then generous and giving;

> The gentleness gives and the fire takes. The gentleness is emanent from itself, and gives a substance that is like itself . . . and the fire swallows this up, but out of it produces light. It gives something nobler than it has swallowed up—gives spirit for substance—for it swallows up the gentle beneficence. . . . Understand the meaning right: God the Father is in Himself the freedom out of nature, but makes Himself manifest by fire in nature. The nature of fire is His property, though He is in Himself the *Ungrund* where there is no feeling nor any pain . . . and draws for Himself . . . another will to go out . . . again into the freedom beyond pain. This other will is His Son. . . . It is this other will which breaks down death as the stern, dark source, which kindles fire and proceeds through fire . . . and fills the primal will which is called Father. . . . Therefore it can dwell in freedom, that is in the Father's will, and make the Father bright, clear, gracious, and friendly. . . . It is the Father's substantiality, it fills the Father everywhere. (*Menschw.* II, v, 6–7)

Desire, hunger for self, opposes the other will which is begotten in pain and suffering; it is hunger which seeks self-satisfaction, a thirst which seeks to be quenched, a sight that would be fulfilled—sensual images which for Boehme are indicative of a deeper meaning. The free will expands, desire draws in.

> Desire has nothing that it is able to make or to conceive. It conceives only itself, and impresses itself, that is it coagulates itself, and draws itself to itself, and comprehends itself, and brings itself from Abyss to Byss, and overshadows itself with its magnetical attraction; so that the nothing is filled, and yet remains a nothing. (*Myst. Mag.* iii, 5)

Will is centrifugal, desire centripetal:

> God . . . can desire nothing in Himself and therefore He brings Himself out of Himself into a divisibility, into a center, in order that a contrariety may arise in the emanation, viz. in that which has emanated, that good may in the evil become perceptible, effectual, and capable of will; namely, to will and separate itself from the evil and to re-will to enter into the one will of God. (*Ird. u. himl. Myst.* i, x, 14ff)

Desire

> is the stern attraction, and yet has nothing but itself or the eternally without foundation. And it draws magically, viz., in its own desiring into a substance. (*Ird. u. himl. Myst.*, iv, 2)

The will tends to posit being in order to give itself to others, to manifest itself in them; desire seeks to possess others to nourish its own being. If the Absolute is the no-thing and the All then desire and freedom are but logical realizations of these ideas. There is one curious aspect, that while the will tends to posit being it is incapable of doing so, for the function of creation belongs to desire, as nature's all.

Desire's dialectical evolution corresponds to that of the will except that it is reversed. The evolutionary cycle is less pure and less rich because desire's life is frustrated. Will is spirit-vision; desire is passion (*Treib, Streben*) obscured by self-consciousness.

Desire is only an hungry will, and it is the natural spirit in its forms. . . . God is without desire as concerning His own essence . . . for He needs nothing. All is His, and He Himself is all. (*Sig. Rer.*, vi, 2)

Desire is the instinctive life which to reveal itself parts from itself and prolongs its life in the spirit. In spirit, not in itself, desire becomes self-conscious, or more exactly that spirit becomes conscious of its own desire. Spirit, however, reveals itself to itself. Both stand together, need each other, imply each other.

If there were but one will, then all essence would do but one thing: but in the counter will each exalts itself in itself to its victory and exaltation. And all life and vegetation stands in this context, and thereby the divine wisdom is made manifest, and comes into form to contemplation, and to the kingdom of joy; for in the conquest is joy (*in der Ueberwindung ist Freude*). But only one will is not manifest in itself, for there is neither evil nor good in it, neither joy nor sorrow; and if there were, yet the one, viz. the only will, must first in itself bring itself into a contrary, that it might manifest itself. (*Myst. Mag.* xl, 8)

Pure desire is incomplete and meaningless. Desire is always for something that can sustain it. Ever seeking to be something, it remains a nothing, perhaps even meonic. As it can find nothing it draws back into itself, tormenting itself. This is Boehme's *Angst*, a significant and powerful conception.

Each thing elevates itself, and would get out of the combat into the still rest . . . and only awakens the combat. . . . In the light of nature there is no better help and remedy for this opposition. . . . Now every taste desires only its like, and if it obtains it, then its hunger is satisfied, appeased, and eased, and it ceases to hunger, and rejoices in itself. (*Sig. Rer.*, ii, 4–5)

The self that aspires for itself kills itself: in willing itself the will limits itself; in desiring itself the will consumes itself. This is the heart of Boehme's dialectic. The ultimate threat is that desire, unless checked by freedom, brings death.

Real life is then struggle and, thankfully, victory. But the truth is that death is the root of life for the threat of death presses in upon life:

> Life proceeds out of death, and death must therefore be a cause of life. Else were there no such poisonous, fierce, fervent source fire could not be generated, and there could be no essence . . ; hence there would be no light, and also no finding of life. (*Theos. Punkt.* i, 68)

Sin is not death; rather, it results from desire, from self-will, from the death that is inherent in desire. Being is a continuing victory, and eternal life the final victory. The central fire is

> the only cause of life and motion of all powers; and without it all would be in the stillness without motion. (*Myst. Mag.* x, 43)

So death begets life.

Life and death, light and darkness, Yes and No, freedom and desire, good and evil! By opposing each other a third is produced, a generative process which reason cannot comprehend but which must be grasped by intuitive intelligence. Discursive reason (*Vernunft*) abstracts, and these abstractions are unreal because by abstracting the life-process is halted. Life is movement which must be grasped by an intuitive intelligence (*Verstand*) comprehending the entire process as well as the act of knowing. In intuitive intelligence no one phase opposes another; each implies the other.

> That cannot enter into particular existence which has no ground, which cannot be apprehended, which dwells in itself and possesses itself; but it proceeds out of itself, and manifests itself out of itself. (*Theos. Punkt.* vi, 7)

Divisibility, manifestation in particular existential forms—these cannot exist alone. Indeed, they need more (*Sig. Rer.*

xiv, 9). In fire all opposites coincide and it is *Verstand* which knows these while *Vernunft* can know only abstractions. True knowing is of the coincidence of opposites. Discovery of the eternal no-thing in which God beholds Himself is God's Wisdom or intuitive understanding (*Gnad.* i, 6), His self-conspection (*Gnad.* ii, 8).

Why does the Absolute thus develop itself? It emerges from the coincidentarious source to become spirit, master of nature and of life. From the primal separation in the *Blick* body results; body is life's concomitant (*Sig. Rer.* iii, 18). To escape death inherent in the fire, life is born as the realization of all the germinal possibilities within the *Ungrund.* (*Theos. Punkt.* i, 64)

> In fire there is death: the eternal nothing dies in the fire; and from the dying comes the holy life. Not that there is a dying, but that life as love arises in this way from the painfulness. The nothing or the unity thus takes an eternal life into itself, so that it becomes sentient, but proceeds again out of the fire into the nothing. (*Gnad.* ii, 32)

Whenever Boehme describes the generation of the supersensual life he must talk of it in cyclic terms. The free will desires; desire is an embryonic will. They oppose, and this opposition gives cyclic movement, life.

> We understand . . . how the light world fills the eternal freedom, or the primal will, which is called Father. . . . We understand also here earnestly and fundamentally how the natural life that wishes to dwell in the light-flaming world, must pass through death and be born out of death. (*Gnad.* iii, 6ff).

This life or movement from unconsciousness to full self-consciousness, a poised tension between life and death with final victory for life in Christ, takes place in man's mind and being.

This is drama, cosmic drama. The formless seeks form but in the movement to form there comes a moment when it is confronted with death. Then it struggles to avoid death by reconciling form (personality) with death. But in Christ, we shall later learn, life is victorious.

Spirit engenders itself in natural form. This proposition is important. In such engendering spirit finds that by getting a "body" it has introduced death into its being. All Boehme's images—from alchemy, folklore, mysticism, and the Bible—were meant to explain this vast struggle which he found in his world, in his self, and in his God.

Divine nature, or God's body, is what the dark unfathomable will is striving towards. Life can only be in body. Abstraction is not life. Life, the Unconditioned's search for conditioned form, the formless's effort to manifest its inherent potentialities, demands some body. This "body" is in Boehme's sense self-consciousness, form, personality, comprehensibility, and such as can be known, felt, willed, and loved. Apart from the chaotic *Ungrund* all essences are conditioned.

When the eternal will has found "bodily" form it has discovered a life of tension and dialectic. This cannot be endured. A new goal emerges—redemption, search for life in which death has been overcome. So another life-cycle begins, another birth is sought. The theogonic struggle is to get form; with it formal limitation is acquired. Now a life-cycle begins within a dialectical existence which looks forward to final removal of formal limitations, to a new birth in a new body.

Here Boehme's break with Neoplatonism is clear. He accepts emanation from the One. But he denies that return is regeneration. If the many were to return to the One salvation would be partial, for death would not have been overcome. Salvation is no retreat back into the primal ground of being, no escape back to *Nirvana,* thus dodging corporeal existence's meonic limitations, but it is, rather, full redemption by surmounting these limitations. His goal was individual form in which meonic trends have been destroyed. Oriental mystics, distrusting individuality, sought to surmount it in the abyss of being; they wanted a freedom from the self. Boehme advanced to a Kingdom where there is a first and a last, where spirits sat down to eat and drink with a risen Lord, where bodies were without death's darksome mystery, where Saint Cecilia plays her lute for the infant Jesus! Boehme, in distinction from Neoplatonic and oriental mystics and in full accord with Western cherishing of personality, sought freedom *for* the self to become a perfect self. He was one mystic who did not want to get rid of his self, only of his sinful self.

As he sat at his writing table he saw in the candle before him on its holder the cycle of all life. The candle had tallow, wax, and wick. Then there was the mysterious fire, the strange separator. Finally there was an unseen world of smoke, gas, air—tallow in a new birth! As the tallow burned it became liquid, then gas; this was life: congealed matter being changed into heavenly matter.

> See in a burning candle, when the fire . . . consumes. . . . There the substance dies, that is in the dying of the darkness it is transformed in the fire into a spirit and into another quality. . . . With the . . . fire the being of the candle passes into the consuming process, into a painful motion in life; and as the result . . . becomes light and shining in a large room. (*Gnad.* ii, 15)

Fire, agent of transformation, shows a process similar to alchemical transmutation which prefigures the redemptive life.

Within being there is hunger for manifestation, and, as no generation takes place without dialectic, Boehme creates his seven natural principles to explain this process. These seven natural principles are not the seven spirits of God (and this needs emphasis because so many Boehme students have mistakenly identified them):

> I have written . . . of the forms of nature. . . . It must not be understood as if the Deity were circumscribed . . . I write only of the properties, how God has manifested Himself through the internal, and through the external nature. . . . These seven properties can be found in all things; . . . In the internal world [they make] the Holy Element. (*Myst. Mag.* vii, 17–19)

These seven natural forms (*Gestalten*) show themselves as the breathing forth, circumscribing, forming, and bringing forth of the Deity into properties.

The circumscribing is the *Fiat*. . . . The desire is the beginning. . . . The whole ground is contained in the passage where it is said God created by the Word. The Word remains in God, and with the *scientia* or desire proceeds out of itself into division. . . . It is the beginning of nature. (*Gnad.* iii, 2)

How this comes about is described in a long and important passage from *Myst. Mag.* in which Boehme's nonconceptual imagery is clear. (Inasmuch as Boehme's views of the seven natural principles changed considerably as he matured, *Myst. Mag.* appears the best of his statements of this doctrine.)

The desire proceeding from the will . . . is the first form, and it is the *Fiat*, or *Let there be*. . . .

The first property is . . . astringent, harsh, impressing, self-conceiving, self-overshadowing; and it makes, first the great darkness . . ; secondly, it makes itself substantial in a spiritual manner, wholly rough, harsh, hard, thick, and is the cause of coldness, and all keenness and sharpness; also of all whatsoever is called essence; and it is the beginning of perceivancy . . . and introduces the contemplation into itself. But the desire in itself brings itself thereby into pain. . . .

The second form or property is the constringency or attraction of the desire; that is, a compunction stirring or motion. . . . Here arises the first enmity between the astringency or hardness . . . or sting of stirring; . . . The desire makes hard, thick, and congeals. . . . Thus the astringency is a mere cold rawness, and the compunction, viz. the attraction, is yet brought forth with the impression. It is even here as father and son; the father would be still; the son stirs the father and causes unquietness. . . .

The third property is the anguish . . . or welling forth, which the first two properties make. . . . In the contrition of the hardness the first sense of feeling does arise, and is the beginning of the essences; for it is the severation . . . in the word of the powers; each power becomes severable and sensible in itself. It is the origin of distinction, whereby the powers are, each in itself, mutually manifest; also the origin of the sense of the eternal mind. For the eternal mind is the all-essential power of the Deity; but the senses arise through nature with the motion in the division of the differentiation of the powers; where each power does perceive and feel itself in itself. It is also the origin of taste and smell. . . . Therefore the divine understanding brings itself into spiritual properties, that it might be manifest to itself. . . . Now we are to consider the working anguish in its own generation and peculiar property; for just as there is a mind . . . in the Word of the power of God, so likewise the first will to the desire brings itself . . . into a mind. . . .

The fourth form of nature is the enkindling of the fire, where the sensitive and intellective life does first arise, and the hidden God manifests Himself: For without nature He is hidden to all creatures, but in the eternal and temporal nature He is perceived and manifest . . . by the awakening of the powers. . . . The true life is first manifest in the fourth form. (*Myst. Mag.* iii, 8ff)

Boehme warns us to

attend and mark aright! I understand here . . . the eternal not the temporal nature. . . . Therefore do not foist in or allege calves, cows, or oxen, as it is the course of irrational reason to do. (*Myst. Mag.* iii, 20)

His point is that life is produced in trinitarian structure, that matter, stars, and man are trichotomous.

These principles, acting dialectically, move to the separation in the fire, the purifier and the separator. Fire is the source of all life (*Sig. Rer.* xiv, 23–34).

The fifth form is light, the triumphant kingdom of God's great love (*Myst. Mag.* vi, 18):

The fifth form . . . is the true love-fire, which separates itself in the light from the painful fire, and therein the divine Love in being is understood. For the powers separate in the fire terror, and become desirous in themselves. In this form is also understood every characteristic of the first three forms, yet no longer in pain, but in joy; and in their hunger or desire. . . . The fifth form has all the powers of the divine wisdom in it. It is the root-stalk of eternal life. . . . It is called the power of the glory of God. . . . By means of this power all things grow, blossom, and yield their fruit. (*Gnad.* iii, 26ff)

The sixth form . . . is speech, namely the mouth of God, the sound of the powers, where the Holy Spirit in the love comprehension brings itself manifestly out of the comprehended powers . . . So there is a sensual effectual speaking of the divine powers . . . by this is understood the five senses, namely, spiritual hearing, seeing, smelling, tasting, and feeling, where the manifestation of the powers work together unitedly . . . as we see in a concert of music, how all the melody . . . is united together. Further we understand in the sixth form the true meaning of the thoughts or percipient senses. For when the spirit has brought itself out of the (separated) qualities, it is in the temperament again. (*Gnad.* iii, 31, 33)

The seventh form is . . . where the sound of the speaking word embodies itself in being, as an entity in which the sound . . . embodies itself for manifest utterance. . . . This seventh form is a comprehensibility of all the qualities, and is properly called the whole of nature, or the formed, expressed Word. It is the inner, divine, uncreated heaven, but stands connected with the divine active birth of the temperament; and is called Paradise, as a growing life of the comprehended working divine powers. (*Gnad.* iii, 37–38)

It is the sabbath within reality in

which the working power of the divine power rests. . . . It is the true image of God, wherein God has perpetually fashioned Himself from eternity into an eternal being. (*Gnad.* iii, 39)

Boehme's description of the life-cycle in terms of seven natural powers came from the ancient astronomers who

have given names to the seven planets according to the seven forms of nature; but they have understood thereby another thing, not only the seven stars, but the sevenfold properties in the generation of the essences. (*Sig. Rer.* ix, 8)

His reference is to the surviving Gnostic systems which placed the planets in the following order: Jupiter, Saturn, Mars, Sol, Venus, Mercury, Luna. Much of Boehme's abstruse symbolism comes to clear light when this point is remembered. Furthermore, these seven forms are like the seven days; the seventh is a day of rest (*Gnad.* iii, 39).

Each form contains the six others within it (*Myst. Mag.*

vi, 24) and all seven are found within all things (*Ibid.*, vii, 68), even in God's name ADONAI (*Theos. Frag.* ii, 10). Superimposed upon these seven forms of nature is another pattern: the first four together make the world's hellish principle while the last three form a divine element (*Dreyfach* ii, 50).

Here then is Boehme's life-cycle which moves through seven forms to a kind of being in which flesh has been transmuted. These forms are his life-cycle, but the shapes of individual beings are ruled by the angels. Boehme gave to angels a peculiar role, naively conceiving of them as having a beginning in the divine center and as arising with the Trinity's "birth" (*Myst. Mag.* viii, 1). They really are what we would call the formed individualized ideas of God in His wisdom. Originally they existed in two principles only and were created from the first principle (*Princ.* iv, 67), being of light's matrix.

> They are the essence of both the inner internal fires. Their powers are the great emanating names of God. All have sprung from the Yes and have been led into the No, in order that powers might become manifest. (*Theos. Frag.* iv, 14)

Angels are the formed powers of God's Word, His outspeaking (*Theos. Frag.* vi, 5), His thoughts (*Theos. Frag.* vi, 5).

> Now, what is angelic form?
>
> As man is created to be the image and similitude of God, so also are the angels, for they are the brethren of men. (*Aurora*, v, 2)

Having human-like form

> every angel is created in the seventh quality . . . out of which his body is compacted . . . for the body is the . . . compacted spirit of nature. (*Aurora* xiii, 33, 35)

They have hands, feet (*Aurora* xii, 78, 83), mouths and an aperture for breathing (*Aurora* vi, 10), no teeth or wings (*Aurora* vi, 17: xii, 84), nor limbs (*Aurora* vi, 12). They eat paradisaical fruit (*Aurora* vi, 17) of the divine power (*Princ.* iv, 68) of God's Word (*Princ.* iv, 5).

Angels help God to rule the world.

> God or the eternal unity rules all things through . . . angels. The power . . . is God's, but they are His instruments whereby He disports and moves Himself, and by and through which He reveals the eternal powers and wonders. (*Theos. Frag.* vi, 7)

Angels are God's wonder-workers, fashioners and shapers of His powers:

> What angels will and desire is by their imagination brought into shape and form, which forms are pure ideas. . . . The divine powers have shaped themselves into such ideas before the creation of angels. (*Theos. Frag.* vi, 7)

Numbering a thousand times ten thousand (*Princ.* xv, 3), they are unequal in rank, ranged in three realms and seven dominions:

> There are seven high dominions in three hierarchies . . . according to the seven properties of nature. Every form of . . . eternal nature has . . . a throne . . . wherein distinctions are understood as well as the will to obedience to the holder of the throne. This dominion they have under their administration as creatures of divine endowments. (*Gnad.* iv, 24–25)

Thrones are like the three principles. Each throne has seven princely hierarchies (*Gnad.* iv, 25). As free angels they have the possibility of falling. Before Lucifer's fall they were able to imagine themselves into the world of matter.

Each angelic realm is ruled by a prince: Lucifer, Michael, Uriel. Of these Lucifer was the most beautiful of all heavenly creatures (*Aurora* xiii, 31) ruling the second kingdom. Angels as such do not fall, but humble themselves before God's great majesty so that the eternal No may not get dominion over them.

Now, what is a principle—this idea that plays so large a

part in Boehme's views of eternal nature? In Boehme's view a principle is an abstraction which is conceivable only in terms of discursive reason. It does not appear to intuitive understanding.

A principle is a life (*Princ.* v, 9), an existence which has become what it was not, a thing which has sprung from a no-thing (*Menschw.* I, v, 9). For when life and movement appear where previously none existed, there is a principle (*Theos. Punkt.* ii, 1) which has only one spirit, one central life, one will (*Seel. Frag.* i, 30).

Boehme saw three principles, three worlds (*II Apol. Tilke,* 40). These three worlds make up the threefold emanation of divine being, deriving from three sources.

> God is the essence of all essences, wherein there are two essences in one, . . the eternal light . . . and the eternal darkness. . . . These are the two principles, the original of which we know nothing of, only we know the birth, the indissoluble bond. (*Princ.* iv, 30)

From Lucifer's fall the third principle came.

> These . . . three . . . are the one God in His wonderful works, who has manifested Himself by this world. . . . We are to understand a threefold being, of three worlds in one another. (*Theos. Punkt.* ii, 32)

These three principles are each other's cause. (*Gnad.* vi, 6)

The third principle which has come is the world of substance, matter, the world of men, of beasts, and of things (*Princ.* vii). It emerges from the first two principles.

> The four elements are a principle of another property, and have another light . . . the sun. But in the pure element the things of this world are only as a figure. (*Dreyfach* v, 116)
>
> The third principle comes from the power of the essences, and has its beginning from the power of fire and light . . . which is the *Mysterium Magnum* wherein all things lie. . . . And it is to be understood that the *Mysterium Magnum* is in itself good, and no trace of evil is to be found in it; but in its process of unfolding . . . it becomes a *contrarium* of qualities. (*Gnad.* viii, 7–8)

The great mystery has come out of wisdom; in it God has seen the forms of the creatures (*Menschw.* I, i, 12), and He created it so He might be manifested in matter (*Princ.* v, 16) in seven days, giving angels dominion over it (*Gnad.* iv, 10). This third principle is still growing

> and therein are . . . created from what is inward the stars and elements, which . . . together with the sun are called the third principle. For the two inward worlds . . . the fire-world and the light-world, have manifested themselves by the third principle; and all is mixed together, good and evil, love and enmity, life and death. To every life there is death and fire; also, contrariwise, a desire of love, all according to the property of the internal world. And two kinds of fruit grow therefrom, evil and good; and each fruit has both properties. They show themselves . . . in every life in this world, so that wrath and . . . evil . . . are always fighting against love, each property seeking and bearing fruit. What the good makes, the evil destroys; what the evil makes, the good destroys. For it is perpetual war and contention . . . each bears and produces fruit . . . each will be lord. . . . The external principle is . . . perpetual war and contention, a building and a breaking. . . . In this struggle . . . growth rises: . . one draws out of the earth its fruitfulness, the other destroys . . . again. In all animals it causes . . . strife; for all animals, and all the life of this world, except man, is only a fruit of the third principle. . . . And all that moves in the world, and man by his spirit and visible body in flesh and blood, is only the fruit of the same essence, and nothing else at all. (*Theos. Punkt.* i, 48ff)

Here, then, is Boehme's dynamic vision of a living, contending world in which all things are made up of Yes and No. He saw that the world moved by this opposition and he believed that only a surrendered humble understanding could know eternal nature; rational reason could not do this because, assertive and arrogant, it sought to resolve antinomies and paradoxes. His metaphysics and logic, if such it may be called, were founded on paradox; he was a dialectical idealist. Yes and No oppose each other and by opposition define and condition one another, "bear" each other. The Yes is strong affirmation, the No is suppression. God too has

Yes and No though from a creature's point of view He is God only in His Love (*Theos. Frag.* ii, 12ff)

Dialectic, holding that one form implies another, that being moves by opposition, is Boehme's basic metaphysics. As the formed Word is spoken forth four stages are to be understood: the unexpressed, unconscious ground, the act of speaking, the meaning, and the spoken Word. These are the four steps in the process of spirit becoming flesh; the chaotic source, the act of embodiment, the embodied self-consciousness, and the totality of manifested being or Wisdom. Boehme's eternal nature was essential to his theology and it saved him from materialist pantheism:

God's love would not have been manifest without the eternal nature, that is, because the fire of love would not have been manifest without the fire of wrath. (*Gnad.* vii, 26)

Boehme's trinitarian structure which dominates his theology came from his mystical insight. Yet trinity was only half of his idea of God. He held as firmly to God's unshatterable unity in His transcendence:

We Christians say that God is threefold, but only one on essence. But that we generally say . . . that God is threefold in person, the same is . . . wrongfully . . . understood by the ignorant, yea, by a great part of the learned. . . . He is threefold in His eternal generation. He begets Himself in trinity; and yet there is but one essence . . . to be understood in this eternal generation, neither Father, Son, nor Spirit, but one eternal life, of God. (*Myst. Mag.* vii, 5, 11, 2)

It became increasingly difficult for him to hold his doctrine of three persons; he held that God is only person in Christ (*Myst. Mag.* vii, 5). This vision is partly heterodox but must be understood in the light of his conception of the meaning of "person."

Here then is Boehme's threefold eternal nature, a world of dialectic, manifested in a created world of strife and evil which is, apart from the mysterious deep of God and from the material world we know, an eternal nature.

Die Schöpfung, itzt am Ziel,
Harret, schweigt noch!—Ihr Gefühl
Wandelt in sich, und vermisst,
Was Geschöpf und Schöpfer ist;
Suchet einen, der mit Geist
Schmeckt und, was er ist, genuesst,
Suchet, der mit Gottesblick
Alle Schöpfung strahlt zurück!

—HERDER

CHAPTER FOURTEEN

TEMPORAL NATURE

BOEHME's understanding of creation, his entire cosmological speculation, found its start in Scripture's opening sentence: In the beginning God created heaven and earth. The key words are "heaven" and "earth" (*Myst. Mag.* x, 47). He had difficulty in conceiving of a world in which good struggles with evil as compatible with God's goodness. The act of world-creation was no problem for him: it happened when Lucifer fell (*Myst. Mag.* xii, 10). Heaven had existed even before the earth was. Basing his vision on the Biblical distinction between heaven and earth he postulated two creative acts: creation of heaven and its angels, creation of the earth and its beasts. Psalm civ gives Boehme the clue when it calls the angels flames of fire.

The term flames of fire denotes the central fire of the eternal nature, in which the creatures . . . stand, as the particular will of a being. But when God would realize his idea in the form of living creature, as in the form of self-will, He put in motion and separated the central fire in eternal nature. Thus the idea became manifest in the fire, which was accomplished through the breathing forth of the Yes. Thus the No, as the emanated will of self-receptiveness, took shape in the outbreathed Yes, in order that the creature might be established in its own will. And thus its own will is understood in the central fire, that is, in the properties of the fire, in which the creaturely life consists. For if this had not been, then Lucifer could not in self-will have broken himself off from the Good, and have fallen. If he had not possessed a volition of his own, then God's power must have fallen. But in this way the creature has broken off from the good and willed to rule in the power and in the properties of the central fire of nature, i.e. in the sphere of transmutation and phantasy; to which the Devil likewise came. (*Theos. Frag.* v, 2–6)

Creation began because the hidden God sought to manifest Himself in all ways. The God who is a nothing which seeks to become a something, who is known and who wants to be known–this God has not yet gotten His will until a created being loves Him. Only then does God come to completion, become a God. So the created world represents a determined (*sui generis*) mode of being which is essential to divine wisdom, to God's effective self-realization:

For all things are risen from the eternal spirit, as a likeness of the eternal . . . which is God and the Eternity, has in its own desire introduced itself into time, so that He is a life in the time, and the time is in Him as it were dead. (*Sig. Rer.* xiii, 2)

Commenting on the six days of creation, Boehme admits that it is the

greatest mystery, wholly hidden from the external reason . . . [for] there is neither night, morning, nor evening in the deep above the moon; but a continued day from the beginning of the outward world even to the end of time. (*Myst. Mag.* xii, 1)

Nevertheless, in six days God created the world's six categories (*Myst. Mag.* xii, 33).

We are to understand by creation . . . that the *Verbum Fiat* has amassed the spiritual birth, and introduced itself into a visible dominion and essence. (*Myst. Mag.* xii, 34)

The resulting world with its separate creatures is a figurement of the inner world. Internal characterizes external; spiritual manifests itself in body, clothes itself in form. (*Sig. Rer.* ix, 11)

Boehme was seeking to reconcile his religious intuitions with the metaphysics of his nature philosophy; he did this with his doctrine of signatures:

> The whole outward, visible world with all its being is a signature or figure of the inward spiritual world; whatever is internally, and however its operation is, so likewise it has its outward character. (*Sig. Rer.* ix, 1)

What, then, is creation? For Boehme creation is *ex nihilo* but in a sense that is far from the traditional: the nothing is the no-thing, the *Ungrund*. Creation is a metaphysical separating.

> It was the *mysterium magnum,* where all things stood in wisdom, in a spiritual form, in a wrestling spirit of love; not in the form of creaturely spirits, but in such a model that wisdom had thus . . . sported with itself. This model the one will has comprised in the Word, and suffered the attraction to work freely, so that every individual power . . . might be brought into a form according to its quality. Thus it is that the divine creative Word . . . has amassed into a compaction of powers. . . . As Moses says: in the beginning, i.e., in the inmassing of the *mysterium magnum,* God created the heavens and the earth, and said, let there arise all manner of creatures, each . . . according to his property. At the word *fiat* the great mystery became compacted into being, that is emerging out of the inward spiritual being into palpable tangible being, and in the compaction lay the attraction belonging to life, and that in two propria,[1] viz. a mental and an ental one. That is (1) a truly living proprium springing from the ground of eternity, and which is rooted in the wisdom of the Word, and (2) a proprium budding forth from the being's own desire as generated in itself, and which forms the growth wherein the vegetative life stands. Through this mysterium the *quinta essentia,* viz. the ens of the Word, originally became manifest and essential, and to it all the three principles were suspended. And here the ens

has separated—what is spiritual passing into spiritual beings, and what is inert into inert senseless beings, as are earth, stones, metal, and the material matter. (*Gnad.* iv, 12–15.)

All things proceed from one "mother" and creation is separation (*Sig. Rer.* iv, 1) into mortal and immortal, life and death, spirit and body. At creation

> the whole essence of eternity moved itself . . . and the whole form was enkindled and stirred, and that in the desire of manifestation; and there the generation divided itself into the flagrant of the enkindled fire into four parts, viz., fire, water, and earth, and the air is its moving, egressive spirit. (*Sig. Rer.* iv, 2)[2]

No new thing came from the earth's creation because God is not a maker in the objective sense (*Myst. Mag.* xix, 27).

> Creation . . . is . . . a manifestation of the all-essential, unsearchable God; all whatever He is in His eternal unbeginning, generation, and dominion, of that is also the creation, but not in omnipotence and power, but like an apple which grows upon the tree, which is not the tree itself, but grows from the power of the tree; even so all things are sprung forth out of the divine desire, and created into an essence, where in the beginning there was no such essence present, but only the same mystery of the eternal generation, in which there has been an eternal perfection. . . . For God has not brought forth the creation that He should thereby be perfect but for His own manifestation, viz., for the great joy and glory. (*Sig. Rer.* iv, 1–2)

In Wisdom God imagined the world to show Himself and the product is the result of His self-desiring. Eternal nature generates rocks and hills and elements; creation is therefore indirect; God first imagined astral forces; these astral forces made the tangible world. Creation is therefore reproductive, self-continuing. God first created the heavenly world and after Lucifer's fall the earth; thus Boehme's fire-world and light-world combine to produce our world. Creation originates in God's desire for manifestation (*Irrth. Stief.* 43), a desire already formed in Wisdom. He created all things out of the no-thing which He Himself is (*Sig. Rer.* vi, 8) and creating the external world is the formulation of the seven natural powers.

Before the creation of creatures the "wonders and powers" were in an ideal world wherein the Spirit sported with himself (*Theos. Frag.* iv, 1). This was Wisdom, His image and counterstroke of the *Ungrund.* The two fires were as yet one fire with two principles in it and the third principle, matter, existing only as possibility. In creation the love-fire became the basis of heaven, and wrath fire of hell. At the word *fiat* substantial reality arose, yet before the *fiat* could take place an event had to happen, Lucifer's fall (*Dreyfach* v, 18; viii, 23):

> When the central fire . . . moved itself, and brought itself into a more considerable desire . . . creation took place. This . . . God put into motion according to both fires. . . . In the course of this motion the hellish foundation of God's wrath broke forth, which God expelled from this working and shut up in darkness. There it remains . . . like a hungry maw full of craving after creation, and would also be creaturely and figurate. This is the cause . . . that Lucifer, the prince of a throne, turned away from God's Love to the central fire in God's wrath, in which he opined he was to rule over God's gentleness and Love. But on this account he was thrust from the central love fire . . . and now possesses hell. (*Theos. Frag.* iv, 3–5)

Lucifer's No, his receptivity to self-centeredness, which led him to put to proof the

> property of eternal nature, and would not live in renunciation, but wished to rule in and with the Holy Name. . . . His creaturely will elevated itself . . . and abused the Holy Name in it. . . . He . . . broke off from the unity. He wished to rule over the Yes with the No, for the No had elevated itself in him and despised the Yes. (*Theos. Frag.* vii, 2–7)

Lucifer imagined himself into the dark matrix (*Dreyfach* ix, 38). He despised humility (*Gnad.* iv, 31) and, having a free will, became self-willed in fantasy (*Gnad.* iv, 29). He fell because of his egocentric will (*Gnad.* iv, 32) which led him to the fire's might (*Theos. Frag.* vii, 1–5) and, rebelling against the meekness (*Myst. Mag.* x, 12), he wanted to possess another principle (*Theos. Frag.* x, 3) and to act in his own name.

So a new principle was made for him; he imagined himself into matter (*Gnad.* iv, 32). He was driven from heaven into a new principle and the actual creation of this world began (*Myst. Mag.* xiv, 17). He was locked out of the first two principles (*Princ.* iv, 73) and a dwelling was made in the darkness for him (*Menschw.* I, v, 21). Now he is the prince of the world of fantasy (*Sig. Rer.* xvi, 15) and full of pride, greed, envy, and wrath (*Aurora* xvi, 79ff). He lost his bride, Wisdom (*Myst. Mag.* ix, 12), and he cannot become an angel again (*Princ.* xvii, 66) because he lost the divine names (*Theos. Frag.* viii, 9). From the loveliest of creatures he became the most hideous.

These then are descriptions of Lucifer's rebellion and the result—the first movement in nature (*Gnad.* vi, 12). God did not plan the fall (*Myst. Mag.* ix, 3) but

> created Lucifer for this harmony, to play with His Love-spirit in Him, as upon the musical instrument of His manifested and formed Word; and this the self-will would not. . . . How came that He would not? Yes, he knew well enough; but he had no sensible perceivance of the Fall, but only a bare knowledge. The fiery lubet, which was potent in him, did egg him on, for it would . . . be manifest in the essence of the wrath . . , in the root of fire. The darkness also . . . desired to be creatural, which drew Lucifer. . . . It drew him not from without. . . . The original of the Fall was within the creature, and not without. . . . So it was Adam also. Self-will was the beginning of pride. (*Myst. Mag.* iv, 9ff)

Breaking away from God's unity

> he was cast with his legions out of his throne, and immediately shut up by the darkness and had been grasped by the fierce pride-wrath of the hellish foundation. (*Theos. Frag.* xiii, 3)

Here the created world arose and on the first day of creation Lucifer was driven out (*Myst. Mag.* xii, 14) and on the third day he was locked in between time and eternity (*Myst. Mag.* xii, 35). This fall was followed by creation.

> God spoke: *let there be light!* and there was light. And with this coming to be light, the Devil's might and strength was wholly withdrawn from him in the essence for here the light shone in the now awakened power, in the darkness; which light the prince of wrath could not comprehend: . . . It was the light of nature, which was useless to him. (*Myst. Mag.* xii, 14)

This Paracelsian light of nature was the quintessence of the other elements (*Princ.* vii, 7), the fiery tincture of the heavenly firmament (*Dreyfach* ix, 93). When God said *let there be light* the sun was created, the dialectical counterpart of Lucifer's darkness. Between Lucifer's darkness and this new light there was again a *contrarium* (*Gelassen.* ii, 10). So the first day's work separated light from darkness.

> The darkness remained in the wrathful property, not only in the earth, but also in the whole deep; but in the light's nature the light of nature did arise . . . from the quintessence. (*Myst. Mag.* xii, 15ff)

All earthly materials were drawn together in one darkness and heavenly materials into one light. Between these natural dialectical forces life was produced.

Light is quintessence, the fifth element, source of the four natural elements (*Beschau.* iii, 21), the pure element (*Epist.* xx, 9). In it the Word became essentially manifest and in it all three principles were suspended (*Gnad.* iv, 15). This light of nature, from which the sun came, was in temperament, or in a state where love and wrath were mutually balanced (*Gnad.* viii, 29).

This natural light was freedom. Boehme understood that creation was more than making a planetary system; he also had to explain how freedom became impaled within the earth's four elements. The elemental earth came to be after Lucifer's fall as the by-product of the creating light (*Aurora* xvii, 9: xxi, 14). By making light he also made the dark. Earth is of no different essence than the stars; indeed, it is like the stars for whatever the natural light is spiritually, that the earth is in its coarseness (*Gnad.* v, 13). Earth became the third element, fire and light already existing. Boehme's four elements were created progressively: fire produced light, light air; fire also produced water and its ashes the earth.

The first day's work substantialized fire's polarities. Between these poles life was created. Freedom and desire thus were projected into the physical universe. Nature's light was made before earth. Here Boehme's solution—if such it be—to the problem of evil appears: the rough earth is a misdirection of freedom which permits light to be known. Goodness consists in order, in nature's subordination to spirit, of desire to will. Evil is the disorder, rebellion, perversion of making spirit nature's servant (*Sig. Rer.* xv, 14). Goodness is spirit victorious over earth's appetites.

On the second day of creation life and death were separated.

> For there the light broke through the darkness, and made the dead body of nature to spring and flourish, and to be stirring and agile. (*Aurora* xix, 2)

The firmament which separates heavenly water from earthly waters was

> the gulf between time and eternity, but that God called it heaven and makes a division of the waters, and gives us to understand that the heaven is in the world, and the world is not in heaven. (*Myst. Mag.* xii, 23)

The second day's work consisted in separating heaven from hell and separating the waters above the firmament from those below the firmament. God created

> the firmament of heaven, viz. the strong enclosure to the darkness of the original matrix, that it might no more kindle itself, and generate earth and stones. And therefore He made the enclosure . . . out of the midst of the waters, which

stays the might of the fire, and become the visible heaven, whence the creatures have proceeded, from whence now the elements fire, air, and water proceed. (*Princ.* viii, 9)

Boehme distinguishes internal, heavenly, sweet, spiritual water of life and light from elemental water. The water above the firmament is the water of eternal life (*I Apol. Tilke,* 259), akin to fire.

For light is also a fire, but a giving fire; for it gives itself to all things, and even in its giving there is life and being, i.e., air and spiritual water; and in this . . . water the love-fire of the light has its life, for it is the food of this light. (*Gnad.* ii, 29)

Spiritual water is the holy element from which the world and its four elements were brought into substantial form (*Myst. Mag.* vi, 5). In this spiritual water above the firmament God's spirit rules and reigns (*Myst. Mag.* x, 52), for it is Christ's body (*Myst. Mag.* x, 57). In this sweet, love-enkindling water (*Aurora* ix, 23) the Holy Spirit works in angels and men (*Myst. Mag.* xxii, 52; xxiv, 24). Through this spiritual water's power to break through death the new man and new world come (*Myst. Mag.* ix, 51).

The water below the firmament is an elemental earthy substance; a misty steam (*Sig. Rer.* iii, 23) which is a witness to the inner water's power (*Myst. Mag.* xiv, 70) and which came to be with Lucifer's fall (*Aurora* xiv, 21). Material water originates in the spiritual world (*Gnad.* iii, 24); without it fire cannot burn (*Myst. Mag.* xiv, 7) and within it the creatures live (*Princ.* xx, 53); from it bodies originate (*Aurora* i, 17). Holy water above the firmament is the dialectical counterpart of elemental water (*Myst. Mag.* xii, 24ff).

Outward water is the instrument of the inner . . . for the moving spirit in the Word is the water which rules the inner water of baptism. Dear Christians, let this be spoken unto you; this is the real ground. (*Myst. Mag.* xii, 26ff)

If the earth's regeneration is to follow, if the fallen elements are to be raised, the two waters must become separate in the final act of world-redemption; to do this they must have already been separated. So Boehme also has two heavens:

> The outward heaven is passive, and the inward works through it, and draws forth an external fruit out of the outward; whereas the inward heaven lies hidden therein in the firmament, as God is hidden in time. (*Myst. Mag.* xii, 29)

On the third day God made life in the midst of death (*Aurora* xxiv, 41), by *fiat* dividing earthly waters so a dry place might emerge on which creatures might dwell. This dry earth grew verdant; life budded through dead matter; grass, herbs, trees, plants sprang forth.

> Thus every essence became visible, and God manifested His manifold virtue with manifold herbs, plants, and trees, so that everyone that does look upon them, may see the external power, virtue, and wisdom of God therein. (*Princ.* viii, 9)

Paradise's verdant creation came as the originally perfect creation was distorted by Lucifer's fall.

> For although many thousand . . . herbs stand one by another in one and the same meadow, and one of them is fairer . . . than the other, yet one of them does not grudge the form of another, but there is a pleasant refreshment in one another; so also there is a distinct variety in Paradise, where every creature has its greatest joy in the . . . beauty of another; and the eternal wisdom of God is without number and end. . . . You shall find no book wherein the divine wisdom may be more searched into . . . than when you walk in a flowery meadow, there you shall see, smell, and taste the wonderful power and virtue of God; though this be but a similitude, and the divine virtue in the third principle is become material, and God has manifested Himself in a similitude. But (this) is a loving schoolmaster to him that seeks. (*Princ.* viii, 12)

The third day's work was the moving life in the midst of the darksome earth's death.

Paradise meant for Boehme life sprouting from death

(*Menschw.* I, iv, 13). Paradise is budding through wrath, love coming from dead matter.

> The holy element budded forth in the temperament through the four elements, and produced through the four elements heavenly fruit, which was pleasant to the sight and good for food, as Moses says. (*Gnad.* v, 9)

This Paradise, a holy fire which emanated from God (*Theos. Frag.* iii, 38), is a pleasurable, divine, joyous world without elemental strife, with no opposition and reaction, but only love-play (*I Apol. Tilke,* 131). The *Ungrund's* longing to be realized is fulfilled by Paradise which has no evil in it and is

> where there is perfection, where there is . . . love, joy, and knowledge; where there is no misery; which . . . neither death nor the devil's touch, neither do they know it; and yet it has no wall of earth or stones about it, but there is a great gulf between paradise and this world. (*Princ.* ix, 7)

Paradise has its own peculiar substance and matter; it is transparent, glistening, composed of a bright, clear, visible substance (*Princ.* ix, 18).

> The depth of this substance is without beginning or end, its breadth cannot be reached, there are neither years nor time, no cold nor heat, no moving of the air; no sun nor stars; no water nor fire; no sight of evil spirits; no knowledge nor apprehension of the affliction of this world; no stony rock nor earth; and yet a figured substance of all the creatures of this world. (*Princ.* ix, 21)

Before Lucifer's fall the world was all paradise (*Myst. Mag.* xxv, 16) but after this event it bloomed only in a small spot on earth (*Dreyfach* xi, 12), the Garden of Eden (*Myst. Mag.* xvii, 8). If nature is to be restored a small section of divine substance must remain within the otherwise corrupted earth.

On creation's fourth day God made the heavenly world of stars and planets. Already in 1612, two years after Kepler's views had been published, Boehme had revealed his Copernican views:

> Some suppose that [the sun] runs about . . . the earth in a day and a night. . . . This . . . is not right. The earth rolls itself about; and runs with the other planets . . . around the sun. The earth does not remain . . . in one place, but in a year runs once about the sun. (*Aurora* xxv, 65ff).

With this fourth day the sidereal birth took place (*Aurora* xxii, 1). Boehme thus gave the world an external, sidereal, and internal birth (*Aurora,* xix, 32). Stars and planets were made from the light created on the third day (*Aurora* xxiv, 1), from the quintessence (*Princ.* viii, 8). Its source was the *Ungrund's* primitive fire, being realized in the natural center through the seven natural powers (*Dreyfach* vi, 44). Each planet had a special role in helping to sustain the created world (*Princ.* v, 10). The sun, though not nature's light (*Aurora* xviii, 125), is still the external world's ruling spirit (*Sig. Rer.* xii, 19) giving the stars their light (*Aurora* ii, 9), and taking Lucifer's place in energizing the world and so becoming the heart of the universe (*Dreyfach* ix, 25), the ruler and king of all nature (*Dreyfach* xl, 40), and the deity within the third principle (*Princ.* viii, 13–23):

> Its rays kindle the . . . earth from which everything grows . . . whereby the magical fire is revealed. . . . Now as the power and rays disclose the mystery of the outer world, so that creatures and plants proceed from it; so, on the other hand, the mystery of the outer world is a cause by which the sun's rays are . . . enkindled. . . . But because the sun is nobler, and a degree deeper in nature, than the mystery of the outer world . . , it penetrates into the outer mystery and kindles it, and thus too kindles itself. (*Gnad.* ii, 23).

Being made of the quintessence of the sun helps to counteract the earth's wrathful elements (*Princ.* xv, 9), enkindling sweet light in them and laying the foundation for eventual regeneration. The sun's vitality is also the universe's basic vitality (*Aurora* xxv, 38), originating the natural powers (*Aurora* xxvi, 12), propitiating wrath's fire and making all love and light (*Dreyfach* vi, 63). Through solar activity the world's hidden mystery of forms and patterns becomes manifest within the substantial world (*Gnad.* viii, 13); from it things get life and substance; it is good to good things and evil to evil things (*Gnad.* viii, 13).

The sun generates the planets and stars which draw their vitality from it (*Gnad.* ii, 26).

> We see . . . that the stars are so greedy and hungry for the sun's power that they introduce their desire . . . into the first three forms, and draw the sun's power into themselves. The sun . . . penetrates powerfully into the stars to receive their desire, so that they get their luster from the sun's power. (*Gnad.* ii, 26)

Each star has its own character (*Aurora* xxv, 25), and projects this individuality into the created world. By the stars good and evil become manifest (*Myst. Mag.* x, 6) in individual aspect (*Myst. Mag.* xiii, 8). As some stars are invisible, so many individual forms are not perceivable by the human mind (*Dreyfach* x, 38). Stars rule by the powers derived from the sun, from the quintessence which dominates the four elements. Stars awaken the dead elements and bring individuality into being (*Dreyfach* vii, 48).

Boehme gave special roles to the planets. His planets were Saturn, Jupiter, Mars, Venus, Mercury, Luna, and Sol. Each rules one of the seven natural powers, each planet being like its form. Saturn begets corporeality (*Aurora* xxvi, 2, 12) and has a dark wrathful quality; it is like the alchemist's lead (*Sig. Rer.* iv, 23). Jupiter is man's power to reason and to think (*Aurora* xxv, 107), begetting life in the divine vitality (*Aurora* xxvi, 17). It is the alchemist's tin (*Sig. Rer.* iv, 29). Mars is hunger, wrathfulness, anger (*Sig. Rer.* iv, 20), symbol of anxiety and gall, the alchemist's iron (*Sig. Rer.* iv, 37). Venus is mildness, humility, spiritual meekness (*Dreyfach* ix, 79), the propagative seed (*Sig. Rer.* iv, 21), the alchemist's copper (*Sig. Rer.* iv, 35, 36). Mercurius is God's active working Word which awakens the creature's life seed (*Clavis* 26); *Dreyfach* ix, 96), producing life and death and leading to the creative life-urge to spirit and essence (*Myst.*

Mag. xiv, 5). It is the active agent (*Sig. Rer.* iv, 30), the alchemist's quicksilver (*Sig. Rer.* iv, 30). Luna is the lustful (*Sig. Rer.* iv, 27) container of the created world's substances (*Sig. Rer.* iv, 27), the alchemist's silver. The sun is the world's perfection—pure gold.

By dominating their metals the planets rule the things which contain such metals, thus activating the earth and making it productive.

On the fifth day God commanded all manner of beasts to come forth, each after its own kind. Out of what were they to come forth? Out

> of the matrix of the earth, that they might be of the essence of earth. . . . Now then if the beasts were merely out of a lump of earth, then they would eat earth, but seeing they are proceeded out of the matrix of the earth by the *Fiat*, therefore they also desire such food as the matrix affords out of its own essence; and that is not earth, but flesh. (*Princ.* viii, 38ff).

Each creature is a mode of divine revelation (*Irrth. Stief.*, 514) and

> must remain in its place wherein it was apprehended in its creation and formed into an image, and not depart out of the same harmony. (*Sig. Rer.* xvi, 18)

Each creature is made after its own kind and

> lives in its mother, whence it has taken its original. . . . It cannot live in another degree. As beasts upon the earth . . . therein they live; and thence they take their food and nourishment. . . . Birds were created in the sulphur of the air, therefore they fly in their mother; also the fishes in the sulphur of the water and the worms in the sulphur of the earth. Thus each thing lives in its mother whence it was taken, and the contrary is death. (*Myst. Mag.* iv, 19ff)

Individual characteristics come from the substantial origin, the outer emerges from the inner.

> For we see that there are good and evil creatures, as

venomous beasts and worms . . . which desire to dwell only in the dark and conceal themselves from the sun. In contrast to them we find many creatures . . . fashioned from the realm of phantasy, as . . . apes and such beasts and birds as play monkey-tricks . . . We find . . . good friendly creatures. . . . By the food and dwelling of any animal we see from whence it came; for every creature desires to dwell in its mother and longs after her. (*Gnad.* v, 21ff)

What is this mother after which a creature longs? It is the creature's formal character within the three principles. In the first principle the mother is the fire's wrath; in the second principle the mother is meek light; in the third principle the mother is the sidereal world. For life each creature must return to its mother, partake of its pure idea and become attuned to its inner state of being.

Whatever idea dominates that is the mother to which the creature must return. As each creature has a sidereal body and an elemental body (*Myst. Mag.* xiv, 2) the sidereal body's star is its mother. Not only does each earthly creature come from this mother but it also seeks nourishment therefrom. This figure of speech means that creatures are nourished by their governing idea: a creature knows only the mother that bore it (*Princ.* ii, 4); the mother only is eternal, the creature temporal (*Aurora* xvi, 13).

The creatures, each made after its kind, are also in the world of conflict, and the struggling, striving of creatures in field and forest is witness to Lucifer's fall and to a corruption within creation.

On the sixth day God, speaking the *Verbum Fiat,* said *Let us make man!* From the mixture of elements and essences already created God made an image to be like Himself to have dominion over fish and fowl, over cattle and crawling thing. God took of the heavenly element and of the earthly, of all the constellations, degrees, and elements, and made a twofold body for man—a spiritual and an elemental. The spiritual body was God's image, clothed with the quintessence; the four elements were the corporeal body. Into these God breathed a living soul, making a man of all three principles (*Myst. Mag.* xv, 17) with a tripartite soul different from that of Plato:

> And the soul . . . consists in three kingdoms: the first is . . . the dark and fire-world. . . . The second is the holy light world. . . . The third . . . is the outward astral and elemental kingdom. . . . (*Myst. Mag.* xv, 18ff).

Yet man does not have three souls, only one.

> And if this were not, then it could not be said, that the soul went to heaven or to hell, if it were not in it. . . . We are in no wise to think that the soul is God Himself. . . . But the soul is the . . . formed Word; it is the spirit and the life of the three principles of divine manifestation. (*Myst. Mag.* xv, 25)

The first man was the finest of God's creatures, creation's secondary goal.

The first six days saw God creating all things. On the seventh he gathered all the essences of the other six properties and made a seventh in which eternal day lies

> whence the days of time are proceeded; and the ancients have called it *Sonnabend;* but it is rightly called *Sönnabend* wherein God's Love does appear and atone the anger; as when the six properties . . . do enkindle themselves . . . they are atoned and reconciled in the seventh. . . . Thereof Moses speaks rightly, *God rested on the seventh day from all His works, and hallowed the seventh day.* (*Myst. Mag.* xvi, 20)

Rest has a special meaning. The divine vitality which entered creation found itself conditioned by it. Each of the six powers had come to be made up of contradictory manifestations. This could not be tolerated; God drew contradictions back into restful unity.

> This rest is the holy heaven . . . where time works in itself, and sets forth for . . . the day of separation, where, at the end of the days of this world, evil shall be separated from the good, each thing shall possess its own heaven. (*Myst. Mag.* xvi, 25)

Departure into creaturely strife and disunity is not permanent; there is promise of a Sabbath at the end of time, a transparent glossy sea before God's throne (*Myst. Mag.* xvi, 27). This Sabbath is a promise of further divine activity when judgment shall be passed on all creation (*Seel. Frag.* xxx, 62).

Creation has proceeded from a *Quall,* which is Boehme's word for reality's dynamic center. A *Quall* is incomprehensible and irrational (*Seel. Frag.* i, 51), a particular source for each particular thing (*Myst. Mag.* viii, 20), the core of individuality (*Seel. Frag.* i, 52). Between this *Quall* and individual beings there lies a hierarchy, a pleroma which goes a long way towards answering but which does not finally solve the problem of creation. Like other theologians, including Plotinus, Boehme finds the gap between the One and the many unbridgeable. The two trends of his thought here emerge in basic conflict; his stubborn loyalty to God's goodness and his equally firm conviction of evil's recalcitrance. He could not admit that evil came from God; nor could he see how anything existed apart from God. His pleroma of causes only pushed his problem further into the background. God must realize Himself on all levels, yet some of the realized modes act contrary to His goodness. Boehme's solution, so characteristic of his mind, is the idea of the "divine within God," or "God so far as He is called God" (*Myst. Mag.* xxix, 9).

This is of course Boehme's permanent problem: why does God allow evil? His answer, the only seeming true answer, is to assert over and over again the goodness of God and the freedom of the human spirit (*Myst. Mag.* xxvi, 34). All his theology is founded on freedom; determined being is devilish (*Myst. Mag.* ix, 31). The only predestination he admits is the idea that all evil creatures within us are predestined to damnation.

Here then is Boehme's world which is at once the magical, organic manifestation of God as well as the object (*Gegenwurf*) of His kingdom of forms. This opposition cannot be tolerated. Tension must be released. The world and man, noblest of the creatures, must be redeemed.

NOTES TO CHAPTER FOURTEEN

1. The glossary in the 1730 edition gives *proprius* as meaning genius, the characteristic nature-spirit, the innate character.
2. This vision of the separation of fire into the elements is not too far from the modern view of the earth's origin.

Il me faut, comme à l'univers, un Dieu qui me suave du chaos et de l'anarchie de mes idées . . . Son idée délivre notre esprit de ses longs tourments, et notre coeur de sa vaste solitude.

—RIVAROL, AS QUOTED BY SAINTE-BEAUVE IN HIS *Memoirs*

CHAPTER FIFTEEN

MAN

THE KEY to Boehme's doctrine of man is Wisdom, especially his description of her as the image of God. Wisdom was the image (*Ebenbild*) or counter-image (*Gegenwurf*) of the unknown God; she was the mother-bride of God and the mother-bride of man and thus the revealeress of God in man and of man in God. She was also the form of the God-image in man, the image binding man to God, and the image revealing God's wonders in man.

This contiguity between man and God is consummated in a flash, *Blick*. Not only does God see Himself in Wisdom (*Princ.* xv, 14) but he also sees man (*Princ.* xvii, 12) through her. In her the Holy Spirit discovers the human image created in the *Verbum Fiat* (*Dreyfach* v, 44).

The *Blick* in which God knows man and man knows God and in which man knows himself is the central act of divine intuition, the act of self-contemplation in God, the divine knowing of creatures, the creature's knowledge of the Creator, and the creature's knowledge of himself. In this creative intuition the "eye" perceives all life's mysteries in Wisdom.

Wisdom is then man's heavenly corporeality (*Busse* i, 27), man's highest essence and element.

That substantiality wherein the virgin of God consists,

Adam had on him; for the spirit of this world was given him, and breathed into him therein; but the essences were paradisaical, and sprung up through the one pure element, which the substantiality contains, and that substantiality the spirit of this world, in Adam, took into itself in its power. (*Dreyfach* xiii, 15)

Wisdom is man's heavenly pattern and image, his archetype,

the image of the heavenly world's substance in the soul's inner ground. (*Myst. Mag.* lvii, 9)

She is the love of Adam (*Gnad.* vii, 33) wherein God unites Himself with man. She is the heavenly Eve (*Myst. Mag.* lxvi, 52) who stands in heaven and paradise, mirroring herself in the soul's earthly qualities, as in the sun. Wisdom is the image of God both in the theogonic system and in man's soul.

And in this . . . is understood the angelic and soulic true image of God, whereof Moses says: God created man in His own image, that is, in the image of His divine imprint, according to the spirit; and in the image of God created He him. (*Gnad.* i, 15)

Boehme's description of Wisdom is philosophical idealism at its clearest:

She is the divine chaos wherein all things lie, viz. the divine imagination, in which the ideas of angels and souls have been set from eternity, in a divine type and resemblance; yet not then as creatures, but in resemblance, as when man beholds his face in a glass; therefore the angelical and human idea did flow forth from wisdom, and was formed into an image, as Moses says: God created him in His image; that is, breathed into it the breath of divine effluence, of divine knowledge, from all the three principles of the divine manifestation. (*Clavis* 19)

Just as Wisdom is God's bride so is she also man's. Here Boehme's androgynous views begin to appear inasmuch as he distinguishes between the female light-nature and the male fire-nature.

The fire-soul must subsist in the fire of God, and be so pure as refined gold, for it is the husband of the noble Sophia, from the woman's seed; for it is the fire's tincture, and Sophia is the Light's tincture. If the tincture of the fire be wholly and thoroughly pure, then its Sophia will be given it; and so Adam received again to his arms his most precious and endeared bride . . . and it is not any longer man or woman, but a branch of Christ's pearl tree, which stands in the paradise of God. (*Myst. Mag.* xxv, 14)

This marriage of Wisdom with man's fire-soul forms the peculiar and in some ways primitive background for Boehme's androgynous man. Original man unites fire and light.

Man should be the image and similitude of God, wherein God should dwell. Now God is a spirit, and all the three principles are in Him; and He would make such an image, as should have all the three principles in Him, and that is rightly a similitude of God. (*Princ.* x, 9)

Boehme gives various descriptions to this divine image in man: the angelical world in him, the idea, the lily-twig, Christ in him. In *Busse* he used the traditional image of German mysticism, *Füncklein;* he also calls it *glimmende Docht,* the glowing candle wick after the flame has been snuffed.

The point of departure for Boehme's idea of the *Urstand,* or the essential man before the fall, is the identification of the heavenly man with the resurrected Christ.

I know the sophister will here cavil with me, and cry it down as a thing impossible for me to know, seeing I was not there and saw it myself. To him I say, that I, in the essence of my soul and body, when I was not yet I, but when I was in Adam's essence, was there, and did fool away my glory in Adam. But seeing Christ has restored it again to me, I see, in the spirit of Christ, what I was in

Paradise; and what I now am in sin; and what I shall be again. (*Myst. Mag.* xviii, 1)

In his soul man has all that God's spirit breathed into him at creation (*Bedenk. Stief.* i, 36), the image which was corrupted. In *Wiedergeburt* Boehme says that regeneration reverses the fall; primitive man and Christ are the same. All men are fundamentally one man; the Vine has branches which get vitality and produce fruit from the same root (*Myst. Mag.* xxiv, 15). Man's self-knowledge comes from the one God-man (*Myst. Mag.* xxiv, 15).

God made man in a pure element, a holy corporeality not of the earth's four elements (*Myst. Mag.* xvi, 6). Adam had a body wherein all the qualities stood in harmony (*Myst. Mag.* xvi, 5).

> None lived in self-desire, but they all gave up their desire unto the soul. . . . They were all tinctured with sweet love so that there was nothing but mere pleasing relish and love-desire and delight between them. (*Myst. Mag.* xvi, 5)

Essential Adam had no strife, no war of opposites, no tension or disruptive dialectic; divine Love illuminated his inner parts as the sun lights the world (*Bedenk. Stief.* i, 36). This inner body was God's dwelling-place, an image of divine substantiality where the soul received God's meekness (*I Apol. Tilke* 233).

> Thus . . . was the first man when he stood in paradise . . . in manner as time is before God, and God in time; and they are distinct, but not parted asunder. As the time is a play before God, so also the outward life of man was a play into the inward holy man, which was the real image of God. (*Myst. Mag.* xvi, 8)

Essential man's inner being, God's image, and his outer being, *limnus* [1] of earth, were not in conflict although the inner kept the outer imprisoned (*Myst. Mag.* xvi, 7) in perfect, undisturbed life in a body as clear as glass, penetrated by the sun's celestial light without darkness or death (*Sig. Rer.* xi, 51).

Essential man had a body because no spirit can subsist without a body, which is the spirit's mother (*Aurora* xxvi, 50). Boehme had no idealist antithesis between body and spirit; body was for him not flesh. It was rather form, definiteness, comprehensibility, that which can be known, willed, and loved, perhaps even personality. Inasmuch as only the *Ungrund* is incorporeal no spirit can exist without definitive form. Boehme's essential man was then no disembodied spirit but a man who eats, drinks, and reproduces.

Boehme develops essential man's physiology from Biblical descriptions of the risen Christ. The kingdom is not one of values and ideas but a joyous, majestic place where the redeemed sit down with a knowable Lord at banquet feast. Entrance into this kingdom is being reclothed in a new body. Adam's two essences

> formed one body, wherein was the most holy tincture and divine fire and light, viz. the great joyful love-desire, which did inflame the essence, so that both essences did earnestly desire each other in love, desire, and love one another. . . . And yet they are not two bodies, but one; but of a twofold essence, viz., one inward, heavenly, holy and one from the essence of time; which were espoused and betrothed to each other, eternally. (*Myst. Mag.* xviii, 17, 18)

Androgynous essential man partook of all spiritual potentialities; man

> is a little world out of the great world, and both the properties are in him. God said after the fall: 'Thou art earth, and unto earth shalt thou return.' (*Epist.* xii, 7)

In his outward being man is a little world of the great world and what the superior is that is also the inferior. Correspondence between the world and essential man implies that the world is like God; God is threefold; the world has three principles; man has body, soul, spirit.

> Man was a mixed person. For he was to be an image of the outer and the inner world, and was to rule by the inner

quality over the outer but as the symbol of God. (*Menschw.* I, iii, 13)

In God's power man was to be lord over creation (*Menschw.* I, iv, 7); his rule was to extend over heaven and earth, in all stars and elements (*Myst. Mag.* xvi, 2); he was innocent, childlike, unconscious of evil, without avarice, pride, envy or wrath (*Dreyfach* xi, 23):

When God had created Adam thus, he was then in Paradise . . . , and this clarified man was wholly beautiful and full of all knowledge; and there God brought all the beasts to him, that he should look upon them, and give every one its name, according to its essence. . . . And Adam knew what every creature was, and he gave to every one its name, according to the quality of its spirit. As God can see into the heart of all things, so could Adam do also, in which his perfection may very well be seen. And Adam and all men should have gone wholly naked, as he then went; his clothing was the clarity of virtue; no heat nor cold touched him; he saw day and night with open eyes; in him there was no sleep, and in his mind there was no night, for the divine virtue was in his eyes; and he was altogether perfect. . . . He was no man nor woman; as we in the resurrection shall be neither. Though indeed the knowledge of the marks of distinction shall remain in the figure, but the limbus and the matrix were not separated, as now. . . . Man was to dwell upon the earth as long as it would stand, . . manage the beasts, and have his delight and recreation therein. (*Princ.* x, 17–19)

He stood in heaven; his essences were in Paradise; his body was indestructible. He knew the divine angelic language and the language of nature (*Seel. Frag.* iv, 7); no fire burned in him, no water drowned him, no air suffocated him, no earth penetrated him—the elements stood in awe of him (*Dreyfach* xi, 23). Neither heat nor cold, sickness nor accident, terrified him. His body could pass through doors (*Menschw.* I, ii, 13). He lived a pure life like a burning oil flame. He had celestial perception and his intelligence passed and comprehended supernatural things (*Sig. Rer.* xii, 2).

Essential man, having no elemental body, needed no

bowels, belly, nor digestive organs. He ate spirit food, magically. The fruit he ate

> was pleasant to the sight, and good for food in a heavenly way; not to be taken into a worm-bag or miserable carcass as is done now in the awakened animal property. . . . In the mouth were the centers of separation. (*Gnad.* v, 34)

In this mouth he ate paradisaical food, which

> also was good. . . . Adam could eat of every fruit in the mouth, but not of the corruptibility, that must not be, for his body must subsist eternally but in Paradise. (*Princ.* xv, 16)

Likewise, essential man drank out of eternal life's source which lies hidden within earthly water (*Princ.* x, 20). This Boehme's general principle is clear, that a creature is nourished by that from which it originates. Animal man eats earth; but eternal man eats of the essential word of God (*Epist.* xlvi, 18). His mind is nourished from the star which is its original; the soul is nourished by the Logos (*Test.* I, i).

> And here we have the great *Arcanum* [2] of feeding spiritually, Dear Sons . . . you have the ground of all essentiality and the essences of all essences. And of this Christ has told us: He wanted to give you the water of eternal life, and would well up in you as a fountainhead (*John* iv, 14) not outwardly from the light-fire, but born inwardly from divine fire, whose image it is. (*Gnad.* ii, 30)

Essential man did not have an earthly body so his reproductive processes were not as now. Androgynous, no sexual act took place. Procreation and reproduction were asexual, without *partie honteuse*. The *Urmensch* or original man loved the divine image in himself. The first man

> was both man and woman before Eve, he had both . . . fire and water, . . soul and spirit, and he should have brought forth his similitude out of himself, as an image of himself by his own imagination and his own love; and that he was able to do without rending the body, for . . . the soul had power

to change the body into another form; and so also it had power to bring forth a twig out of itself, according to its property, if Adam had stood out the trial. (*Seel. Frag.* viii, 2)

Primitive Adam, in whom death was not yet real, really had no need of reproducing; he just lived on, for he was man, the species and individual together.

Boehme's originality appears best in his doctrine of fall and sin. Following his own ideas rather than churchly doctrine he rejected Adam's temptation as the first revolt against God; he understood that eating fruit was but logical result of a creature already fallen. He posited a fall before history and one in history. The transcendent fall happened when Adam slept.

Before he slept Adam had looked on God with a steady *Blick,* with open eyes his divine consciousness was not momentary—*Augenblick!* He was sleepless because the dialectic of sleep and wakefulness had not risen. Tired of unity, Adam slept and his imagination turned away from God. He broke consciousness away from God. He wanted

to contemplate . . . what evil and good was, how it would relish and be, in the unlikeness of the essence. (*Myst. Mag.* xviii, 28)

The knowledge of good and evil is of separateness and strife, and Adam

brought his will and desire from God into selfhood and vanity; and broke himself off from God, from His divine harmony. (*Myst. Mag.* xix, 3)

What Adam willed he got; when he contemplated plurality he got disharmony and dialectic. In his sleep this became possible.

Two things resulted from Adam's sleep: first he lost divine consciousness, the divine image; second he received a new kind of life—existence—which is marked by dialectical tension between opposing forces. This is where the *turba*[3] reigns. (*Bedenk. Stief.* 356a)

Adam was in the angelical form before the sleep; but after . . . he had flesh and blood; and he was . . . a lump of earth. . . . With his eyes he apprehended the light of the Sun and knew the first image no more. (*Princ.* 32, 33)

Sleep was succumbing to this world's powers, and Adam became a slave to just those powers which previously had served him. Now the elements ruled in him.

A further result of Adam's sleep was sexuality (*Bedenk. Stief.* 363). He was weakened and divided. Eve was made for him during his sleep. He was therefore guilty of adultery with regard to the Virgin Wisdom. In sleep he left Wisdom and got a new mistress. This suggests that he lost the original image of God (wisdom) and got an image of himself. He knew that he was alone; and God said it was not good for man to be alone; so another image was made (*Seel. Frag.* viii, 3):

When impotent Adam fell asleep the second creation of man began

for God took the tincture of the water, as a twig out of Adam's soul, and a rib out of Adam, and half of the cross that was Adam, and made woman of them. (*Seel. Frag.* viii, 5)

Adam fell asleep in eternity. He awoke in time. A new kingdom appeared, history began. Tensions grew, and Eve, who battled Adam's will and became the instrument of his temptation and of his fruitfulness, appeared. Man became sexual; he searched for the lost unity; his sexual eros was, however, a deceptive illusion.

The tincture is the longing, the great desire after the Virgin . . . but it is the divine inclination. . . . The masculine seeks her in the feminine, the feminine in the masculine. (*Princ.* xiii, 39; 46; 48)

Erotic love is illusion. In a memorable myth Boehme tells of its deceptiveness. The lover

supposes that he has gotten the virgin; he grasps with his

clutches, and will mingle his infection with the virgin, and he supposes that he has the prize, it shall not now run away from him; he supposes now he will find the Pearl well enough. But it is with him as with a thief, driven out of a fair garden of delight, when he has eaten his pleasant fruit, and wants to eat some more of the good fruit, and yet cannot get in, but must reach out with his hand, and yet cannot come at the fruit for all that; for the gardener comes and takes away the fruit; and thus he must go away empty, and his lust is changed into discontent. (*Princ.* xiii, 40)

The gardener is paradise, the fruit is the lost unity, the theft is the illusion of re-achievement in erotic experience. Adam's fall, then, did not result from sexual misuse; on the contrary, for Boehme, sex followed the fall. The original sin was that man broke away from the consciousness of God in sleep.

Sleep is, however, not punishment alone but also the promise of the future deliverance. In Adam disunity was possible—uncontested and undecided. When once contest has been invited and risk incurred then deliverance also becomes possible. Sleep points forward to Christ's rest in the grave (*Myst. Mag.*, xix, 5). Newborn man has to return back through Adam's sleep to awake in eternity, when the continuous *Blick* shall be restored.

The transcendent fall has repercussions. Adam lost divine unity, gained sexual disunity—a yes and no in life itself. Adam now ate the fruit that Eve presented to him. And with eating he changed. A new substance enters his being; a new mode, existence, is entered in upon. By eating earth he consumed the earth's dark death. He became part earth. He got the quality of inertia, decomposition, and death inherent in the earth. After the transcendent fall Adam's body

had not then such hard gristles and bones; O no, that came to pass first when mother Eve did bite the apple and also gave to Adam; only the infection and earthly death, with the fainting and mortal sickness, stuck in them; the bones and ribs were yet strength and virtue. (*Princ.* xiii, 13)

By eating earth he got a worm-carcass or *Madensack*. And

now in this body he is nature's child (*Aurora* xxvi, 78) and now he belongs to Lucifer's kingdom (*Letzte. Zeit.* I, 74).

Man's consciousness of nakedness shows that he knows that he has sinned and fallen. He is now ashamed of his body. Other animals have coverings; only man is naked.

> When Adam and Eve . . . beheld themselves . . . they perceived the monstrous images and bestial form . . ; they took notice of the stomach and guts, into which they had stuffed the earthly fruit, which began to take effect, and they saw their bestial shame; and then they did lift up their minds towards Paradise, but they found it not; they ran trembling with fear, and crept behind the trees; the world has stirred their essences in the spirit with the earthly fruit. And then came the voice of God in the center of the gates of the Deep, and called Adam, and said: 'Adam, where art thou?' And he said: 'Here am I; and I am afraid, for I am naked.' And the Lord said, 'Who told thee that thou art naked? Hast thou eaten of the tree whereof I said unto thee that thou shouldest not eat thereof?' (*Princ.* xvii, 84)

Man's sense of nakedness is, then, a clue to his consciousness of sin. Before the fall he had been transparent; his body had been crystalline, pure; now he knows that he is naked. Man loves and yet hates this coarse body. Man is captivated by vanity for his body all the while that he is ashamed of it

> because it acquired such a monstrous form in its body. . . . From this has arisen human shame by which man is ashamed of his members and also of his naked form, so that he must borrow his clothing from earthly creatures. . . . This cloak is full proof to him that he is not at home with his soul in this aroused vanity. (*Wiedergeburt* ii, 19)

Adam and Eve sewed fig leaves together to cover their shame, their coarse flesh and bones, the disease-ridden carcass. But nakedness is their sense of not-belonging in an earth-body (*Princ.* x, 6–7).

This borrowed clothing, together with the awakened earthliness, and subjugation to the powers of heat and cold, is a plain and full proof that man is truly not at home in this world. For all earthly appetites, cares, and fears, together with this false clothing, must perish and be severed from the soul again. (*Wiedergeburt* ii, 19)

Nakedness unlocks Boehme's atavism; man remembers his primitive, essential unity and his angelical form.

Another subjective clue by which man knows his alienation from this world is his anxiety (*Angst*)—a conception whcih Kierkegaard popularized but in another form. Anxiety is the tension between man's two wills. Man remembers his lost unity; he longs for his primordial freedom as he lives a life of torment and death (*Gnad.* iii, 5). Anxiety is the source-spring of hell-fire in a sensitive heart (*Tab. Princ.* 39), the cause of sadness and joy (*Aurora* xiii, 118). Without anxiety there would be eternal darkness (*Menschw.* II, iii, 13), an idle nothing (*II Apol. Tilke,* 141). Adam's fall made man sensitive to painful distinctions, basically the distinction between God and nature (*Gnad.* iii, 5); if man wants knowledge of God he must dwell in anxiety's house in his soul (*Menschw.* ii, vi, 12). Anxiety is

a root of feeling, the beginning . . . of mind, a root of . . . all painfulness . . , a manifestation of the eternal unfathomable will in the attraction . . , a cause of dying . . , the very root where God and nature are separated . . . [where] the manifest sensible life arises. (*Gnad.* iii, 5)

The fall was not because man was sensual; rather man became sensual because of the fall!

From the fall man also got his two forms of knowing—reason (*Vernunft*) and the understanding (*Verstand*). A new knowledge came with the fall which became separate from his divine knowledge—reason. Reason had an astral origin (*Menschw.* III, ii, 3) and is the world's spirit in man (*Sig. Rer.* viii, 3). Reason is a noble thing which is blind without God's spirit (*Menschw.* iii, v, 3). Inasmuch as reason comes from the stars it cannot search deeper than the stars (*Epist.* lv, 4) and however fine reason may become it still partakes of God's wrath (*Seel. Frag.* i, 84) and can know nothing about divine things (*Gnad.* ii, 2). Reason can know nothing of God's kingdom (*Dreyfach* xvi, 22), of the tree of faith (*Menschw.* III, viii, 7), and cannot come to certainty (*Sig. Rer.* xv, 22) but always stands in doubt (*Epist.* xii, 22). Reason breeds all disputation and strife (*Test.* II, i, 1–9) and runs around in circles (*Myst. Mag.* ii, 4) and becomes the tool of self-will and pride.

Understanding (*Verstand*) originates from the holy element (*Sig. Rer.* xiii, 8) and is the inner world's life, a free will (*Myst. Mag.* xxix, 1), and is Wisdom in her government of man (*Myst. Mag.* xxxv, 13).

> God has appointed . . . one master . . . which can alone manage the soul of the great world . . . and appointed a type of its likeness as the reason over this officer, which represents . . . what he is to do and make; and this is the understanding, viz., God's own dominion wherewith he rules the officer. Now the understanding shows to the officer what . . . each thing is. (*Sig. Rer.* viii, 3)

In understanding man can search all things and even penetrate with it into God's Wisdom for by it God draws man (*Myst. Mag.* iii, 8). Understanding is man's inner life (*Clav.* 99) and comes from the inner light (*Myst. Mag.* xi, 25).

Finally, Adam's fall brought the great *turba.* The *turba magna* is the wrath and aroused vehemency of dumb nature, the poisonous source which produces freaks, sports, poisons, and other false expressions of the divine vitality.

> Each form of nature . . . received its property in its hunger, and therein it is not annoyed or molested. . . . But if the will enters back again into the birth of the other properties . . . [then] is the abominate and *turba* born; for this will is entered contrary to the course of nature into a strange essence, which is not of its property. (*Sig. Rer.* xiv, 77)

When the *turba* was awakened fire and brimstone rained out of heaven (*Myst. Mag.*, xliv, 26); Lot's wife, by the *turba*, became a pillar of salt. The *turba* is the third principle's potential power to fall back into wrath again, the ultimate threat of existence.

These, then, are the preliminary results of Adam's fall; one other yet remains. With Adam sin appeared.

Although sin originates in Lucifer's fall (*Aurora* xiii, 116) it entered man after Adam's fall, proceeding from Adam's self-willed separation from God to the selfhood in all his Cain-like sons (*Gnad.* ix, 61):

Thus . . . may be known what sin is . . . Namely, when the human will separates itself from God into an existence of its own, and awakens its own self. . . . For all into which the will enters, and will have as its own, is something foreign to the one will of God. For all is God's and to man's own will belongs nothing. But if it be God's, then all is its also. Thus we recognize that desire is sin. For it is a lusting out of one into many and introduces many into one. The will possesses, and yet should be will-less. (*Myst. Punkt.* iii, 16ff)

Before the fall there had been but one man with one will—now many men had many wills.

Each particular fire burns in accordance with the character of its own being; and here separation and enmity are born. . . . Covetousness is sin, for it is a desire to be out of God. . . . Pride is sin, for it will be a thing of its own, and separate itself from God. . . . Seeing . . . we are in God but one in many members, it is against God when one member draws itself away from the other, and makes a Lord of itself. . . . Pride will be lord and God alone is Lord. Thus there are two lords, and one separates from the other. All therefore is sin . . . that desire possesses as its own, be it meat or drink. (*Myst. Punkt.*, iv, 9ff)

In a remarkable figure of speech Boehme says that the Devil strewed sugar upon Adam (*Princ.* xvii, 93)

and that sugar he shall eat eternally, and frame his will continually therein to get other sugar. . . . And hereby it is signified to the ungodly, that they shall also eat the same sugar eternally, which they have continually baked here, with their blasphemies, cursing, robbing, and taking the sweat of the needy and miserable to maintain their haughty pride. (*Princ.* xvii, 94)

Instead of seven sins Boehme has but four: arrogance, avarice, envy, and wrath (*Aurora* xiv, 47). Arrogance longs

inspoken into the mother of all men and as a living power embodied it in the eternal covenant, and has fulfilled the covenant by introducing the Divine Being into human quality. (*Gnad.* viii, 23)

From eternity Christ has been eternal love in man (*Gnad.* vii, 31), coming to us for our salvation and as long as the soul loves He is in man's heart (*Gnad.* ix, 63). He is never extinguished. He thrives on the trials of unbelief and is like a glowing wick after the candle has been snuffed. He is the inward light, *Fünklein,* which can become fanned into the flames of consuming Love.

Boehme's psychology, by insisting that this divine spark is essential for the creation of human nature, departs from that of Sebastian Franck and Hans Denck. Boehme's Christ is redeemer and sperminal Logos (*Irrth. Stief.* 25); He is restorer of unity as well as indwelling Word. All men share in the Christ within: not all choose to unveil Him fully. All beings share the eternally spoken Word; not all share the Word made flesh, that is, the Word projected into the third principle.

Here Boehme's refusal to identify his second principle with the second person of the Trinity makes sense. The Christ of history reawakens and rekindles the soul's innermost ground. His drawing power, or tincturing, attracts the inner Word. Like cures like—this is the old formula.

Boehme's doctrine of the soul is complicated. Like Plato, Plotinus, and Schelling he held that the world had a soul, an oversoul, which the eternal essences have made from the divine vitality (*Seel. Frag.* iii, 4). This world-soul participates in all three principles (*Dreyfach* ii, 5) and binds them, giving them unity. The soul's task was to keep all in balance, in harmony. The soul, not deriving from the four elements, has been

breathed into man . . . by the moving spirit. Which original is before the light of life . . . out of which the light of God is enkindled . . ; therefore the soul is God's own essence or substance. (*Princ.* iv, 20)

The soul is begotten by the interaction of the first two principles, wrath and love.

> The soul . . . is the roughest thing in men; for it is the original of the other substances or things. It is fiery, harsh, bitter, and strong, and resembles a great and mighty power, its essences are like brimstone; its gate or seat out of the eternal original is between the fourth and fifth forms in the eternal birth. (*Princ.* xiii, 30)

Man's soul lives in his heart but dominates his brain (*Seel. Frag.* viii, 7, 8). Wherever man is influenced by divine vitality, there is soul (*Seel. Frag.* vii, 9); in man the soul hovers between hell and this world (*Princ.* xvii, 7), capable of being swayed by either. It is demonic in the sense that it can be good or evil (*Princ.* x, 14).

After Adam's fall the soul's imagination became external (*Irrth. Stief.* 346), losing its holy divine *Ens*, its holy substance and spiritual qualities (*Gnad.* vii, 11), becoming blind to God (*Test.* I, i, 21). It is bound by three strong chains (*Princ.* xxv, 8) which infect it with worldliness (*Dreyfach* xiii, 8). It has self-will, possessing a light of its own, and stands in the sun's light (*Princ.* xiv, 11), surrounded by love, wrath, and this world's spirit (*Bedenk. Stief.* 71).

Man's spirit derives from God and the constellations (*Aurora,* preface, 98), ruling and dominating man's mind (*Aurora,* v, 39), and helping him to search the divine deep (*Aurora* xi, 71). Each element has its spirit: fire-spirit, water-spirit, air-spirit, and earth-spirit (*Princ.* vii, 35). Each spirit "eats" of the mother that bore it, seeking the maternal substance as fulfillment for its longing (*Epist.* xxxi, 20). Not all external world spirits are of the Holy Spirit (*Myst. Mag.* viii, 19); some have fallen through self-will.

Boehme's man is threefold and he has fallen on each of the three aspects: his body is corrupt earth, his soul has a burning hunger, his spirit has led itself into world dominion. He needs total regeneration.

The four elements produce four complexions (*Theos. Frag.* xii, 17). Fire governs the choleric, air the sanguine, water the phlegmatic, earth the melancholic.

Fire's choleric complexion makes courage, sudden wrath, aroused pride, and arrogant self-centeredness. Air's sanguinity is subtle, friendly, joyous, of uncertain courage, changeable, easily persuaded, witty. Water's phlegm is fleshly, coarse, feminine, frugal, stubborn, dull. Earth's melancholy lives in the tension between light and darkness, good and evil, dominated by tragedy and anxiety (*Complex.* 3ff). In as much as the melancholy complexion comes from earth it shows its dark chamber of death and puts man on the boundary between life and death, waiting for permanent release (*Complex.* 40).

Boehme's anthropology with its distinction between essential man and existential man explains man's present situation on the boundary between life and death, Yes and No, as son of God and child of earth (*Princ.* xx, 82). Man

has two worlds in him. The property to which he turns himself, to that world he is introduced, and of that world's property will he eternally be, and enjoy the same; either a source of light-world gentleness, or a hostile source from the dark world. Here he buds and grows in the middle world between the light-world and the dark-world; he may give himself to which he pleases. The essence which obtains the dominion in him, whether fierceness or gentleness, the same embraces him, and it hangs unto him and leads him; it gives him morals and will, and unites itself wholly with him. (*Theos. Punkt.* iv, 22–23)

External man was created a tool and instrument of the internal (*Sig. Rer.* xv, 18), and the gross, corporeal man was not God's image but a horrible monster (*Myst. Mag.* xvi, 1),

a house or husk of the spiritual man, in which the spiritual man grows. . . . The outward gross body . . . shall not inherit the Kingdom of God (*Clavis* 14ff).

Christ came to help redeem man's inner spirit (*Theos. Frag.* xii, 17) and this inner man is Christ's loyal and obedient servant (*Myst. Mag.* lxxi, 55).

Natural man, standing on the "limit between life and death," as Boehme called it, has two properties, both of which draw him and desire to have him. . . . Man is drawn and held of both; but the center stands in him, and he has the balance between the two wills (*Princ.* xxi, 20).

That kingdom to which he gives himself, to that does he become subservient (*Princ.* vii, 2). God has produced in man a creature of two wills (*Dreyfach* vi, 66) who is both good and evil (*Aurora,* ii, 9), alive and dead. In man the name Jesus fights the dragon in combat between typical wrath and typical love (*Theos. Frag.* xi, 13ff). Whoever wins, wins forever (*Princ.* xvi, 42). Before the fall Yes was manifest in man's essence; afterwards it was concealed (*Gnad.* xiii, 37). Yet

> Man is not so altogether corrupt that there should not be any possibility at all left in him. (*Epist.* xlii, 49)

He still can be redeemed (*Menschw.* I, xiv, 19) and redemptive action is grounded in the divine image within his own being; he is capable of comprehending everything in his heart (*Princ.,* preface, 2; xvi, 32) because he has a free will (*Princ.* xxii, 15; *Dreyfach* vi, 68). He can live in health (*Sig. Rer.* ix, 69) because he can release the curse laid within the earth (*Sig. Rer.* xi, 85).

Since man is also created of earth and of astral spirits (*Princ.* xvi, 24), and since the rule of earth and stars has made him a hypocrite and sinner (*Princ.* xvi, 28), he tends towards being a devil. God said that He would put enmity between the woman's and the serpent's seed. This enmity is powerful within man, not outside of him. Man seeks an earthly kingdom (*Myst. Mag.* lv, 43) and remains blind to God's works (*Epist.* xlviii).

Great theological systems usually meet in trying to define man's role in the world. Boehme's man is the key to his world for he is an individual and personal image of God (*Sig. Rer.* x, 3) and an image of the world itself (*Myst. Mag.* ii, 5). Though man is God's image by natural right, he is not so in fact; the image has become obscured by rebellion against God's will. Man, impaled in existence, is deeply moved by life's inadequacy. He longs for a better world.

This longing establishes his superiority to the beasts (*Gnad.* v, 26). Man also desires earth, but differs from the animals in wanting a better earth. The perception of animals is circumscribed by desire and instinct; they do not ask concerning either their origins or their destiny. Man does. Man surpasses the beasts because he can go beyond himself. This is his true freedom.

Boehme's man is in some ways the signature of all things, who by understanding the language of nature knows God's formed words. When Adam walked through the garden he named the things he saw into reality. But Adam fell. Now he no longer understands nature's words. A principle of distortion has entered reality and man longs now for wholeness. He lives in the hope of the restoration of the totality of that lost image; this totality which is the New Man in Christ, restorer of the fallen, distorted image.

NOTES TO CHAPTER FIFTEEN

1. *Limnus* is the purest earth-essence.
2. *Arcanum* is mystery.
3. *Turba* is the aroused wrath in nature, a poisonous source, which destroys everything.

Wirt als ein kint,
Wirt toup und blint,
Din selbes iht
Muoz werden niht;
Al iht, al niht trib über bor.
—FROM THE *Dreifaltigkeitslied*

CHAPTER SIXTEEN

REDEMPTION

THE DOCTRINE of Wisdom defines Boehme's exposition of Incarnation and redemption for if Wisdom is the form through which and in which God completes Himself then Wisdom is finally the form by which He restores a fallen world. To maintain his realism (theologically considered) Boehme refused to identify Mary with Wisdom. If the incarnation was not in a real person, if Christ did not become man in Mary, if He did not put on the corrupt earth, then He could not have helped man. What Christ did not adopt as His own He could not redeem.

Many have taken upon themselves to write of the Virgin Mary, and have believed that she was not a daughter of the earth. To them . . . has been presented a reflection of the eternal virginity, but they have come short of the true mark. Some have simply supposed that she was not the daughter of Joachim and Anne, for Christ is called the seed of the woman, and indeed is, and He Himself attests that He came from above, from Heaven; He must therefore, according to them, be wholly born of a heavenly virgin. But this would profit little to us poor children of Eve, who have become earthly and carry our souls in an earthly vessel. Where was our soul, if the Word of Eternal Life had not taken it to itself? If Christ had brought a soul from heaven, where was our soul and the Covenant with Adam and Eve, by which the woman's seed was to bruise the serpent's head? If Christ had willed to come and to be born wholly from Heaven, He would not have needed to be born a man on earth. (*Menschw.* I, viii, 1)

Wisdom, the hidden God's instrument of self-manifestation, assumes her role as revealeress also in the Incarnation.

Mary's body is the receptacle of her soul, her soul is the receptacle of Wisdom, and Wisdom is the receptacle of the divine Logos. Each corporeal form is the receptacle of the higher spirit which is produced and realized within it. Wisdom is God's body (*Epist.* xxxi, 48) and so bears the Son, the eternal will's first manifestation. Mary unites the divine and human nature which was disrupted in Adam. In her betrothal between Wisdom and man is again possible, making the second Adam historically present in the *Benedictus* when wisdom reunited herself with Mary.

Christ has truly, in the body of the Virgin Mary, attracted to Him our human essences, and is become our brother; yet these human essences cannot comprehend the eternal Deity, only the new man, born of God, comprehends the Deity. (*Princ.* xiii, 41)

When the Holy Spirit announced the conception Mary had the total God within her.

And for this cause God became man, that He might in Himself generate anew the soul of man again, and might redeem it from the chains of fierceness of anger, and not at all for the bestial's body's sake, which must melt into the four elements, and come to nothing; out of which nothing will remain. . . . But in the new man (which we attract on to our souls in the bosom of the virgin) we shall spring forth and flourish again; and therein is no necessity nor death. (*Princ.* xxii, 22ff)

The Incarnation's purpose is ultimate resolution of the tension between life and death. How does wisdom enter Mary? Here Boehme allegorizes:

God said to Adam and Eve: the seed of the woman shall bruise the serpent's head, and thou, serpent, shall sting him in the heel (*Gen.* iii, 15); that is, in the wrath of God thou shalt slay him, but he will bud forth out of death and bruise thy head, that is, will take away your power and overcome your wrath with love. . . . In this same sign the highly precious Virgin of the wisdom of God, in which Christ, as the breaker down of death, was to become a true man, deprive death of its power, and destroy the devil's sting; he was to tread the winepress of the fierceness and wrath, and enter into the wrath as into the center of fire and extinguish the fire with His heavenly blood. (*Menschw.* I, vii, 10)

In Mary Wisdom brings the Logos to a new form; Christ is eternal but in Mary He became man. No new God has thereby been created; He merely became man (*Dreyfach* vi, 79). Wisdom's reunion with humanity is no abrupt inbreak but rather realizes a theogonic act. Unity was broken by Lucifer and Adam; the image of union restores the lost unity, yet this image—or better, this remembrance—of union has been present in man as prophecy and judgment. When Adam broke unity God directly gave a new promise:

God spoke again into our poor fallen soul in Paradise, immediately after the fall, the Covenant and root of His highest Love and Grace, through the Word, as the center of Grace to corruption, and to the new generation. (*Myst. Mag.* lvi, 25)

This has been continued in history by the carriers of the covenant, a spiritual lineage by which Abraham's faith was invested in Isaac according to the inward ground (*Myst. Mag.* lvi, 28). There was difference between the image in the line of the covenant and the restoration in Mary:

The works of the law were before God in the mirror, till the life was born again from the covenant and the fulfillment came. Then the works of the mirror ceased, and the works of the fulfillment of flesh and blood . . . began again; for in Mary was the beginning. (*Menschw.* I, ix, 16)

In the Incarnation Christ again brought the improperly compounded, disunited essences into full harmony.

Boehme's Christology was dialectical; his Christ was androgynous. If the fall resulted in the loss of unity, then the Savior (whole-maker) restores the image to fullness and makes that image available for all men.

> The new birth in sum is this: that the angelical image must be born again which God created in Adam. God formed Adam in the image of God, and though He knew that he would not stand, yet he appointed Him the Savior who could bring him again into the first image, and therein establish him forever. (*Myst. Mag.* xix, 21)

As the fallen Adam was androgynous, so also the second Adam, for He restores unity to the fallen image:

> And when Christ on the cross had again accomplished this redemption of our virgin-like image from the divided sex of male and female . . . he said: *it is finished* . . . Christ turned back Adam into his sleep from the vanity, and from the man and woman, again into the angelical image. (*Myst. Mag.* xix, 7)

Male and female, having parted in Adam's sleep, reunite themselves in Jesus. The male and female principles

> were indeed united in the incarnation . . . so that they were inseparable, but the true ens of the soul, which the Word assumed in the name JESUS, was of us men from the female tincture . . . which was severed from Adam (and put into the woman) that this property in the light might transmute . . . the fiery masculine property again into the live and divine humility, and that the masculine and feminine property might be quite changed into one image again: As Adam was before his Eve, when he was neither man nor woman, but a masculine virgin. (*Myst. Mag.* lvi, 20)

Here the incarnation gets special meaning. Christ became man in the woman but He was born male. Manhood comes from the Father, womanhood from Mary.

> Christ was born of a virgin, that He might sanctify the woman's tincture again, and change it into the man's tincture, that the man and the woman might be one image of God,

and no more man and woman, but masculine virgins. (*Myst. Mag.* lvi, 46)

Here even in the incarnation a manifestation of Boehme's Yes and No is apparent, the conflict between the hidden God of wrath and the known God of Love. Let man

ascribe the male to God the Father, viz., to the first principle, where God's Word does manifest itself in the fire-world, which is the first center of the creature; and the female let him ascribe to God the Son, viz. the second principle, where the divine eternal Word does manifest itself in the light of Love. . . . In this manner fire produces light. (*Myst. Mag.* xxiii, 45)

As expected reunion follows the process of division. Fire and light had separated (*Gnad.* vii, 17ff); in the fall Adam got fire and Eve light (*Myst. Mag.* xix, 17; xxii, 43, 44); In Christ both were again united.

When an androgynous Christ is thus posited the traditional bride-mysticism makes more sense. In Christ each sex finds what it lacks to be whole. Boehme sees in sex a shadowy, vague, incomplete prototype of final unification.

We understand, then, the incarnation of Christ in a natural way, like that of all men. . . . Christ in nine months became a perfect man and at the same time remained a true God, and was born into this world in the manner and mode of all Adam's children, by the same way as all men. And that, not that He needed it—He could have been born magically—but He desired and was destined to remedy our impure, animal birth and entrance into this life. He was to enter into this world by our entrance, and lead us out of the earthly quality. For if He had been born magically in a divine manner, then He would not by nature have been of this world. . . . How then would He have willed to suffer death, and enter into death and break it to pieces? . . . He is truly the woman's seed, and He entered into this world in the natural way, like all men; but went out by death in the divine way, in the divine power and essentiality. . . . For the earthly part, which He received from His mother Mary into Himself, into the divine nature, died on the Cross to earthly nature. The soul was thus in the essentiality of God, and descended as a conqueror into the hell of the Devil, that is, into the fierce wrath of God, and quenched it with God's love and gentleness that characterize the divine love-essentiality. . . . And this was the reason that God became man, in order that He might lead us out of death into the life eternal, and quench with His Love the wrath which burned within us. (*Menschw.* I, x, 9ff)

So Christ became man in the woman's seed (*Myst. Mag.* xxvii, 26), conceived of Mary's will naturally (*Princ.* xviii, 96), yet sinless (*Princ.* xxii, 36), drawing human flesh, soul, and spirit to Himself in Mary (*Dreyfach* xi, 26)

Christ cannot be known from the letter of Scripture (*Buchstaben*) or reason (*Menschw.* I, i, 10). Only the regenerate man who has put on Christ's God-manhood as his own can know His person (*Myst. Mag.* xxxvii, 30). Boehme has a divine and human nature in Christ (*Irrth. Stief.* 420, 438) but not in the traditional sense; he sees that all men partake of the formative Word (*Irrth. Stief.* 131), but only the faithful partake of the formed Word. In Adam the formative Word was made, but He had not yet taken on flesh (*Epist.* xii, 58). In Jesus this happened, so Christ is the formed Word.

Boehme's Christology was also dualistic: his Christ had two natures, a formative Word beyond corporeal existence and a formed Word in Jesus. In Jesus Christ the judgment implied in man's consciousness of his nakedness—man's knowledge of losing the *imago dei*, the image of God,—is altered. Nakedness is poignantly revealed in Christ's nakedness. However, Christ is not just the restoration of the lost image, not merely sentimental reminder of a lost ideal; He is a new being, partaking of both human tragedy and of eschatological hope. In Him the new birth gets its new body.

Why did God become man? Boehme has some new answers to Anselm's old question. God sent Jesus to open the gate of the birth in man's life so he might be reunited with God (*Princ.* iv, 39). He sent His Son to overpower the dragon-source and wrath in man and so to redeem man from the No (*Theos. Frag.* xii, 12). He had to take on all three principles or else His saving, redeeming work would have been incomplete (*Taufe* I, iii, 5, 6). Moreover, Christ had to take on human form so God could create an androgynous man:

Only the male kind was circumcised, and in the same member that is an abomination before God and a shame of the soul, for impregnation was not destined to be bestial. Circumcision is thus a sign and figure, intimating that this member should be cut from man and not appear with him in eternity. And Christ had to take on the form of a man, though inwardly He stood in a virgin image, that the purpose of God might stand. For the man's or the fire's property must rule, and the woman's or the light's property must soften his fire and bring it into a gentle image of God. (*Menschw.* I, vii, 13)

In the incarnation Christ also sanctified the female principle:

In Eve . . . God established His Covenant and brought His Word thereinto, that the woman's seed (i.e. the heavenly seed which the Word was to reintroduce, and in which God and man were to be again one person) should bruise the head of the power of the serpent's spawn and the Devil's will, and destroy the Devil's works. (*Gnad.* vii, 19, 20)

In Boehme's view Christ's work was victory over darkness and No, over the wrath.

In man the name Jesus fights against the dragon. This combat is not a creaturely thing . . . It is a combat between Yes and No, between the typical wrath and the typical love, between the first and second principles. (*Theos. Frag.* xi, 14, 15)

Why was combat necessary? Why did Christ have to suffer and die? Because

the human will must be broken and slain, and through death be introduced again into the holy name. Christ, accordingly, had to die and bring the human will through death, through hell, and through this foundation, because the self-assumption of a will cannot subsist in God. If a will is to subsist in God, it must be impatible and non-suffering, so that it may be able to dwell in fire and yet not be laid hold of by the fire. (*Theos. Frag.* xi, 19)

In this connection Boehme repeats an image as old as Origen, which is, perhaps, the heart of his theology:

> As the sun in the elements presses through everything, and kindles itself in the elements, and yet its light remains free; or as fire through-heats iron, and yet becomes not iron, but the iron is only an object in which the fire elevates and inflames itself; so pure also must the will be which is to possess God's unity; no assuming may be in it. (*Theos. Frag.* xi, 20)

Christ is the tincture that transmutes God's wrath into Love. Boehme says that He was the guiltless Lamb (*Irrth. Stief.* 436) but He did not pay the price in sacrifice for man's enormous sin. Boehme understands that the inner Christ never did die (*Princ.* xxii, 54), as the legalist view of the atonement demands:

> When Christ died on the Cross, the name JESUS did not also die. . . . No, it cannot be, the Eternity does not die, only the spoken Word. . . . The anger of God was set on fire and did wholly die. (*Sig. Rer.* xii, 3ff)

Only by conquering the third principle could He conquer self-will.

Why did He have to die? In order to rise again in a new form of life (*Princ.* xxv, 13). He entered death and brought man out of darkness into the freedom of the divine life.

> Therefore Christ had to die, and with the soul's spirit pass through the fire of eternal nature, that is, through the wrath and hell of the eternal nature . . . and make our soul a way through death and wrath, in which we might with Him and in Him enter through death into the eternal divine life. (*Menschw.* I, iii, 7)

He had to take the four congealed elements back into nature's fire, reheat them, and pour them out in a new form without the dark wrath (*Dreyfach* v, 142). Through His death the cherub's sword was broken (*Menschw.* I, vii, 3) and the serpent's head bruised (*Sig. Rer.* vii, 24). The Devil was vanquished (*Princ.* xxiii, 9) and man released from bondage, death, and corruption (*Sig. Rer.* vii, 44). Christ destroyed our death in His (*Menschw.* I, vi, 4), tinged humanity with His blood (*Epist.* xxxviii, 14), opened up a gate for all (*Dreyfach* vi, 95), restoring the image corrupted in Adam (*Gnad.* ix, 87).

The resurrected Christ symbolizes the original and the final perfection of man, the first-born after death (*Myst. Mag.* xli, 11). Christ has incorruptible flesh, and in Him sin has been removed as possibility by forgiveness. What Adam lost Christ restored.

For by human works sin had come into the world, and so also it had to be slain by human works. (*Gnad.* ix, 59)

This refutes the premise of Anselm's view by claiming that, though the sin be great, it was not great enough to demand a God as payment. Originating with man, sin had to be appeased by man. God cannot undo what man has done.

If it will enter then it must do it in the manner and form as it went out, for it brought itself into false desire and lust. Even so likewise it must introduce itself again by returning into a sorrow and conversion, and in the sorrow of repentance again introduce itself into a divine desire which is called faith. (*Myst. Mag.* xxvii, 35)

In a lovely reapplication of the parable of the good Samaritan, Boehme said,

The fair image fell among murderers, that is, among the harsh spirits of nature . . . These held the image captive and drew off from it the robe of Paradise and left it lying half-dead. Now there was need of the Samaritan, Christ. And that was the cause that God became man. If the harm could have been healed through the speaking of a Word or a word of forgiveness, God would not have become man. (*Menschw.* III, vi, 2)

By forgiveness and reconciliation Christ restored man's

The new man is also androgynous, neither ,iving in marriage. He enters a real kingdom, ritual body, to sit down to a banquet of sacra- Christ's new body and blood. All his horrible ve been removed. Nakedness and anxiety are *urba* has been removed. Profane love has been to holy love (*Bedenk. Stief.* 325) and wedded v love spiritually. This is a far cry, indeed, from al dream of *Nirvana.*

living Word of life the resurrected Christ dwells in eart (*Dreyfach* xi, 88). This becomes the basis of tion.

> refore it is said: watch, pray, be sober, lead a tem- e life, for the Devil . . . walks about as a roaring lion, ing whom he may devour (*I Peter,* v, 8). Follow then after covetousness, money, goods, power, and honor, for Christ we are not of this world. For therefore it was that rist went to the Father . . . in order that we should fol- w Him with our hearts, minds, and wills; and hence He ays that He will be with us all the days, even to the end of the world (*Matth.* xxviii, 20). . . . We must force a way out of this world, out of the earthly man, and give up our will to His Will, and introduce our imagination and desire into Him; then we become pregnant in His virginity . . . and we are new-born in Christ in ourselves. For as death passed upon us all by Adam, so the Word of life passes upon us all from Christ . . . Christ need not first leave His place and enter into us, when we are new-born in Him; for the divine being, in which He was born, contains everywhere the second principle. Wherever it may be said that God is present, there it also may be said that the Incarnation in Christ is present too; for it has been revealed in Mary and thus inqualifies backwards to Adam and forwards to even the last man. (*Menschw.* xii, 19)

If Christ in the second principle is in everything, why must man turn to Him? Indeed, Jesus lives within all as unchange- able Love and to this indwelling Christ man turns.

> In every man . . . the word of promise . . . must be- come . . . a being, and this is accomplished in repentance

and conversion. God says in Isaiah (1, 18): Though sins be as red as scarlet, if ye turn, ye shall be white as s This takes place when the kingdom of Grace is manife in the kingdom of nature. . . . When the poor sinner pents, God comes in Christ's spirit and brings forth a r son out of Christ's flesh and blood in him . . . And t commences the gestation of the new man. (*Gnad.* x, 4ff)

Christ speaks His Being into all men but not all want hear His Words (*Gnad.* xiii, 4) nor do all respond by con prehending His essence within them.

Man's foremost response to Christ's work is repentance departing from the sin of pride and from the pride of sin (*Irrth. Stief.* 297). Repentance is the quieting of man's false imagination (*Gnad.* xiii, 7) for

no longer to be doing is the . . . best repentance. This . . . is when . . . the soul begins to be still from imagining. . . . There is no judgment from without upon it, but only in its own judgment. . . . For imputed Grace from without is of no effect. . . . The imputed Grace . . . must be manifested in us, in the inward ground of the soul, and be our life. . . . Repentance should not be put off till the end, for an old tree takes root badly. If Christ is not in the soul, there is no Grace nor forgiveness of sins. Christ Himself is the forgiveness of sins who with His Blood transmutes in our soul the introduced abominations. (*Gnad.* xiii, 7ff)

Repentance leads to prayer, man's second response to Christ's work.

Real prayer is not the habit of repeating the words of prayer; no, such verbalizing without heartfelt devotion and divine desire is merely an outward act, an external word-carving. (*Gebet* i)

There is true prayer and false prayer, the latter dependent upon the nature of him who prays. Prayer is a discipline in which the will is transformed and can enter into the divine will and become saturated with divine Love (*Dreyfach* xii, 25). Prayer without Love is unavailing (*Dreyfach* viii, 13) because it is the soul's hunger for God's primordial will

(*Dreyfach* xvi, 47). Man must not come before God with naked breath and idle words; he must come converted from his false way of life:

> We must want to depart from all arrogance, falsity, wrath, envy, and stubbornness. We must want to yield our whole heart and soul to God, the Holy Spirit, so that He is our repentant activity and our desire in prayer. He shall enclose our will and desire in Himself, leading them to God, so that we may die to our false vanity and desire in the Death of Christ, which has been declared to us all, being born in the spirit of Christ to a new will, mind, and loyalty to God. And we shall henceforth come before God with our new will and birth in such a power of righteousness and purity, like His children which He has dearly bought through the Blood and Death of His dear Son, regenerating them in His Spirit. (*Gebet* 10)

Through such prayer the inner Christ is awakened and God's enkindled fire-wrath is quenched (*Aurora* xvi, 11, 12).

Man's third response is true faith. In a fine passage Boehme describes what he means by true faith.

> Now, faith is not an historical knowledge, that man should frame articles to himself and depend on them alone, and force his mind into the works of his reason; but faith is one spirit with God, for the Holy Spirit moves in the spirit of faith. True faith is the power of God, one spirit with God. It works in and with God. It is free and bound to no article, save only to the true love, in which it gathers the power and strength of its life; human delusion and conjecture are of no consequence. For as God is free . . . in such a sense that He does whatever He wills, and needs give no account about it; so also is the true faith in the spirit of God. It has no more than one inclination, viz., to the Love and Mercy of God . . ; it seeks not itself in carnal reason, but in God's Love . . . It regards the earthly life as nothing . . . It gives itself up in humility to the will of God . . . It makes where there is nothing, and takes where nothing is made. It is operative, and no one sees its being. It is mighty, and yet is the lowest humility. It possesses all, and yet embraces nothing more than gentleness. It is thus free from all iniquity and has no law, for the fierce wrath of nature has no in-

fluence upon it. It exists from eternity, for it is comprehended in no ground. (*Menschw.* III, i, 2–4)

Faith, one of the powers of God (*Princ.* vii, 3), is born in a resigned man's will (*Menschw.* I, xi, 8). It is the essential Word in men from which the incorruptible flesh is made (*Gnad.* ix, 98). Where faith is absent the Word has no essence (*Test.* I, ix, 42).

Persecuted by his church, Boehme bore little love for the outward heap of stones which could neither save nor redeem (*Menschw.* I, xii, 3). But he cared with all his heart for the mystical seed in the believer's heart (*Myst. Mag.* xxxvi, 60).

The whole titular Christendom is turned into mere sects and orders, where one sect despises and brands another as unrighteous. And thus they have made of Christendom a mere murdering den, full of blasphemies about Christ's person; and have bound the spirit of Christ . . . to the forms and orders of disputation. (*Myst. Mag.* xl, 94)

In the churches self-seeking rules; each wants to be master.

In the stone-houses of the churches, cathedrals, and cloisters . . . they do counterfeit somewhat of Christ, seeing that they there read the writings which the Apostles left behind them; but afterwards in their preaching . . . they foist in the kingdom of nature, with brawling and disputing; and spend their time with disputing, confuting, and contending about sects (and different mental idols and opinions), in so much that one party is brought wholly to condemn the other, and the ears (and hearts) of the hearers are so infected with gall and bitterness that one sect wilfully opposes another, and cries it down for devilish; whence nothing but wars and disdainful provocations do arise, to the desolation of countries and cities. (*Myst. Mag.* xl, 98)

A Christian has Christ on the inward ground (*Gnad.* x, 37) and so has the church in his heart (*Myst. Mag.* xxxvi, 60). The real church is Christ and He dwells in us (*Menschw.* I, xiii, 3). To go into a world-church without the inward Christ can make no one good (*Test.* I, preface, 6) as Satan often leads penitents to church believing it is a real church when it is only a bawdy-house (*Myst. Mag.* lxii, 45, 36) for God's concubines.

This hard word was compensated for by Boehme's description of the inner church of the spirit which is Christ's image on earth (*Sig. Rer.* xi, 54) and His mother (*Sig. Rer.* xi, 35). There are two churches, Cain's and Abel's (*Myst. Mag.* xxvi, 25; xxvii, xxviii); Cain's rides high; Abel's dwells within it. The true temple is Divine Love (*Myst. Mag.* lxxiv, 26) and where Love becomes visible the Church of Jesus Christ is.

Boehme's order of salvation is within and the means of Grace are subjectively adopted. External forms are unnecessary. Since Christ lives essentially within the regenerated soul (*Myst. Mag.* xxxix, 9) He nourished and sustains him by means of His sacraments. A Christian hungers for Christ's members (*Myst. Mag.* lviii, 52), wanting Christ's sustaining nourishing food.

> The testaments of Christ are nothing else but a loving bond . . . wherewith God in Christ binds Himself to us and us to Him. (*Wiedergeburt* viii, 2)

Boehme's metaphysics, with its earthly and heavenly substances, determines his sacramentarian views:

> The outward heaven is the . . . conception of . . . water. . . . The holy water is yet continually separated from water under the firmament. This holy water is that of which Christ told us, that He would give us it to drink; that should spring up in us to a fountain of eternal life. The holy heavenly corporeality does not consist therein; it is the body of Christ which He brought from heaven, and by the same, introduced heavenly, paradisaical essentiality into our dead . . . body; and quickened ours in his. . . . In this heavenly essence the Testaments of Christ consist (*Myst. Mag.* x, 56)

This holy essence is eaten by the soul and the earthly mouth does not chew it with its teeth (*Seel. Frag.* viii, 3ff). The outward meal is a remembrance of the inner (*Seel. Frag.* viii, 3). Sacraments are not sin offerings or sacrifices (*Myst. Mag.* xxvii, 43) but a feeding on God's essence.

Boehme, the Protestant, held two sacraments: baptism and

the supper. While Schwenkfeldian ideas are sometimes expressed by Lutheran phrases like *Unwürdig, Taufbund,* Boehme's words really are superficial.

Circumcision and baptism are one act (*Myst. Mag.* xl, 10) and baptism is made with the heavenly water in which God's flaming Love-word has incorporated itself. The body is baptized with elemental water, the spirit with heavenly water (Sig. Rer. vii, 67) by means of the Holy Spirit (*Test.* I, ii, 39). The minister baptizes with outward water while the Holy Spirit baptizes with the water of eternal life (*Princ.* xxiii, 37). Boehme does not distinguish infant or adult baptism; he says that all sinners need continuous baptism (*Theos. Punkt.* viii, 9).

The Supper is the sacramental meal by which Christ's body is fed to man's soul (*Dreyfach* xi, 75). It was instituted by Jesus in the upper room.

> When they met together and made known the wonders of the Lord, and sat together with a fervent spirit; then, after exhortation one of another, they distributed the Lord's Last Supper, as He had commanded them: They took bread and brake it, and ate of it, and thereby and therewith have commemorated the Lord's Death; in like manner also they took the cup, and drank of it, and commemorated the shedding of His Blood; saying one to another, Take and eat the Lord's Body, which was given for us on the Cross. So also they did with the cup; they took it in their hand, and drank of it; for the uppermost of the congregation began, and said to the other, Take the cup and drink the Blood of Christ our Lord, which He has shed for us on the Cross for the remission of sins. . . .

Here Boehme sets forth a democratic supper without priestcraft; there is no sacrificial thanksgiving:

> He gave not . . . the earthly substance . . . which was despised, buffeted, spit upon, scourged, and slain. . . . He gave them His holy body, His holy flesh . . . whereby the Disciples were capable of receiving Christ, and became members of His Body. (*Dreyfach* xiii, 10ff)

In the Supper man is nourished by light, drowning the wrath

and so becoming incorporated in the Love which is Christ. He draws Christ to and within Himself.

The reborn man, in a new body, the production of which is the aim of Boehme's soteriology, again achieves the total human image foretold in Scripture and promised in faith. He gets again what Adam lost, a body of harmonious elements and equivalent Love. This is eschatological man. To achieve this total human image by restoring Adam's pristine essence to man was the second covenant's purpose.

> God has decreed a day, in which He will bring the essence of the old and first Adam through the fire, when it shall be released from vanity, from the craving of the Devil and from the wrath of eternal nature. We understand further how God has brought again into us His holy being . . . in the true pure Love, and has rekindled His Love . . . and generated a new image. (*Menschw.* I, xii, 10ff)

Salvation is thus healing us, making us whole. Our earth body puts on Christ's essence only after death; but our soul can put on His heavenly flesh and blood here and now (*Gnad.* viii, 97ff). External flesh cannot be regenerated until after the general resurrection on the last day; but the inner man's new birth begins with his faith and proceeds through a process of repentance, resignation, ethical regeneration to expectant hope (*Princ.* xvi, 48). The new birth is acquirement of a new will (*Myst. Punkt.* iii, 25) which is the expressed name JESUS (*Tab. Princ.* 72). When the soul leaves the third principle and goes into the second it stands in Jesus' heart (*Dreyfach* iii, 49); man, therefore, departs from his animal nature (*Princ.* xxi, 70), enduring suffering, trial, and tribulation (*Menschw.* II, vi, 12) as Christ did, for to be newly born we must follow Christ (*Gnad.* ix, 116). The newly born person is wisdom's child and has become whole again (*Myst. Mag.* lxvi, 47).

The redemptive struggle continues in man. Christ has opened up a gate (*Gebet* 31) but not all men enter in. Christ offers a new birth in a new body but the earth is ever yet present.

> So long as the earthly man lives, the soul is . . . in dan-

ger, for the Devil has enmity with it . . . . and reaches . . . after the fire of the soul; here fighting is required. (*Menschw.* II, vi, 11)

The world is full of the Devil's snares set to catch men (*Dreyfach* xiv, 20). The elemental earthly life is still at enmity with the newborn man; death is still present (*Myst. Mag.* lii, 13–14).

The noble image must always be in strife against the outer reason-life, and the more it strives, the greater grows the fair tree, for the image co-operates with God. (*Menschw.* III, viii, 7)

The crown of victory is set upon the revived soul which, however,

as soon as it transpires, is immediately laid aside as a crown, just as one crowns a king—afterwards the coronation must be proven by trial. So it happens with the soul since she is still surrounded with the house of sin, for, if she were to fall again, then her crown would be defiled. (*Busse* 27)

Believing man is regenerated only in his inner nature; in his external body the struggle continues (*Bedenk. Stief.* 50ff). Sin still cleaves to flesh and many, like David, become so strong that they fall again (*Gnad.* vi, 33). No one is excluded for there was no ordaining regarding any individual soul, merely a general predestination in Grace (*Gnad.* xii, 9). Man is free. His life is a battlefield of two wills, a fateful duel.

As a twig grows out of the earth, and the essence flees from the earth, and is drawn up by the sun till a stalk . . . is produced out of it, so also does God's sun in His power always draw man's lily, i.e., the new man, from the evil essence. (*Menschw.* II, vii, 12)

There is no dodging or avoiding this struggle; it takes place in all men; none are free of it. This inner Christ

shines for all peoples, for one as well as another: for one

people in His revealed Name, and for another in the name of the one God. He draws them all. (*Gnad.* xiii, 18)

At this dawning those heathen Christians who have true knowledge shall be judged more vigorously, especially those who conceal and hide the Light by false interpretations; who persecute one another. Christians live just as selfishly as the heathen.

Why then will we wrangle here about a knowledge of the gifts? In Christ are all the treasures of wisdom. If we have Him we have all; but if we lose Him, then we have lost all, and ourselves too. The one ground of our religion is, that we love Christ in us, and love one another as Christ has loved us. . . . But this love is not manifest in us unless Christ become man and be manifested in us. He gives His Love to us so that we love one another in Him. (*Gnad.* xii, 21ff)

The end shall come again to the beginning. Life's wheel shall revolve. To live in Love is to live in Eternity (*Dreyfach* xviii, 21) and to live in Love is to dwell in God (*Seel. Frag.* i, 46). Here is freedom beyond existential dialectic, a true rest, a sabbath beyond selfhood's iniquity and worldly evil (*Myst. Mag.* xl, 32).

Man now still lives in time and temporal evil shall continue until the golden age (*Seel. Frag.* iii, 21) when all secrets shall be manifest (*Myst. Mag.* xxxv, 2), all desires known. This is Enoch's time.

Boehme, like so many great Christians, felt that this age was near. His own time was that of the seventh seal—six already had been broken—but soon the new day's dawn—which he had seen in vision—would become actualized and hell's horrors would stand revealed (*Dreyfach* xv, 2, 3). Then will come the thousand years of God's peace (*Seel. Frag.* i, 4), ending the distinctions in time and history. Then will the disharmony of the third principle be removed; the *magna turba* in the earth will pass. Sin's power will be broken. The sleepers will be awakened (*Dreyfach* v, 130), wrath will be changed into Love.

The last judgment is . . . an ingathering by the Father of

all beings and of all that He has brought forth through His Word. Into whatever anything in free will has separated itself, into that will it enter. (*Gnad.* vi, 86)

When this youngest day comes wars will cease, elemental strife will pass. Life no longer will be made up of Yes and No in conflict. Yes and No will be melted, fused into one wonderful joyous harmony. As Boehme wrote in the copybook of a friend:

Weme Zeit ist wie Ewigkeit,
Und Ewigkeit wie die Zeit,
Der ist befreyt
Von allem Streit.

Ach Gott, wo soll ich weiter fragen!
Er ist bei keiner Kreatur.
Wer führt mich über die Natur?
Wer schafft ein Ende meinem Klagen?
Ich muss mich über alles schwingen,
Muss mich erheben über mich:
Dann, hoff ich, wird mirs wohl gelingen,
Dass ich, o Jesu, finde dich.

—ANGELUS SILESIUS

EPILOGUE

JACOB BOEHME had seen eternity's dawn. This red-flaming vision of a new spiritual world lit up the darksome shadows of his age and of his heart. He saw Yes and bitter No in all things—in his war-torn Lausitz homeland, in his sin-buffeted self, and in his riven church. This was the one pole of his vision.

The other pole was never quite projected in full perspective into his temporal consciousness but it persisted with a stubbornness which Gregory Richter could not comprehend. Boehme's dawn was no mist-shrouded breaking of a worldly day; it was sunrise to *eternity*. His ultimate vision, never really expressed in his writings but ever implicit, was of universal spiritual unity in the bonds of peace. The Yes and No which he saw were provisional, passing prelude to a world ultimately at peace with itself. Although he never formulated this part of his vision in the utopian terms which some of his contemporaries employed, still this sabbath was the heart of his sight.

His sun had dawned! But what a Sun it was! As his follower, poet Angelus Silesius, wrote:

Jesus, ew'ge Sonne,
Aller Engel Wonne,
Was für Freude muss es sein
Wenn du kommst ins Herz hinein.

Jesus, Sun of Righteousness and Prince of Peace, had dawned in Boehme's heart to a new eternity. This was a dawning to a new age and a new world.

Boehme—and now, perhaps, we may want to call him the "blessed Jacob"—was a Christian mystic on whom the gracious Spirit had descended. However maligned by Gregory Richter, he stood in the line of prophets who, without benefit of priestly ordination, had seen the mystery unfold itself. Boehme, though, was neither classical nor oriental mystic; he had climbed no ladders nor escaped the wheel of reincarnative births. Closing his eyes and mouth—as mysticism originally suggests, perceiving the great mystery, he was led to penetrate beyond the breach between man and woman, between creed and creed, and between God and the world. Plotinus, typical classical mystic, had been four times transported into ecstasy. Not Boehme, however. He claimed, on the contrary, that God had come down into him. Thus did he reject classical mysticism's ascending Gothic, the mysticism of hierarchies, fashioning instead a properly Protestant mystical genre of descending Agapé. He wanted nothing of ladders, pilgrimages, levels, stages, degrees, hierarchies—the ascending steps of an ambitious faith seeking to seize and to know the Godhead. For between medieval mysticism and Boehme there towered Luther and his *simul iustus et peccator,* for the reformer had centered the attention on the psychology rather than the mechanics of repentance, as Boehme's tracts on *Busse* show.

Some insist that mysticism implies *Nirvana,* that is, that the self must be destroyed by being lost in the abyss of pure being. This is posited on a view which sees selfhood as evil. Boehme was aware of this danger for he wrote:

> But her [Sophia's] marriage to the Soul is not immediately consummated nor is that image which was distorted in Paradise immediately restored. Here is dangerous ground for man, since both Lucifer and Adam fell at this point, which may happen again because man is still firmly bound by vanity. (*Busse* 32)

Not only did Boehme disclaim *Nirvana;* he asserted that it was man's chiefest sin.

Nirvana is the necessary religious goal of monism. It appears only within those metaphysical systems which consider the self's finitude evil *per se*. What this means, in short, is that the doctrine of sin defines the dualism which the mystic seeks to resolve. And the solution to the problem of evil is mediated to the mystic by the metaphysical environment in which he happens to dwell.

The Greeks had formulated the problem of evil by assuming that matter was evil; this made them seek, therefore, to become fleshless. Buddhism, identifying evil with suffering selfhood, had sought to void the self in apophatic pantheism. Orphic deliverance had been by transcending individuality in esoteric orgiasm, a holy bestiality. Stoicism had sought to harmonize individual reason with the universal mind. The Neoplatonists had sought deliverance by intellect through supra-rational apprehension of Truth. Each way had been determined by its view of evil which issued from the metaphysical climate which surrounded it.

It is, perhaps, clear that the prevailing metaphysical climate conditions the view of evil which in turn determines the religious quest. Flesh, self, matter, ignorance, suffering—each has been exorcised. But this is negative, for these goals are obtained by some scheme of negation, a point of view which was clearly expressed by Pseudo-Dionysius:

> We shall obtain ecstasy by denying or removing all things that are—like as men, who, carving a statue out of marble, remove all the impediments that hinder the clear perception of the latent image and by this mere removal display the hidden statue itself in its hidden beauty.[1]

In contrast to this negative mysticism, Boehme sought a new man who was a regenerated son of God. Selfhood, individuality, conditioned existence were for him not evil *per se*. So he did not seek to remove these "impediments" because he did not believe that they impeded. He knew that his lily could become a perfect lily only because it welcomed the energies of earth, air, and sun, only if it grew to full individual perfection from within. To be a lily was not in itself evil. What Boehme wanted for himself and for his world was not to get rid of the multiplicity of finite forms but simply to remove the great curse within reality which prevented the multiplicity of God's wisdom from becoming expressed in forms. His was a world-redeeming not a world-escaping faith!

This mystical revolution—and that is what it really was—was wrought when Boehme, freed from a medievalism which had been shackled by Greek metaphysics, sought to combine the new cosmology of the Renaissance with his Lutheran Bible. The medieval church had sought to get man to heaven. But Boehme's Bible told him that Christ had commanded us to love! Now, *love is a this-world ethic!* It is not an ethic of renunciation. It takes place within time and we do not wait for death to become lovers. Wrath and love—his temporal Yes and No—were both present judgments within a world of time, and their resolution could be accomplished within history without ecstatic transcendence.

Boehme's mind, surrounded by a theological climate almost as dry as the Sahara, knew that religion was more than creed-hawking, system-building, and confessional apologetic; it was love! He approached the task of externalizing this faith, which is basically an irrational one, with bold, fresh, and uninhibited mind, one that was not trained in the schools and knew neither the Lombard's *Sentences* nor the Philippist *Loci Communes.* And as a consequence he fashioned a theology whose images and terms were in full rebellion against the usual theological categories, thus pointing forward towards the future liberation of theology by the subjective language of romantics like Schleiermacher. This fresh, bold, venturing spirit brought Boehme much pain and discomfort—but it is also the index of his greatness.

Boehme's Yes and No were within his self, too. He was indeed the first significant voluntarist because he sought removal of the divided wills within his being. The Neoplatonists had understood the place of will in the processes of ideation and knowing; Augustine had known that the achievement of consciousness was an act of will; Duns Scotus and Occam had given will prominence in their epistemologies. But Boehme saw in his divided self both fire and light, both egocentric libido and yielding love, and he knew, not that one will was necessary for consciousness, but that two wills were wanted.

> Without dialectic no thing can become manifest to itself. If nothing resists it, then it continually proceeds from itself; it does not return to itself again. . . . If the natural life had no dialectic . . . then it would never ask for the ground from which it came. (*Beschau.* i, 8–9)

With Eckhart will had been a means of knowing God, and in the late sixteenth century will had meant knowledge for control; the unity sought in Counter-Reformation mysticism was unity of control, implying the new psychology of Loyola's *Spiritual Exercises.* This voluntaristic monism could not produce self-consciousness and Boehme's problem with regard to the Trinity, posited for the first time in Christian history, was to produce a self-contemplating God known by a God-contemplating self.

The traditional trinitarian view describes how God acts *vis-à-vis* His creation; it does not show how He knows Himself. Boehme's theogony is therefore an unusual attempt to show how both a self-contemplating God comes to know Himself and then, after creation, how He knows and is known by His creatures. To do this Boehme had to conceive of God's inner life as both conscious and beyond consciousness; he had to postulate his nonrational *Ungrund,* an idea—if so it may be called—which follows from the difference between the *deus occultus* and the *deus absconditus.*

The *deus occultus* grew from the union of Dionysian mysticism and nominalism as in Gerson's *Considerationes de mystica theologica,* holding that God is hidden from man, and man, knowing only that God is, can know positively only what God is not. The Lutheran-Boehmist *deus absconditus,* however, posits not so much a God hidden *from* man as a God whose mysterious depth is unknown both to Himself and to His creature—a God who is to some degree a mystery.[2] Boehme's formulation of his fundamental problem is put in language as clear as that of any philosophical theologian; he wrote:

> Had the hidden God, who is merely one Essence and Will, not led Himself by His Will out of Himself, had He not brought Himself out of eternal comprehension in the *temperamenta*[3] into a differentiation of wills, and had He not led the same differentiation into a subjectivation of natural and creaturely life, and did this same differentiation not stand in strife in life, how then would the hidden Will of God, which in itself is single, become manifest to itself. (*Beschau.* 1, 10)

Boehme, then, sought to explain how a self-conscious God and a self-conscious creature came to be.

By thus postulating a dark mysterious point of identity behind God's consciousness Boehme raised an aspect of God which is neither nature nor spirit, subject nor object, thought nor being, but the unity of all contradictions. When once a *coincidentia oppositorum* is thus postulated then two basic laws of thought are abnegated: the law of contradiction and the law of the excluded third. A new logic appears. Aristotle had asserted that where there is disparity there can be no love.[4] But Boehme saw deeper. He understood that where there is no disparity there can be neither love nor self-consciousness. To love one needs both a lover and a beloved. Love implies, nay demands, separate persons—lovers, selves. If love be man's chief end then selfhood cannot be evil *per se* nor is self-consciousness evil *per se,* as classical and oriental religions hold. This was Boehme's fundamental insight for he saw that love demanded two self-conscious beings who were capable of freely directing their own loves beyond themselves. Oriental and classical religions denied the validity of finitude and personality and they considered limitation and differentiated existence as evil. Not so Christianity, however much it may have been formulated in Aristotelian terms. Boehme's vision of a loving kingdom where there was a first and a last, where perfected selves sat down to eat heavenly manna with their risen Lord, while not unique with him, was, however, unfamiliar ground for oriental and classical mystics. Boehme, by validating self-conscious personality, also validated the Christian ethic of love. Surely this achievement, while shared with other great spirits within Christendom, is great enough for so simple a man, the humble and meek little cobbler of Görlitz.

Boehme has been victimized by a false reputation. Surely we have quoted enough from his pen—however inadequate translation may be—to dispose of the popular notion that he had an "apocalyptic obscurity" in his style. He wrote clear German, sometimes a German of more-than-average merit, and whatever obscurity there was issued from the inadequacy of language rather than from paucity of vision or littleness of mind. His vocabulary, as has already been said, was not the usual verbiage of theology; herein, however, lies its value. Writing before man had acquired precision in describing subjective states, writing with little allegory, he yet managed to convey his profoundly inwardized vision of the nature of consciousness and of the world.

Perhaps, when the ultimate sunrise dawns to final eternity, Boehme's vision that all things consist of Yes and No will prove to have been close to the ultimate truth. Our physicists, immersed in their tables and formulae, working their slide-rules and calculating their logarithms, know that an atom is the dynamic equipoise of plus and minus and when the *temperamentum* is disturbed by the flaming fire-flash —a truly cosmic *Blick* and *Blitz*—chaos ensues. Stripped of its nonessentials Boehme's vision is proven each time an atom is split.

Not only were atoms made up of Yes and No, plus and minus, but our human society also was split into affirmation and negation. Boehme lived his earthly course on the banks of the Neisse river in eastern Germany, and today the fateful Neisse-Oder line splits two worlds apart. Living thus on the boundary of East and West his vision of binding Love may yet prove capable of bridging the chasm of our riven world. It yet may prove a *sunrise to eternity.* As he would have said,

"To this end may God help us all!"

NOTES TO EPILOGUE

1. *Myst. Theol.* tr. Rolt., 194–195.
2. Hinc Verbum factum est et sapientia dei abscondita et exinanita, ut nostram quoque hanc pessimam sapientam absconderet et examiniret, quae est plena vanitate errore et peccata. Luther in *Werke*, Weimar edition, I, 34.
3. This is harmony without dialectic or contrary wills.
4. *Eth. Nic.* 1165. b.17

BIBLIOGRAPHICAL NOTE

Biographical materials about Boehme are for the most part confused and untrustworthy, especially the earlier materials. The first critical analysis was Will-Erich Peuckert's *Das Leben Jakob Böhmes,* Jena, 1924. Here the early materials were scanned and the background well integrated, although full use was not made of Boehme's own letters. Richard Jecht's *Jakob Böhme–Gedenkgabe der Stadt Görlitz,* 1924, presented the new materials from various sources in the Görlitz Archives. There are at least eighteen references to Boehme in the official records, and we know as much about him, in the objective sense, as we do about his slightly older contemporary, William Shakespeare. The best source, however, is Boehme's own writings.

The several collected editions of Boehme's writings contain seven tracts which deal with biographical materials. These have been translated and published by Francis Okeley, *Memoirs of the Life of Jacob Behmen,* Northampton, 1780. The first of these tracts is von Franckenberg's *De Vita et Scriptis,* which has been often cited in our work. Dr. Peuckert has traced all of Franckenberg's materials back to even more remote sources, except of course those materials which he made up. The second of these tracts is Dr. Weisner's *Wahrhaftiger Relation,* the account by a Breslau physician which was sent to the Boehmist groups in Amsterdam in 1651. It is trustworthy, although limited. The third tract, and the most reliable, is Dr. Kober's *Umständiger Bericht,* a longish account by Boehme's personal physician which was written in November, 1624, the month of Boehme's death, and therefore the earliest work we have. It is fully trustworthy and contains detailed descriptions of Boehme's illness, his last hours, and eight supplementary documents as follows: a) Dietrich's letter to Kober, b) Dietrich's Questions to Boehme which we have paraphrased in our work; c) the eulogy given at Boehme's funeral; d) Boehme's widow's petition to the Council; f) Michael Kurtz's account of the funeral; g) Michael Kurtz's eulogy; and h) specification of certain questions prior to absolution.

The text of Boehme's writings, although the product of much labor by the early editors, still presents major problems.

The printed versions are clear enough, but the problem arises from the relationships of these versions to the several manuscripts. Variants exist in the manuscripts. Furthermore, the British translations made by the commonwealth-period Boehmists were most likely made from printed Holland-Dutch versions and so were not direct translations from Boehme's German.

When Franckenberg first listed Boehme's writings his chronology was not fully correct. And we are not sure that all Boehme's works have survived. In 1675, Beets, publisher of the German versions, inserted an advertisement in the back of one of Franckenberg's books saying that a tract, *Der Krauter der Natur,* was known to have existed. What a find this would be to discover that Boehme was also an early botanist! Boehme himself says in *Apol. Richter* something about his book on the noble Sophia which he also mentions in *Letzte Zeit* I, 1, 2. He also refers to several small treatises which he had given here and there and kept no copy of.

Werner Buddecke has found most of the manuscripts that were available to the early editors and he has catalogued them in his *Verzeichnis.* Also he has collated these with the early printed editions.

The manuscripts were originally gathered by a wealthy Amsterdam merchant, van Beyerland, who, after much trouble and with considerable luck, finally got these writings to Holland where he proceeded to translate them into Dutch. All of Boehme's works except *Irrth. Stief.* and *Aurora,* along with *Sig. Rer.* and *Myst. Mag.*—works of his maturity—first appeared in Dutch. The last three appeared in German editions. The manuscripts were handed down to Beyerland's heirs, and Franckenberg brought out an edition in succeeding years. In 1682 Gichtel brought out his famous edition, erroneously called the first, which was reset and brought out

THEOSOPHIA REVELATA.
Das ist:
Alle Göttliche Schriften
des Gottseligen und Hocherleuchteten Deutschen THEOSOPHI
Jacob Böhmens,
Darin die allertieffesten Geheimnisse GOttes und seines Wesens; der ewigen und zeitlichen
Natur und Creatur; Schöpfung der Engel und ihrer Hierarchien; des Falles Lucifers und seiner
Legionen; der Schöpfung dieser Welt und des Menschen, und alles was Leben hat; samt des verführten Menschens
Fall; Insonderheit das Kündlich-grosse Geheimniß JEsu Christi, mit der Mutter der himlischen Wiedergebärerin und seiner heiligen Oeco-
nomie unter und mit uns Menschen, im Glauben der neuen Geburt von oben; benebenst dem wahren Fundament Christlicher Religion
und der Gottseligkeit, den Liebhabern der Weisheit, aus ihren verborgenen Schätzen, gründlich entdecket werden.
Alles nach dem wesentlichen Grunde der Dreyen Principien Göttlicher Geburt in der Seelen,
und Sein Selbst-Offenbarung in Dreyheit und Weisheit; auch nach dem Prophetischen und Apostolischen
Zeugniß, und dem wahren Sinn und inwendigen Verstande der gantzen heiligen Schrift,
deren 7 Siegel Apoc. V. alhie eröffnet liegen.
Aus des Auctoris wieder gefundenen eigenen Originalien, und denen von Alters darzu gehörigen vielen Copeyen,
welche man nunmehro alle mit einander conferiret, mit vieler Arbeit aufs neue treulich corrigiret, und mercklich verbessert.
Anbey mit des Hocherleuchteten nunmehro seligen Mannes Gottes
JOHANN GEORG GICHTELS,
Eines Gottseligen und erfahrnen Kenners dieser Schriften,
Geistreichen Summarien und Inhalt jeden Capitels, dem Gottbegierigen Leser zu einem
ausgebornen Lichte, im Verstande des Gemüths, ausgezieret.
In Beyfügung des Auctoris J. B. ausführlich-erläuterten Lebens-Lauffes und dienlichen Registern.

Gedruckt im Jahre des ausgebornen grossen Heils 1730.

TITLE-PAGE OF THE 1730 EDITION

under Glusing's editorship in 1715. Then Johann Wilhelm Ueberfeld re-edited the works, compared them with the manuscripts, modernized the spelling, and brought out the 1730 edition in ten volumes which is the standard. We have used it, and it is now in process of being made available in a modern German edition. The Schiebler reprints of the 1682 edition are not critical.

Of the vast literature on Boehme Koyré's is the only work of comprehensive scope and Benz's the most penetrating. The best interpretations still are the lectures which Franz von Baader made on Boehme, especially on *Gnad.*, the work of his deep maturity.

In our opinion—and the reader may take it for what it is worth—most interpreters have made two mistakes: first, they have failed to see his growth, his ability to discard ideas when they no longer suited him; and secondly, they have failed to appreciate Boehme's own understanding of his categories, of the "joints" in his system. The fatal mistake, made by Hegel and so many others, is to identify the seven spirits of God with the seven natural powers.

INDEX

Paris: An Urbane Guide

Paris: An Urbane Guide to the City and Its People

PETER DE POLNAY

HENRY REGNERY COMPANY
CHICAGO

FIRST PUBLISHED IN ENGLAND BY W. H. ALLEN & COMPANY

MANUFACTURED IN THE UNITED STATES OF AMERICA

LIBRARY OF CONGRESS CATALOG CARD NUMBER: 78–105122

FIRST PUBLISHED IN THE UNITED STATES BY HENRY REGNERY COMPANY 1970

Contents

Introduction

In the Neolithic Age elephants lived on the slopes of Belleville, huge mammoth-like creatures nearly twelve feet high and fifteen long. They used to go down to drink in the Seine, taking the road that today roughly corresponds with the avenue Mathurin-Moreau and the rue de la Grange-aux-Belles. In 1903 during the construction of the Métro Porte-des-Lilas-Villiers, the molar tooth of an elephas primigenius was found; pre-historians completed the pattern. If the elephants did indeed take the shortest cut to the river, then they must also have lumbered along the future rue Saint-Denis, the road the kings of France were later often to take.

Blaise Pascal said: "Rivers are roads that move." Paris was born in the Cité, where two roads meet, one the East-West river road, the other the North-South land road. When the Cité became too small, the inhabitants grouped themselves on both banks of the river along the North-South road, which became the rue Saint-Jacques on the Left and the rue Saint-Martin on the Right Bank. The North-South road was joined together by two wooden bridges across the river, Le Grand-Pont (now Pont-Notre-Dame) and Le Petit-Pont, still on the same site with the same name. Over the two bridges passed the great road connecting the Loire with the plains of the North. From the start Paris remained a circle crossed by two perpendiculars: the river road and the land road.

Today, as in the days of the Romans, all the routes nationales begin in the Place du Parvis-de-Notre-Dame in the heart of the Cité, which is the heart of France.

In 50 B.C. when Caesar came to conquer Gaul, the Cité was inhabited by the tribe of the Parises or Parisii who hailed from Asia. Labienus, Caesar's lieutenant, marched on the Parisii, his legions vastly outnumbering the tribesmen. Before joining battle with the Romans, Camulogène, the chief of the Parisii, burnt all the bridges and the houses of the settlement; then he perished in the fight. Thus Paris was born out of defeat and fire, for that burnt-down village was its first ancestor. Not for nothing is "Fluctuat Nec Mergitur" the motto of the town.

Between the second and the fourth centuries an entirely Roman town stood on the site of the burnt village. On the distant hillock of Montmartre (Mons Martis to the Romans, Mons Martyrum to the Christians because of the martyrdom of SS Denis, Rustique and Eleuthère) stood temples of Mercury and Mars. Inside the Roman town, which spread on the Left Bank from the Seine to Mons Lencotitius (Montagne Sainte-Geneviève), lived about fifteen thousand souls. The town was called Lutetia. The Right Bank remained marshland. The rising little city took the fancy of the Emperor Julian the Apostate, who lived there from 351 to 361 A.D. It is said that he built his palace on the site nowadays known as Les Thermes de Julien; but that is not certain.

Within the town the Romans built a theatre (the site of the Lycée Saint-Louis), an arena (rue Monge), and baths, the ruins of which are beside the Cluny Museum in the rue du Sommerard.

"I was in winter quarters in my dear Lutetia," wrote Julian in a letter. "Here winter is less rigorous than elsewhere. The people have it that this is caused by the sea breeze that reaches Lutetia. . . . Sea water is less cold than fresh water. In this land you find excellent vineyards and fig trees, which are protected with straw in winter. The natives take the gifts of Bacchus because he is the father of joy. Their usual drink is water from the river, which is clear and limpid. As they live on an island, it would be difficult for them to procure any other water."

Fig trees are still to be found at Argenteuil, and straw is still used as protection against the cold.

After the invasion of the Franks, the town lost the name of Lutetia and was called Paris after the long-extinct, small tribe of the Parisii.

During the reign of the Franks, the Parisians suffered heavily from their cruelty and treachery. Chilpéric II outdid his kinsmen. In August 584, envoys appeared in Paris sent from Spain by the Visigoth ruler whom Grégoire de Tours, the great chronicler, refers to as the King of Spain. The emissaries came to arrange a marriage between the Visigoth king and Rigonthe, Chilpéric's daughter. Chilpéric ordered a large number of Parisian families to leave their homes so as to accommodate the envoys in a dignified manner. The poor people were herded together, put into four-wheeled wagons and driven out of town. Those who clung to their homes were put to death. It was rather modern in conception and execution.

Chilpéric agreed to the marriage, and gave his daughter a fine dowry. Queen Frédégonde added a large quantity of jewels, gold and silver. Fifty wagons were needed to carry the daughter's baggage south. The escort consisted of four thousand men. Ducs Domegisellus, Ansoalde and Bladaste, along with Wadon the High Chamberlain, were sent with the bride to guide and protect her. The cortège left Paris through the southern gate. The axle of one of the carriages broke and the superstitious populace cried out: "Mala hora!"

Having travelled the distance of three leagues, tents were pitched for the night. When darkness fell, a group of soldiers stole about a hundred horses and disappeared into the forest. The horses all wore gold chains and bits. On the second night, still more horses vanished. On the fourth, some of the gold and silver went too. The nobles who were there to protect their princess set the example, and, wherever Rigonthe and her suite passed, the cottages of the poor were destroyed and their beasts driven away. In Poitiers several noblemen abandoned her, taking a fair share of the dowry with them. None the less Rigonthe continued on her journey. On arrival in Toulouse she heard of her father's death. He had been assassinated on the order of his wife Frédégonde. On hearing the news, the three dukes and the High Chamberlain decamped with the rest of the treasure. Rigonthe had to give up the idea of marriage, and all that was left for her was to seek refuge in the convent of Sainte-Marie-de-Toulouse.

Such was life under the Franks.

After the dismemberment of Charlemagne's empire, Paris became the capital of the kingdom which from then on was called France. The town continued to expand along the North-South road, the Cité still remaining the centre of the town. On the Right Bank the North-South road cut across the new East-West road (rues Saint-Antoine and Saint-Honoré), and where the two roads crossed became known as la Grande Croisée de Paris. Churches rose, among them Saint-Julien-le-Pauvre and Saint-Germain-des-Prés, the oldest surviving churches of Paris—building started on both before 1170—unless one considers Saint-Pierre of Montmartre, started in 1134 and finished in 1147, when Montmartre was well outside the boundaries. Notre-Dame, though begun in 1163, was finished only in 1330. The little church of Saint-Julien-le-Pauvre, without belfry and transept, was one of the twenty churches built in the vicinity of Notre-Dame during the Middle Ages which, with the exception of Saint-Julien and the remains of the chapel of Saint-Aignan in the rue des Ursins, have all disappeared.

Already in Roman times Paris was a walled city, but the town continued consistently to expand beyond the walls. It was King Philippe-Auguste who in 1188 decided to construct a final wall round Paris, a wall intended to give the town its definitive size and shape, and which became known as the Enceinte de Philippe-Auguste. Excavations in 1896 in the rues Clovis and Cardinal-Lemoine revealed a section of this wall, about nine feet thick; at regular intervals of about two hundred yards stood a tower. (One such tower can still be seen at 29 rue Guénégaud.) The wall had five gates on the Right Bank. Starting from the Quai des Célestins, it reached as far as the Portes Saint-Denis and Saint-Antoine; then in a half-circle it enclosed the Louvre and stretched back to the Seine.

The western end of the wall was on the Left Bank, somewhere near the French Academy, where at the time stood the Tower of Philippe-Hamelin, later known as the Tour de Nesle, of sinister reputation. The wall was carried as far as the Porte Saint-Jacques and joined the river at the height of the Port-de-Saint-Bernard. On the Left Bank the enceinte had about thirty towers and six gates.

Remains of the Enceinte de Philippe-Auguste can be seen at the Palais de Justice (Tour de l'Horloge), the flagstones of the Cour Carrée of the Louvre between the clock and the south entrance giving on the Quai du Louvre, in the rue de Rivoli behind the statue of Coligny, at 135 rue Saint-Denis, at 11 rue du Temple and elsewhere.

Paris refused to stay put. The next attempt to halt it was the Enceinte of Etienne Marcel, completed by Charles V, who took the wall more to the east to join up with the fortress of the Bastille. As Paris continued to outgrow its walls, new ones were built. For instance, the Portes Saint-Martin and Saint-Denis are part of the Enceinte of Louis XIV. From the time of Julius Caesar until 1841 when the fortifications were built, Paris had nine different walls, each trying to contain the town; but whenever outlying places and villages were officially included within the city in an attempt to give it a definite limit, new agglomerations sprang up beyond them. In brief, the effect was contrary to aim and expectation, as though the walls were in constant pursuit of the expanding town. Such is also the story of the suburbs, which are still on the move and, it seems, will never stop.

Neither walls, ramparts, bastions, fortifications nor octrois (toll-gates) could stem the tide; the town expanded, pushing all obstacles out of its way. The reason for this was aptly put by E. Babize in 1930. "England," he said, "goes to India, Germany to America, Italy colonises Africa, and France immigrates to Paris."

In the eighteenth century, in accordance with the Plan of Bretez, also known as the Plan of Turgot, a new enceinte was thrown round Paris, the Walls of the Fermiers Généraux, the "tax-farmers" who did very well for themselves in their work of collecting the revenue. One evening, after a game of chess in Voltaire's drawing-room at Ferney, the guests told stories about robbers, and Voltaire was asked to tell one too.

"Mesdames," he said, "once upon a time there was a fermier général . . . ma foi! I forget the rest."

Those walls were to stay until 1860.

One generally pictures old Paris as a dark, sordid town with dark houses clustered round the churches and dark crimes committed in narrow alleyways. In the sixteenth century Torquato Tasso, the Italian poet, visited Paris as a member of the suite of Cardinal Luigi d'Este. The spoilt son of Renaissance Italy did not think much of the city. In letters to his friends in Ferrara he complained of the awful climate, the monotonous fog and the inhabitants who were as changeable as the weather. A few church spires attracted him; the houses not at all; and the only things he praised and admired were the gay windmills of Montmartre.

On the other hand, Rodolphe Boutenais, a lawyer from Châteaudun who became advocate to the Great Council of Paris towards the end of the same century, wrote a poem in Latin in praise of Paris, entitled *Lutetia*:

"Here on the summit of the mountain where Saint-Denis and his companions were put to death"—he was alluding to Montmartre —"still flourishes a village that took its name from the martyrs, the friends of Christ. Here stone is quarried to which is added plaster, so useful in the construction of our houses, whose brilliant whiteness transforms Paris into a town wearing a cloak of snow. The constant use of this mixture keeps the flames away, and to it we owe the peace of our town, its beauty and resistance to fire."

You have only to look at the buildings that have recently been cleaned to be able easily to visualise Boutenais's Paris as a town wearing a cloak of snow.

In the days of Philippe-Auguste, clothes and horses' harness were covered with gold, silver and jewels, but people lived poorly at Court and even more poorly elsewhere. The royal palaces had neither marble nor polished floors; carpets were unknown: the king and his courtiers walked on straw.

"For the salvation of our soul and the souls of our forebears," wrote Philippe-Auguste, "we hereby give the usage of all the straw of our room and house to the poor who dwell in the Maison-Dieu in front of the great church of Notre-Dame, whenever we leave the town and sleep in some other place."

The same monarch shared with the Provost of Paris the spoils of the condemned, including the clothes they wore at their executions; supervised the gaming houses and brothels, which paid him toll; and attached women to the Court, who, known as the Royal Prostitutes, wore special dresses to distinguish them from other harlots, and whose main task was to keep the bodyguard happy.

The people paid tolls and taxes on practically everything. Already in the time of Saint-Louis, at the toll-gate of the Petit-Châtelet payment was exacted in respect of the rare monkeys that entered the town. If a merchant imported a monkey for sale, he paid 4 deniers, but a laudable exception was made in the case of jugglers. If the monkey danced for the toll-collector in the Passage du Petit-Châtelet, no duty payment was demanded, and if on top of that the juggler sang a song that pleased the collector, he too was exempted from tax.

Pigs abounded in the streets of Paris. They roamed the town, eating all the filth and offal for which they could wish. These scavengers were very useful, for they fed well, cleaned up some of the mess in the streets and, once they had become fat and appetising, provided succulent food for the people, who thus doubly benefited from them, until one day, near Saint-Gervais, a pig unfortunately found itself between the forelegs of a horse ridden by Philippe, the eldest son of King Louis-le-Gros. The horse threw the prince, who died of his fall, and the bereaved king stopped the pigs' free progress and forbade them to wander in the streets. An exception was made for the pigs of the monks of Saint-Antoine; as long as each carried a bell, they were free to run about, though never more than twelve were allowed out together. They became known as the Privileged Pigs.

Another and often more dangerous obstacle to free circulation was the number of streams running in the middle of the streets. There were no pavements and no gutters. When it rained, the streams turned into torrents, especially down the streets dropping from Montmartre and on the Left Bank from the Montagne Sainte-Geneviève. The streams, of course, swept filth and dirt along. They were still running in the middle of the eighteenth century, and Restif de La Bretonne, that inexhaustible chronicler of the Paris of his day, relates a scene he witnessed in the rue Montmartre where he saw such a torrent. (One wonders whether Restif ever slept, since he seems invariably to have been at hand whenever and wherever anything happened in Paris.)

It was night: he preferred to stroll about at night. The torrent in the rue Montmartre was in full flow. Although there was a moon, the town was in darkness. It was an old, barbarous custom, as he says, not to light the street lamps when there was a moon, in spite of the fact that its light could not penetrate into the narrow streets because of the high houses. Few people were abroad in the night. Fearlessly, he walked on, his aim the rue des Vieux-Augustins (now rues d'Argout and Hérold), his intention to cross the covered sewer there. He called out to two women on the other side of the torrent, busybody that he was, not to cross the stream before they reached the sewer. They were mother and daughter. The daughter did not listen to his wise words—so few people seemed to—but tried to wade across. She fell, and the torrent took her along. The mother shrieked. Restif entered the mire, which was the messy stream from the Halles, risking being thrown over by its force. Restif of course, who always emerged victorious, pulled the girl from the torrent, and, seeing that she had fainted, carried her home to her lodgings and modestly vanished before the grateful mother could thank her daughter's saviour.

The custom of not lighting the street lamps when there was a moon was still in existence when street lanterns were changed to street lamps in the 1770s. By 1780, twelve hundred street lamps shed their light every moonless night. Householders had to pay for their lanterns, and later their street lamps, every twenty years. The citizens complained that this tax was greater than the expense of lighting the town.

The streets were covered in mud, which turned black and smelly at mealtimes when water was discharged from the pitchers, in spite of the sulphur and salt used against mud and stench by the municipality. The mud was now and then carted away in wheelbarrows by private contractors. When it snowed, the mud froze, and the streams were covered in ice. It was bitterly hard work to clean the streets when it thawed.

Until the eighteenth century, houses were known after their ensigns. If they had none, then they were referred to as the house next to such and such an ensign, or the second or third house after the ensign. In 1726 street numbers began to be used. Noblemen objected to them, for they found it humiliating to live, say, at number 10 with a tradesman at number 11. Tradesmen did not care for street numbers either: they feared new taxes. In 1797 street numbers became obligatory. All houses were given numbers, starting on the right side of the street and ending on the left. For example, in the rue Saint-Honoré the house on the right corner of the rue de la Lingerie was number 1, on the left corner number 730. Street names were given officially only from 1726 onwards: until then tradition alone had kept their names alive.

Paris under the kings was poor in public gardens but rich in private ones, especially on the Ile-Saint-Louis (Ile-des-Vaches in the Middle Ages). True, there were the public squares of Grève (now de l'Hôtel-de-Ville), Chevalier-du-Guet (rue Jean-Lantier), Sainte-Opportune, Sorbonne, Parvis-de-Notre-Dame, and Croix-Rouge among others, but they were cluttered with the stalls of fishmongers, butchers and bakers, leaving little room for the strolling Parisian. Henri IV and Richelieu were each moved by the poverty of open space, but the contributions of the good king and the great cardinal amounted only to the Place Dauphine and the Place Royale. Still, the Parisian had the laughing countryside just beyond the walls, and there he repaired to drink, eat and dance in the guinguettes* that surrounded the town like the enceinte.

The Revolution, the Empire and the Restoration all contributed to the growth of Paris, but the great feverish impulse came with the Baron Haussmann, Prefect of the Seine for seventeen years, who was led, guided, helped and pushed by his sovereign, the Emperor Napoleon III. The Walls of the Fermiers Généraux were demolished, and the outlying villages of Montmartre, Batignolles, Belleville, Ménilmontant, Reuilly, Les Gobelins and Montrouge attached to the capital; and thus in 1860 the Paris of twelve arrondissements turned into the Paris of twenty. The Emperor was happy. Once the walls were gone and the villages swallowed, the town sprawled, as it were, all over the place, and the villages quickly lost what little rusticity they still possessed.

To the Emperor and his indefatigable Prefect, progress seemed the answer to all ills. "Du petit au grand" was their motto. By the 1860s they could boast of new, large, beautifully paved streets and boulevards, flanked by new houses of equal grandeur. New buildings rose daily. The rue de Rivoli and the Place de l'Opéra were conceived. The Hôtel de la Paix (now Grand-Hôtel) and the Hôtel du Louvre were erected with their hundreds of rooms for the foreigners who flocked to admire the new Paris with its modern

* Guinguettes: taverns with gardens where one danced, named after Guinguet who owned such an establishment in the 1670s in Ménilmontant.

cafés, some with twenty-four billiard tables, rightly calling themselves the biggest in the world. On top of all this appeared the large stores like the Louvre, Pygmalion, the Belle Jardinière, and the Bon Marché, which revolutionised commerce and brought in a new era in shopping which Emile Zola ecstatically praised in his *Au Bonheur des Dames.*

The lovers of old Paris still grind their teeth when speaking of the baron. The "haussmannisation" of Paris remains a deadly sin in their eyes. "Think," they say, "of all the old streets that vanished, the old stones that were destroyed and the squares and the private gardens that had to disappear." They forget one thing, that the wide boulevards of the Baron with their trees and the houses that flank them are not as ungainly a sight as the huge lifeless barracks and skyscrapers that would have sprung up if the prefect and the emperor had left the matter to our age. Anyway, many old streets are left as witnesses of the past of Paris.

Paris has several times been invaded, yet little physical damage has been caused to the town by enemy hand. Its worst ordeal, and the worst destruction it suffered, was caused by the Parisians themselves during the violence and horrors of the short-lived Commune of 1871.

"You cannot govern against Paris; you cannot govern without Paris," observed Léon Gambetta to Louis Andrieux, Prefect of Police; who, remembering the Commune, was of the opinion, however, that if one day a government ruled France according to the wishes of only the Parisians, they would govern against France.

I

The Halles I

The district of Les Halles lies in the first arrondissement and dates back to the twelfth century when it belonged to the new parish of Saint-Germain (Saint-Germain-l'Auxerrois). In the reign of Philippe-Auguste a chapel was built in the Halles dedicated to St Agnès, and paid for by Jean Alais, a burgher of Paris and chief of the mystery players. Alais had lent money to the King who did not repay him in cash but gave him the right to levy 1 denier on every panier of fish brought into the Halles. Alais did so well that he donated the chapel out of sheer remorse. The chapel received relics of St Eustache from the Abbey of Saint-Denis. It soon changed its name to Saint-Eustache, and the newly created parish took the same name. The population of the Halles grew so fast that Saint-Eustache had several times to be enlarged. It was eventually pulled down to make room for a much larger church. The foundation stone of the present church was laid on August 19, 1532, by Jean de la Barre, Comte d'Etampes, Provost of Paris. Saint-Eustache is to the Halles what Notre-Dame is to the Cité, and in dignity ranks next to it.

At the time when St Louis was in the Holy Land, a strange personage arrived in the Halles who took the church by force. He was a Benedictine monk called Jacob, who came from the Abbey of Cîteaux (Côte d'Or), leading thirty thousand men, a miscellaneous horde consisting of shepherds, beggars and ordinary people who had joined him on his progress. Most of them were armed. Jacob evicted the priests and anointed himself bishop. The clergy of Paris did not dare intervene. Was he a visionary, a plain adventurer, or a madman? Nineteenth-century socialists liked to think of him as a revolutionary and a social reformer.

Jacob, whose followers camped and lived around the church, was a preacher of strength. He, the simple monk, had seen the angels, and the Blessed Virgin had visited him in his cell in the Abbey of Cîteaux. He was at Saint-Eustache to execute her holy commands. He and his aides used the confessional to discover which of the parishioners had worldly goods. The people of the Halles, who were already known for their good humour and gaiety, were delighted with the monk until his armed men began to take their money and possessions, including wives and daughters.

As suddenly as he had arrived, Jacob and his flock left Saint-Eustache and set out for Orleans. No more was heard of him. The priests of Saint-Eustache returned to the relief of the population. When there was no fear of his return, the Bishop of Paris excommunicated him and his followers.

During the reign of Charles VI, the English, the Burgundians and the Armagnac faction took their turn in ill-treating and killing the people of France. The Parisians suffered most, and the Armagnacs were the worst offenders. The merchants of the Halles preferred to be put to ransom by the English and the Burgundians, and the Armagnacs used to say to them, "If it were the English or the Burgundians you would not complain so bitterly."

The Armagnacs wore armbands. They wanted, as a chronicler put it, to enrol the saint, and went to Saint-Eustache and put a band round the arm of his statue. A young Parisian pulled off the band, then destroyed it. The Armagnacs cut off his hands and banished him from the capital. In May 1418, when the Burgundians entered

Paris, many Armagnacs were massacred. The overjoyed people of the Halles rose against the defeated foe, women and children calling them treacherous dogs while they were put to the sword.

Their hands still dripping with the blood of the Armagnacs, the parishioners of Saint-Eustache formed the confraternity of Saint-André. Its members wore garlands of roses. Their purpose was to butcher the prisoners who were behind lock and key in the several prisons of Paris. With the shout of "Kill the Armagnac dogs!" the brotherhood, followed and assisted by their women and children, burst open the prison gates. Great carnage took place inside. They murdered the Armagnac prisoners in the prisons of Saint-Eloy, For l'Evêque, Saint-Magloire, Saint-Martin-des-Champs and the Temple. They were a tough lot, the good humoured people of the Halles.

The Provost of Paris tried to stop the slaughter, but they answered him, "In spite of your justice, sir, your pity and your motives, God curse all who feel for those false Armagnac traitors." They were as good as their words. In less then twelve hours, five hundred and eighteen prisoners were killed, among them five bishops, several magistrates, Chancellor de Marle and the Constable of Armagnac, for whom they made an armband out of his own skin.

The address of the Church of Saint-Eustache is 2 rue du Jour. This is a short street of wholesale butchers, and the gutters often flow with blood, though nowadays only for a legitimate reason. In the old days it skirted the Enceinte of Philippe-Auguste and was named rue Raoul Raisolle.

The Place du Pillori du Roi was in the centre of the Carreau de la Halle, as the Halles Centrales were known until 1775. From the thirteenth century onwards, butter, cheese and bread, laid out on straw, were sold in the Carreau. Fish was laid on wooden boards, hence the fishmarket was known as Parquets.

The Royal Executioner, who lived in the House of the Pillory, received—indeed, collected in person—the revenues for the booths and sites of the Carreau. Followed by his lackeys, he took the rent from every vendor, and as each stallholder paid, a lackey marked the back of his smock with a chalk, the colour of which was changed every day.

Between the pillory and the gibbet stood a high stone cross, beside which bankrupts and debtors received their green bonnets from the executioner. The pillory, which was inside a one-storey-high tower with casement windows, consisted of a wooden post and frame, fixed on a platform raised several feet from the ground. In the centre of the platform was placed an iron wheel full of holes, into which were pushed the heads of the "patients" who on market days spent three hours there for the edification of the populace. Every half hour the wheel turned, and the patients, of course, with it. The practice was abolished by Louis XVI.

The first pillory was built in the thirteenth century. The gibbet was often in use. Even an executioner perished on it. In 1418, Capeluche, Royal Executioner who had struck the Duc de Bourgogne, a Child of France, was hanged in the Place du Pillori; he himself explained to his late assistant how to set about his task.

On April 1, 1516, Fleurant, another executioner, beheaded a condemned man rather clumsily, having several times to strike his blows. The awful sufferings of the victim caused indignation among the onlookers, who started stoning the executioner. The petrified man rushed down into the cave under the pillory, to which the populace set fire, burning him to death. A new pillory had to be erected.

Jean Montagu, Superintendent of Finance to Charles V and Charles VI, was beheaded in the Halles on October 17, 1409, and his body hanged at Montfaucon, a locality between La Villette and the Buttes-Chaumont, then outside Paris, famous for its gibbet erected in the thirteenth century. On November 12, 1411, were executed Colinet de Pirex and his six accomplices for having let the Armagnacs cross the bridge at Saint-Cloud which they should have defended. Five of the traitors were beheaded, the sixth hanged;

Pirex himself was drawn and quartered, and what was left of him hung from the gallows. The heads of the accomplices were exposed on spikes in six different places in the Halles.

The most spectacular execution was that of Jacques d'Armagnac, Duc de Nemours, which took place on August 4, 1477. He had been judged by Parliament for lese-majesty to Louis XI, who was not a man with whom to trifle. Nemours awaited the day of his execution in an iron cage in the Bastille. The preparations took eight days and a large crowd camped out in the Halles so as not to miss the entertainment. On August 4 the heat was intense. Taken from the iron cage, Nemours was hoisted on a horse caparisoned in black, then led to the Halles. The fishmarket was hung with black cloth. It had been scrubbed with vinegar to remove the smell of fish. There Nemours made his confession, while a meal of wine, white bread and pears was served to the officers of the King and the gentlemen of Parliament. After Nemours had received absolution, he was led to the gibbet and beheaded. By order of Louis XI, Nemour's two young sons were tied to the scaffold so as to be the first to receive their father's blood.

With lighted torches, one hundred and fifty Cordeliers (Franciscans) approached the gallows, and the bleeding remains were put into a coffin. Then chanting De Profundis, they carried the coffin to their church on the Left Bank (now 15-21 rue de l'Ecole de Médicine). The unfortunate sons were led back to the Bastille where they were fustigated once a week and had a tooth torn out once a month. One went mad and died in prison; the other was released and later killed in some obscure battle.

The people of the Halles loved their church, but also their amusements. Their Sunday entertainment was going to the Théâtre de l'Hôtel de Bourgogne in the rue Mauconseil, which they rightly regarded as their theatre since it was in their district. Vespers in Saint-Eustache had to end at three o'clock to give them time to walk to the theatre. That tradition dates back to the end of the sixteenth century when Jean du Pourtalais, an actor of the Hôtel de Bourgogne, beat the drum announcing the play too near the church walls. The priest objected. The following Sunday the actor behaved even more rashly, beating the drum during the sermon. Annoyed at the disturbance, the priest raised his voice; the drum beat louder and the congregation lost interest in the sermon. The priest sallied out and said to Pourtalais, "How dare you drum while I preach?"

"Who authorised you to preach after the play has begun?" Pourtalais riposted.

The congregation left the church and gathered round, enjoying every second of the argument. When it became heated, the priest drew a knife with which he split the drum. He turned back to continue the sermon. The actor ran after him and pushed the drum over his head. Retaining his dignity, the priest entered the church and told a deacon to free him. Then he looked round. Not one member of the congregation was left: they were all at the theatre. Next Sunday, services finished at three sharp, and thereafter no drum beat outside Saint-Eustache before the end of vespers.

The best loved priest of Saint-Eustache was called Merlin, who before his death called the fishwives to his sickbed and recommended his nephew, who was also a priest, as his successor. The Archbishop of Paris designated another priest for the position, which so enraged the people that they stopped him from entering the Halles. This happened during the reign of Louis XIII, whose Queen was Anne of Austria. Soldiers were sent to escort the new priest into the church, but the public resisted, and since the parishioners were known for their temper, the soldiers withdrew. (The Halles were always treated with leniency in the days of the Kings.) The parishioners had won, but they had no priest.

The fishwives of the Halles had their own corporation, and were officially known as the Dames des Halles. Vulgarly, they were called poissardes. They did not enjoy a good reputation; they were noisy, foul-mouthed, jealous of their privileges, and not loath to fight. The police often had to warn them. A police ordinance dated August 22, 1738, threatened them with large fines and prison if they continued insulting the passersby. The Ladies of the Halles took no notice. They were privileged to go in a body to congratulate the King, the Queen and the royal Princes, and to present the monarch with a bunch of flowers when a Child of France was born, or on the occasion of a royal marriage or a victory; also on New Year's Day, when they were served with a huge dinner, presided over by a Court official who gave them a money present in the King's name. When Saint-Eustache found itself without a priest, they decided to put their case before Anne of Austria.

When those hefty women came into the august presence, one of them said in a loud, excited voice, "Our good priest Merlin named his nephew as his successor. In any case, the Merlins have always been the parish priests of Saint-Eustache, son following in the father's footsteps." The Queen laughed, then referred them to the Archbishop, who did not give in until the population of the Halles was on the point of revolt. Thus was the nephew appointed parish priest.

Nowadays, on New Year's Day, the Dames des Halles bring their bunch of flowers to the President of the Republic and are duly photographed for the press.

The shop at 2 rue Sauval, known as the Pavillon des Singes, belonged to Jean Poquelin, Upholsterer to the King. Above the shop on January 15, 1633, was born his son Jean-Baptiste. Eleven years later the upholsterer bought another house at the corner of the rue des Petits Piliers, which disappeared when the new pavilions were constructed in the last century, and the rue Jean-Gilles (today rue de la Réale), where he moved with his family. His son, though hereditary Upholsterer to the King, did not follow in his father's footsteps, but went on the stage, taking the name of Molière. Yet he was buried as Jean-Baptiste Poquelin.

Molière died on February 17, 1673, his last performance being in *Le Malade imaginaire*. Because of their immoral profession, actors were not buried in consecrated ground; none the less Molière received the sacrament of Extreme Unction. Two nuns from Annecy were staying, guests of the actor, his wife and their daughter, in his house at 40 rue de Richelieu. The Archbishop of Paris, François de Harlay de Champvallon, did not know how best to act. Molière headed the King's troupe of players, and the King had admiration and affection for him, yet an actor remained excommunicated even in death. The parish priest of Saint-Eustache refused to have the funeral service in his church, though Molière had been one of his parishioners. In vain the Abbé Benjamin, Molière's confessor, declared that he had died a good Christian. The priest remained adamant and the Archbishop did not force the issue.

Armande, Molière's wife, Michel Baron, Molière's pupil, and the Abbé Benjamin went to Versailles to see Louis XIV, who was well acquainted with Saint-Eustache, where he had made his first communion. The argument they put to the King was that the parish priest of Saint-Eustache was denying justice to Jean-Baptiste Poquelin, Upholsterer-Valet to His Majesty, therefore a Crown official. In short, the priest was showing lack of respect for the King. Louis XIV "recommended" to the Archbishop that Molière be given a Christian burial.

"We have," the Archbishop notified the priest of Saint-Eustache, "given permission for the late Molière to be buried according to Christian rites in the cemetery of his parish, on condition that it should be without pomp, with only two priests and not during daylight. No solemn religious service is to be permitted in the parish or anywhere else."

Molière was buried on the night of Tuesday, February 21. An immense crowd assembled in front of the house in the rue de Richelieu, which frightened Armande, who, on the advice of her friends, threw a hundred gold coins through the window, begging the people to pray for the soul of her husband. She spoke in so touching a voice that the cortège was able to move off in respectful silence. The coffin was accompanied by a hundred torch-bearers.

As the procession reached the Halles, an onlooker enquired who was being buried. "Molière," a fishwife replied.

"Monsieur Molière to you," shouted one of her colleagues from her window.

In the year 1684 Paris was full of strange rumours. Within four months twenty-six young men between the ages of seventeen and twenty-five had disappeared. Gossip had it that they had been killed by assassins in the pay of some foreign princess who, on her doctor's recommendation, took a bath of blood every day to help cure the liver ailment from which she suffered. The story reached the ears of Louis XIV who spoke to de La Reynie, his police lieutenant, who in turn put one of his agents called Lecoq on the case. Lecoq had a smart son, a broad-shouldered, intelligent fellow of the right age. Father decided to use his son as the bait. L'Eveillé, as the son was nicknamed, was dressed up as a rich young man; he had a gold chain round his hat, and two gold watches protruded from the pockets of his silk breeches.

L'Eveillé strolled along the streets, the quays, and visited the gardens of the Tuileries and Luxembourg. On the fifth day he saw a remarkably pretty girl, accompanied by an old woman, in the Tuileries. They entered into conversation, then the duegna took him apart and told him in a whisper that the girl was the illegitimate daughter of a Polish prince and a milliner of the rue Saint-Denis. The prince had been murdered by brigands during a journey to Poland, and the girl had inherited all his substantial worldly goods. The old woman suggested that L'Eveillé should marry her.

The young man said he was the son of a rich physician and it was arranged that he should meet the old woman that same night after dark outside the church of Saint-Germain-l'Auxerrois, when she would introduce him to the girl's mother. In fact, she took him to the rue Courtalon in the Halles. There was no mother, only the girl, who received him in "deshabillé galant". She was such a lovely sight that he forgot all about his mission. His father and his men were outside the house, awaiting his signal. The son was too busy cuddling and kissing.

The princess left the room, promising to return. L'Eveillé was intrigued by a screen, which he tried to move but which seemed to be nailed to the floor. He shook it hard, and it collapsed, revealing a wardrobe which he threw open. There on twenty-six silver salvers lay twenty-six human heads. Worried by the silence in the house, the father and his men burst in; and just in time, for the girl had reappeared, accompanied by six armed bandits. The policemen swiftly disarmed them.

The girl belonged to a business association run by a rich Englishwoman, who was never caught. Young men were enticed to the house and killed. Their heads were cut off, and sent, dried and embalmed, to Germany, where they were used for the study of phrenology. The bodies were sold to medical students in Paris.

The so-called princess, the duegna and their henchmen were sentenced to death and hanged.

The Halles wake up when others sleep. The maraîchers (market gardeners) in their huge two-wheeled carts used to be the first to arrive; the meat porters began work soon after midnight; and all the odd hands needed by the Belly of Paris were hired long before daybreak. It has always been the custom of the Halles for goods and work to be paid for on the spot and in cash, so there was plenty of ready money. Already in the Middle Ages, the Halles were famous for their cheap eating places, open all night. They drew the reveller, the crook, the deserter, the escaped convict and all who preferred darkness to light. Prostitutes were part and parcel of the way of life. The night was theirs. Those in the Halles were the cheapest in Paris. Some of them would give themselves for even a plate of soup and boiled beef. (The tradition of the low sums paid to prostitutes in the Halles has not died out. A streetwalker, say, of the Madeleine district, who there would accept nothing under 60 francs, drops her price to one-third if she goes to the Halles to add a little more to her earnings.)

A porter received a tip every time he delivered meat, and it was by no means rare to spend part of it on a woman between errands. In that noise, bustle and gaiety, the prostitute felt at home. Besides, if business were bad she could pick up vegetables fallen from a basket or a bit of offal dropped from a panier. At dawn the prostitutes withdrew, for at dawn came the Dames des Halles to open their stalls and booths. The fishwives were warm-hearted, willing, generous women, always ready for a temporary husband or lover. The prostitutes would have had little chance with them around.

Restif de La Bretonne liked strolling in the Halles—naturally at night. That assiduous chronicler of Paris-at-night was drawn by all he deplored. He was horrified by the debauchery in the Halles; therefore he could not keep away. He shuddered at the sight of men smoking or sleeping in corners, of fallen girls hobnobbing with cardsharps and billiard players. There were fights, and insults rent the air.

One dark night he caught sight of a fair-haired girl, practically the prisoner of an old bawd trying to ply her with eau-de-vie. The girl refused, the bawd insisted. "You both come with me," Restif addressed them sternly, and taking the girl by the hand, he led her out of the Halles. Following hard on their heels, the bawd suggested that he take the girl for himself, but he was too pure a man for that. They crossed over to the Left Bank, where lived the Marquise. (This good lady whose name was never divulged spent her time saving the fallen women whom he brought her. She was probably a figment of his vivid imagination.) The Marquise, having just finished writing a letter, appeared on the balcony. Restif made the usual sign, the door was opened, and the girl was ushered in. Immediately, a bed was made for her, a proof that the Marquise had taken her under her protection. Meanwhile the bawd was still waiting outside in the street.

"Fly," said Restif when he reappeared, "or the Marquise who lives here will have you arrested."

The bawd fled.

On another occasion he saw the Night Watch arresting a woman, who was young and good looking. A crowd surrounded them, and Restif felt pity for her. "I am an honest woman," she protested. "Anyone can check on that. I will give my name and address."

The unfortunate woman was sobbing loudly. Restif, however, knew how to treat the Watch. He was probably himself a police spy. "Gentlemen, I know this lady and will accompany her home," he said. The Watch withdrew. "Why did they arrest you?" Restif asked, walking beside her.

She was, she explained, a married woman. An unpleasant and ugly man had fallen in love with her and, because she scorned him, the man became angry and decided to avenge himself. She had been on business to the Palais Royal, and had run into him as she was crossing the Halles on her way home to the Faubourg Saint-Antoine. He followed her until they met the Watch, when he shouted for all to hear, "Mon Dieu! Here is the Watch! Run!" She stood her ground, however, and the man denounced her to the Corporal of the Watch, saying she had attacked and wanted to rob him. He had then disappeared in the crowd. Restif formed the conclusion that she was an adventuress, but none the less took her home. She lived near the church of Saint-Paul. She told her husband a similar story, though this time she turned the ugly man into a complete stranger whom she had never seen before. She whispered into Restif's ear that it was preferable thus to describe him to her husband.

When Restif left, he found the man himself waiting for him in the street. The man said terrible things about the woman. Restif called him a liar and a calumniator, addressing him from such moral height that the man had no answer. Restif returned to the house, where the woman was now alone, and begged her to tell the truth. She swore that she had already done so.

"You tried to seduce the woman," he said to the man, who was still outside. "If you dare to molest her again, I will speak to her husband."

The man drew his knife.

"You have been judged," Restif said. "Look out, calumniator." Never again was the man seen in the neighbourhood.

One night in the 1750s the Duc de Foix, the Duc de La Ferté and Monsieur de Camardon were in a place of debauch in the Halles. Monsieur de Camardon suggested to the Duc de La Ferté that he should bring his wife to the Halles to have a look at the brothel of either Louise Darquin or Madelon Dupré, both of whom had a high reputation in whoring circles. The Duc de La Ferté did not find the proposition acceptable, in fact considered it in bad taste. His wife, he said, was not the woman to visit places like that. Camardon replied that not only the Duchesse de La Ferté but also the Duchesse de Foix would come to one of the brothels. He was willing to bet 100 pistoles. The bet was accepted.

Five days later Camardon went to see the Duchesse de Foix, who was his sister, to tell her that he had arranged to take Madame de La Ferté to the fair of Saint-Germain, but not a word would be said to her husband. Would his sister join him on the same condition? She agreed, and Camardon set out in a carriage with the two ladies. In the Halles a wheel broke. Camardon offered to take them to the house of a decent bourgeoise with whom he was well acquainted, while they waited for another carriage. He took the duchesses into a clean, well-furnished suite of rooms where they were received by a dignified lady. By messenger Camardon sent a letter to the ducal husbands, asking them to come to the brothel of Madelon Dupré where there were new girls, each one a fresh discovery.

The husbands arrived post haste and nearly collapsed when they saw their wives being entertained by the Dupré. The wives themselves became furious when their outraged husbands explained where they were. Camardon, however, soothed their feelings when he explained why he had taken them there. He beckoned to the Dupré, who at once had an excellent dinner served. Camardon had attended to that detail too.

The duchesses began to enjoy themselves and, after the meal, asked to be shown the girls. The Dupré called them in one by one, and made each walk past the table, displaying her charms; some of them even paraded again at the request of the husbands, who were laughingly scolded by their wives. Before they left, the duchesses congratulated the Dupré on her taste, and for the rest of their lives boasted of the pleasant day they had spent in a brothel.

In the early part of the reign of Louis XV, a market gardener from Orleans introduced red cabbage to the Halles. Nobody seemed to want it. People then were as conservative in their habits as they are today. A cabbage was green and not red. All their lives they had eaten green cabbage, and they would not change their habits just because a maraîcher from Orleans had the stupid idea of growing that red stuff. However, the Orléanais had a genius for publicity. He awaited the right moment.

His opportunity came in 1721 when the old Duchesse d'Orléans, widow of Monsieur, Louis XIV's brother, died. On the next Sunday, as the ladies of society arrived at the still not completely finished church of Saint-Sulpice (begun in 1646, façade finished only in 1745), a lackey in black approached them, handing each a sealed envelope and announcing in a mournful voice, "Her Royal Highness the Duchesse d'Orléans died last night. With her last breath she charged me to hand a letter to each of her friends who comes today to Saint-Sulpice."

There was one lady who could not resist looking at the letter during Mass. On her knees, she tore it open, and with bowed head surreptitiously read the contents.

"Tender friend," the letter said, "I cannot render a better and more valuable service than to leave you my favourite recipe on how to use red cabbage in cooking.

"Cook a medium sized red cabbage in four pints of bouillon with two slices of cooking apple and an onion stuck with clove, and add two glasses of good red wine. Sprinkle generously with spices and let it simmer for several hours."

The letter was signed, "Charlotte Elizabeth of Bavaria, Duchesse d'Orléans."

The lady tittered, for it was the sort of last gift that one might expect from a German princess. The other ladies could resist no longer, and read their letters too. They were identical. Of course, there was no lackey in black at the door when they came out.

The "Chou rouge à la d'Orléans" made the maraîcher's fortune. The story reached Versailles, the King tasted the red cabbage and grew to like it, and it was to become one of Madame de Pompadour's favourite dishes, which she often prepared herself for the King.

II

The Halles II

The Church of the Innocents was built in the twelfth century, and though it was demolished in 1786, the church and the adjoining cemetery, which was condemned at the same time, remain the symbol of Paris of the Middle Ages. Their memory seems to lift one back into the dark alleyways that twisted round the church, the cemetery, the charnel house and the arcades, and to conjure up a picture of Death leading the way in a Danse Macabre to the grave, kicking his legs with equal gusto whether his partner was mighty or poor.

The fifteen arcades on the site of numbers 1, 3, 5, 7 and 9 of the rue de la Ferronerie were painted in their whole length with frescoes representing the Danse Macabre. They were known as the Arcades des Charniers. The first charnel house was built in the fourteenth century. It was several times rebuilt, the last occasion being when the rue de la Ferronerie was reconstructed around 1668.

There were fifteen frescoes, seventeen with the introduction and the conclusion, and each contained two groups, each group consisting of two figures, one of them invariably Death with his grinning skull. Death was in animated conversation with thirty living creatures: in the first with the Pope, in the second with the

Emperor, in the next with the Cardinal, then the King, the Patriarch, the Constable, the Archbishop, the Knight, the Bishop, the Squire, the Abbé, the Magistrate, the Schoolmaster, the Burgher, the Canon, the Merchant, the Carthusian, the Sergeant, the Monk, the Usurer, the Physician, the Lover, the Lawyer, the Minstrel, the Parish Priest, the Labourer, the Cobbler, the Child, the Clerk, and finally the Hermit. Under each picture were verses containing the dialogue between Death and the living person. The verses were by Jean Gerson, Chancellor of the University of Paris. The frescoes were painted in vivid colours.

Paradoxically, the cemetery was the hub of life in the Halles. People on their way to the Carreau stopped with their beasts, lovers met beside the tombs, and, in spite of the putrid smell, fashionable folk took their evening stroll within the high walls that Philippe-Auguste had thrown round the churchyard.

Not only the parishioners of the Holy Innocents but also those of the adjoining parishes were buried in the cemetery. Most churches dumped their dead there. The dead belonged mostly to the poorer orders. From the sixth century onwards, the privileged classes were buried in their own parish churches, or in the chapels of abbeys, priories, convents, colleges, seminaries and hospitals. The Cemetery of the Innocents in general catered for those who were thrown into the fosses communes, the paupers' graves, each grave, shaped like a long trench, remaining open until it was full. The pestilential stench can be imagined. It was said, in praise of the cemetery, that its earth was of such excellence that it devoured a corpse in nine days. There were those who maintained that it took only twenty-four hours. Louis de Beaumont, Bishop of Paris, who died in 1492, insisted in his will that earth from the Cemetery of the Innocents be placed in his coffin.

The fosses communes were about sixteen to twenty feet deep. The dead lay in them, covered in shrouds. They could not afford coffins. When the trenches were full, earth was shovelled on the bodies and when the bones had been eaten dry they were taken to the charnel house. The galleries and cloisters all served the same purpose. The empty ditches were filled in, then new paupers' graves were dug. And so it went on. Each patch was either part of a grave or would soon become so. In winter the criminals and ruffians of the cours des miracles (thieves' kitchens) used to warm themselves by burning bones in the cemetery. As if emphasis were needed, a marble skeleton sculptured by Germain Pilon stood in the middle of the cemetery. Neither bones nor stench deterred the crowds. Haberdashers had booths under the arcades; public letter-writers sat on the tombs, waiting for customers; and prostitutes hung around for the same reason. The bereaved, after all, needed consolation.

Women who wanted to retire from the world often took up their abode in the cells of the Church of the Innocents. Each cell was walled up after the recluse had entered, leaving only a small aperture through which she could contemplate either the church or the cemetery, depending on the site of her cell. Once a day a few crumbs were pushed in through the hole. Once in, you stayed for life. Alix la Bourgotte, a nun of the Hospital of Sainte-Catherine, entered a cell of the Innocents in 1420 in which she died forty-six years later. Louis XI paid for her tombstone in the cemetery, and the epitaph ended with:

> Elle trépassa céans en son séjour
> Le dimanche vingt-neuviesme jour,
> Mois de juin, mil quatre cent soixante et six.
> Le doux Jésus la mette en Paradis.

The record goes, however, to Agnès du Rochier, daughter of a rich Paris merchant who, in 1403, was walled up in a cell of the Church of Sainte-Opportune nearby in the Place Sainte-Opportune. (The Church was demolished in 1790.) She remained thus entombed from the age of eighteen to her death at the ripe age of ninety-eight.

Not all who were walled up chose that existence because of their devoutness. Renée de Vendômois, who in the reign of Charles VIII married the Seigneur de Souidai, fell in love with one of the

King's archers whom she loved with such fierce passion that she had her husband murdered. Parliament condemned her to death but Anne de Beaujeu, the King's sister and Regent of France, changed the punishment to perpetual reclusion in a cell of the Innocents, where she remained until her death.

"In the name of Our Lord and the Blessed Virgin, let me speak with you!" cried a man from the cemetery as Henri IV rode past in his coach. The man was François Ravaillac who had several times tried to have speech with his King.

Ravaillac was the son of humble parents. Born at Angoulême in 1578, he was as a child already drawn to religion, and was happier in church than in his father's cottage. He wanted to become a priest but his parents' resources were inadequate; they lived mostly on the alms of the neighbours. The son had to earn his living. He started as a valet de chambre, in time he managed to set up as a petty provincial solicitor, "solliciteur de procès", and he also taught children to read and write. He was thrown into prison by creditors. He had visions in his cell, and when he came out he sought to join the Society of Jesus, but was rejected. He took to writing madrigals and sonnets.

Slowly, he reached the conclusion that it was his destiny to save the Pope from the convert from Navarre who now ruled France and who sooner or later was bound to declare war on His Holiness. He, poor François Ravaillac, was sent by Heaven to enact the part of the Church's principal champion and protector. He made no secret of his views and spoke of them to all and sundry. He went to Paris with the half-formed intention to kill Henri IV. But, by temperament, he was no murderer. He appeared in the Louvre and asked to be admitted into the King's presence. His request was refused; he insisted, and was thrown out. He came back, and the Marquis de La Force ordered that the strange, uncouth fellow should under no condition be admitted. The King was within earshot and said to the Marquis, "Do not treat him badly." Ravaillac left, ready to return to Angoulême, but in a tavern in the Halles he had overheard some priests and soldiers discussing the King. They had, quite wrongly in fact, thought that his conversion was only skin-deep and that he might one day turn against the Pope. In Angoulême Ravaillac remembered that conversation and decided that it was his duty to return to Paris to save the Pope from the King.

The angel of revenge arrived in Paris unarmed, but when he was refused a room at the inn of the Cinq-Croissants in the vicinity of the Hospital of the Quinze-Vingt near the Porte Saint-Honoré, he picked up a knife from a table and hid it on his person. He hung around the Cemetery of the Innocents, called to the King when he drove by and made other efforts to see him. What he really wanted was to explain to him that he was misguided, that he should repent and leave the Pope alone. As he found no opportunity to speak to the King, he decided once again to leave. He took the road to Angoulême. (All his journeys were made on foot.) When he reached Etampes, he stopped before a Crucifix at the entrance of the town. The Crucifix spoke to him and told him that he was shirking his duty. So Ravaillac turned round and retraced his steps to Paris.

There had already been fifteen attempts on the life of Henri IV. In spite of his vitality and laughter, he had the presentiment that he would die by the hand of an assassin. Foreboding lay heavily on him on the morning of May 14, 1610. Sully, his minister, was ill. He desired to see Sully, yet he could not bring himself to leave the Louvre.

"You must not go," the Queen (Marie de Medici) begged him. None the less he set out for the Arsenal to visit Sully. "I have much to tell him," was the reason he gave.

Ravaillac, who had spent the night at the Inn of the Trois-Pigeons at the corner of the rue Saint-Honoré and the cul-de-sac Saint-Vincent (now rue Saint-Roch), was already roaming the Halles.

The royal carriage was an open one with its floor so near the ground that nobody could have crawled under it. Above it, supported by eight pillars, was a canopy. The curtains were thrown outside the carriage and almost brushed the ground as it bumped along. The Duc d'Espernon sat on the King's left, in front of him by the doors were the Duc de Montbazon and the Comte de Roquelaure, next the Marquis de La Force, the Maréchal de Lavardin, Monsieur de Liancourt, the Marquis de Mirebeau and finally the principal squire. Thus the carriage was pretty full. The King had his arm around the shoulder of the Duc d'Espernon. The coachman asked the King which way he wanted to go to the Arsenal.

"Go past the Cross of Trahoir," replied the King, "then through the streets of l'Oratoire, Saint-Honoré and de la Ferronerie."

The carriage arrived at the end of the rue Saint-Honoré and turned into the rue de la Ferronerie, where it had, however, to stop because of a cart loaded with straw which had broken down and which almost took up the width of the street in front of the cabaret known as the Salamandre. One of the two footmen who walked beside the coach had dropped behind to tie his garter. The King was reading a letter from the Comte de Soissons which Espernon had handed him. Trying to pass the cart, the coachman drew close to the shops which were tenanted by ironmongers. Before one of the shops (now 8 rue de la Ferronerie), which had for its sign a crowned heart pierced with an arrow, was a mounting-block, and from it jumped Ravaillac, who, with the stolen knife, struck the King between the armpit and the left breast. Then he struck again, this time the knife reaching the King's heart. The Duc de Montbazon clasped him in his arms. "Sire, what is it?"

"It is nothing," said the King. "It is nothing," he repeated, almost inaudibly.

France lost a great king and Ravaillac was executed a fortnight later.

Louis-Sébastien Mercier, the author of *Tableau de Paris* and many other works, often repaired to the Cemetery of the Innocents. Mercier evokes Paris of the second half of the eighteenth century with the same force as does Restif de La Bretonne, but while Restif speaks mostly of himself, Mercier sees only Paris. He writes with such detachment of his native city that one imagines him as a foreign visitor, preferably a Swiss, glaring at Paris from the outside, uninfluenced by any affection.

The public letter-writers of the Charniers, he says, had to lead the lives of theologians, though they were more useful because they were the keepers of the tender secrets of the servant girls whose declarations of love they put to paper. Theirs was no easy life. In winter they blew on their frozen fingers; in summer they sweated under their bob-wigs, and were surrounded by the evil smell and the bones of the dead. They had to provide ink, paper, wax, grammar, syntax and style, all for 5 sous. A petition to the King or the Ministers cost 12 sous, for the style had to be more distinguished than in a letter, say, to a shepherd in a distant village, who in any case would need the help of the local priest to find out what his loved one's heart was murmuring.

The public letter-writers, Mercier observed, were the Ministers' most diligent correspondents. He saw no handwriting but theirs on a Minister's writing table. At the beginning of the reign of Louis XVI, the ordinary people thought they had a king after their heart (they were not far wrong), so petitions were sent by the thousands. When the course of events estranged the King from his people, the public letter-writers of the Charniers, who during the boom had bought new bob-wigs, now found their stalls deserted by petitioners. They turned back to the love-sick servant girls whom they had neglected while the going was good.

Mercier, watching the scribes at work in the stench of the cemetery and the charnel house, was fascinated by the servant girls treading their way through putrid bones, past gaping graves with rotting bodies, to whisper to the writers their declarations of love.

The inhabitants of the Halles had clamoured for over two centuries to have the Cemetery of the Innocents closed. A decree of the Parliament of Paris, dated January 1, 1766, forbade burials inside the town, but this stopped nobody from dumping their dead in the

Cemetery of the Innocents. However, in the year 1785 a householder in the rue de la Lingerie went into his cellar, where he found rats devouring a corpse. He turned on his heels, wanting to get away from the stench as quickly as possible. A rat bit him as he escaped, and the unfortunate man died within two days. When the police arrived, they filled their nostrils with scented cotton wool before venturing into the cellar. The foundations of the building had given way under the impact of the loose earth of the cemetery, which, because of the continuous digging, had moved as if shifted by a minor earthquake. Among the foundation stones a number of corpses was found in the company of regiments of rats. In short, the dead had moved back with the earth into human dwellings. The Council of State condemned the church and the cemetery, and that, one might say, put the final stop to the Paris of François Villon.

In January 1786, the demolition of the church began. The bones of the dead were taken to the quarry of Montsouris beyond the Barrier of Saint-Jacques, and were inhumed on the Left Bank beside a house known as la Maison de la Tombe-Issoire. The galleries of the Charniers were turned into shops, the soil of the cemetery was carted away and the ground filled with fresh earth. It became the Market of the Innocents (of the Charniers only two arcades remain, 11-13 rue des Innocents) and to the Square des Innocents the Fountain of Pierre Lescot and Jean Goujon was transferred from the corner of the rues aux Fers (now rue Berger) and Saint-Denis.

A gentleman called John Scott, who was to write a book entitled *Picturesque Views of Paris* with drawings by Frederic Nash, visited the Market of the Innocents in 1818. "It is here that the costume and manners of the lower orders of Paris, the gaieties and gallantries of porters, footmen, cook-maids and market girls may be contemplated." He admired the fountain in the middle of the Square des Innocents because "of that want of superfluous ornament which often distinguishes the French school".

The fountain was erected in 1551 according to the designs of Pierre Lescot and Jean Goujon. It is supposed to have replaced an ancient one of the thirteenth century, mentioned in an old agreement between Philippe le Hardi and the Chapter of Saint-Merri. The fountain originally had only three arcades, but when it was moved into the Market, Augustin Pajou was employed to execute a fourth, and "its great merit is proved by the impossibility of distinguishing which of the four is the supplement." The lions and basin were added after the move, and "are not so much esteemed as the other parts of the monument; the water by which the fountain is fed, and falls finely down the slope of the steps, comes from the Canal de l'Ourcq." Goujon had placed a naiad: Pajou added three of his own. "The Lions assist the cascade by vomiting from their open mouths torrents of the foaming liquid." The fountain is still in the Square des Innocents, as also is an arch of the cemetery: the first, a comparative newcomer; the second, one that was left behind.

The Church of Saint-Merri in the rue Saint-Martin belongs also to the district of the Halles. It escaped the fate of the Church of the Innocents because its cemetery was suppressed in 1520, the parishioners being buried thereafter in the Cemetery of the Innocents.

In 1832 a barricade was erected in front of Saint-Merri, a few yards from the intersection of the rues Saint-Martin and Aubry-le-Boucher. The red flag floated on the barricade and Maréchal Soult mobilised the garrison of Paris and the Garde Nationale to restore order. The revolutionaries were not many in number, and the rising lasted only from June 5 to 6. June 5 was the day of the burial of the popular General Lamarque, who died from cholera, his last gesture being to kiss the sword given to him by the Bonapartist officers of the Hundred Days. That apparently was as good an excuse as any to rise against King Louis-Philippe. The rising was swiftly put down by the troops, and only the barricade of Saint-Merri still held out on June 6. An old hand of the July Revolution, whose surname was Jeanne, led the men and threw back ten assaults by the military. Shots were fired from windows and from behind doors. The bells of Saint-Merri tolled the whole day long. At six in the evening the troops attacked from three different directions. Jeanne and his men tried to force their way through the attackers, but most of them were bayonetted to death. For decades the district bore marks of the fighting.

The parents of Georges Cain, the curator of the Musée de Carnavalet from 1897 to 1918 who wrote delightful books on Paris, had known an old lady who lived near Saint-Merri. She trembled with fear whenever she went past the door of the tenant who lived on the ground floor of her house. Her friends could not understand her persistent fear, and Cain's parents asked for the reason. Many decades before, her husband had fought with the Garde Nationale on that famous June 6, while she, hearing the firing, was at home waiting for him in anguish. Suddenly a man on a stretcher was brought into the house. She rushed downstairs. The wounded warrior was covered with a blanket which she lifted, expecting the worst. It was the ground-floor tenant, wounded in the jaw.

"Oh, what joy," she cried, "that it's only you, Monsieur Vitry."

He never forgave her.

The porters of the Halles, known as Les Forts and also as the seven hundred muscular fellows, belong to a corporation that depends directly on the Préfécture de Police. Each fort has his number and each team its chief. Their fame and the respect that their presence inspires are even greater than those of the Dames des Halles. Their number was usually seven hundred and thirty-five, a hundred and six dedicated to butcher's meat, a hundred to poultry, a hundred and ninety-one to butter, eggs and cheese, fifty-four to fruit and vegetables and a hundred and eighty to fish. The remaining hundred and four were inside the pavilions. (Average figures for the 1920s.) Every fort carries a medal on which is engraved the coat of arms of Paris.

They have always been famous for the pride they take in their work, their good humour, huge appetite and loud laughter. One is struck by their bonhomie, which does not desert them while they carry the heavy carcases. The aprons of the meat porters run with blood, their necks have the muscles of an ox, and one cannot but feel that nothing pleases them more than lifting weights from which most people would shrink. Nowadays they too turn up at the Elysée on New Year's Day, wearing their large hats.

The forts, like all other workers of the Halles, radiate gaiety, and the visitor wonders why they are so conspicuously different from other manual workers, The forts, like the fishwives, have their own —in every sense valid—explanation. They deal with reality. The carcase of a sheep or a panier groaning with turbot exists as an entity. It is not just a cog in some great wheel. It stands on its own and you know what will become of it, whereas the workman in a factory has no connection with the final result. Moreover, the forts work in the open; they are paid after every errand; tips abound, and the eating places and bistrots are at their elbows. They are not herded together, there is no workbench, and each errand is personal to the man who runs it. When he lifts meat off the hook, or has it slung over his shoulder, he expands like a virtuoso waiting for applause.

The lorries are cleared of boxes, often faster than the commission agent expects, so that the tips are generous, and the forts rush off to the bistrots for a drink of muscadet. In this age of doctored wine, the innkeepers of the Halles would not dream of serving the sort of wine that is offered by some of the bars of the boulevards. Only the best will do for the people of the Halles.

In the rue Antoine-Carême used to gather the Hommes Sauvages, who sold herbs, foliage and fern. They were called the Wild Men because their merchandise came direct from suburban gardens, picked generally while the owners were still asleep or while they were absent from home. In this age of supervision and control, the

Hommes Sauvages have mainly disappeared, though there still remain the little old men who walk round the streets, clutching a small bunch of flowers or herbs which nobody seems to buy. As the hours pass, so the flowers wilt and the herbs turn sickly, yet they go on clinging to them until the Halles become deserted under the midday sun. Their bus or métro fare from the suburbs costs more than the money they ask for their withered goods.

The Hommes Sauvages may have gone, but a new, brisker trade has sprung up in the Halles: vendre à la sauvette. This form of trade is based on running away. The vendors, usually Algerians or Tunisians, turn up in the Halles a few minutes before the vegetable stands close, when the greengrocers practically give away their left-over wares. The vendors hire a handcart which they fill with their purchases and push uphill, generally in the direction of Montmartre. They are not of a retiring disposition, but stop in some busy market street, preferably in front of a greengrocer's, shouting their cut-throat prices, pushing cabbages or lettuces under the noses of housewives on their way into the shop. Their price is a quarter of what they would pay in the shop, so trade is brisk and profitable until the irate greengrocer telephones the police. Since the police sirens and the flashing lights of the police cars warn them in time, they bolt, leaving behind the handcart which in any case carries the owner's name who, when notified by the police, will come and fetch it, only to hire it out under the same conditions the next day. It does not amuse the Paris police to confiscate vegetables: they would prefer to catch the vendors themselves, but they are landed as a rule only with the goods, and it is a piteous sight to watch the smart, white-gloved policemen picking up cabbages and cucumbers and, with a gesture of disgust, throwing them inside their vehicle for distribution to the hospitals.

Handcarts are not strictly necessary. You can hold in your arms as many vegetables as you can carry and accost the passersby on the pavement. On Sunday mornings in the rue Montorgeuil the police suddenly appear, and the vendors dash into the rue Etienne-Marcel. A North African, with a policeman hard on his heels, will slow down as he passes a possible customer, and whisper fiercely, "4 francs the lot."

Around the turn of the century, it was the practice of the gendarmes who had caught a deserter from the army to march him through the streets of the Halles before taking him to the military prison. When they reached the rue de la Ferronerie, one of the gendarmes would take the prisoner's cap and pass it round. The tradesmen, porters and fishwives would then fill it with coins, which the gendarme would give to the deserter. Often the poor soldier would burst into tears at the sight of such kindness.

Though deserters are no longer taken through the Halles, the habit of generosity has not died out. When a man comes out of prison and finds his way to the Halles, everybody, including the prostitutes, give him food, drink and money on the understanding that tomorrow he will look for work. If he returns the following night in the hope of being helped again, he will find all hearts and purses closed to him.

In 1810 Napoleon went to the Halles and walked round, contemplating the inadequate number of pavilions, the crowds, the carts jostling each other and the horses practically unable to progress. He turned to Bélanger, the architect of the new cupola of the Halle-au-blé. "I don't like this mess. The place lacks design. There is no discipline here. This market is not worthy of the capital of an empire." In February 1811 he signed a decree concerning the embellishment of Paris. Article thirty-six mentioned the Halles. A vast covered market was to be built, extending from the Market of the Innocents to the existing pavilions, which would be demolished. Nothing came of it. Under Napoleon III were constructed the pavilions that have survived to this day, but soon there were the same crowds, the same lack of design and discipline. Traffic jams became insufferable, long before the coming of the motor lorry. Napoleon's grandiose plan was finally shelved.

Since life is one half-measure after the other, nobody has adopted the Emperor's conception of the Halles. Had his plan been followed, the Halles would not have been condemned to extinction. For the Halles are going. The days of onion soup and chips are numbered, and while the authorities and the Municipal Council debate the future of the terrain, the bulldozers are waiting to erase eight hundred years of history, habits, customs, laughter, courage and gaiety. The meat market is moving to La Villette; fish, vegetables, cheese and fruit to Rungis, near Orly; many of the old houses will come down, bistrots and restaurants will close, and even the girls of the rue de Cygne, who for generations were famous for their large breasts, for only women with voluptuous shapes were accepted in the street, will have to look for a new beat. If you go today to the Halles and speak to the people and ask them what they intend to do after their world has vanished, they change the subject, and you feel as though you are enquiring after the health of a patient in a hospital for incurables.

III

Cabarets, Restaurants, Cafés and Brasseries

Paris has always been the gastronomic centre of France. There is no special kudos in that, for throughout the ages Paris has remained the El Dorado to which all provincials flocked, a French Klondyke. Naturally, since the provincials knew only the cooking of their own regions, they still prepared regional dishes when they cooked in the capital. Hence Paris benefited from the good dishes of the provinces; and as a result, you find in Paris every possible variety of French food. "Why," asks the Parisian, "should I travel when all the fine dishes of France are on my doorstep?" To travel from, say, Nantes to Dijon is expensive and takes time, whereas in Paris you can do that with two tickets d'autobus—culinarily speaking, of course.

In the beginning there were no restaurants. Meals were eaten in the cabarets and hôtelleries, which were taverns, eating houses and inns. The guests sat at the same tables (which were not yet called tables d'hôtes, a refinement that was to come much later). There also were the rôtisseurs, the cook-shops, where food was bought to be taken home.

In the rue de la Huchette, which is still with us in that beehive of old streets between the Quai Saint-Michel and the Boulevard

Saint-Germain, the rôtisseurs were already flourishing in the fourteenth century, though strictly speaking it was the street of the apothecaries: their sign a lamprey. The rôtisseurs were more sought after than the apothecaries. On his return to Italy, Father Bonaventura Calatagirone, General of the Franciscans who was instrumental in the signing of the Treaty of Vervins between Henri IV and Philip II of Spain, spoke glowingly of the cook-shops in the rue de la Huchette, the only marvels, he affirmed, that he had found during his long journey. The Infidel's reactions were no different. The Turks attached to the different Ottoman ambassadors found nothing more agreeable than to go to the rue de la Huchette and inhale the wonderful smells. It was in a cabaret of the rue de la Huchette that the Abbé Prévost d'Exiles wrote *Manon Lescaut.*

The oldest cabaret one knows of was La Pomme de Pin, which opened its doors around 1400 in the Cité on the spot where nowadays one of the pavilions of the Hôtel-Dieu stands, giving on to the rue de la Cité and the rue de Lutèce. François Villon was a client, but Villon was no ideal customer from the cabaretier's point of view, as these lines show:

> C'est bien disné, quand on s'échappe
> Sans débourser pas un denier,
> Et dire adieu au tavernier
> En torchant son nez dans la nappe.

Rabelais also visited it. Boileau, Molière, Racine and La Fontaine often met there. Edmond Beaurepaire described it as a joyous academy, where even the greatest minds could not help getting drunk at least twice a week.

When Guillaume Colletet, academician and poet, was hard up—a frequent occurrence—he wrote flattering poems either to Cardinal de Richelieu or some other powerful patron. One day he asked Desbordes-Gruyn, proprietor of the Pomme de Pin, whether he would give him credit on a poem he intended to write to the Cardinal.

"On condition you finish it tonight," the cabaret-keeper replied.

"If that's the only condition, then serve me at once with your best burgundy."

Colletet got to work and wrote a long and pious poem, entitled *Les Couches sacrées de la Vierge*, which on second thoughts he dedicated to Jean-François de Gondi, first Archbishop of Paris. The prelate was so impressed by the poem that he presented Colletet with a silver statuette of Apollo.

"It's silver all right," Colletet said to Desbordes-Gruyn, "but how can we turn it into the silver you pay with?"

The silver Apollo remained the inn sign till Desbordes-Gruyn's death. The Pomme de Pin survived into the eighteenth century.

A cabaret-keeper needed a certificate from his guild, the municipality and the King's Attorney. The guild had five holidays a year —Easter, Whitsun, Assumption, All Saints and Christmas—when the cabaret-keepers who sold only drink could remain open, but those who served food had to close. Some of the cabarets were outside the Walls like the Hôtel de Stockolm in the rue de Buci, where one dined for 18 sous (100 sous equalled 5 francs), and next door the Hôtellerie de l'Eau in the rue de Bourbon-le-Château, where the price was 20 sous. In the Mouton Blanc near the Cité, Molière, Racine, Boileau, La Fontaine, Lully, Mignard and Dufresnois used to gather, and at 10 rue Childebert (now rue Bonaparte) a wine merchant called Chamfort cooked meals for painters. Two fried eggs there cost 3 sous.

The cabarets, as later the cafés, were generally frequented by people of the same profession or trade. Men like Racine or Boileau would not have entered a cabaret where, for example, tailors drank. In the eighteenth century in the rue de Richelieu, one Charlotte Bourette kept the Café Minerve, patronised by men of letters. She was known as the Tenth Muse because she addressed in verse her literary customers, who replied in kind. One wonders what her verses were like when a glass was smashed or some distinguished man left without settling his bill.

Also in the rue de Richelieu was to be found the Taverne Anglaise, where for the first time in Paris roast beef was served with boiled vegetables. It was very expensive, for boiled potatoes and vegetables were considered a curiosity. Nearby in the Galerie Beaujolais of the Palais Royal at the restaurant called Les Trois Frères Provençaux, General Napoleon Bonaparte and Paul Vicomte de Barras were often present in the days after the Revolution. At the time of the Directoire in the Café Hardy, rue de la Grange-Batelière, déjeuners à la fourchette (cold collations) were served.

The first café in Paris and in the world was established by Procopio dei Coltelli, a Sicilian, in the year 1686 in the rue de l'Ancienne Comédie. The Café Procope is still in the same place, though it has become a restaurant. La Fontaine, Voltaire, Benjamin Franklin, Danton, Robespierre, Bonaparte, Balzac, Victor Hugo, Gambetta, Verlaine and Anatole France were among its clients.

Yet the old cabarets were slow to die, their strength the excellent wines they served. "Mon Dieu, how witty the French are," observed the Prince de Ligne to his companion Count de Poelnitz, as one night they were leaving a Paris cabaret.

"It isn't difficult with the wines they have," the Count answered.

The table d'hôtes was the forerunner of the restaurant, its heyday the second half of the reign of Louis XV. The customers all sat at the same table, and the latecomers were put at the bottom. The meek and the modest fared badly. You needed a strong personality to make your presence felt. The table d'hôtes was the happy hunting ground of overbearing men who learnt quickly to come early and take the best seats at the top of the table. When the meal was served, they took such large helpings that little was left for the well-behaved, modest guests. The strong men knew that those at the lower end of the table would not dare to complain; and they seldom did. The servants, for there were no waiters yet, were under the influence of the bullies, whom they admired in any case, and they saw to it that they got the best morsels and that their glasses were always full. As with food, so with conversation, which mattered so much in the eighteenth century. Those at the top of the table chatted, argued and related anecdotes. Down at the bottom, conversation was carried on in whispers, and even that could meet with disapproval from the top. To broach a subject or start a discussion at the lower end was strictly frowned on. The hard core of the tables d'hôtes victimised foreign visitors who were not versed either in French or table d'hôtes habits. The Germans and the Swiss were the worst sufferers. The English found a simple way round. They sent out for their food and dined in the peace and quiet of their rooms at the inn. For the polite traveller and diner-out, the restaurant came as a gift from above.

According to Reichard's guide book, published in Weimar in 1805, a Parisian called Boulanger in 1767 conceived the new-fangled idea of serving fresh eggs and poultry on separate tables, without cloths. Over the door was written: "Venite ad me omnes qui stomaco laboratis et ego restaurabo vos." From Boulanger's offer to restore their stomachs with food, according to Reichard, the word restaurant originated: a good anecdote though shaky etymology.

The habit of eating in restaurants spread, to the detriment of the cabarets and tables d'hôtes. The food was good and varied. In 1788 an English visitor noted in his diary the bill of fare of the Restaurant Beauvilliers. There were a hundred and seventy-eight different dishes, which included soups, roasts, entrées and puddings. The favourites were fricandeau with spinage, veal en papillotte, choucroute, soused herring, partridge with cabbage, and duckling with white turnip. In short, the sun of gastronomy was already shining on the Paris whose good people were preparing themselves for the Revolution and the Terror.

Prices were similar to those before the First World War; between the reign of Louis XVI and Sarajevo, one paid roughly the same in good restaurants. At Beauvilliers a meal cost about 4 francs, a bottle of Clos-Vougeot or Chambertin or Hermitage came to 4 livres (about 4 francs), and Beauvilliers was considered an expensive restaurant; so much so that in his Guide Book Reichard recommended the traveller to avoid it and to frequent third-class restaurants, where "conversation is pleasant and often edifying."

The Revolution gave restaurants a new impetus. The great houses of the aristocracy were closed and their chefs, if they were lucky not to be despatched in the wake of their masters, found themselves out of work. The fortunate ones opened restaurants on their own which did remarkably well, since the Revolution brought into Paris, and also created, a large number of military men, deputies and officials. Thus were born some of the famous names in the history of gastronomy, like Naudet, Meot, Robert (of Sauce Robert fame) and Véry, whose famous restaurant in the Boulevard Magenta lasted long enough to suffer damage at the end of the nineteenth century from an anarchist bomb. Deharme, another chef of the old order, kept the Marmite Perpétuelle in the rue des Grands-Augustins. The Perpetual Pot simmered for eighty-five years without the fire ever going out. Day and night, juicy capons were cooked in the pot, and as one was taken out, a fresh one took its place. The capons were eaten with coarse salt.

In the rue de la Harpe, Leblanc, also a chef of the old régime, kept a cook-shop-cum-restaurant, his whole ground floor filled with Bayonne hams, even the smallest weighing no less than twenty pounds. The curtains were drawn to keep out the flies, and an enormous black and white cat presided over the hams, its task to keep away the mice. Leblanc was a modern-minded cook in the sense that he despatched his ham pâtés all over France.

However, the true moderniser was Marie-Antoine Carême, perhaps the most gifted of the chefs. He was born in a hut in the rue du Bac, one of twenty-five brothers and sisters. He was still a boy when a pastry cook took him in out of charity. Because he worked hard and seemed intelligent, Robert took him over, eventually passing him on to La Guipière, chef to Murat, King of Naples. La Guipière, to whom Carême dedicated his *Memoirs*, died in the retreat from Moscow, the poor man probably freezing to death while trying to heat a casserole. Carême became Napoleon's cook, then Talleyrand's, and was the head chef at the banquet given in 1814 on the Plain of Vetus for the Allied sovereigns. For the rest of his life he was considered the premier cook of France. For some time he acted as chef to Emperor Alexander I. He revolutionised pastry, which before his time was heavy and, therefore, expensive. By creating the thin, flaky pastry known as pâte à choux, he broke down, as it were, the social barriers, bringing cake within everybody's reach. The heavy, expensive cakes that the working-classes used to chew on Sundays in the guinguettes gave way to the light, cheap choux à la crème, thanks to Carême whose greatest pleasure, as he often declared, was to watch little urchins in the streets devouring pastry made from his recipes. He wrote *Le Patissier royal* in 1825 and *Le Cuisinier parisien* in 1833, the year of his death, when he was forty-nine years old.

For those who could afford little for food, the nineteenth century produced several interesting restaurants, two of which certainly deserve mention.

In the rue de la Gaîté in Montparnasse, the Maison des Acacias had a distinctive renown, for there the food was sold by auction. Neither the plats du jour nor the other dishes were priced; there was no bill of fare; in fact, the prices were left to the clients, the highest bidder receiving each dish. The waiter might bring in a smoking stew and shout, "How much?" Each dish had a reserve on it. "5 sous," the waiter would call, pushing the plate under a hungry customer's chin. The customer might examine it, sniff it, look at it from every angle, eventually perhaps refuse it. "6 sous," someone might call, and after brisk bidding it would be knocked down to, and put before, the most reckless guest. There was only one snag: frequently the dish became cold before the auction finished. As at a sale, the bidding often became acrimonious, in which case the dish was put up again. It was not unknown for the unadventurous to leave the restaurant with an empty stomach.

In the rue du Départ, a street created in 1849 between the Boulevard du Montparnasse and the second Montparnasse Station which was still under construction, a certain Monsieur Cadet, known to his clients as père Cadet, established another restaurant for modest purses, La Grande Californie. It was certainly big, with its four entrances, enormous hangar-like dining-hall, two inner courtyards and a garden. The clientele could not be called distinguished. It included tramps, pickpockets and beggars. Plates, cutlery and glasses were attached by chains to the long tables. The customers sat on low benches, and père Cadet, assisted by his heavily limping wife, gave them copious food inexpensively. Because it was she who collected the money, the clients nicknamed her Mother-Five-and-Three-Make-Eight. They were obliged to leave their hats, coats and parcels in one of the courtyards, for the Cadets refused to have smelly objects indoors. It was also forbidden to cut and chew tobacco in the dining-room. Cadet was a strict believer in hygiene, and La Grande Californie smelt, like a prison, of disinfectant.

It was a self-service restaurant in that the clients lined up before the kitchen, took their food and moved into the dining hangar, where they sat down if there was room, or ate standing. In one of the courtyards cigarettes made of stubs were sold. The usual meal, consisting of soup and braised beef with carrots, cost 3 sous, a sausage 2 sous, and a soup alone 1 sou. Some of the more luxurious dishes came to as much as 4 sous. A journalist asked Cadet how he managed to feed his clients so cheaply. "Quantity is my secret," he replied, and truly enough around three bullocks, ten calves, five or six sheep and thirty rabbits were slaughtered daily by his butchers on the premises. He employed fifty females just to clean the vegetables and peel the potatoes, and over three thousand casks of wine were sold in a year.

Every day Cadet distributed several hundred plates of soup to the needy. He became one of the first mayors of the fourteenth arrondissement. La Grand Californie closed its doors in 1866 to the great regret of its habitués.

In those almost pioneer days of popular restaurants around 1850, an enterprising restaurant-keeper set up his establishment in the rue de la Huchette. He had the original idea of giving free tobacco with meals. He expected thereby to attract a large number of guests. Indeed he did, and was soon ruined.

The cafés evolved too. In the seventeenth century the Parisians gathered on the Pont-Neuf; at the end of the eighteenth in the Palais-Royal; and during the Romantic Period, that is the first half of the nineteenth century, on the Boulevard des Italiens and the Boulevard Montmartre. The boulevard first called Coblenz, then de Gand or des Bains-Chinois, took the definite name of Boulevard des Italiens when the Italian Opera House established itself in the rue Favart on the site of the present Opéra-Comique; its cafés became the centre of attraction of the boulevardiers. After the Baron Haussmann all the inner boulevards became their meeting places and hunting grounds. Only near the Madeleine was there any peace and quiet.

The Café de la Régence and the Café Turc were the meeting places of domino and chess players. Farther out in the Boulevard Bonne-Nouvelle, the Grand Café de France was patronised by billiard players. It had nine tables. The Café de Mulhouse and the Café de l'Europe catered for commercial travellers and tradesmen. The literary gents still went to the Café Procope as in Molière's time, and the bohemians, needless to say, spent their evenings in the Café Momus of *La Vie de Bohème* fame in the rue Saint-Germain-l'Auxerrois.

The financiers, whose number was legion in the Second Empire, patronised the cafés of the rue de la Chaussée d'Antin. The smart set frequented such places as the Café Anglais, the Café de Paris, La Maison Dorée, and the Café Tortoni, especially Tortoni, which had seen the citoyens, the incroyables, the dandys (*sic*) and the lions: fundamentally the same noisy young men, though belonging to different decades. Tortoni had the best ices. Fashionable folk arrived in carriages and were served with ices without having to alight. Not for anything would people of fashion have been seen in the more modest cafés near the Portes Saint-Denis and Saint-Martin.

On the Left Bank the Café d'Orsay in the rue de Lille was the favourite of the officers of the Imperial Guard during the First Empire. It became a literary resort after the Restoration, Alfred de Musset being one of the regulars. He used to get drunk on absinthe. A full tumbler always stood before him. With glassy eyes he would contemplate the beverage, seemingly afraid of it. Lifting the glass to his lips, he would put it down without tasting it. After going through the motion at least five times, with sudden decision he would swallow the lot and call for another. The café owner, a retired butcher, often approached his table, begging him to drink no more, saying it would only harm him. On such an occasion Musset rose from the table, and leaning against the wall, said in a contemptuous voice:

"Back to the meat stall!"

Then he sank back on the banquette.

With the advent of gas lighting, cafés with gas lamps became the fashion, even in the outlying districts. In Batignolles, before it was attached to Paris to become part of the seventeenth arrondissement, the Café du Gaz was the most popular. Of course, smart people did not visit suburban cafés, leaving them to small rentiers, retired army officers and tradesmen.

The sedate customers took soft drinks or coffee, known as gloria if served with a drop of brandy; in such cafés wine and alcohol were not drunk except in some such form. "Family liqueurs," inoffensive sickly stuff, were also served, and bavaroise with milk was the only food available. Smoking was prohibited.

As the century approached its end, so café habits changed. By the 1890s women appeared in cafés, not only on Sundays with their families but on weekdays too and alone, though always wearing hats. In the cheaper cafés and brasseries, men did not remove their hats; they smoked cigars, which were more favoured than cigarettes. Posters covered the walls and in spite of the spirit of the Revanche, frankfurters and Munich beer were in demand. Choucroute à toutes heures came into its own. (Surely from that derives the hackneyed story of the café that advertised five o'clock tea at all hours.)

In working-class estaminets, cider was chiefly drunk; the customers kept their caps on. Vermouth, coffee, absinthe and hot wine all cost 2 sous. In short, the cabarets, whose offsprings were cafés, restaurants, estaminets and brasseries, had reverted to type. They had again become what they had been in the beginning: popular drinking places, and not as select as in the seventeenth, eighteenth and early nineteenth centuries. Where they were different was in the matter of publicity, which in the old days was unnecessary.

The Café Foy in the rue de la Chaussée d'Antin, managed by a Monsieur Nigaud before the Bignon brothers made it famous, had among its clients Bouffé, director of the Théâtre du Vaudeville. He was nicknamed "C'est pour moi" ("It's on me"), because, when it came to paying, he had his drinks chalked up. He drank large quantities of champagne. Came the day when Nigaud asked him to settle his enormous, outstanding bill, adding that he would not be asking for it if the café had been doing well, but alas that was not the case. Bouffé said that Nigaud's trouble was that he did not know how to sell himself. He needed publicity, and Bouffé offered to take charge. He would invite the best known journalists in Paris, and do all the talking. Nigaud would only have to provide adequate food and drink for the distinguished company. Deeply moved, Nigaud thanked Bouffé and put the bill back into his pocket.

Bouffé was as good as his word. A few nights later, after the show at the Vaudeville, he appeared in the café with a group of his down-at-heel actors, whom he introduced as famous journalists. Nigaud served them with an excellent meal; and champagne flowed till five in the morning, when he sent them home in fiacres, at his expense. In the morning he bought every Paris newspaper, but of course there was not one word about the Café Foy. He complained bitterly to Bouffé. Were they really such influential men?

"Didn't you recognise them?" Bouffé asked. "The tall one was Théophile Gautier, the bearded one Emile de Girardin, the one with the long moustache Alexandre Dumas, the little old man Nestor Roqueplan, the fat man who sang so lustily was, of course, Lamartine, the giant Eugène Sue himself, and the one who looked the very picture of health Dr Véron in person. What more do you want? Aren't they illustrious enough for you?"

"But they haven't written about me."

"You should invite them more often."

"Never. I'd go bankrupt if I did," said Nigaud, holding out the bill.

"C'est pour moi," said Bouffé, waving it away.

The brasseries de femmes were at their height between the Franco-Prussian and the First World Wars. They were not so much brasseries as unauthorised brothels. There were two categories, one for men, who were mostly soldiers, commercial travellers and tradesmen, the other for Lesbians. The waitresses wore low-cut bodices and skirts above the knees. As a prelude, the client ordered a drink from the waitress he fancied. When she brought the drink she sat down beside him. There were no silly games or pretensions. Once the price was settled, they went either down to the basement or up to the first floor, depending on where a room was free; the more discreet rooms were reserved for the local tradesmen who did not want to be observed by anyone in the neighbourhood. The customers who had not the wherewithal for a few minutes of love stayed in the brasserie, ogling and pinching the waitresses. However, short shift was made of such unprofitable clients. In the brasseries for Lesbians, decorum was a little more observed.

In 1891 the police raided the Brasserie du Divorce in the rue Saint-Séverin, and the manageress, the cashier and the concierge were hauled before the Tribunal Correctionnel (Tenth Chamber). The prosecution used the waitresses as witnesses against them. The oldest was seventeen. They were simple, provincial girls, picked up by the concierge, who pimped for the establishment. The girls were told that they would be employed simply as waitresses, and one cannot but wonder at their lack of curiosity when on arrival in the brasserie they were dressed up immediately as Arcadian shepherdesses, to quote the manageress's words. They wore nothing under their short skirts, and, if they showed repugnance, the cashier scolded them, saying that they were not business-minded. The manageress and the cashier were sentenced to six months' imprisonment and the concierge to three.

The women who ran brasseries de femmes had a strong sense of publicity. They advertised in the newspapers and had business cards distributed in their district. "The most elegant dress is the simplest," announced the Brasserie du Sénat. "You can see our simply dressed ladies every night." The Grande Brasserie de la Seine: "All Paris throngs to see our pretty Women Doctors noted as much for their healing power as their charms." The Brasserie des Sorciers: "Here your fortune is told by famous fortune-tellers. Visit our basement where our fortune-tellers seek the Stone of Philosophy."

The great pastime in a Lesbian brasserie de femmes in the rue Grégoire de Tours was to watch the girls fighting each other with razor blades and to lay bets on them. The girl who first drew blood by cutting the other on the leg was declared the winner. The waitresses were as proud of their scars as were duelling Prussian students. Often they bled like pigs, but that only added to the gaiety of the evening. If a kind-hearted customer tried to intervene, they turned on him in fury.

The café-concerts were in the same tradition, though there were always women stupid enough to imagine that they were employed because of their singing voices.

"You sing well," the manager of a café-concert said to one of the artistes, "but you are too severe with the public."

And he cancelled her contract.

IV

Joan of Arc in Paris & the End of English Rule

At the beginning of September 1429 Joan of Arc left Rheims, where Charles VII had been anointed (sacré) King of France. Until her coming into his and France's life, he was piteously called the King of Bourges. She joined the Court at Saint-Denis, then with King and army advanced as far as La Chapelle, an ancient borough dating back to the time of Sainte-Geneviève and enclosed by high walls. Joan spent the night in an old building known as the Logis de Sainte-Geneviève, situated behind the Church of Saint-Denis-de-la-Chapelle (now 96 rue de la Chapelle), confident of taking Paris from the English.

On the morning of September 7 she rode with the King, followed by the troops, along the rue du Coq (prolongation of the rue de Clichy). They reached the windmill of the village of Batignolles, where battle was joined with the English, after which Charles VII withdrew to Saint-Denis, having again lost faith, but Joan took the army to the adjoining village of Monceaux, determined to besiege Paris the next day. (Monceaux lost its "x" as recently as the last century.)

When day broke she left part of her army in the village and

marched with the rest on Paris. They took the old Roman road which today roughly corresponds to:

rue de Lévis,

rue du Rocher,

the present corner of Boulevard Haussmann and rue de l'Arcade, where she crossed the watershed of Ménilmontant on the Bridge of Arcan (the watershed ran from the Hill of Ménilmontant, crossed the Champs-Elysées and reached the Seine at Chaillot. Now it is the main underground collector of drainage on the Right Bank),

rue de la Ville-l'Evêque,

rue de l'Arcade and the rue des Mathurins, which cross each other, cutting across the orchard of the Monks of the Holy Trinity known as the Mathurins, whose farm was on the site of the present number 39 rue des Mathurins,

rue Vignon,

rue d'Argenteuil,

and then reaching the Enceinte of Charles V at the present Place du Théâtre Français.

According to the *Registre des délibérations du Chapitre de Notre-Dame*, her force consisted of twelve thousand men, three hundred chariots and six hundred assault ladders, as well as siege ordnance, including cannons, barrels of gunpowder and stone cannonballs. With the grinding noise of the men-drawn chariots, the army reached the Porte Saint-Honoré (161 rue Saint-Honoré). Joan chose the Porte Saint-Honoré because there the walls appeared to be more vulnerable than at the Porte Saint-Denis, which was strongly fortified. She lined up her army behind the Butte Saint-Roch, levelled down by the Baron Haussmann when the Avenue de l'Opéra was constructed, and the Butte des Moulins, also levelled down, where now rues Sainte-Anne and des Petits-Champs meet. (The Butte Saint-Roch was between the Avenue de l'Opéra and the rues Thérèse and des Pyramides.) The cannons were dragged up on the two hillocks because there they were out of reach of the English cannons at the Porte Saint-Denis.

Before the Porte Saint-Honoré, Joan of Arc was wounded in the leg by an English arrow, yet she still wanted to continue the siege, but on the King's order the army commanders forced her to abandon the battle. She returned by the same route to Monceaux, then to La Chapelle, where she rested in the Logis de Sainte-Geneviève. Deeply dejected, she contemplated the jealousies of men and the untrustworthiness of the King. Her work, she thought, lay in ruins.

Eventually she took the road to Saint-Denis. On arrival she went straight into the Abbey church and prayed "humbly and devotedly". She hung up in the church, as an ex-voto offering, the armour she had worn when she was wounded.

In those turbulent times, crime was rampant and cruelty stalked the town. On December 15, 1427, Sauvage de Fromonville, a nobleman, was brought before the English Regent because he did not belong to the English Party. The Regent summarily condemned him to death and appointed Pierre Baille, Grand Treasurer of Maine, to preside over the execution. That worthy refused to allow the condemned man to receive the Last Sacrament. He personally hurried him up the ladder and, when he was already under the rope, struck him over the head with his stick, then belaboured the hangman who had dared to enquire why his victim had been refused confession. The hangman was so frightened that he omitted to take all the necessary precautions. As a result, the rope failed to hold and de Fromonville fell to the ground, still alive. Unimpressed and unmoved, Baille ordered him to be taken up the ladder again. This time the rope held.

After Joan's unsuccessful siege of Paris, misery and hunger descended on its inhabitants. Under the pretext of taking a walk outside the Walls, many Parisians passed through the city gates; once they reached the countryside, they took to robbing and killing. Ninety-eight such strollers were caught, twelve were hanged and eleven were taken to the Halles to be beheaded. When it came the turn of the eleventh, a young man of twenty-four, a girl broke through the crowd and, calling out loudly, claimed him as the man she intended to marry. She had probably never seen him before and was acting out of pity. She was so lovely and begged for his life so touchingly that all present were moved, and he was taken back to the prison of the Grand Châtelet, where he was set free on condition that he married her. If a woman was to be executed and a man stepped out of the crowd, offering to marry her, she was set free. Thus young girls escaped death more often than their elders.

The Seigneur de la Bottière discovered that his wife had a lover who was none other than his neighbour. He invited him to dinner, then after the meal took his wife and the lover for a walk. When they reached the woods, the husband killed them both. Shortly afterwards, he was apprehended, judged and condemned to be beheaded. He declared to the judges that every one of them was a cuckold, and that because he had refused to be one of them, they, the cuckolds, had decided to get rid of him. Such, he maintained, was the only reason for the death sentence. He refused to have his eyes bandaged, but took the executioner's sword and ran his fingers along the blade. Then he turned to the executioner and said, "Dispatch me quickly, my friend. It's up to you and your skill. The blade is well sharpened."

Not all noblemen behaved as exemplarily as the Seigneur de la Bottière. Nearly two hundred years later, another nobleman, whose name is not recorded, was sentenced to death. He had committed several crimes, including robbery. When he mounted the scaffold, he grabbed the Franciscan friar who had come to confess him, and threw him into the crowd. Then he went for the hangman and bit his neck. It took some time to overpower him. As a punishment for his outrageous behaviour, the hanging was cancelled and he had to undergo the more painful ordeal of being drawn and quartered.

In 1431 the ten-year-old Henry VI of England was sent to Paris to be anointed King of France in the Church of Notre-Dame. He entered the town through the Porte Saint-Denis. The city gate was decorated with the coats of arms of England and France. The magistrates and the Provost of the Merchants received him in their scarlet robes under a canopy of sky-blue silk sprinkled with golden fleurs-de-lys. When the cortège was formed, it was carried by four magistrates. The little monarch walked under the canopy, and the crowd thought that the procession resembled that of Corpus Christi.

Nine champions and nine damsels, accompanied by a multitude of knights, moved in front of the canopy. In their midst marched an impostor whom the English had taken in the battle of Beauvais. He pretended to be a prophet, and the people believed in him because he had stigmata on his hands and feet similar to those of St Francis. They had venerated this man like a saint. Now he was roped like a common thief.

Twenty-four heralds and twenty-five trumpeters walked before the King, who was encompassed by five ecclesiastics, a cardinal and four bishops. The procession stopped at the Fountain of Ponceau in the rue Saint-Denis. Three young girls represented sirens, and in the middle of the fountain rose a colossal artificial tiger-lily that spouted wine and milk through its petals. Whoever succeeded in pushing his way through the throng could drink as much as he wanted. A tableau represented savages dancing in a small jungle. (The same pageant was shown fifty-one years later on the occasion of Louis XI's entry into Paris.)

Beyond the Fountain of the Trinité, which was at the corner of the rues Saint-Denis and Greneta, extended a long wooden stage on which a mystery play based on the life of Our Lady was enacted. Farther on, another mystery play showed the life of St John the Baptist. In the Cemetery of the Innocents a stag hunt was improvised, the stag having been locked up there the night before.

In front of the Grand Châtelet a boy of the same age as Henry VI held a court of justice. He wore two crowns and was flanked by other boys dressed as princes of England and France. This pageant was much applauded, though some of the more patriotic spectators complained that the "king" more often consulted the English "princes" than the French ones.

The procession passed in front of the Hôtel de Saint-Paul, where

Isabeau of Bavaria, widow of Charles VI and grandmother of Henry stood in a window. The little king doffed his hat to her. She bowed, then turned away and cried; and well she might for all the calamities she brought on France.

Next Sunday the King was anointed in Notre-Dame by the Cardinal of Winchester. Then he returned to the Palace of the Louvre, where he dined at the round marble table at the end of the banqueting hall. The royal suite and the guests dined in the same hall. So dense was the crowd on the staircase that neither the representatives of the University and of Parliament, nor the Provost of Paris himself, could force their way up. They had to wait until a passage was opened for them, but by then their seats had been taken by cobblers, mustard-makers and their like. A useless tussle ensued. If a guest was strong enough to remove one of the interlopers from his own seat, the man immediately pushed another guest off his chair and took his place. Thieves had also managed to find their way into the hall, where they reaped a fair harvest. The entertainment that followed the banquet was on a mean scale, and the consensus of opinion was that Parisian burghers and merchants treated their guests more lavishly when their children married.

When on April 3, 1436, the troops of Charles VII appeared at the Porte Saint-Jacques, the defenders were so impressed by the size of the French King's army that they decided to open the gate. However, the key was in the keeping of the Bishop of Thérouanne who, with the Bishops of Lisieux and Paris, was a staunch supporter of the English. The problem was solved by lowering a long ladder. The first to climb it was the Seigneur de l'Isle-Adam who planted the King's banner on top of the gate with the cry, "Town conquered!"

The Parisians sided with Charles VII; the three Bishops, the Provost and the Captain of Paris with the English. About four thousand Parisians collected beside the Porte Saint-Denis; with three divisions, the English advanced along the rue Saint-Martin, shouting, "St George! St George! Death to the French traitors!" The

Bishop of Thérouanne commanded one of the English divisions. Another division, led by the Provost, marched towards the Halles. The Parisians threw chains across the streets to impede their progress, and, from the windows, the women and children threw tables, logs, stones and boiling water on them. Surprised to find the Porte Saint-Denis so well guarded, the English retreated into the Bastille. Meanwhile the royal troops infiltrated into the town, and once they were inside, the Parisians in their zeal pulled down the Porte Saint-Jacques, shouting, "Saint-Denis! Saint-Denis! Long live the noble King of France!"

The Parisians were pleasantly surprised by the royal troops' agreeable behaviour. They had feared the worst, yet the King's men neither looted nor molested them. They considered it a miracle for which they thanked St Denis. (The troops had strict orders to behave well, and any of them found pillaging, or even entering a burgher's house, were hanged on the spot.)

The English were in such vast numbers behind the walls of the Bastille that their food soon ran out. Paying an enormous ransom, they were allowed to leave Paris. They did not want to be seen in the town, so they left across the fields on the other side of the enceinte. The Parisians gathered on the walls to watch them go. The Bishop of Thérouanne, who departed with the English, was loudly jeered by the populace.

The King of Bourges was now truly King of France, and she who had been the mover of it all was burnt at the stake in Rouen less than two months later.

V

For l'Evêque

At 19 rue Saint-Germain-l'Auxerrois stood the prison of For l'Evêque, the building taking up the space between the street and the Quai de la Mégisserie. It had earlier been the ecclesiastical court of the Bishops of Paris, Forum Episcopi, hence For l'Evêque. It was a cosy sort of prison, as prisons go, and the defenders and admirers of the old régime like to harp on the easy life prisoners led there.

If a book or pamphlet were published without royal permission (privilège du Roi) and the author happened to be a distinguished man like Voltaire, Diderot or Mirabeau, he was sent to the Bastille or to Vincennes; the bookseller and printer went to For l'Evêque, and the colporteur, who was hardly more than a newsvendor, to Bicêtre. A writer could gauge his importance both in society and literature by the prison to which he was sent. Many must have sobbed in deep disappointment when they discovered that the Bastille was not their destination. Generally, the prisoners in For l'Evêque were a miscellaneous lot in so far as there were among them debtors, hoodlums, actors and actresses, noblemen, forgers and pimps. No dangerous criminals were sent there.

Lack of room was the most disagreeable feature. The four-storey house, with its slate roof and two turrets was approximately thirty feet wide and a hundred and fifteen feet long. Around two hundred and fifty people were usually crowded into it. The cells were less than six feet square, which makes it difficult to visualise how the prisoners managed to throw large dinner parties and entertain lavishly. That they did so is clear from the records, however. Mlle Clairon (Claire-Josèphe-Hypolitte Legris de la Tude), the famous actress, seemed to receive the whole of Paris society at her princely table at For l'Evêque, to which actors and actresses were specially privileged to be sent since they belonged to the Royal Household (Chambre du Roi). They went there without police escort to purge their contempt for whatever they had done; they never stayed long and were occasionally allowed out to perform.

For l'Evêque had no governor: the man in charge of the prison was the Concierge, who writers on French prisons, like the late Frantz Funck-Brentano, have compared to the master of a family boarding-house. Except for the chaplain and the clerk, he paid every member of the staff, and kept his staff as small and as cheap as possible. He employed only two warders, whose duties included guarding the gates. Rules of 1690 and 1717 obliged him to pay them 100 livres a year each, and since dogs cost less than men, he kept an imposing number of large dogs, which mounted guard at the gates when the warders were busy elsewhere, and acted as bodyguards to the Concierge when he made the rounds of cells and dungeons. They jumped at the throats of prisoners who made threatening gestures.

The Concierge had no true authority. In eighteenth-century Paris there were several houses of detention run by private individuals, the best known at Picpus, presided over by Mme Marie de Sainte-Colombe, where Louis de Saint-Juste was once locked up for petty theft. The position of the Concierge of For l'Evêque was no higher then hers. Prisoners who had enough money were looked after and served by their own servants; the rest by old women who lived on tips.

The Lieutenant of Police strictly forbade gaming in prisons, especially the game of faro. He had For l'Evêque in mind when he issued the order, for the prison was famous for the faro parties given by the inmates. On January 14, 1724, two lieutenants of the Constabulary and two clerks of Parliament accompanied Police Commandants Divot and Delafosse to For l'Evêque. They climbed to the third floor, where in the cell of three detained officers, Chapelain, Dumontois and Delalande, they found an elegant company of sixteen playing faro for high stakes. Dressed in an expensive linen dress, Mme de Coade, herself in prison for illegal gaming, ran the party. Among the gamesters from outside the gaol were Mme de la Marre, wife of the Procurator of Parliament, Causanel, a lieutenant in the Régiment de la Ferre-Infanterie, and the Chevalier de Sauvegrain. Consternation was mutual. The guests, however, recovered quicker than the police, burst out of the cell and made good their escape before the police could catch them. The inmates could not be arrested because they were already detained, so the six officers withdrew empty-handed.

Jean Noiseux was a violent man who loved fighting. When arrested, he drew his knife on the police, who managed to disarm him only after a fierce fight. The police had arrived to take him to For l'Evêque on his parents' demand, because they feared that "he might disgrace the family". Prison life did not change his habits. The Concierge at the time was called Chevallier. On November 5, 1728, he wrote to the Lieutenant of Police: "This man is drunk every night and spends his time inciting prisoners to sedition. At ten o'clock last night when the cells were already locked, he kicked up such a row in his cell that his cellmates had to call for help." Chevallier had gone upstairs to stop the noise, Noiseux had grabbed him by the collar, and if the two warders and the dogs had not followed, the Concierge would surely have been injured, for the dogs had had to bite hard before the prisoner let him go. Therefore,

Chevallier earnestly begged the Lieutenant to have Noiseux transferred to another prison, preferably the Châtelet. The Lieutenant wrote in turn to Cardinal de Fleury, the King's Minister, pointing out that the Concierge and his warders would not feel safe until Noiseux were removed from For l'Evêque. So small was the power of the Concierge that if he, his two men and many dogs were unable to master a prisoner, all he could do was to implore the Lieutenant to have the man removed. Noiseux was in fact transferred to Bicêtre.

A certain Chevallier (no relation of the Concierge) was put into For l'Evêque for forging lottery tickets. He continued his work in prison. A man called Luron came regularly to fetch the fresh tickets and put them into circulation. In his cell Chevallier had all the apparatus he needed, and fellow prisoners came to watch him at his work, which they found most instructive.

Prisoners received anyone they wanted. In the seventeenth century serious efforts were made to exclude mistresses; by the eighteenth they were abandoned: the mistress reigned supreme.

In the 1720s a fellow called Saint-Louis, known also as Louis Legrand or La Planche, was brought to For l'Evêque. He specialised in letter-writing, his letters being addressed usually to rich foreigners. Prison dampened neither his ardour nor his industry. He wrote, for instance, in these terms to the Ambassador of Modena:

"Monsieur, One of your friends has described you as a most amiable person in whom I can have enough confidence to introduce a young lady, fifteen years old. You are only asked to be discreet because of her parents. I do not sign this in fear that it might fall into wrong hands. Be good enough to let me know through the emissary whether you are interested in the little lady."

Here is a reply from a rich Englishman:

"I am sensibly grateful for your offer. It is not my habit to meet young ladies; however, if the young person of whom you give such a favourable account would like to come around at five o'clock after dinner, I would receive her with pleasure. . . ."

In another letter written to Mme Berrichon, who kept a shop at the corner of the rue de Grenelle and the Barrière de Grenelle, he proffered the name of a gentleman interested in her daughter, a Monsieur de Bontemps who, being a nobleman, could be of practical help to mother and daughter. There was no cause to worry about the daughter's honour and reputation, for the nobleman would personally defend them.

Saint-Louis plied his trade, which also included finding women from outside for his fellow prisoners, until the Concierge secured his transfer to Bicêtre.

A young lady, Anne Thiebaut, complained to the Lieutenant of Police that on a visit to another young lady held in For l'Evêque for debt, she had stopped for a meal with her friend, and that while they were dining merrily, another detainee, the Chevalier de Faiol, had burst in and insulted them. The nasty old man had shouted as if they were deaf, and would have beaten them had not other prisoners restrained him. Since Mlle Thiebaut was obliged to visit her friend regularly, she begged the Lieutenant to impose silence on the Chevalier, so that she should not have to listen to insults and coarse language unfit for the ears of a young lady of her station. The Lieutenant was in a dilemma. How could he impose silence on a prisoner in For l'Evêque? What would be the point of issuing an order that the Concierge would be unable to carry out? After due reflection the Lieutenant found the sensible solution: the Chevalier de Faiol was set free.

Ladies visiting friends in prison had to put up with a lot of unpleasantness because of the Concierge's lack of authority. At the time of Mlle Thiebaut's complaint, the Concierge also appealed to the Lieutenant. A man called Garnet, famous for the scandal he created in cabarets, was now a prisoner in For l'Evêque. "He causes constant trouble," wrote the Concierge. "He fouls the beds of other prisoners, incites them to revolt, ill-treats the warders. . . ." The Lieutenant took a less lenient view of Garnet: he was transferred to the Châtelet.

Into the interesting world of For l'Evêque entered in 1770 Clotworthy Skeffington, second Earl and sixth Viscount Massereene in the Peerage of Ireland. He was then twenty-seven years old. In his early days he had been a man of fashion: "The most superlative coxcomb Ireland ever bred" (Thicknesse, 1770). He "spent an ample fortune in the most wretched dissipation" (Croft, 1780). In a suit as to the validity of his will, the jury at Carrickfergus found that he had been insane at the time he made it. One witness said that "on the death of his favourite dog he had given positive orders that fifty dogs should attend the funeral in white scarves, and that all dogs in the parish should also be present."

He arrived in Paris in 1770 in the hope of curing his spleen, the English ailment much admired in France. It was known too as melancholia. Within a few weeks he was in debt to Parisian tradesmen to the tune of 376,732 livres. His own version was that he had been cheated at cards, but it is most unlikely that he would have sat down to play with tradespeople, or that they would have pursued him for card losses. In any case Lord Massereene refused to pay his creditors, saying that they had robbed him and that he would not give them a sol. Aware that he had a large income and vast estates in Ireland, the tradesmen assumed, quite erroneously, that a little coercion would bring results. They had him arrested and put into For l'Evêque, believing that the overcrowded prison into which the sun never penetrated would do the trick. They did not know their man.

Lord Massereene quickly settled down. With a large income one could do well for oneself in For l'Evêque, as he proceeded to demonstrate. The best cook-shops sent in food and wine, and since he could afford to entertain lavishly, his cell was full of visitors, mostly English. Since the prisoners had the run of the entire building from morning to evening, he took plenty of exercise in the court-yard and up and down the stairs. When he felt in need of women, his friends and servants provided him with as many as he wanted. He kept open cell, sent carriages to fetch his women, and paid their jewellers' and dressmakers' bills and for their boxes at the Opéra. He indulged in every pleasure and lived without a single worry, which was more than could be said for his creditors who, in accordance with the law, were responsible for his basic keep; he had only to pay for the extras. The tradesmen appealed to the Procurator General, begging him "not to permit any visitor to see milord except for those who attend to his business affairs, especially no member of the opposite sex, for as long as milord has company that amuses him he will not attend to his debts." The Procurator General replied that the Concierge was the sole master at For l'Evêque and that it would be impossible to impose a measure that went against all the traditions of the prison.

Another solution had to be found, The creditors' expenses rose steeply. Seven years after the arrest, the debt stood at nearly 1,000,000 livres, so they conspired together in sending to Lord Massereene two ruffians, Verdier and Jullot, to persuade him that with 1,000 écus they could bribe both warders. All he needed was a disguise, which they would provide for him. Lord Massereene fell into the trap. It was decided that the escape should take place at seven in the evening, when it was already dark, on March 17.

He was dressed in a grey suit, his face half hidden by a vast cravat and high collar; he wore false whiskers and a hat with a large brim. What he did not know was that Verdier and Jullot had sent an anonymous letter to Dinant du Verger, the Concierge, informing him about the plot. The Concierge hardly knew how to act; he was not used to prisoners escaping. He appealed for help to the Lieutenant of Police, who sent a police inspector with a handful of men. They hid between the prison gates, and when milord appeared they jumped on him, threw him down, tied him, and dragged him into one of the rat-infested, underground dungeons. The creditors congratulated themselves. Everything had gone as planned. Milord would certainly capitulate and settle his debts.

Once again they misjudged their man. Lord Massereene shouted from the dungeon to all who were willing to listen that he was ready to stay there until he reached the ripe age of ninety, but that on no condition would he pay his debts.

The British Ambassador protested at Court, and Massereene was released from the dungeon and sent back to his cell, where the gay life recommenced. By 1780 the creditors' expenses had risen to nearly 2,000,000 livres. However, another danger was in the offing for milord. Louis XVI, in the days of his reforming zeal, sought to improve the lot of prisoners, and since For l'Evêque was badly overcrowded he decided to have it razed to the ground. By a royal decree of August 30, 1780, criminals were to be transferred to the Châtelet and debtors to the Hôtel de la Force, a spacious prison at the corner of the rues Pavée and du Roi-de-Sicile. On the day of moving the creditors waited in the street in the hope of catching Massereene. It is not known what they intended to do if they caught him, but by then they were unhappy, disillusioned men. Accompanied and surrounded by friends, he ran the whole way from For l'Evêque to the Hôtel de la Force. The creditors had failed again. Life in the new prison was as pleasant as in the old; and the debt rose to 3,000,000 livres.

Lord Massereene married in prison Marie-Anne Barcier, the sister of another detainee. She came every morning to spend the day with her husband.

On July 14, 1789, the debtors in the Hôtel de la Force heard the boom of the cannon in the Place de la Bastille. Massereene grasped the situation better than the other prisoners and incited them to break out collectively. Some protested that, being unarmed, their task would be hopeless. Massereene brushed aside the objection. He led them up the stairs, where they tore down the iron banisters and, now well armed, they marched to the gates. Because of the troubles in Paris a detachment of infantry had been sent to the Hôtel de la Force. The officer in charge called to the advancing prisoners: "One step more and my soldiers will fire!" Massereene stepped forward. "If you kill me, you will, according to law, be responsible for my debts." Everybody in Paris knew about the colossal sum he owed, and the officer let the prisoners go. Thus ended nineteen years of incarceration of a man who had been imprisoned because of his debts and let free also because of them.

The party reached the British Embassy. The first thing Lord Massereene did was to offer his companions a copious meal with excellent wines. A few days later he was smuggled out of France, and before the end of the month he landed in Dover with his wife. He died in 1806 without having evinced any desire to see France again. The Hôtel de la Force was demolished in 1850.

VI

From the Cours des Miracles to the Procession of the Fat Ox

The first cour des miracles, or courtyard of miracles, was established in the rue de la Grande-Truanderie, which took its name from the truands (beggars, vagrants) who infested the street and the neighbourhood, which was known as la Truanderie. The street was also called Via Mendicatrix. The name cour des miracles was a mocking reference to the fact that these people who limped round the neighbourhood, their arms or legs in bandages, shouting from pain, fainting, often blind, were miraculously as hale and hearty as the next man when they returned to the yards in which they lived.

Around 1350 another group of beggars and thieves was set up in two adjacent houses, the larger containing twenty-four rooms, in the rue des Francs-Bourgeois. The wretches who lived there paid no duties or taxes whatsoever, and were referred to as free citizens; hence the name of the street. The houses were known as the Little Houses of the Temple or the Almshouses of the Francs-Bourgeois. A burgher, le Masurier, had given them to the Grand Prior of France for the purpose of accommodating forty-eight poor.

Henri Sauval, author of the truly monumental *Histoire et Recherches des Antiquités de la Ville de Paris*, which was published in

1724, forty-eight years after his death, by Claude-Bernard Rousseau, called them the wicked poor, for they were neither impressed by, nor grateful for, the charity they received. They stood in the doorways, insulting the pedestrians, kept the neighbours awake at night with their awful din, and stole anything on which they could lay their hands. The almshouses became refuges of debauch and prostitution. When, however, the big private mansions began to rise in the rue des Francs-Bourgeois in the seventeenth century, the inmates were forced to leave. They dispersed in groups all over the city. Their number had considerably increased since the fourteenth century. The cour des miracles of the rue de la Grande-Truanderie being full, they created new crumbling, filthy thieves' kitchens for themselves. Some went to the Cour de Roi-François in the rue du Ponceau, some to the Cour Sainte-Catherine nearby or to the Cour Brisset and the Cour Gentien in the rue de la Mortellerie (now rue de l'Hôtel-de-Ville); others to the Cour de la Jussienne in the rue de la Jussienne, near the Chapel of Sainte-Marie-l'Egyptienne (demolished in 1792)—crumbling, filthy thieves' kitchens all of them, with yards that had always been inhabited by thieves, beggars, rogues and the wicked poor.

The cours des miracles multiplied rapidly. They spread as far as the rue Saint-Honoré, Bourg Saint-Germain, Faubourg Saint-Marceau and the Butte Saint-Roch. The most populated was between the rues Montorgeuil and Neuve-Saint-Sauveur (rue du Nil). This was a foul conglomeration of narrow alleyways and horrible shacks, built of mud, each housing about fifty families with their children—legitimate, bastard and stolen. In 1630 the Town of Paris decided to cut a street through the neighbourhood between the Impasse Saint-Sauveur and the rue Neuve-Saint-Sauveur (now part of rue du Louvre), but nothing came of it, for the masons who began work on the new street were soon manhandled by the rogues.

One of the rules of the inmates of the cours des miracles was never to keep anything for the morrow, so whatever they earned by begging or thieving was spent the same evening. Their days invariably ended in drunkenness. The women prostituted themselves for a sol or just for pleasure. They went to church only to steal, to cut purses or to pick pockets (most people carried their purses attached by a string or a ribbon to their belts), yet they had some form of faith. At the bottom of one of their yards was a painting of God the Father which they had stolen from a church and took to worshipping. Men who had given women of the yard handsome children were paid by other women to lie down with them so that they too should have good-looking babies to take out when begging. A pretty babe in arms was a handy asset.

Each yard had a school for thieving. A rope, to which were attached a purse and small bells, was stretched across one of the mean rooms, used specially for the purpose. The apprentice had to be able to cut the purse string without the bells tinkling and without moving his body. If he failed he was beaten; if he succeeded he was declared a master, yet was still beaten. It formed part of his schooling to become immune to beatings, which were a hazard of life once he started to exercise his skill. The new master would be taken to some crowded place like the Cemetery of the Innocents, and would be ordered to try out his art in his teachers' presence, perhaps on a woman praying on her knees before the Virgin, her purse hanging loosely from her belt, or on someone else whose purse seemed easy to cut. As he approached the prospective victim, the teachers' trick was to shout to all and sundry, pointing at the new master, "Look, this fellow is a real purse-cutter! He's going for that poor creature there!" Everybody's attention was of course drawn to the young thief, and the teachers joined with the crowd in pouncing on him, kicking and beating him. It was part of his training not even to glance at his companions who, while he was being belaboured, reaped an excellent harvest of purses and the contents of pockets. His own colleagues denounced him more loudly than the rest, calling him by every vile name of which they could think. Then in the noise and the pushing they and the new master vanished one by one. After that final test, the new master joined one of the groups, and from then on he was considered a fully-fledged purse-cutter and pickpocket.

No one was allowed to operate alone because in a group it was more difficult to be caught. If one gang saw another in a church or a street, they went elsewhere; it was not in their interest that too many thieves should congregate in one spot. They arrived for work, however, individually. Each night the head of the yard designated the different places to be visited the following day. An intelligent system was evolved. In each district there was a hiding place, which might be behind a doorway, in a stable, or anywhere that the uninitiated would not notice. Groups consisted of either six or twelve men, but because they were not allowed to arrive together, and because no man could know how many intended to go to any one place, each went on his own in the morning to the hiding place in the district he had in mind, where only a dice was hidden. The first arrival turned the dice from square one to square two, then went off to the appointed place. The next man turned it to square three, and so on until square six was reached. If there were a seventh arrival, he would see that the group was complete, and know that he must go elsewhere. If the group was to consist of twelve men, two dices were left in the hiding place.

An Academician, who was a friend of Sauval who relates the story, in his young days discovered such a lair of dice in the Halles. He rose at dawn and hurried to the hiding place, where he turned the dice to square six even if it were on square one. He was proud of having reduced the number of those who went to the Halles to cut purses or pick pockets.

The ruffians of the cours des miracles were known as the Argotiers, and their thieves' language as argot. It was said that the language had been invented by debauched scholars. Their world was the Royaume argotique.

In 1255, the Hospital of Quinze-Vingt was founded, beyond the Porte Saint-Honoré, by St Louis. It was for the blind, who took to begging in the rue Saint-Honoré, which was conveniently sited near the hospital and on the route taken by the maraîchers to the

Halles. The blind often begged at night, when the market gardeners passed with their carts, because they knew them to be generous men. However, because they could not be seen in the dark, or easily identified, they always had with them a boy who was supposed to hold a lighted lantern to his face when he heard the trundle of a cart. In their unlit darkness the blind beggars fretted about whether they could trust the boys, who might be indolent or simply forgetful, and they were known to ask passersby whether the light was shining strongly enough. Street-women were among their most constant benefactors, and to show their gratitude the beggars recommended them to any men who gave them alms.

In the Hôtel d'Armagnac at 1-33 rue des Bons-Enfants, there took place on the blind peoples' feast days a thrilling game, which invariably attracted a large audience. Four blind men and a pig were let into an enclosure in the courtyard. Each blind man was armed with a big stick, and the pig was promised to the one who succeeded in killing it. There ensued the spectacle of the blind hurling themselves at the spot where they heard the pig grunting, while the pig ran round in circles, trying to escape them. "There he is, the dirty pig!" one of them would cry, but as the pig was by then at the other end of the pit, the blind man would find himself, in the general excitement, belabouring one of his mates. The audience rocked with laughter at such fun.

After a while the blind were disentangled and allowed to rest. Then they were at it again. Rarely did one of them manage to hit the pig, let alone kill it. Often they gave up, not because of the blows they had received, but because of the laughter of the onlookers.

When St Vincent de Paul was the priest of the parishes of Clichy, du Roule, de la Madeleine and d'Antin, he heard of a market in infants near Notre-Dame, where foundlings were sold to beggars.

One could buy a baby for 8 sols. The beggar took away his purchase, and broke its arms and legs so as to arouse more compassion in the hearts of those whom he would accost with the poor, unfortunate child. St Vincent persuaded the authorities to abolish that infamous practice, and prompted by the misery and suffering of foundlings, he created the Oeuvre des Enfants Trouvés, the foundling hospital of Paris.

To his Sisters of Charity he gave a recipe for a soup for a hundred needy:

"Fill a large pot with five buckets of water, put into it twenty-five pounds of bread, seven quarters of fat, four pints of peas, white turnips, leaks and onions, and salt, for 14 sols. The lot will not cost more than 100 sols for a hundred people. It should be distributed in bowls."

On the feast days of SS Leu and Giles, the inhabitants of the rue aux Ours raised a high pole in their street and tied to the top a basket containing a fat goose and 6 écus. They smeared the pole with grease and promised the goose, the money and the basket to whoever could reach them. In spite of the grease there were plenty of competitors, but as with the blind and the pigs in the Hôtel d'Armagnac, it was rare that anyone succeeded. There was a difference, however; if no one reached the basket, the person who climbed nearest to it was at least given the goose, the basket and the money being kept for the next holiday.

Each district, each profession and each guild had its own patron saint or saints. The Town of Paris celebrated the feasts of SS Denis, Marcel and Geneviève; the University, SS Nicolas and Catherine; the Sorbonne, St Ursula, and the six guilds of the tradespeople had a patron saint each. Drunks fervently celebrated the feast of St Martin. Loose women celebrated the feast of St Mary Magdalene. In the fifteenth and sixteenth centuries to ask for medlars in a church was considered proof of enormous stupidity, and it was the custom on the feasts of SS Simon and Jude to send simple people to the Temple for this very purpose. They were assured that the saints would see to it that they received the fruit. What actually happened, however, was that their faces were blackened with soot by lackeys hired for the purpose, and a good time was had by the onlookers. In Mid-Lent, the apprentices in the Halles were sent to kiss the bas-relief of a sow on the wall of a house; as they leaned forward to do so, their noses were banged into the wall. For the rest of the day they over-ate and got riotously drunk.

On the feast of St John footmen and maidservants danced through the streets, often behaving scandalously. In contrast, at the Hôtel de Ville, the aldermen and the Provost of the Merchants gave a magnificent supper followed by a ball for their families and friends at which they danced respectably to the music of violins. On Christmas Eve the common people were so intoxicated that Notre-Dame was guarded by the Watch. It was said in the seventeenth century that those who went to Midnight Mass did not seek God but groped for Him. On Easter Sunday, when canary-bread was distributed in the almshouses, there was again a great deal of drunkenness among spectators and recipients. However, the populace behaved at its worst on the feast of Epiphany; and respectable people in the reign of Louis XIII deeply regretted the passing of the good old days of Charles V, when the masses were still decent and behaved respectfully.

At 54 rue Quincampoix there was a famous cabaret called l'Epée de Bois, where the Dancing Masters and Violin Masters met. In 1658, Cardinal Mazarin, by letters patent, instituted the Community of Dancing Masters and Violin Masters, who continued to meet at the Epée de Bois until 1661, when it was incorporated into the Royal Academy of Dance, merging eight years later with the Royal Academy of Music to form what became known as the Opéra.

The cabaret remained a meeting place of musicians and dancers until 1719 when John Law of Lauriston, the monetary reformer and originator of the Mississippi Bubble, set up his bank in the street. The Epée de Bois turned into a rowdy tavern, where those who wanted to make quick money spent what they hoped to make. John Law believed in credit as a universal remedy and in paper money equalling the value of gold. He advocated a central bank that would have the monopoly of collecting taxes and issuing public loans. The bank's capital would be provided by selling shares to the public.

He offered his plan to Scotland, England and Savoy; all three rejected it. Then he thought of France, which was on the verge of bankruptcy following the death of Louis XIV. Philippe d'Orléans, the Regent, jumped at the plan, and Law founded his bank, which did well at first. Almost everybody who could afford to do so bought shares in the bank. Flushed with success, Law created the Compagnie des Indes, which received the monopoly of external trade, and as a result of the fever of speculation, shares originally valued at 200 livres rose to 20,000. An unlimited number of bank notes was printed and put into circulation. The shakier the enterprise became, the faster the printing machines worked.

Then came the collapse. Law could not pay dividends, and the frightened shareholders turned their shares into banknotes, and their banknotes into gold and silver—until the supply of gold and silver ran out. Law and his bank, which had amalgamated with the Compagnie des Indes, went bankrupt. Only banknotes under 10 livres were honoured. The bank closed its doors and there followed a riot. Law had lost his own fortune too in the course of his grand design. He left France and, in 1729, at the age of fifty-eight, he died a pauper in Venice.

Indirectly, a broker named Lacroix was one of his victims. Lacroix had made a vast sum of money while the going was still good. A German, Count Antoine de Horn, assisted by de Miles, a Piedmontese nobleman, and de Tournai, the son of a French banker, decided to bag the broker's fortune. They chose the simplest method. On Good Friday, 1720, they met him at the Epée de Bois on the pretext of selling him an estate. The French accomplice stayed in the street as a look-out while in a private room upstairs his colleagues murdered Lacroix in cold blood. A waiter, hearing strange noises, opened the door, saw the corpse, locked the door and rushed out to give the alarm. The Piedmontese climbed out through the window, slid down a drainpipe, and got away before the police arrived, but was caught shortly afterwards in the Cemetery of the Innocents. The German followed him out through the window, sprained his ankle as he landed on the ground, and was arrested on the spot. In spite of de Horn's excellent connections (he was distantly related to the Regent, and his brother was a ruling prince in Germany) six days after the murder he and the Piedmontese were broken on the wheel in the Place de Grève.

It was the habit of beggars to carry sticks. Sticks and canes made no special impression in a world where men of quality carried a more dangerous weapon, the sword. Disbanded soldiers, ruffians and rogues all begged in the daytime. To beg was a recognised way of earning a living, there being no stigma attached to it as long as the beggar stuck to asking for alms. It often happened, however, that when a humble beggar found himself alone in an alley with a charitable person who had stopped to give him a coin or two, the beggar's stick turned swiftly into an arm. Down it came on the victim's head, and by the time he had recovered, his possessions and the beggar were gone. Now and again these rogues operated in bands. Then there was no question of begging: they attacked like a pack of wolves, though usually only after dusk. Thus the system of gangs evolved.

The gangs approached a house at night and threw pebbles at the windows. If no irate householder leaned out, they knew that the house was uninhabited. One gang leader, Raffia, collected around him youths between the ages of fifteen and eighteen. He and his mob specialised in robbing goldsmiths and silversmiths, who at night hung in front of their shops large glass cases, each one lit by two candles, which contained their finest jewels. Raffia was sixteen years old. Dressed as a peasant, his technique was to stand open-mouthed in front of a glass case, staring at the jewels with the admiration one expected from a stupid peasant who had never before seen anything so fine. The people who passed probably smiled in pity mingled with condescension at the simple fellow wearing a cotton cap. However, Raffia excelled at cutting glass. His associates boasted of his having extracted jewels unnoticed from practically every jeweller's case in Paris. Eventually he was caught, and confessed to all his thefts. When he was taken to the scaffold in the Place de Grève, he loudly proclaimed that his mother was an honest woman who knew nothing of his misdeeds; he offered his life to God, being unafraid of death, but feared that his mother would die of shame. He burst into tears.

"Set your mind at rest," said the Clerk of the Court. Again Raffia recommended his mother to him as he mounted the ladder.

It was the custom for a condemned man to be taken to the main door of Notre-Dame, where the Clerk of the Court read out his sentence, a taper was given him and he made amende honorable. Then he was lifted into a cart, and in the company of the hangman and the priest who would confess him, he rode to the Place de Grève, where the gibbet awaited him. The magistrates who had sentenced him held themselves in readiness at the Hôtel de Ville, which overlooked the place of execution, in case he wanted to reveal something of importance before he died. Many condemned men took advantage of this possibility of delaying death. They entered the building and spent as much time as they could in spinning yarns, adding details that were untrue, inventing crimes they had never committed. A clerk took down all they said. When they could think up nothing more, they were led back to the hangman. There were several who then asked to be taken back to the magistrates because they had forgotten to confess to some of their worst crimes. Some thus succeeded in keeping death at bay for many hours.

In 1764 a certain Pierre Padoix had the capital idea of denouncing as accomplices a number of decent residents of Saint-Germain-en-

Laye. He was kept the whole night in the town hall, waiting for the arrival of the good people who in the morning were brought in in chains, among them a surgeon and his wife. Padoix accused the woman of complicity in his crimes, and she was taken to the Châtelet, where she died of shame the same day. When Padoix was taken to the gallows he confided in the Lieutenant of Police that the folk of Saint-Germain-en-Laye were innocent, that he had invented the whole story, and would he thank the magistrates for the excellent supper and comfortable night at the Hôtel de Ville? There is a record of a condemned man who was given there a meal consisting of an omelette, a chicken, a salad, a pound of bread, a bottle of wine and three coffees.

It was the custom in Paris, originating in the Middle Ages, for the crowd in the square, and the people in the windows and on the roofs, to intone the Salve Regina when a condemned man appeared on top of the ladder. After the last verse the executioner did his job. Now and then the chant was interrupted by a loud shout of "Vive le Roi!" as a messenger arrived on horseback at full gallop from Versailles, waving a letter of pardon.

In 1731 the King's pardon saved the life of one, Boulleteix, who had killed a companion in an affray. His head was already in the noose when the messenger arrived. He was untied and taken to the Café Marchand in the Quai Le Pelletier (now Quai de Gesvres), where he was given several glasses of wine while the Clerk of the Court passed round his own hat, collecting money for him. On the next Sunday Boulleteix went to the Place de Grève and begged from the crowd. The nearness of death "had turned his blood," his face was the colour of saffron and "a number of decent people gave him money."

A citizen discovered one day that his silver forks were missing. He accused his servant girl of stealing them. Though she protested her innocence, he brought his complaint before the Courts. The girl was sentenced to death, then hanged. Six months later the forks were found in the nest of a magpie. In the Church of Saint-Jean-en-Grève (demolished before the Revolution), at the corner of the Place de Grève and the rue de Lobeau, the repentant citizen had a daily Mass offered up for the poor servant girl. It came to be known as the Mass of the Magpie.

In 1830 a murderer called Verdure was executed. His brother, who was among the spectators, afterwards went to a low cabaret, where he laughingly showed his friends four watches he had stolen from onlookers while the guillotine did its work.

At around the same time, a criminal called Lacenaire, who had served several sentences, used to dine in a small and cheap restaurant frequented by artists and men of letters. Lacenaire had a remarkably fine handwriting and took temporary employment with a firm of letter copyists. He begged all and sundry in the restaurant to give him work. He had fallen on hard days and would copy anything at a very modest rate. Out of sheer kindness two young playwrights gave him their play to copy. The next day he brought back the manuscript, declaring that he would not do the work.

"I read the play," he said. "I find it stupid."

With all the thrills and spectacles that Paris offered, the Parisian was loath to undertake journeys. He was convinced in any case that dangers of many sorts lurked beyond the city walls. In the 1760s an anonymous writer wrote a little leaflet on the Parisian's reactions if he ventured out of the town. It was entitled *Le voyage de Paris à Saint-Cloud par mer, et le retour de Saint-Cloud à Paris par terre.* The distance between Paris and Saint-Cloud was under ten miles.

The Parisian who undertook the journey took his food with him, lest the food of that distant world might be poisonous. He took leave of family and friends, offered up prayers to all the saints, and went on board the small galleon that plied between Paris and Saint-Cloud. Impressed by the vessel and the large expanse of water, he enquired when he could expect to sight East Indiamen. Passing Chaillot, he already imagined himself in the Levant, far from his own people. He shed a tear, thinking of his street. He caught sight of a fish: it must be a dried cod. The Cape of Good Hope would shortly heave into view. When he saw the smoke from the glass-works of Sèvres, he became convinced that it was from Mount Vesuvius.

On arrival in Saint-Cloud he went straight into the first church to thank the Lord for having reached his destination safe and sound; then he wrote a long letter to his dear mother, describing the dangers of the voyage. He looked less elegant than at his departure, for having sat on a coil of ropes, the seat of his velvet breeches was covered in tar. He strolled round Saint-Cloud, meditating on the mysteries of Nature and on the existence of life beyond the gates of Paris.

The return journey by land filled him with awe. He discovered to his disappointment that neither cod nor herring were caught in the Seine. When he saw the Bois de Boulogne he felt sure that ancient Druids dwelt there. The hillock Mont-Valérien was the true Calvary, which cheered him up as proof of his being still among Christians, and when he caught a glimpse of a stag, then of a peacock, he congratulated himself on having seen all God's wonders. When the coach halted at the Château de Madrid, he knew that he was in Spain. Throughout the journey he remained a true patriot, never for a moment denying his origins. Yes, he was a born native of Paris, his mother sold cloth at the Barbe d'Or and his cousin was a notary.

On reaching his home he was received with acclamation, and his aunts, who had not been near the Tuileries for twenty years, the Tuileries being in another neighbourhood, congratulated him on his courage and spirit of adventure.

Of the different hearty amusements of previous ages, the nineteenth century retained the Procession of the Fat Ox. Learned men of the century thought that it derived from the festival of Isis and

Osiris; butchers thought that it was to advertise their trade and have fun at the same time.

The procession took place during the three days preceding Ash Wednesday, and set off each day from a different point, perambulating the principal streets of the Right Bank, then repairing to the Hôtel de Ville, the Préfecture de Police and the Tuileries, where King Louis-Philippe beamed at the ox. The procession ended at the Porte Saint-Antoine. It was escorted at front and rear by two detachments of mounted gendarmes. After the first piquet of gendarmes came a military band, followed by twenty butchers on horseback, dressed as armed Mamelukes. Behind them came the Boeuf Gras, moving at a slow pace, its horns gilded and decorated with festoons, its body covered with a white blanket with embroidered gold fleurs-de-lys. On its back was a small gilt saddle in which sat a child, winged and armed like Cupid. Four ropes, concealed under garlands of flowers, were fastened to the animal's neck, held at equal distance by four strong men accoutred like savages—covered from head to foot with flesh-coloured silk, and wearing short petticoats of tiger skin. They carried clubs decked with flowers.

The procession stopped before every cabaret, and drinks were served in profusion. With the crowd mingled butchers dressed in white, each carrying a bottle and glass for those who were either not permitted to leave the ranks or who could not reach the inns.

At the end of the third day the much acclaimed beast was slaughtered.

VII

In the Marais

The pride of the old district of the Marais is the Place des Vosges. The square has preserved its seventeenth-century elegance and dignity. If Henri IV returned—he was assassinated before it was finished—he would recognise it as the square designed under his supervision by the architects Androuet du Cerceau and Claude Chastillon. He might regret the trees in the garden because they interfere with the splendour of the view; however, the good and kind King would admit that in the Marais, where trees do not abound, the children who play in the square need the trees' shade in summer.

Officially declared a square in 1605, it was called Place Royale, a name it kept until the Revolution. In 1792 it was changed to Place des Fédérés, the following year to du Parc-d'Artillerie, then de la Fabrication-des-Armes, des Vosges in 1800 because Vosges was the first among the departments to pay the new, heavy taxes, once more Royale in 1814, de la République in 1830, des Vosges from 1831 to 1852 when it reverted to Royale, and from 1870 onward des Vosges again.

In 1338 Pierre d'Orgement, Chancellor of France, built a large turreted house, surrounded by a high wall, on the north side of what is the present square. His son Pierre, Bishop of Paris, sold the house in 1402 to the Duc de Berry, brother of Charles V who two years later exchanged it for a house owned by Louis d'Orléans, situated between the rues Saint-Antoine and de Jouy of today. Following the assassination of the Duc d'Orléans by the partisans of Jean-sans-Peur in 1407, the house was bought by the French Crown and became known as la Maison royale des Tournelles. Charles VI often visited it from his palace of Saint-Pol. After him the Duke of Bedford, English Regent of France, resided there and embellished it. His wife died in the same house in 1432. Kings Charles VII, Louis XI and Charles VIII lived in it, and Louis XII died there on January 1, 1515. François I summoned the burghers of Paris to Tournelles when he needed money.

Henri II found Tournelles "mean, insalubrious and nauseating", and used it for short stays only, generally during journeys. On July 1, 1559, between the present rues de Sévigné and Birague, the King, wearing the colours of Diane de Poitiers, jousted with Gabriel de Lorge de Montgomery, Captain of his Scots Guards. Montgomery's lance lifted the King's vizor and penetrated into the brain through the eye. Henri was carried to Tournelles where he died after ten days of awful agony.

The dying King forgave Montgomery, who left for England and became a Protestant. A Valois can forgive, but not a Medici, and Catherine de Medici, Henry II's widow, bided her time, waiting to avenge herself on the man who had accidentally killed her husband. Montgomery returned to France, and was eventually captured after desperate resistance in Domfront (Orne). On Catherine de Medici's insistence, he was sentenced to death, tortured, and dragged in a tumbril to the Place de Grève, where he was executed on June 26, 1574.

Catherine de Medici persuaded her son Charles IX to have Tournelles pulled down, and, when royalty left the district, the deserted gardens became a horse market, the horse-copers bringing beggars, thieves and tramps in their wake. The once-royal neighbourhood virtually turned into a cour des miracles. The area served another purpose too, for men of rank and fashion found it an ideal place for duelling.

The most famous duel of all concerned the Mignons, Henri III's pretty boys. On April 27, 1578, at five in the morning, three Mignons, Quélus, Maugiron and Livarot, met Balzac d'Entragues, Ribérac and Schomberg, partisans of the House of Guise, in truly mortal combat. Balzac d'Entragues was the only one unscathed. Livarot's wounds kept him in bed for seven weeks. Maugiron and Schomberg died on the spot, Ribérac the next day. As for Quélus from whom the whole idea had emanated, he languished for thirty days in the Hôtel de Boissy in the rue Saint-Antoine, where he was visited every day by the King, who offered 100,000 francs to surgeons if they saved him, and gave a similar sum to Quélus, who was the best loved of his Mignons, to encourage him to fight death and make survival worthwhile. When he died Henri broke down and cried for days. The people of Paris were amused and thought it was a huge joke.

Another famous duel took place on the night of January 26-27, 1614, between Philippe Hurault du Marais and the Marquis de Rouillac. Each had his second fighting with him. They fought with sword in one hand, holding a burning torch in the other. The Marquis de Rouillac was the sole survivor.

Cardinal de Richelieu wanted to extirpate duelling. Notwithstanding a royal edict, on May 12, 1627, a savage duel was fought between Messieurs de Montmorency-Bouteville, de Chapelles and La Berthe on one side, and Messieurs de Beuvron, Bussy d'Amboise and Buquet on the other. Bussy was killed and La Berthe wounded. Beuvron and Buquet fled to England, and Montmorency-Bouteville and Chapelles, who made good their escape on horses lent by Baron de Chantel, were captured in Vitry-le-Brûlé, now a parish of Vitry-le-François (Marne), and brought back to Paris. In spite of the influence at Court of their friends and relations, they were beheaded in the Place de Grève thirty-five days after the duel.

The last notorious duel in the Place Royale was fought on December 12, 1643, between the grandsons of Henri de Guise and

Admiral de Coligny. It was not a case of family feud, nor intended as revenge for the Massacre of St Bartholomew: it was because of a row over two women. Coligny lightly wounded Guise, who grabbed his adversary's rapier with one hand and ran him through with the other. Thus died the last of the Colignys. Guise's friends regarded it as a most chivalrous duel.

By that time the Place Royale had reverted nearer to its origins, and was inhabited by quality, though women of easy virtue roamed beneath the arcades at night. In his *Historiettes*, Gédéon Tallemant des Réaux relates that the Duc de Candalle, son of the Duc de l'Espernon, offered a soldier a piece of gold if he would have intercourse with one of those women in the full sunlight of noon in the middle of the square. The soldier was as good as his word, and when the performance began all the great ladies appeared at their windows to watch the spectacle.

When Louis XIII died, Richelieu had a statue erected to him in the middle of the square. The Cardinal found a bronze horse which Catherine de Medici had in her time ordered from Daniel de Volterre, a pupil of Michelangelo. She wanted a statue of Henri II, but nothing came of it. Briard fils now sculpted a larger-than-life-size statue of Louis XIII which he mounted on the bronze horse that now looked no bigger than a pony. On the marble plinth was inscribed:

"To the glorious and immortal memory of the most high and most invincible Louis the Just, XIII of the name, King of France and Navarre. Armand Cardinal and Duc de Richelieu, his principal minister in all his illustrious and generous schemes, heaped with honours and gifts by so good a master and generous monarch, had this statue raised as an eternal mark of his zeal, loyalty and gratitude."

A wag coined a less fulsome inscription: "He had the hundred virtues of a lackey and none of a master." And for the tomb of the King this epitaph was suggested:

Ci-gît le Roi, notre bon maître
Qui fut vingt ans valet d'un prêtre

The eternal mark of Richelieu's zeal was melted down during the Revolution; in 1819 a white marble statue of the King by Cortot and Dupaty was erected in its place and is still constantly visited by the pigeons.

In the Hôtel d'Aubray, 12 rue Charles-V, built in 1620, resided Marie-Madeleine d'Aubray, Marquise de Brinvilliers, born in Paris in 1630, who both by birth and marriage had the world at her feet. Her social position was such that she could have had everything anyone could normally want. Yet she wanted a little more: in fact to watch others die a horrible death.

She was a small, round-faced woman whose blue eyes radiated kindness, and whose skin was praised by her contemporaries for its whiteness. Her father, Dreux d'Aubray, was civil governor of the Grand Châtelet, where the Paris parliament, a judiciary body, met. Her husband, Antoine Gobelin, Marquis de Brinvilliers, was the last of the Gobelins. They were originally dyers from Rheims who settled on the Left Bank, and made a vast fortune. The village of Les Gobelins was called after them. Antoine de Gobelin was too rich to have anything to do with business. Marie-Madeleine and her husband lived in fine style. She took the Chevalier Godin de Sainte-Croix as her lover, and under his great influence, together they concocted potions consisting of vitriol, poison of adder and arsenic. Police Lieutenant Nicolas-Gabriel de La Reynie, who under Louis XIV organised the Paris police, wrote of her, "Who would have believed that a woman brought up in an honest family, and whose figure was so fragile, could go to hospitals for the fun of poisoning the sick to observe the effects of her poison?"

She gave François Roussel, one of her lackeys, a slice of ham which made him feel "as if his heart were stung". Her father, shocked by the way she carried on with her lover, had Sainte-Croix put into the Bastille, but he did not remain there long. The Marquise decided to punish her father, but succeeded in killing him off only after the tenth dose. Then, with the connivance of a servant, she poisoned her two brothers.

She remained a quiet little woman with a sweet smile and the patients in the hospitals looked forward to her visits. In 1670 Sainte-Croix died of natural causes, and not of poison as was later suggested. When an inventory was taken, bottles and powders were found in the turret of 5 rue de Hautefeuille where he had mostly lived. The contents of the bottles and the powders were tried on animals, which died in terrible pain. The Marquise fled to England, later moved to the Low Countries, and was supposedly arrested in a convent in Liège by Desgrez, an agent of de La Reynie, who had come to the convent disguised as a priest. However, the truth was that a French spy, Descarrières, had found out where she was, arrested her and brought her back to Paris. A full, written confession of her misdeeds was found on her. She had poisoned more people than the authorities suspected.

She was executed in the Place de Grève on July 16, 1676, after having made amends and due apology in Notre-Dame. (During her incarceration she behaved with decorum, and her piety was sincere.) She wore only a shift, and a rope tied round her neck. The large crowd included ladies of fashion, the Marquise de Sévigné among them. "It is, is it not, a beautiful spectacle?" she called to them from the tumbril. Bare-footed she mounted the scaffold. The executioner took a leisurely quarter of an hour in preparing her for death; he shaved her hair, set the trap, turned her head towards the gibbet, then turned it away, almost more of an agony than the hanging itself. After she was hanged, her body was burnt and her ashes scattered. "The next day," wrote Madame de Sévigné, "the people came to look for her bones because they thought her a saint."

Today the Hôtel d'Aubray is occupied by the Sisters of Bon-Secours-de-Troyes, and in the court of honour, where Sainte-Croix used to throw his weight about, an old nun stands, waiting to give an injection to a patient, for injections are given free to the poor of the neighbourhood. If you enter the house and look up at the winding staircase with its wrought-iron rails you may see another nun coming down to minister to the sick. The past has truly been scattered to the wind.

By the second half of the eighteenth century, the Marais had lost much of its elegance. Its new inhabitants were the poorer, but very conservative, small nobility. Bigoted, and bemoaning the awful morals of their day, despising its worldliness and the wickedness of the fashionable Faubourg Saint-Germain, they hated the philosophers, and read only novels of chivalry and the *Mercure de France*. They spent their time playing cards for small stakes and abhorring the mutinous poor of the Faubourg Saint-Marcel who filled the cabarets of Vaugirard on Sundays.

During the Empire, the Marais continued to decline, yet it was in the Marais, in the cul-de-sac Saint-Pierre (now rue Villehardouin) where history was nearly changed. The year was 1812.

On October 22 a sergeant of the Paris garrison arrived in Dr Dubuisson's mental home at the Barrière du Trône (now Place de la Nation). He came to deliver a message to General Malet, who was detained there by the Emperor's orders. "Compiègne," the sergeant whispered. That was the code word of the conspirators. The general nodded: he had been waiting to hear it for a long time.

Claude-François de Malet, born at Dole (Jura) in 1754, had been a musketeer under the old order, but rallied to the Revolution and fought with the Army of the Rhine, then with the Army of Italy; he was made a general of brigade in 1799. He became hostile to the Consulate, then to the Empire. In vain Napoleon tried to win him over to his cause, but Malet conspired against him, and in 1808 was put into the prison of La Force in the Marais, where he continued to plot the downfall of the Emperor. In time he got himself transferred to Dr Dubuisson's mental home.

After the sergeant's departure the general sat down to dine with the other inmates. Someone observed that surely tomorrow news would arrive of a victory in Russia: Paris had been without news for some time. After dinner Malet played his usual game of whist, and retired towards ten. He waited until eleven, then tiptoed out into the garden. It was pouring with rain. He let himself out of the grounds, using a stolen key, and vanished into the night in the company of the Abbé Lafon, a fervid royalist who was also a detainee. The Abbé carried a leather box crammed with papers, the proclamations of the Provisional Government. The two men hurried along the rue Saint-Antoine, crossed the Place des Vosges, took the rue des Minimes, reached the rue Neuve-Saint-Gilles (now part of the rue de Turenne), then turned into the rue Villehardouin, where they entered a hovel. The Abbé Caamano, a pock-marked Spaniard, was waiting for them. The hovel was in ideal surroundings for conspirators, being close only to large gardens, convents and monasteries. Malet donned the general's uniform that the Abbé Caamano had laid out for him, signed the proclamations and orders, then had a quick meal accompanied by a glass of claret.

At eleven-thirty a naked man stepped out of a fiacre and burst into the house. This was Rateau, a corporal of the Guard of Paris, who, in his excitement to put on the elegant uniform of an adjutant which Malet had promised him, had discarded his corporal's uniform in the cab. Rateau was twenty-eight years old.

At dawn Malet was ready to leave. The Abbé Lafon had in the meantime had second thoughts and did not want to follow him. "Too late," said Malet, "the guillotine is at the door." At half past four, followed by faithful Rateau, he arrived at the barracks of Popincourt, where he announced to Colonels Rabbe and Soulier that Napoleon had been killed on the ramparts of Moscow and that the Provisional Government had made him military governor of Paris. On his orders Generals Guidal and Lahorie were released from La Force, Guidal designated as Minister of Police and Lahorie as Prefect of Police.

Malet hurried on to General Hulin, the military governor of Paris, whose residence was in the Place Vendôme.

"You are under arrest," Malet informed him.

"Show me your orders," Hulin replied.

"Here they are," said Malet, breaking his jaw with a pistol shot.

Hulin's wife appeared, wakened by the bang; Malet told her to look after her wounded husband. Then, still accompanied by Rateau, he crossed the square to the office of the staff of the Paris garrison. Commander Doucet, Chief of Staff, and his adjutant, Laborde, hesitated to accept orders from Malet, who immediately drew his pistol. They had, however, noticed his movement in the looking-glass, and sensing that something was wrong, managed to overpower both him and Rateau. By then messengers had arrived from General Hulin.

Tied with ropes, Malet was dragged to the balcony and shown to the troops in the square. Guidal and Lahorie were arrested.

The conspirators were tried at once. No lawyer dared defend them, and with dignity Malet conducted his own defence.

"Who are your accomplices?" the President of the Tribunal asked.

"The whole of France, including you had I succeeded."

All the conspirators—fourteen in number—were sentenced to death, and on October 29, in six fiacres, escorted by gendarmes, they were taken to the Plaine de Grenelle, the usual place for military executions. When Malet faced the firing squad he called to the soldiers: "It is my privilege here to give you orders. Aim! Fire!" He shouted, "Long live liberty!" as he fell.

One of the fourteen was an old captain called Borderieux who had seen many campaigns. He had followed Malet because it was a captain's duty to take orders from a general. He did not quite understand what it was all about.

"Long live the Emperor!" was his last cry.

VIII

The Bastille

The Bastille (see Illustration 30) was built to form part of the Enceinte of Charles V at the end of the rue Saint-Antoine. Hughes Aubriot, Provost of Paris, was charged by the King with the supervision of the new fortifications, and it was he who laid the foundation stone of the Bastille on April 22, 1369. The fortified Castle of Bastille-Saint-Antoine was finished in 1383 in the reign of Charles VI. The rue Saint-Antoine became a cul-de-sac with the Castle at the end, and to leave Paris one had to take the rue de la Bastille to the new Porte Saint-Antoine. The Bastille had two towers at the start, constructed with the object of strengthening the defence of Paris against the English. In time two further towers were erected, parallel with the first two. Eventually their number increased to eight. At first they were connected by drawbridges only. The walls came later. The whole was surrounded by a moat.

A guard was always mounted at the entrance gate facing the rue Saint-Antoine. The gate opened on the Courtyard of the Governor, whose mansion was later built in the sixteenth century, and a moat separated the courtyard from the Castle proper, to reach which one had first to cross a drawbridge guarded by a sentry. Past the guard-house was a high gate, beyond it the Great Courtyard, to enter which five more gates, each with a sentry, had to be passed, and two drawbridges crossed. The Great Courtyard was a hundred and twenty feet long and eighty feet wide. The windows of the prison officials and clerks gave on to the Great Courtyard and when there were too many prisoners some of the privileged ones were transferred to rooms adjoining those of the clerks. Strictly speaking, there were no cells in the Bastille. It was no ordinary prison.

Alongside the building that housed the officials and clerks rose the Tour de la Comté; next came the Tour du Trésor, so named because in that tower was guarded the treasure the Duc de Sully had collected for Henri IV. An arcade followed which in the days of Charles VI was still the city gate. Inside the walls lodged the prison staff. The old chapel beyond the arcade had been turned into prisoners' quarters. At the corner stood the Tour de la Chapelle, one of the two original towers, the other being the Tour du Trésor. A wall ten feet thick, raised to the height of the towers, contained the prisoners' rooms.

On the other side of the wall was the Courtyard du Puits, where a new building was erected in the seventeenth century. Five steps led to the entrance door, beyond it a staircase to the suites upstairs. To the right of the staircase was the entrance hall to the stately room where the Ministers and the Lieutenant of Police or the higher officials interrogated the prisoners. The room was known as the Chambre du Conseil. In an adjacent room were kept the prisoners' papers and belongings. Behind the Salle du Conseil lodged some of the high officials, their deputies and some of the turnkeys.

On the left of the entrance door downstairs were located the kitchens, pantries and the laundry. Their doors gave on the Courtyard du Puits. Above the kitchens were three rooms on each of the three floors in which were kept privileged prisoners and the sick. The King's Lieutenant had his suite above the Salle du Conseil, the Major (Deputy-Governor) on the second floor, and the surgeon on the third.

On the other side of the Great Courtyard near the Tour de la Liberté, so called because of the dungeons in its cellar, lived the bulk of the prisoners. Each had one large and one small room, their windows overlooking Paris.

The chapel was on the ground floor. In the walls were three heavily barred recesses, and against the walls were two similarly barred wooden closets, from within which, one at a time in each closet or recess, the prisoners heard Mass. They pulled the curtains aside at the Sanctus and drew them at the Postcommunion. There were two Masses daily for prisoners, and since only five could be present at a time, if there were more than ten prisoners in the Bastille they were unable to go to Mass every day, unless there were those who refused or did not feel like going. In matters of conscience there was no compulsion.

Beyond the chapel rose the Tour de la Bertaudière, followed by the apartments of the Assistant-Major, the Captain of the Gate, some servants and turnkeys. Nearby stood the Tour de la Bazinière, but to reach it one had to pass a guardhouse and go through a heavy gate. If one followed the alley one reached the Tour du Coin at the angle of the Courtyard du Puits. In the building beside the tower lodged the cooks, the scullions and lackeys. The rooms above theirs were rarely used. The Courtyard du Puits was only twenty-five feet long and fifty wide, with a well in the middle into which the cooks threw all the garbage, and, since they kept chickens in that small enclosed space, the well was filthy and the water undrinkable. The Tour du Puits faced the rue des Tournelles, and the entrance to the Castle was between the Tours de la Bazinière and de la Comté.

The towers were about seventy-two feet high. Four of them faced Paris, four the Faubourg Saint-Antoine. They were connected by high walls, along the tops of which the prisoners were allowed to stroll by permission of the Lieutenant, though invariably accompanied by a guard. The thirteen pieces of ordnance atop the walls were fired on feast days and occasions of national rejoicing.

Though from time to time prisoners were held in the Bastille, it remained a military fortress until Cardinal de Richelieu turned it exclusively into a place of detention. His first prisoner was Charles Leclerc du Tremblay, brother of Father Joseph, the Grey Eminence.

It was not defamatory to be locked up in the Bastille, for all prisoners were detained under a "lettre de cachet", which was really a letter of introduction from the King. However, such a letter was not something that one sought. It was short:

"Monsieur le Gouverneur, Sending to my Castle of the Bastille Sieur (name followed) I write this letter to tell you that it is my intention that he should be received by you and kept in safety until my new order. The present having no other purpose I pray to God to keep you, Monsieur le Gouverneur, in good health."

Beneath the King's signature was that of the Minister.

The prisoners' rooms were cold and humid in winter, hot in summer. The furniture in the reigns of Louis XIV, XV, and XVI consisted of an iron bedstead with mattress and green curtains, two tables, two jugs, one fork, one spoon, a tin goblet, brass candlestick, a pair of snuffers, chamber-pot, two or three chairs and now and then a rickety armchair. The prisoners received a provision of matches, one tinderbox, flint and one candle each day. The rooms were swept weekly and the sheets changed fortnightly. Each room had treble doors, all locked.

The price of food was according to a tariff from 50 livres down to 2 livres and 10 sous a day. Laundry and candles were included in the price. The lowest rate permitted no more than the tipping of the turnkeys and servants, so that those who could afford only that lowly sum were really fed by the prison. The food was prepared by a chef who was the Governor's steward. He had a cook, a scullion and a sawyer of wood under him. The food was cooked with little care and the rations were meagre, providing the Governor with his goldmine, according to the prisoners. On meat-days, the midday meal included soup, boiled beef and a vegetable; on fast-days, soup, fish and two vegetables: in the evenings on meat-days, a slice of roast meat, a stew and a salad. The prisoner who paid the highest tariff received half a chicken extra for his dinner, or a pigeon or a rabbit, all of them smelling of cabbage; on fast-days, a dish of eggs, a vegetable, and a pudding which was hardly worth 2 sous. Sunday's dinner consisted of soup, boiled cow, which the steward had the cheek to call beef, and four small pies; for supper, there was a slice of roast veal or mutton, a small plate of beans, full of bones and turnips, and a salad. The cooking oil, just good enough for street lamps, was nauseating. Now and then the prisoners were given mutton chops or tripe and spinach, and on fast-days carp, either fried or poached. On the feast days of SS Louis, Martin and Epiphany, even the non-paying prisoners received half a roast chicken or a pigeon.

Daily all prisoners were supplied with a pound of bread and a bottle of wine which tasted like vinegar. The cutlery was poor, one needed influence to be allowed silver knives and forks. Worst of all was the tasteless, badly cooked food. The prison officials had no supervision whatever over the kitchen, as it was directly under the control of the Governor. A few rich prisoners were occasionally allowed to have food sent in from eating-houses. It cost three times as much as could ever be paid for prison food, however. The ordinary, non-paying, prisoners received five logs a day in winter; the privileged ones had as many as they wanted.

(Thus groused the Sieur Brossays Du Perray who was long detained in the Bastille in the reign of Louis XV.)

Day and night, the sentry inside the Bastille rang a handbell every hour to show that he was awake. The night patrol rang a handbell every quarter of an hour. The bridges were drawn between ten and eleven at night; if a King's Messenger arrived, a bridge was let down whatever the time.

On arrival in the Bastille the ordinary prisoner was searched, and his clothes, luggage and linen carefully examined to see whether there were hidden papers concerning the reason for his arrest. Men of rank usually escaped such close scrutiny, but were asked to hand over their knives, razors, scissors, watches, canes, jewels and money. Then the prisoner was taken to an apartment and locked behind three doors. If he had no servant of his own, he had to make his own bed and fire. Dinner was brought at eleven in the morning and supper at six in the evening.

At the beginning of his detention, books, paper, and ink were withheld from him, and he was not permitted to go to Mass or for a walk, nor to write letters, not even to the Lieutenant of Police on whom his fate in the Bastille depended. Permission to write to the Lieutenant was normally given when the prisoner petitioned the Major, and, once this privilege was granted, he was then allowed to Mass, though only every second Sunday. In his letter to the Lieutenant the prisoner might ask for authority to write to his family, to receive their reply and to keep his own servant in the Castle. One had to apply to the Lieutenant for the smallest trifle, and his decisions depended on the detainee's case.

The Bastille possessed a library founded by a foreigner who was a prisoner there in the first decade of the eighteenth century and who died within the walls. Some of the prisoners had the privilege of visiting the library; others had the books brought to their rooms.

The fate of the prisoners was in the hands of the Lieutenant and the Ministers. They were not discouraged to write to the King. Many did so: none received a reply.

During his detention Brossays Du Perray spoke to old prisoners who had been, or had known those who had been, contemporaries of the Man in the Iron Mask. All they could tell him was that the Governor always stood in his presence, which seemed to confirm that he was of royal blood. However, this was only hearsay since none of them could have been present. The mask was not of iron but of black velvet.

When Louis XVI came to the throne, many prisoners were released, among them an old man who had been detained for forty-seven years. The old man thought he was dreaming. His legs had become so weak, and his eyes were so unaccustomed to the harsh light of liberty, that he had to be helped into the carriage that was to take him home. The shaking of the carriage exhausted him, and on arrival he had to be lifted out. There he was in his street, but his house had long been pulled down, and a public building stood on the site. The whole neighbourhood looked different and he saw no familiar face.

He plied the other old men of the district with questions about his family. They could not help him. He went to see the man he had worked for before his detention but did not recognise him. Slowly it transpired that his wife had died thirty years before and that his children had left Paris long ago. Shattered, the old man waited on the Minister and begged him to be allowed back to the Bastille. The Minister took pity on him, and the retired porter of the house that had been pulled down was attached to him, so that he should have near him someone to whom he could speak of his wife and children. The old man turned the bedroom he was given into a replica of his room in the Bastille. It was not the same thing, and he died soon after.

On July 2, 1789, the Marquis de Launay, Governor of the Bastille, reported to Monsieur de Villedeuil, Minister of State, that the Marquis de Sade, who was then a prisoner in the Bastille, had been shouting through his window to the people in the rue Saint-Antoine that the prisoners were to be butchered and murdered and that the people should come at once to their help. The Governor, therefore, felt compelled to withdraw all de Sade's privileges, including that of walking along the walls. Undismayed, de Sade constructed a sort of loudspeaker from a tin pipe used for emptying water, and continued vociferating through his casement window. People assembled in the street, and he abused the Governor and urged them to come to his help, otherwise he would be massacred.

He gave his version in a letter, complaining that, because of a little trouble he had caused, the Governor had seen fit to denounce him. According to the Governor he had harangued the populace, shouting that preparations were in progress to butcher the prisoners, and exhorting them to pull down that monument of horror. "It's all true," he added.

On July 4, the Marquis de Sade was sent to the madhouse of Charenton, and the one to be massacred was the Governor when the Bastille was taken ten days later.

Vast crowds visited the Bastille from July 15 onwards, and their number was so large and their behaviour so unruly that Soulès, a moderate, who was appointed Governor by La Fayette, stopped further visits and wrote to the Municipal Council explaining his reasons: "Such damage has already been done by them to the fortress that it will cost at least 200,000 livres to have it repaired." Danton, who the night before had been made Captain of the National Guard, was so incensed by Soulès's letter, and convinced also that a moderate like him would let the enemy back into the Bastille, that he went to the Bastille at the head of a shouting mob, where he collared the new Governor and dragged him to the Hôtel de Ville. Soulès's order was rescinded and visitors flocked again to the Bastille. Later, public dances were held there, wine flowed to the sound of fiddles, and the printed patterns on chintzes of the epoch showed the ruins of the Bastille with the inscription: "Ici l'on danse!"

IX

Fiacre, Coachman and Omnibus

Already in the eighteenth century traffic had become a problem. In vain did the exasperated passenger shout, "Whip them, coachman!" The fiacre remained stuck to the spot, since the coachman had enough sense to appreciate that horses could not fly. In time the expression "fouette, cocher!" came to mean that the passenger hailed from the provinces, for only provincials still had faith that the whip would open a passage through the congestion. This is not to imply that Paris coachmen were more reluctant to use their whips than were their counterparts in the country. They used them on their own horses, other coachmen's horses, on fellow coachmen, indeed on pedestrians. In brief, the whips were always at the ready, yet their use did not hasten the flow of traffic. Then, as now, the streets of Paris were often invincible.

Here dustmen barred progress with their carts and bins; yonder a wagon laden with heavy stones was waiting beside a construction site to be discharged, or a shaft-horse might have fallen. As one lot of chaos sorted itself out, water carts appeared, moving in slow procession and stopping in front of every house. Then the heavy wagons from the country, laden with fruit or vegetables, got in everybody's way; their drivers appeared frequently to be asleep, but as their seats were practically on the shaft, they could hardly see in any case where their horses were taking them. The horses knew the way, but theirs was a ponderous progress. Washerwomen were among the worst traffic offenders, their vehicles staying for three to four hours outside a house while inside they made out the laundry list. (A laundress's cart, it is recorded, once kept as many as four hundred carriages waiting.) The never-too-patient coachmen would suddenly succumb to their passengers' entreaties or their own fury, and try to whip their way through the pedestrians, who might not find time to run for safety.

There was little respect for the pedestrian. The running footman pushed him out of the way, the dogs cavorting beside their master's carriage caused him to trip, and if a coachman or a gentleman driving his own equipage felt that the pedestrian was somehow to be blamed for the delay, the poor fellow received the full impact of the driver's anger, generally imparted by the whip.

One day in the year 1776, as Jean-Jacques Rousseau was taking a stroll in Ménilmontant, a Great Dane, running in front of a berline, charged straight into him and bowled him over. The dog's master did not bother to stop, but next day, discovering who the victim was, sent a servant to him.

"My master would like to do something for you, sir," the servant said. "He charged me to find out what you want."

"I want him to keep his dog on a lead," replied Rousseau, dismissing the man.

Coachmen, like the carriages and horses, were the reflection of their masters' rank and station. One saw at a glance whether the turn-out belonged to a courtesan or a duke, a President of Parliament or a financier. Even the words used to instruct a coachman differed from class to class. On leaving the theatre, the inhabitants of the Marais ordered their coachmen to take them to their lodging; those of the Ile-Saint-Louis to their house; and those of the Faubourg

Saint-Germain to their mansion. The élite of the Faubourg Saint-Honoré simply said, "Go!"

Outside the theatres lounged the aboyeurs, the barkers, who sprang to life when the show was over. In booming voices they shouted, "The coach of Monsieur le Marquis!. . . . The coach of Madame la Comtesse! . . . The coach of Monsieur le Président! . . .", their voices reaching the cabaret where the lackeys were drinking and the billiard saloon where the coachmen were arguing.

In 1640 Nicolas Sauvage of Amiens had the original notion of putting at the public's disposal, at certain points of the town, carriages with coachmen and harnessed horses. He brought his idea to Paris. The first such point, or cab rank, was outside an inn in the rue Saint-Martin called Au grand Saint-Fiacre. Hence the fiacre. Apart from sedan chairs, which could be hired from 1617, the only other vehicles for hire before the fiacres were the carosses à 5 sols, but they had no ranks, and one had to search for them or go direct to the coach-house. They were a haphazard enterprise. An order of Parliament promulgated in 1622 forbade their use to soldiers, pages, workmen, lackeys and all other liveried persons, so as to safeguard the comfort of the citizens.

In the eighteenth century, the fiacre was no elegant turn-out. The coachmen were proud that the horses came from the royal stables, albeit only after the animals had become too old or afflicted for further work. The miserable beasts had to work eighteen hours a day, constantly under the lash of the whip. They were seldom rubbed down, and pulled their cabs emaciated and dirty. Their happiest moment was when some lover took the cab and sat in it behind drawn curtains with his mistress, because then the fiacre pulled into a side street and remained stationary while the tryst lasted.

Foreigners were revolted by the shabby cabs and skinny horses, comparing them with the cleaner and smarter cabs of London, Brussels and Amsterdam. The fiacre owners themselves were dissatisfied with the irksome police regulations. One day they drove in procession to Choisy to petition Louis XVI. The Court was unpleasantly surprised to observe the arrival of eighteen hundred empty fiacres: not a reassuring sight. The petition was not accepted, the fiacres were ordered back to Paris, the four leaders were imprisoned and their leader sent to Bicêtre, which was both gaol and lunatic asylum.

The fiacres often broke down; none the less one had to pay the fare. They were not allowed to ply outside Paris without paying special dues. The fiacre owners continued bitterly to complain of their daily tax of 20 sous, and their vehicles remained dirty and rickety well into the nineteenth century.

Between 1830 and 1855 new fiacre models appeared: citadines, urbaines, deltas, cabriolets compteurs, lutéciennes, cabriolets milords, thérèses and les cabs. The old, yellow cabriolet gave way to the coupé, a small carriage that became the most popular, much to the regret of the old coachmen. "All these coupés, all these modern carriages," they said, "will never last. You take a good old cabriolet not because you want to reach your destination quickly but because you want to chat to the coachman." Yet the coupé won.

In the middle of the century the Compagnie Générale was formed. It came to own most of the fiacres in Paris. They had a hundred and sixty employees in their office, a hundred and sixty inspectors to check on the coachmen, nine hundred workmen in their coachbuilding yard, a hundred and eighty blacksmiths, nine hundred cleaners and nine hundred grooms and stable boys. The company was run by efficient men who brought order and system into the world of fiacres. They chose their horses with care and trained them scientifically, starting with three hours of work a day, because they appreciated that if a horse was overworked at the beginning, it might die before it reached the target of staying out, say, from seven in the morning until midnight. The horses were well fed and kept clean, since that too was in the interest of business. "In Paris," one of the managers observed, "you need powerful horses accustomed to privation and misery." The company succeeded in controlling all their interests with the irritating exception of the coachmen themselves.

The fiacre coachmen were born rebels, always ready to fight and, when possible, to cheat boss and passenger. They hated the entire world, including the Préfecture de Police, though when summoned there—a frequent occurrence—they grovelled abjectly. That did not stop them cursing the authorities the moment they were allowed to go. They came to the capital from Lorraine, Normandy, Auvergne and Savoy. There were hardly any Parisians among them. Some of them came because they loved horses. They were the good and decent coachmen with whom owners and police had little trouble. They had but one aim, namely to put aside enough money to buy their own turn-out, an object achieved by quite a few of them. However, they were not the typical Paris coachmen.

The drunks formed a large proportion. Between fares, they rushed into the nearest cabaret to swallow a "canon" of wine. Yet they drove well and seldom had accidents, driving being second nature to them. They were not disliked by passengers and did not ill-treat their horses. "A drunkard's horse is never skinny," says an old French proverb. The drunk chose the life of a coachman because it gave him a sense of freedom and independence. He was the master and the ruler while he sat on the box and held in his hand the badge of his importance, the whip.

A third category, known as the bohemians, consisted of a recalcitrant group who took to the trade thinking that it entailed little work and even less control. The bohemians were in constant trouble with their employers and the police, and frequently ended up either in the gutter of unemployment (during the last century the workless were still free to starve to death) or in prison. They were disappointed men, for a coachman's life was not as easy as they had hoped. They were not wine drinkers like the friendly drunkards. Absinthe was their beverage and in their language strangling a parrot meant swallowing a glass of absinthe. The horses could fall down dead as far as they were concerned. In the days of the Second Empire a fiacre of the Compagnie Générale failed to return to the coach-house one night. In the morning an inspector was sent out to look for it. He found it at a street corner, minus coachman and horse. On the previous evening, the coachman had taken the horse out of the shafts, sold it in the street, then gone off on a huge drunken spree. On being arrested in a tavern near the Fortifications and hauled before a magistrate, his defence consisted of but one sentence, "I felt like having a night out."

The career of a coachman fascinated men in different walks of life. Even those in whose lives the horse as such played no part hankered after the whip and the box. Among coachmen, many oddities were to be found, such as waiters, barbers, wigmakers, water-carriers, dismissed schoolmasters, clerks, bankrupt photographers, unfrocked priests, and in the 1860s there was an ambassador's son who preferred the life of a fiacre coachman to that provided by his station.

In Alphonse Daudet's *Sapho*, the heroine's father was an old, drunken fiacre coachman, and one night, as she and her lover left the theatre, they ran into him. His list of woes was long. The woman he had married, after deserting his daughter and her mother, had been taken to hospital, business was bad, and money increasingly scarce. However, he still held the whip firmly in his hand. Since his daughter had had several influential lovers, he wondered whether she needed a coachman. He would not mind driving her horses. She explained that she had no carriage. "Tant pis alors," he said and swaggered off.

On September 16, 1855, Monsieur Juge, Director of the Ecole Normale of Douai, was on a visit to Paris with his wife. They took a fiacre in the Place de la Concorde and drove to the Bois de Boulogne. The coachman, whose name was Collignon, overcharged them, and M Juge, who disliked being done, went to complain at the Préfecture de Police. On September 22, Collignon was ordered to call on him to refund the excess charge. It was a matter of only a few francs. Collignon bought two pistols. Two days later he sold all his chattels and went to 83 rue d'Enfer (now rue des Ursins), where M Juge was lodging. The two men spoke calmly, without raising their voices. Collignon paid, but as M Juge bent over the table to sign the receipt, Collignon whipped out a pistol and shot him through the head. As Mme Juge threw herself on her dying husband, Collignon fired at her also, but missed. He raced down the stairs and out into the street, where he was caught by a policeman who had heard the shots.

On November 12 he appeared at the Assizes, and neither there nor in prison showed the slightest regret or remorse; not even when led to the gallows.

Towards the end of last century, a certain lady retired from brothel keeping. She had done remarkably well, though she had started on the lowest rung of the ladder, in a provincial establishment near the military barracks. With industry and acumen she had worked her way to the top. She had had the advantage of a clever ponce, whom she married in the course of her career, and he advised her on business matters, looked after her interests, pimped assiduously, and in short was her right arm in every sense. Now all that was over. Their fortune was big enough to enable them to turn their backs on the past, and they bought a private mansion in the centre of the capital. Yet both she and her husband felt rather isolated in fashionable Paris. (Fashionable in those days was used as a French word.) She tried everything she could think of to make herself noticed by the quality. She bought good furniture and pictures by winners of the Prix de Rome, took the best box in the theatre and left nothing to chance. Nevertheless her isolation continued. Then one day she heard that a famous private coachman, who had been in the service of a distinguished nobleman, was looking for a job. She promptly sent for him.

The coachman, of course, knew about her. He asked for double the wages that he would have accepted elsewhere. She agreed. He was willing to drive only every other day. She agreed to that too. He needed a stable boy who would also fetch his meals from the house and not the sort of food with which servants were satisfied. Again she nodded her consent.

"There is one more condition," the coachman said. "I am not driving your husband."

In the 1860s a story circulated in Paris which was probably true. It serves to reveal the coachman's mentality. A gentleman won a large sum of money at his club. He left after midnight and took the coupé that he hired by the month. When he reached his house he found that his wallet was missing. It must have dropped out in the carriage. He hurried to the coach-house, where he found the coachman feeding the horse, not yet having looked inside the cab. The gentleman opened the door, saw the wallet lying on the seat, and said to the coachman, "Thank God I found my wallet. It contains all this. I won it at cards tonight." He showed the coachman the imposing bank roll and gave him a good tip. After he had left the coachman went to the back of the coach-house and, in his despair at having missed the chance of a lifetime, hanged himself from a rafter.

The Compagnie Générale also hired out carriages for private use. A barouche with two horses cost 1,200 francs a month in the second half of last century, plus 150 francs for the coachman, and, if one wanted a footman on the box, that was 6 francs a day extra. A page cost more because of the epaulettes, and the company even provided powdered personnel on demand. They had a beauty parlour on the premises. If required, they provided bells for the horses. At weddings, there was no extra charge for the flowers worn by the coachmen in their buttonholes and those which decorated their whips.

The smart young set liked hiring pony-chaises, which had a rather dashing appearance. They drove the chaises themselves, usually to show off in the Bois de Boulogne. The bloods had to pay in advance, whereas for a family barouche the paterfamilias was not required to settle before the end of the month.

Public transport was one of Blaise Pascal's ideas. The name omnibus orginated from him too. He spoke of it to the Duc de Roannez who in 1661 obtained a concession from Louis XIV. The first omnibuses appeared in the streets of Paris eleven years later. The itineraries were fixed by the King. The coachmen wore the livery of the Town of Paris, and the fleur-de-lys was painted on the doors of the coaches. There were three lines, each served by seven carriages. The first plied between the Porte Saint-Antoine and the Luxembourg; the second between the Place Royale (Place des Vosges) and the Church of Saint-Roch; the third between the Luxembourg and the Church of Saint-Eustache. The coaches had to ply between the different districts at regular intervals, and it was laid down that the passengers be charged for their seats only, and at a moderate price.

The first omnibuses had room for six passengers; later, two more seats were added. The coaches were strictly reserved for the members of the middle classes. Now and then a nobleman might ride in one, but that was such a rare and untoward event that it was likely to be reported in the gazettes. The lower orders were not permitted to use the coaches, which lasted for fifteen years, then vanished from the streets.

Pascal's idea was not resurrected until 1826, and not in Paris but in Nantes, where it had such a signal success that Monsieur Baudry, who was responsible for the venture, wanted to start a similar enterprise in the capital. Baudry, however, had a revolutionary past (he was mixed up with the Carbonari) and Delavau, the Prefect of Police, eyed him with suspicion. The Prefect also saw political dangers in a venture that sought indiscriminately to cater for all classes. Instead of Paris, therefore, Bordeaux became the next city to have omnibuses. They were again so successful that Debelleyme, the new Prefect of Police, gave his fiat to the venture, and the Enterprise Générale des Omnibus was founded in Paris.

The first omnibuses had fourteen seats. A ticket cost 5 sous, the same sum as in the time of Louis XIV. The heavy coaches, shaped not unlike a gondola, were drawn by three horses. Each coach had three trumpets worked by a foot pedal which called the passengers in lugubrious tones. In 1853 appeared the impériales (top-decks), where smokers, students, and workmen preferred to travel. One paid only half price on the top deck.

In time, only two horses were used to draw an omnibus; but at every incline—there were thirty-one on the company's itinerary—an extra horse was harnessed to the omnibus to help it up the hill. The heavy horses were brought from Normandy, Perche, Ardennes and Brittany. Geldings were preferred. The same pair of horses always worked together and had the same coachman. Each omnibus had ten horses attached to it which worked in five relays, a relay extending no longer than sixteen kilometres. In this way the horses endured, some remaining at work at the age of fifteen in spite of having been every day in harness.

Pickpockets reaped an agreeable harvest on the omnibuses. The women specialised in slitting pockets. The men preferred purses, using a string with a tiny piece of lead on the end. The technique was to allow the weighted string to drop into a purse when a passenger opened it to pay the fare, and later to whisk away the closed purse while the victim was staring through the window, otherwise distracted. If the purse resisted, the pickpocket waited for a sudden stop, when he fell over his victim and, apologising profusely, grabbed it. At the next stop he lifted his hat to the passengers and stepped off the omnibus.

The omnibuses and the army of horses they required made traffic even more difficult in Paris. What, people moaned, would it be like in a hundred years' time? There would be so many horses that traffic would come to a complete standstill.

X

Belleville & Ménilmontant

The villages of Belleville and Ménilmontant were inhabited by market gardeners, vine growers and farm labourers. Theirs remained a completely rustic world until the villages were attached to Paris in 1860 by the Baron Haussmann as the nineteenth and twentieth arrondissements (now separated by the rue de Belleville). In one sense the two villages had always been a part of Paris, for they were the Sunday resort of the Parisian working class, who brought their wives and sweethearts to fill the guinguettes and cabarets, spending the day in eating, drinking and dancing. It was a day in the country away from their narrow streets and cobbles. Their wedding feasts, too, were celebrated in the guinguettes of Belleville and Ménilmontant, which formed the same parish, cut across by the rue de Ménilmontant, the high street of the commune. The guinguettes of Ménilmontant were less noisy and rowdy than those of Belleville. The villagers were inordinately proud of the fine view they had of Paris from their hillock. Between 1836 and 1868, the rue de Belleville was in fact called the rue de Paris.

The heights of Belleville were known as the Haute-Courtille, courtille in old French meaning a house with a garden. The lower part of the Grand' Rue de Belleville (now rue de Belleville) was forbidden to traffic on Sundays. The famous guinguettes in the street were Boeuf-Rouge, Coq-Hardi, Sauvage, Gallant Jardinier, Carotte Filandreuse and the cabaret of Papa Dénoyez, who inherited the popularity of Ramponeau, a cabaret-keeper of legendary fame who has a street called after him. The Basse-Courtille was the rue du Faubourg-du-Temple. There was a saying in the eighteenth and early nineteenth centuries that "To see Paris without visiting the Courtilles is like going to Rome without seeing the Pope."

Around 1780 a captain of artillery named Detienne retired to Ménilmontant, where he bought a house. He laid out a vegetable garden on the flat roof, where he grew melons, celery and cabbage. This was considered so surprising and out of the ordinary that provincials went to stare at it as part of their sightseeing tour of Paris.

The rue de Ménilmontant rises from the boulevard of the same name. Number 4 was a dance hall, Aux Armes de France, which in 1856 changed its name to Salle Giffard and became a political café where local enemies of the Second Empire plotted. In the early days of the Third Republic the Salle Giffard was still used by those who regretted the fall of the Commune. Number 27 was also a dance hall, le Bal des Grands Pavillons, as was number 40, le Bal des Barreaux Verts, which was renowned for the good manners of its customers. In dance halls and guinguettes behaviour was usually rough. If you wanted to dance with a girl, you approached her, or even took her from her partner if you thought you could win the ensuing fight. In the refined atmosphere of the Bal des Barreaux Verts, however, a man who wished to dance with a girl first presented her with a rose, which he sent by a waitress. If the recipient were willing, she pinned the flower to her bodice.

For centuries the village of Ménilmontant depended on the parish of Saint-Jean-Baptiste-de-Belleville. As the population of Ménilmontant grew, and it grew fast since the population of Paris spilt out into it, the priest of Saint-Jean-Baptiste had a modest chapel built at 69 bis rue de Ménilmontant, in 1823. When Ménilmontant became a parish on its own in 1847, the chapel became the Church of Notre-Dame-de-la-Croix, in honour of a statue of Our Lady who was invoked under that name as the patron saint of the oratory of the country retreat of the Monks of Sainte-Croix-de-la-Bretonnerie at Ménilmontant. The oratory and the country retreat were destroyed during the Revolution, but the statue was saved, having been hidden at Bagnolet in the Department of Seine-Saint-Denis. The small Church was enlarged between 1863 and 1869, aesthetically speaking not a happy period in French church architecture. During the Commune, the Church of Notre-Dame-de-la-Croix was turned into a club, where on May 6, 1871, the murder of the Archbishop of Paris and the massacre of the hostages was decided on by public acclamation.

The rue de Belleville rises from the Boulevard de Belleville. Towards the end of last century it boasted a funicular railway notorious for its technical troubles. On Sundays and Mondays, the street was probably busier than any inside the capital. At number 8 stood the Bal de la Folie-Dénoyez, the annexe of the tavern, which at weekends was crowded well before noon by Parisians in search of fresh air and a garden, which however would have had little meaning for them were not food and drink also provided. Next door to the tavern was the Follies-Belleville, a music hall. Shops remained open on Sunday and Monday because of the large influx of visitors. At number 17, a hat shop, the Halle aux Chapeaux, gave away a free beret with every hat bought. This was to attract the custom of workmen, whose usual headgear was the beret. At number 18 a cabaret called Grand Condé changed its name to Grand Mirabeau in 1792. Its attractions consisted of four cellars, nearly a hundred feet long, two saloons, an orchard and a yard with a well, giving it an irresistible country air and appeal. The Théâtre de Belleville was at number 46, and at number 94 was found the farm of the Priory of Saint-Martin-des-Champs, known as la Ferme de Savy.

Around 1764, Marshal of France Maurice of Saxony fell in love with Mme Favart, wife of Charles-Simon Favart, the playwright, who had married her in 1745 when he was thirty-five years old and she eighteen. Favart survived both the love affair and his wife. She remained with him until her death at the age of fifty-five. He lived to the great age of eighty-two and was buried in his garden at number 112.

At 139, at the corner of rue Lassus, stands the Church of Saint-Jean-Baptiste-de-Belleville which with the cemetery was considered the heart of the parish when Belleville was still a far-away village. The original church was built in 1635 on the site of a chapel that had been erected in 1548. In time it was pulled down, and the present church was not completed until 1859. It received several hits in May 1871 when the Government troops fought their way into Paris. The terminus of the funicular railway was in front of the church. There was one more music hall, the Lac Saint-Fargeau, before one reached the Haute-Courtille.

The guinguettes of the Haute-Courtille stood side by side, their gardens separated only by hedges. Wine flowed and the kitchen ranges, usually in the gardens, looked more like forges. Meat roasted on the spit was the customers' favourite. Each guinguette had its orchestra. Noise never ceased from Sunday morning to Monday night, when silence fell on the Haute-Courtille. Paul de Kock, the French writer of the last century, often went to the Haute-Courtille. "The gardens of the wine merchants," he wrote, "are lit up only on Sundays and Mondays." For him the Haute-Courtille was a place of drunkenness and nothing else. He described in his novels scenes of violence among drunken groups of workmen which ended with knifing and killing. "One is so accustomed to their shouting that one no longer pays attention."

The most famous feature of the rue de Belleville and the Haute-Courtille was the Descent from the Haute-Courtille which used to take place on Ash Wednesday. Early in the morning, every available fiacre, cabriolet, char à banc and barouche was hired by Parisians to go to the Haute-Courtille. Then, in a fine state of intoxication, they swept down in their vehicles along the length of the rues de Belleville and du Faubourg-du-Temple, not stopping until they reached the boulevards. They went armed with sugared almonds, flowers, eggs and flour, which they threw at the watching multitude. It was necessary to be in good voice, for vociferation was part and parcel of the entertainment. Over a thousand carriages took part in the procession, and the onlookers were estimated at tens of thousands. All windows on the route were let for the occasion, the taverns had already filled the night before, and excitement was intense.

"In 1803," wrote Lord Redesdale in his *Memories*, "Lord and Lady Yarmouth were detained in France—he interned at Verdun—when war was declared after the rupture of the Peace of Amiens, and their second son, Lord Henry Seymour, was born in Paris in 1805. . . . The Lord Henry was a very eccentric personage. Unlike his brother, Richard Lord Hertford, who was a handsome man and in his youth a dandy of the 10th Hussars, Lord Henry was singularly ugly, even grotesque. . . . He was a hero of the various Salles d'Armes, a famous fencer and athlete, and the founder, or at any rate, one of the founders of the French Jockey Club."

A French nobleman was supposedly the real father of the Lord Henry, who was rich and enjoyed practical jokes. He offered a friend a cigar into which he had put a few grains of gunpowder. The cigar exploded after a few puffs, burning the friend's face and hand. Lord Henry laughed loudly. The incident nearly caused a duel. Lord Henry was not keen on duelling. Once a French army officer boasted of his duels to him, observing, "I'm a very unfortunate man. I have fought ten duels and killed all my adversaries."

"I am more unfortunate than you," Lord Henry replied. "I have fought only one and the first shot killed me."

He also was the founder of the Société d'Encouragement et Amélioration de Chevaux en France. He owned a famous racing-stable and was immensely popular in Paris, particularly among the ordinary people, who much admired the eccentricities of the

Englishman who had been born in Paris and spent most of his life there. He had moments of great generosity, and when he died he left the bulk of his fortune to the Paris hospitals. The Parisians nicknamed him Milord l'Arsouille (blackguard, debauchee, also used as term of endearment), and wherever he appeared crowds gathered, shouting "Vive Milord l'Arsouille!"

In the days of Lord Henry's fame there came to Paris a strange personage, Charles de La Battut, son of an English apothecary and a French emigrée. He was born in 1806. The apothecary, being married to another woman, could not recognise him as his son, but succeeded in persuading an impoverished Breton nobleman to adopt him. Hence the name of de La Battut. On the death of the chemist, the illegitimate son inherited 100,000 livres and went to Paris to make a name for himself. He strove hard to be recognised as an eccentric, hoping to emulate Lord Henry, but as he was noisy and vulgar, he made little headway, though he tried everything, including the Descent from the Haute-Courtille on Ash Wednesday, driving a char à banc drawn by six horses with piqueurs blowing hunting horns. His huge carriage led the procession downhill. He showered sugared almonds and money on the crowd, and all he got in return was the shout, "Vive Seymour! Vive Milord l'Arsouille!", for anything so spectacular, the people believed, could only have been conceived by Lord Henry.

Charles de La Battut used to arrive on the heights of Belleville on the night of Shrove Tuesday, bringing a party of the prettiest Parisian actresses to the Bal de Saint-Martin, a cabaret and dance hall of repute, and while supping and drinking and making a lot of noise, he waited for his hour of glory, the Descent from the Haute-Courtille. He drove the char à banc down the rue de Belleville year after year, yet to his chagrin the people still acclaimed him with the heartbreaking shout, "Vive Seymour! Vive Milord l'Arsouille!" He did what he could to disabuse them, leaving the char à banc outside his house in the Boulevard des Capucines the whole day long, but people merely thought that Lord Henry had changed domicile.

In 1835 de La Battut's money ran out, and still unrecognised by the Parisians, he left for Naples, where he soon died. Many decades later the theory was evolved that Charles de La Battut had never existed and that the name was a pseudonym of Lord Henry who on such vulgar excursions did not wish to appear under his own name. Lord Henry, however, hardly had the temperament to appear under a name other than his own. Still, one wonders how an English apothecary in the early part of the last century could have left so much money to an illegitimate son.

When the ruined de La Battut ceased appearing on Ash Wednesdays at the Haute-Courtille, people lost interest in the Descent, for without Milord l'Arsouille it had lost its meaning and lustre. The last procession took place in 1836.

As far back as 1852 the Municipal Council of the two villages protested against the invasion of workmen who, instead of coming only on Sundays, bringing their hard-earned money to spend in guinguettes, began to infiltrate the rustic scene, taking lodgings and settling with their families. The natives did not want their villages to become working-class districts. However, with the "Haussmannisation" of Paris in full swing, thousands of workmen's lodgings and huts were pulled down to make way for the new boulevards, squares and wide streets, and the workmen moved in large numbers into the two villages. Rural Belleville and Ménilmontant became in fact working-class districts, and a hotbed of those who plotted against Napoleon III. In May 1871 Belleville was one of the last strongholds of the Commune, ferociously resisting the troops of the legal Government of Versailles.

The last of the combatants of the already almost defeated Commune were entrenched in Belleville in the rue Haxo. On May 26, 1871, Emile Gois, Colonel of the Commune, went in the company of a brother officer to the Prison of La Roquette in the rue de la Roquette, leading a firing squad consisting of as many as thirty men.

In the prison were detained the hostages of the Commune. Gois asked for fifty to be delivered up to him. They were assembled in the prison courtyard, where the roll was called. Some of the prisoners brought their luggage, believing that they were being transferred elsewhere. There were among them priests, gendarmes and four civilians suspected of treason, by which was meant supporting the legal Government. Emile Gois first wanted to have them shot on the spot, but was persuaded by his men to take them to Belleville.

As the hostages were marched out of the prison, a vast crowd awaited them in the street, hurling invectives at them and throwing filth in their faces. The women especially excelled with their curses and the choice ordures they flung at them. At the corner of the Boulevard de Ménilmontant an even more hostile crowd was waiting. Onlookers stepped into the road and, with the encouragement of their escorts, hit the hostages. At the Carrefour Oberkampf there was a violent scuffle.

The cortège reached the rue Haxo and stopped before the villa at number 85. At the window were two members of the Commune; on the other side of the Fortifications, only a few hundred yards away, German soldiers were playing waltzes on their accordions. An eighteen-year-old girl, dressed as a zouave, had followed the procession from the prison, showing great zeal in insulting the hostages and spitting at them. In a loud voice she had promised to kill them all. She now grabbed a rifle from one of the soldiers and shot dead the Abbé Planchat, founder of a charitable institution. The two members of the Commune leaned out of the window and gave the sign. The remaining hostages were pushed into the garden and the fusillade became general. When the corpses were counted, there were fifty-two and not just fifty: the wardens of La Roquette had delivered two too many. Among those who perished in the massacre were eleven priests and Jesuit Fathers and thirty-six gendarmes. The corpses were thrown into a trench in the grounds.

In 1872 the Jesuits bought the Villa of the Hostages and put a railing round the trench. The names of the victims were inscribed on a tablet, and a memorial chapel was erected in 1936.

By the end of the last century Belleville and Ménilmontant had lost the last vestiges of their rural past. They acquired a far from savoury reputation. The taverns were no longer filled by artisans relaxing after their work: local hooligans had taken over. To hail from Belleville or to speak with a Belleville accent was no recommendation. The same went for Ménilmontant. The criminals of the neighbourhood were young, as too were the ponces and streetwalkers. The district had become one in which crime and prostitution were the privilege of youth. The young hunted in packs and lorded it in the taverns with their aggressive behaviour. Their crimes had the impetuosity of their age.

One afternoon in 1913 a youth named Lucien Picard went to a tavern in Ménilmontant at 107 rue des Haies. He stopped in the doorway and fired two shots. One bullet killed a girl of eighteen, Amélie Van der Heyden, known as Mélie, the other lodged in the shoulder of Alexis Lecca, known as Cricri. Attracted by the shots, a posse of police arrived on the scene with swords drawn. Mélie's corpse was carried to the local police station, and while Picard was being escorted to the central police station, a crowd of about twenty young men followed, led by the wounded Cricri, who asked a friend in the crowd, one Ernest Renard, to avenge Mélie's death, which he could not do himself because of the bullet in his shoulder. Calmly, Renard approached Picard, whom he stabbed with a long stiletto, the blade penetrating deep into the right lung. Picard was taken to hospital. Both Cricri and Renard were arrested and taken before Police Commissioner Deslandes, but as Cricri was wounded, he too was escorted to hospital.

From questioning the witnesses, Deslandes discovered that Mélie was the daughter of an honest artisan of Belgian origin. They lived in Montreuil-sous-Bois (arrondissement de Sceaux), where she had met Picard and left the parental home to become Picard's mistress.

She had remained faithful to him, in the underworld meaning of the word, until she met Cricri, whose brother was the lover of Casque d'Or. Casque d'Or was a prostitute of repute. She had started her career by picking up men in the Bois de Boulogne who were then robbed by her male accomplices. She had caught the public imagination, and had been much publicised, even making appearances in music halls until the police intervened. It had been a feather in Mélie's cap to become, as it were, Casque d'Or's sister-in-law. Moreover, Picard was only a burglar whereas Cricri was a fully fledged apache who had an exalted position among the young criminals of Ménilmuche (Ménilmontant in their language).

Commissioner Deslandes went to see Picard in hospital. Picard looked enormously proud of himself.

"I am a killer from Montreuil," he boasted. "I won't have a little apache from Ménilmuche take my girl. That was why I killed her."

XI

Monceau & Batignolles

In the seventh century the Merovingians, who had made Paris their capital, hunted in the thick forest that spread from Montmartre to Saint-Cloud, taking in the hamlets of Passy, Chaillot, Roule, des Ternes, Monceau and Batignolles. Though farmers slowly established themselves on the edge of the forest, the game reserves remained, and deer, stag, hare and rabbit caused much damage to the cultivated land. The Revolution did away with the reserves. Because of its sandy soil Batignolles was covered with vineyards. By the eighteenth century Monceaux (as it was then spelt) had become a flourishing agricultural community. The dairy farmers were known as nourrisseurs, and their farms provided Paris with milk. Streets like Cardinet, des Moines and Jouffroy were dairy farms before Monceau was urbanised. After the Revolution one of its first paved streets took the name of rue des Fermiers (now 16 rue Jouffroy—91 rue de Saussure). When Baron Haussmann attached the outlying villages to Paris, Monceau and Batignolles were engulfed in the new seventeenth arrondissement, which also took in des Ternes and Epinette. The limits of Monceau are rue Des Renaudes, Boulevard de Courcelles and rues Lévis and de Tocqueville; of

Batignolles, Boulevard des Batignolles, Avenue de Clichy and rues La Condamine and Lemercier.

In 1753 Laurent Grimod de la Reynière, a fermier général, bought the château of the village of Monceaux (22 rue Legendre). He had waxed scandalously rich on the salted meat he supplied to the army of the Prince de Soubise during the Seven Years War. But he made good use of his fortune. He built a mansion at the corner of the rue de Bonne-Morue (now Boissy-d'Anglas) and Avenue de l'Elysée (now Avenue Gabriel), and fed extremely well. He was a glutton of the first order, and gave dinner and supper parties the excellence of which still echoes down the centuries. Gluttony in fact killed him. He died in harness with a napkin round his neck and foie gras on his plate.

His son Alexandre-Balthazar-Laurent not only followed in his father's footsteps but took the art of gastronomy so seriously that at one time his parents had him locked up by lettre de cachet in the monastery of the Canons of Domèvre. His parents were enraged by the "philosophical breakfasts" he gave and also because of the fortune he spent on food. He was a lawyer by profession, but gastronomy and literature remained his chief interests. His main works were: *Reflexions philosophiques sur le plaisir, par un célibataire* (1783), *La Lorguette philosophique* (1785) and *Almanach des gourmands ou Calendrier nutritif* which he published from 1803 until 1812. An anonymous versifier wrote:

> Grimod, tes vers valent moins que ta prose,
> Et cependant ta prose ne vaut rien . . .

Grimod was born with deformed fingers. A Swiss, to whom he paid a life pension, made him artificial fingers which he used with great dexterity when eating, writing and drawing.

During the carnival of 1783 he gave a "funereal and lugubrious" feast that ended with a supper of seven courses, each consisting of a meat dish prepared in twenty-two fashions. The number of guests was twenty-two. They were forbidden to speak. The dining-room, hung with black drapery, was heavy with incense. The footmen, dressed as choir boys, sang dirges, and a coffin stood behind the table. When at seven in the morning his wife looked in, on the arms of her lover the Baron de Breteuil, Grimod received them with a quotation from a poem by the Abbé Delille: "And these two great débris console each other."

His prodigality forced him to sell the Château de Monceau to one, Juvet, a Paris apothecary. The château changed hands several times before Haussmannisation destroyed it.

The parkland beside the village of Monceau belonged to the royal family. Henri IV used often to stroll through it; Louis XIV came there to hunt. In the reign of Louis XVI the land became the property of Louis-Philippe-Joseph, Duc d'Orléans, known to history as Philippe Egalité. He was Duc de Montpensier until the death of his grandfather, Louis Duc d'Orléans, and Duc de Chartres until the death of his father, Louis Philippe, Duc d'Orléans. Philippe Egalité was the richest landowner in France. Struck by the prevailing Anglomania, he introduced into France horse-racing in the English style; he also wanted an English park, and appointed Carmontelle, a pupil of Le Nôtre, to turn the unkempt parkland into an English garden. "I want a picturesque garden," he said, "a land of illusions," adding that "Only illusions can amuse one." (One wonders whether he remembered those words as the tumbril took him to the guillotine on November 6, 1793, only nine and a half months after his cousin Louis XVI, for whose death he had voted.) When the English garden was completed the natives named it la Folie de Chartres.

Ruins, pagodas, empty tombs and pyramids were built. Water was brought to the park and cascaded from artificial rocks, the sheep pen was copied from Marie-Antoinette's at the Petit-Trianon and the cowshed was in white marble. The botanical garden was filled with exotic plants. The park contained a white pavilion, a blue pavilion, a temple of Mars, a temple of Love, and baths. In a deep artificial grotto the Duc d'Orléans gave supper parties, and his orgies reminded old people of those of his forebear, the Regent; also in the grotto he held evenings of evocation directed by Cagliostro, an Italian charlatan, at which the guests evoked the dead, though only distinguished dead like Diane de Poitiers, Mary Stuart, Ninon de Lenclos and Mlle de la Vallière. Under Cagliostro's guidance they appeared and gave satisfactory answers to the questions put to them.

Now and then Marie-Antoinette visited the park. On her last appearance, on the eve of the fateful departure for Varennes, she picked a large bunch of roses.

Attached to the land and their customs, the peasants of the village of Monceau frowned at progress, and were incensed when the Duc d'Orléans wanted to drain a smelly marsh. Their cattle had always gone there to drink and from time immemorial they had washed their linen in the filthy yellow water. Soldiers had to protect the workmen.

During the Revolution the park became the property of the nation. The nation neglected it. Napoleon gave it to his High-Chancellor, Jean-Jacques, Duc de Cambacérès, in the hope that he would look after it, but the expenses being too heavy, Cambacérès swiftly returned it to the state. In 1805 Pope Pius VII visited it while in Paris for the coronation of Napoleon. Marie-Louise used to take the little King of Rome there. Her imperial husband, who had little love for the English, referred to the park as the Chinese garden. In 1811 he thought of turning it into a zoological garden, but the Russian campaign made him abandon the plan.

In 1830 the property was restored to Louis-Philippe, Duc d'Orléans, who had become King of the French. When the Boulevard Malesherbes was built, a large part of the estate was expropriated and the park ceded to the Town of Paris. It is now but one-third of its former size. The sites beside the park were sold to private individuals on condition that they built their mansions with gardens and with the same wrought-iron railings in front. They remind one, wrote a contemporary, of Piccadilly in London. Somehow the spirit of England lingered on. The owners of these English-looking houses sent their babes into the park with uniformed nurses, who pushed them in English perambulators, while their English dogs dragged their footmen from tree to tree.

Batignolles developed differently. No rich people lived there and prices were low, for no toll gate existed between the village and Paris. The district became the haven of retired tradesmen and officials. "To spend sixteen hours a day for thirty years in a shop," wrote Alexis Martin, "and live above it in a narrow room, and put aside with great difficulty a sum large enough to bring in 3,000 to 4,000 francs a year to enable you to retire to Batignolles, was in the last century the dream of most Parisian shopkeepers." Batignolles was a quiet little backwater, the Siege and the Commune its only upheavals. The rentier of Batignolles was described as a man who liked his soup hot, wore thick felt slippers, plugged his ears with cotton wool, and, leaning on his cane, floated gently down the stream of life. He lived in a small flat, with small rooms; the walls were papered and looking-glasses abounded. If there were an alcove, he pushed his bed into it; if not, then the bed was curtained. Pious pictures hung on the bedroom walls even if the householder was an agnostic. The parquet floors were waxed.

The little rentier of Batignolles went twice a week to the café to play a game of dominoes, though only with his equals. His favourite café was either A la Grande Marquise at 113 rue d'Orléans or Au Moka at 5 rue de Lévis. When he dined out he chose a cheap restaurant. He passed the ambulant soup vendors with his nose in the air: their soup was good enough for workmen but not for a retired shopkeeper. He loathed new ideas, used snuff, abhorred tobacco, never missed the Sunday family dinner, rose early, retired early, and was willing to discuss politics provided one agreed with him. He died between seventy and eighty. Eugène Scribe and Eugène Labiche made fun of him in their plays.

Civil servants were also plentiful in Batignolles, though even Batignolles was often not cheap enough for them. In 1860 the Deputy of Batignolles, Paul Dupont, a printer, read out in the Chamber of Deputies the daily budget of a civil servant earning 2,200 francs a year:

One loaf of bread	francs 0·75
One litre of wine (watered)	0·40
Meat, vegetables	3·00
Heating	0·06
Laundry	0·25
Lighting	0·03
Coal for kitchen	0·20
Schooling for two children	0·50
Clothing for family	0·80
Unforeseen	0·05

To that had to be added 400 francs a year for rent if the two children were of different sex (300 if of the same, and therefore in a smaller flat), so that the total annual outgoings came to nearly 2,600 francs. Paul Dupont's speech brought no result, yet somehow or other the poor civil servant managed to bring up his children on the yearly deficit.

Batignolles suffered from lack of water. In 1837 when the rentiers began to take up residence, a limited company was formed to supply water to the expanding village. A twenty-horsepower steam engine was installed in the village of Clichy beside the Seine. The water was pumped into a reservoir in the rue Capron, from where it was distributed by water carriers. They trudged along the streets with buckets on their backs, shouting "A l'eau-eau! Porteurs d'eau!" There was a surcharge of 1 sou a floor. Thus those who lived, say, on the fifth floor paid heavily for the commodity. The water carrier stopped in the courtyard, called "A l'eau-eau!", and the tenants shouted down. Then he climbed the stairs, if necessary to the top, even if only to deliver a litre or so for one person. If there was water left in the bucket he tried all other doors on the floor in the hope of not having to descend with unsold water. He fared worst in the houses where there were servants, for servants were a cruel lot. They waited until he reappeared in the street and only then called out their requirements, so that he had again to climb the stairs. In Batignolles as elsewhere, the water carriers were mostly Auvergnats or Savoyards. They belonged to the poorest section of the population, and if a father caught his daughter speaking to a water carrier, she was severely punished.

Next to water carriers, and in competition with them, were the well cleaners, who earned almost less. There was a well in practically every second courtyard.

A curer les puits
C'est peu de pratique
La gaigne est petite
Plus gagner ne puis

So they sang, as with their hooks, buckets and ropes they arrived to make the wells as clear as fountains.

During the Siege of 1870-71 the water carriers had to fill their buckets in the evening, carry them to spots chosen by the authorities and leave them there until the morning, so that water was at hand if a fire broke out. They received practically nothing for the work.

Street lighting came to Monceau and Batignolles in 1776. The lamps were filled with thick oil made of animal fat; the wicks were of cotton wool. The lamp-posts were sixteen feet high and just over sixty yards apart. They were lit between November 1 and April 1. Pickpockets and housebreakers, therefore, operated mostly in summer. The lamps were taken down during funeral processions so that the wreaths piled on top of the high hearses should not brush them. In 1855 the first gas lamps appeared in Batignolles. Householders installed gas in their kitchens and on the staircase, but not in the apartments because they feared that gaslight would make curtains and upholstery fade. By 1873 the oil lamps had disappeared and gas alone reigned, apart from a few lanterns that remained until the First World War in the Passage Geofroy-Didelot, and rues Lebouteux and Cardinet. To be able to read his newspaper in the light of street lamps was a new and inexpensive pleasure for the little rentier of Batignolles who liked to relate the story of the Arab who, when asked what he admired most in Paris, replied, "The stars you put at night into your lanterns."

XII

The Bois de Boulogne

To the north-east of mediaeval Paris spread the vast forest of Rouvray. The thick and dark forest harboured bandits, outlaws and other criminals. The inhabitants of the surrounding hamlets kept well away.

Arnaud Catelan, a troubadour from the South who, like the trouvères of the North, sang his ballads "se baladant" from château to château, acquired such a reputation that his fame reached King Philippe le Bel in his Château de Passy, not far from the forest of Rouvray. The King asked the Countess of Provence, whose protégé Catelan was, to send him to Passy for a season. The Countess wrote back to say that Catelan would be bringing gifts of sweet wine and fragrant herbs of the Midi. When Philippe was notified that the troubadour had reached the edge of the forest, he sent the captain and men of his guard to escort him safely to Passy.

The captain and his men, who very likely had not had their pay for some time, took immediate advantage of the situation and the darkness of the forest. They killed Catelan in the belief that he was bringing valuable presents to their master. All they found in his baggage were sweet-smelling herbs and wine. On their return to Passy, they told the King that they had not found him, though they had searched the entire forest. The King assumed that Catelan must have decided to take a roundabout route to avoid travelling through the forest.

Days passed, but no troubadour turned up. The captain, however, began to exude sweet-smelling scent, and his men, unaccustomed to the wines of Provence, lolled about in drunken stupor. Philippe became suspicious and decided to get at the truth, using the method of his time—torture. Captain and men confessed to their crime, the corpse was found in a meadow, and the murderers were hanged. Philippe had a stone cross put up where Catelan was killed. The meadow still bears the name of Pré Catelan.

Jacques Hillairet, probably the most thorough and accurate historian of Paris, discounts the story of the troubadour and attributes the name of the meadow to Théophile Catelan or Catalan, who was Captain of the Royal Hunt towards the end of the reign of Louis XIV. The cross might have been erected in memory of Pierre Belon, a distinguished herbalist, who was assassinated in the forest in 1564. With other artists and savants, Belon had been quartered by Henri II in the Château de Madrid.

Still, the legend of the troubadour has retained its fragrance whereas the herbalist and the Captain of the Royal Hunt are rarely remembered.

Whatever the truth, banditry remained the order of the day.

Du Guesclin, Constable of France, returning to Paris, took a short cut across the forest. He had a heavy escort and got safely through. His baggage, less carefully guarded, fell into the hands of brigands. He told his King, Charles V: "Sire, it is a shame that only two leagues from your capital one cannot travel in safety." In spite of his remonstration, the forest remained the hideout of bandits.

When the English were chased out of Paris, the routiers—disbanded English soldiers who had no desire to leave the fair land of France after the Hundred Years War—took over from the bandits. One such, Robert Knolles, set himself up in the Château de Saint-Germain and pillaged the neighbourhood, coming as far as the

Seine, burning, looting, killing, setting fire to the abbey of the village of Auteuil.

The man who eventually pacified the forest was Olivier le Daim, Surgeon Barber to Louis XI. The King gave him the hunting rights of the Preserve of Rouvray. In order to protect his game, le Daim cleared the forest of marauders and put an end to brigandage. After all, it was more worthwhile to preserve a fine stag or a wild boar than some poor traveller.

His successor was Jacques Coictier, appointed personal physician to Louis XI in 1470. Coictier acquired great influence over his suspicious, superstitious master, and knew how to take advantage of him.

One day Louis XI said: "Coictier, you who seem to know such a lot, tell me how long you will live."

"Sire, I will die a week before you."

After that no medical man was better looked after by his patient than Coictier by his King.

The King often came to see him in the Preserve of Rouvray. He inaugurated in person the church that Coictier had built, and signed a royal edict giving the new parish the name of Boulogne (now Boulogne-sur-Seine), by which name also the forest was to be called.

Towards 1530 after returning from his captivity in Madrid, François I entrusted Girolamo Della Robbia with the construction of a château in the Bois de Boulogne. The château brought him no luck: he died of loving too vehemently the pretty Ferronnière whom he had installed there. The ordinary people called it the Château de Faïence; the King, the Château de Boulogne; and the courtiers, disgruntled by its distance from Paris and its lack of the facilities for spending the night offered by Saint-Germain-en-Laye and Fontainebleau, spoke of it as the Château de Madrid, to remind their sovereign lord of his enforced stay in that town.

Henri II kept Diane de Poitiers in the château, and Charles IX had children there by Marie Touchet and Mlle de la Béraudière.

Henri III, the King of the Mignons, had a bull ring constructed in the grounds. Henri IV closed it and restored the château to its original use by installing Gabrielle d'Estrées, and other royal mistresses after her departure.

In his delight when Queen Margot agreed to a separation, he gave her the château for life. She had a road cut through the forest, still known as Allée de la Reine-Marguerite, to facilitate her visits to the Abbey of Longchamps. After her death the château lost its importance. Louis XIII came to it but seldom. It is recorded that on December 15, 1610, he killed two wolves in the forest, and seven years later he bathed at Auteuil, catching a chill. In 1656 Mazarin turned it into a workshop for weaving stockings. In 1793 it was declared national property, then was sold for 648,000 francs to a citizen, most inappropriately named Leroy, who razed it to the ground. Now only the name remains.

The Château de Bagatelle was built for Jean d'Estrées, Marshal and Vice-Admiral of France, the nephew of Gabrielle d'Estrées. Later it belonged to Mademoiselle de Charolais, granddaughter of the Great Condé, whose whim was to have herself painted in the garb of a Franciscan monk. Voltaire wrote a quatrain:

Frère Ange de Charolais
Dis-nous par quelle aventure
Le cordon de saint François
Sert à Vénus de ceinture?

In 1777 the Comte d'Artois, the future Charles X, bought Bagatelle from the Prince de Chimay, and made a bet with his sister-in-law, Queen Marie-Antoinette, that he would not only have the house pulled down but have a new one erected while she was away in Choisy. The Queen stayed for sixty-four days in Choisy, and on her return indeed found that a new pavilion had been built and that the gardens had been turned into an English park watered by the Seine. There was, however, one trifle about which Artois did not care to boast. Bélanger, the architect, who had orginally estimated the cost at 600,000 livres, spent more than double to get the work finished in time. The pavilion came to be known as the Folie d'Artois.

The Revolution declared it national property. The Directory sold it to one, Lhéritier, who turned it into "a branch of Mohammed's Paradise", though even under this guise it failed to prosper. In 1806 Napoleon bought it, and now and then he lunched there; his son, the King of Rome, was often taken to the gardens; and to Bagatelle came Josephine to make the child's acquaintance.

After the Restoration, the future Charles X named it Babiole and gave it to his son, the Duc de Bercy, after whose assassination it became the property of his widow, Marie-Caroline, until the Revolution of 1830. In 1835 it was sold to Lord Yarmouth, later the fourth Marquis of Hertford, brother of Milord l'Arsouille. He bought it for 313,000 francs, less than a quarter of the sum that Artois had spent on it. From Lord Hertford, Bagatelle was to pass to Sir Richard Wallace of Wallace Collection fame.

Lord Redesdale has refuted in his *Memories* the generally accepted belief that Sir Richard was the brother of Lord Hertford. It would certainly have been strange for Lady Hertford (the fourth Marquis's mother) to have named both her sons Richard, even if one of them was illegitimate. The truth is that Richard Lord Hertford, when a mere boy, had an affair with a Scottish girl called Agnes Wallace. Richard Wallace was their son. Lord Hertford made a home for his mistress in Paris, and, when he parted from her, the child was placed with a concierge in the rue de Clichy, where he ran wild in the street until he was about six years old. The child was shown to his grandmother, Lady Hertford, who took to the clever little boy and decided to bring him up. This was much against the inclinations of her son, though in time Lord Hertford became so fond of him that he made him his agent and representative at auctions and sales of works of art.

When Lord Yarmouth bought Bagatelle, it was rumoured to be the scene of orgies. "Many of the stories," wrote Lord Redesdale, "were started by the rather second-class English Society. These stories lost nothing in the telling and so Bagatelle came to be looked upon as a sort of Parc aux Cerfs." On the other hand, J. Laffitte, a French contemporary who wrote a book called *Un Coin de Paris* about the sixteenth arrondissement, which includes the Bois de Boulogne, described Lord Hertford as a misanthropist.

Lord Hertford was a fervent art collector. When two acquaintances asked leave to fight a duel in the grounds, he politely replied that he had not the slightest objection to their shooting each other, but could not trust their skill so far as to risk his statues. He had in his park statues by Pigalle, Lemoyne and Houdon.

Lord Hertford died in 1870, leaving the residue of his large estate to Wallace "for all his care and attention to my dear mother and likewise for his devotedness to me during a long and painful illness I had in Paris in 1840 and on all other occasions."

Wallace was created a baronet in 1871 in recognition of the great services he had rendered the English colony in Paris during the Siege. He married Mlle Castelnau, by whom he had one son, who was an officer in the French army. Sir Richard died in Paris in 1890, Lady Wallace seven years later.

She left Bagatelle to her secretary, Sir Henry Murray Scott, who sold it to the Town of Paris in 1904, the building to be used for temporary exhibitions of works of art, and the grounds for collections of trees, shrubs and ornamental plants. Lady Wallace of course left the contents of Hertford House to the nation: hence the Wallace Collection.

Sir Richard left his mark on Paris too. In 1871 he gave eighty fountains to the Town of Paris. Sculptured by Lebourg, melted down by Barbizat, each cost 675 francs. The first was put up in the Boulevard de la Villette. When he made his generous present of the fountains, he thought more of the thirst of horses than of pedestrians. He probably knew the old Parisian saying: "Paris is a Paradise for women, a Purgatory for husbands and an Inferno for horses."

XIII

The Oldest Profession

Prostitution had its ups and downs throughout the history of Paris. There was never a dull moment. The Kings of France, often from a sense of morality or deep piety, would suddenly decide to extirpate it. They regarded the prostitutes as members of a corporation. If you disband a corporation, it ceases to have members; if the corporation resists, then violence must be used. On that principle the existence of loose women was frequently in danger. Charles VIII ordered them to be burnt; Marshal of France, Pierre Strozzi, had eight hundred thrown into the river; and in 1635 the Civil Lieutenant of the office of the Provost of Paris warned them "to leave the town and the faubourgs or to be shaved and banished for life without any redress." They remained.

Prostitutes had a comparatively quiet time under Henri III, the King of the Mignons, who was indifferent to women whatever their profession. St Louis, the first King to bring some order into prostitution, was also the first to forbid them to dress like decent women. This was because, at a Mass, his wife, Marguerite de Provence, had given the kiss of peace to a richly clad lady standing next to her; then to her horror the Queen discovered that the woman was a common prostitute.

In 1367 the Provost of Paris designated special districts for prostitutes. The one called Glatigny was situated on the north side of the Cité beside the Seine, and faced the Place de Grève. It formed a sort of quadrilateral based on the rue de Glatigny (absorbed in part by the Hôtel-Dieu), the rue des Marmousets (rue Chanoinesse and part of the Place du Parvis-Notre-Dame), rue de Saint-Pierre-aux-Boeufs (part of the rue de la Cité), rue d'Arcole, rue aux Fèves (part of the rue de la Cité), rue de la Licorne (part of the rue de la Cité), and rue des Deux-Ermites (part of the Place du Parvis-Notre-Dame). That warren of hovels and mean streets became the bastion of vice, the realm of bawds, whores and ponces. Since in outlook malefactors and their like were not far removed from them, they too flocked to Glatigny. It became dangerous to hazard into that busy world next door to Notre-Dame. The police of Paris, still insignificant in number, hardly dared to enter it. The good burghers of the town protested in vain. The priests of Notre-Dame fared no better, although occasionally the Provost issued an ordinance which was not however enforced. Eventually, in 1518, Queen Claude, touched by the laments of the clergy, raised the matter with her husband François I, who ordered the destruction of Glatigny. François was known to his subjects as a man whose firmness could easily change to complacency, so before he could rescind the decree, the burghers of the Cité, armed with spades, pickaxes, hammers and mattocks, moved into Glatigny, and within twenty-four hours had destroyed all the hovels. Next day the Bishop came in procession to exorcise the evil that had resided there so long.

An even worse district was Hueleu, the other neighbourhood set aside for harlots. The name Hueleu derived from Hurleur, which originated from Hue Leu or Hugues Loup, who lived in the twelfth century and gave his name to the district that was outside the Enceinte of Philippe-Auguste. The streets of the Grand-Hueleu and Petit-Hueleu did not disappear until the Boulevard Sébastopol was constructed a hundred years ago. The Hueleu district took in parts of the rues Saint-Martin, Saint-Denis, Greneta, aux Ours and du Bourg-l'Abbé.

The same François I who had Glatigny demolished apparently favoured Hueleu, for in 1532 a prostitute of that district, known as Jeanne Belle-Fille, who had been insulted by other harlots who had called her a sorceress and accused her of "having commerce with the Devil", was taken under his august protection. On pain of death and a large fine, the inhabitants of Hueleu were forbidden to molest her. She waxed rich, acquired houses, farms, woods and fields, and the royal arms of her protector were displayed on all her possessions. Charles IX made the Provost of Paris personally responsible for the closing of Hueleu, which was effected on March 27, 1565.

With the two districts closed, the prostitutes invaded practically the whole town, but they soon found a district of their own again in the rues des Gravilliers, Pastourelle, des Vertus, Phélipeaux (swallowed by the rue Réaumur), Froimantaux (Place du Carrousel) and Quincampoix. As the song had it:

Dans la rue des Gravilliers
Elles y sont par milliers.

Dans la rue Pastourelle
Autant de putains que de maquerelles.*

Dans la rue des Vertus
Autant de coupeaux que de cocus.

Dans la rue de Phélipeaux
Ce n'est rien que ribaux.

C'est la rue Froimantaux
Petit rue, grands bordeaux.*

Prostitutes were not allowed to exercise their profession in their lodgings; nor were they permitted to hawk their bodies after

* Maquerelle: bawd, hence maquereau: ponce; bordeaux: houses of prostitution in old French.

nightfall. When the couvre-feu (curfew) was rung they had to leave the inns, where in the fifteenth and sixteenth centuries they plied their joyless task, and return to their lodgings. They were enjoined by the police to go home quietly, to make no noise, not to upset the neighbours, to sneer at nobody, to keep their doors closed and to receive no visitors. On the Day of Assumption in 1417, Margot la Bourgeoise, Catherine du Soleil and Marguerite de Lestre, all three of them prostitutes, were caught in their rooms with clients. The Provost fined the women 40 sols each, half of which went to the King, half to the poor.

The harlots took picturesque names, and because they often got into trouble with the authorities, their names survive, whereas the names of many honest burghers and their sober wives go unrecorded. Prostitutes at the end of the Middle Ages had names like Thomase la Courtoise, Jehanette la Commune, Perette la Vilaine, Catherine aux Lardons, Etiennette la Chèvre. Somehow those names convey the flavour of the period better than those of respectable citizens.

In 1393 a harlot gave birth to a daughter. An accomplice took the child to the Porte Saint-Martin and left her outside the Walls. He had pushed a piece of linen down the child's throat so that she would be unable to cry and attract attention, but an hour later the dog of a passing hunter discovered the baby, who appeared to be dead. A large number of peasants joined the hunter, who carried the child to the Priory of Saint-Martin-des-Champs (now Conservatoire National des Arts et Métiers, 292 rue Saint-Martin) and placed her on the altar of Our Lady. By then the crowd numbered over four hundred. Joined by the monks, the people prayed to the Virgin, begging her to intercede for the poor little thing who had died unbaptised, and lo! the child moved, opened her eyes, dislodged from her throat the linen, and cried out. She was baptised in the Priory because the crowd was so dense that she could not be carried to the parish church. She was christened Marie. The Priory bells were rung, a Te Deum was sung, and little Marie died three hours later. The monks kept vigil over her corpse until the next day when she was buried with great pomp beside the altar of Our Lady. That was the origin of the veneration of Notre-Dame-de-la-Carole at Saint-Martin-des-Champs where a confraternity was formed in memory of little Marie. (Carole derives from Carolus, as Charles VI was King of France at the time.)

Until the end of the sixteenth century it was the custom to inflict punishment on harlots caught in streets where decent people resided. First a straw hat was pushed down over the harlot's forehead, who was then lifted on a donkey, but facing the tail, onto which she had to hold. To the sounds of drum and fife, she was paraded round the town. Jeering crowds and laughing children accompanied her, and when almost the whole populace had insulted her, she was returned to Hueleu. After the practice had ceased in Paris, it was implanted into Brussels by the Ducs de Bourgogne of the House of France.

In the reign of Henri IV prostitutes moved into the rue de la Perle, which in those days was still at the very extremity of Paris. A crucifix had been erected there and was known as the Crucifix-Marque-Eau because it marked the height of an inundation of the Seine. Following the arrival of the whores, the people called it Crucifix-Maquereau. The prostitutes used to complain bitterly of decent women who, by their competition, were spoiling the trade. Nowadays, they said, a woman kept by a courtier or a Superintendent of Finance earned greater respect than an ordinary prostitute, though her profession was the same. When a prostitute died she was buried like a dog, whereas a kept woman received a funeral of such pomp that one wondered whether debauch were the greatest virtue.

The complaints were not unfounded. The fees of prostitutes rose, along with other prices, in the reign of Henri II. Five sols became the price, rather a tempting sum, which induced three ladies of the Court to go to a place of debauch to discover whether they were considered worth that sum. They wore masks while giving themselves to all and sundry. One of them was recognised however by her cobbler who, even in the heat of love, remained true to his last. He remembered the shoes she was wearing, for it was he who had made them. He had no opportunity to give her away since the ladies themselves boasted of their escapade and showed the 5 sol pieces to their acquaintance.

The Order of the Filles-Pénitentes was established in the parish of Saint-Eustache, and in 1572 the convent was transferred to buildings next to the Monastery of Saint-Magloire in the rue Saint-Denis. When in 1497 Simon, Bishop of Paris, drew up the rules of the Filles-Pénitentes, he intended that only fallen women and girls should be received in the convent, but before being admitted they had to swear on the Gospels that they had not prostituted themselves with the aim of finding shelter there. The Filles-Pénitentes looked after their charges so well that it seemed an easy way out of abject poverty and misery to prostitute oneself for a while in order to find a peaceful life and regular meals in the convent. If it was discovered that a woman had lied, that she had not been a bona fide prostitute, she was chased from Saint-Magloire. The Parliament of Paris regularly sent the harlots condemned for life to take up their abode within the convent.

It also happened that girls who led a decent life were sent to the convent. Their parents wanted to get rid of them, perhaps because they were ugly and had no dowry. Swearing that they had led a life of debauch, they were admitted though untouched virgins. This became so much the practice that in the end all newcomers were examined, and the virgins rejected.

Condemned men on their way from the Châtelet to the gibbet at Montfaucon stopped with their escorts in the courtyard of Saint-Magloire, where the nuns prayed for their intentions, then gave each of them three slices of bread and a glass of wine. Thus fortified, they continued on their last journey.

The Order of the Filles de la Madeleine, known as the Madelonnettes, received in their convent in the rue Fontaines-du-Temple not only dissolute women sent by the Parliament, whom they lodged in cells with barred windows, but also adulterous women who remained in the convent until their husbands were ready to forgive them. Another function of the nuns was to educate young girls and widows whose virtue was not too steady, and look after then until they found husbands. Unlike other Orders, the Madelonnettes put no obstacles in the way of repentant women and girls who wanted to join their congregation. The nuns lived by charity; they had no other income. Their convent was closed in 1790 and turned into a prison in 1793.

Louis XIV tried to solve the problem of prostitution by creating the Hôpital Général, but this helped so little that he issued orders, countersigned by Colbert and registered by the Parliament of Paris on April 29, 1684, to control "women of public and scandalous debauch".

In the eighteenth century, as the New World was still conveniently distant, a number of women were transported to Louisiana, like the Abbé Prévost d'Exiles's Manon Lescaut. Enlightened men of the time were, however, concerned to find a better answer. Nicolas Restif de La Bretonne, who still remains the bugbear of French literary men, rushed straight into the fray with what he considered to be a final solution. He thought himself far greater than Jean-Jacques Rousseau, and his writings of more lasting value. He gave his views in *Le Pornographe*, published in London in 1770.

All streetwalkers and other prostitutes were to be assembled in spacious, comfortable houses on the outskirts of the town, to which they would be taken in a friendly manner, and without compulsion. The houses would be called the Parthénions. Kept women could join them, but if they misbehaved their lovers were to be punished.

Each Parthénion would have a council of administrators chosen from among men who had been municipal councillors (échevins). Under them would serve the governesses, superannuated prostitutes chosen for their kindness and "douceur". None of the administrators, whose tenure of office would last six years, could enter the house as a client.

Women would not have to reveal their names when entering a Parthénion; governesses would be forbidden to enquire. Only the state of their health would be examined scrupulously. If ill, they would be cured. No newcomer over twenty-five would be admitted. The Parthénion being a refuge and an asylum, no father could remove his daughter, who could refuse to see her parents if they called.

A Parthénion would have two gardens, one through which the clients could sneak in, the other in which the girls could promenade. There would also be a number of wide passages. The first would be for the oldest women, none of whom however would be over thirty-six. The second would be for those between twenty-five and thirty, the third for women between twenty and twenty-five, the fourth for the eighteen to twenty age group, the fifth for the sixteen to eighteens, and the sixth for girls between fourteen and sixteen, of whom only those would be allowed to have clients who temperamentally were ripe enough to receive them. Virgins below fourteen, whether brought in by their parents or arrived on their own, were to be brought up by decent women and to choose whoredom only if they felt suited for it.

The prettier girls would be on one side of the passage, the rest on the other. If a man wanted the same girl regularly and paid for a daily ticket, the girl would be set aside for him. Such girls would live separately, but could communicate with others who were not on duty in their passage or in the communal room. If a regular lover ceased to come for a week, in other words bought no ticket for seven days, he would lose his mistress.

However much in love, a young man might not contemplate marriage to an inmate of a Parthénion, even if he were thirty, though a man of mature years who was completely master of himself would be heard by the administrators, and permission to marry might be granted to him if such a marriage were not too harmful to his interests.

The governesses would be forbidden to admonish girls; only the administrators could do so. Two sentries would be posted at the entrance of the first garden, which would be full of trees and shrubs, so that the client could flit unobserved from tree to tree until he reached the house. Once inside, he would present himself at the box office, and remove the mask that a customer would have to wear to enter a Parthénion, so that the governess could have a good look at him. Having bought a ticket, he would then be ushered into a dark room, from which he could see the communal room belonging to the corridor of his choice. His arms, cane and mask would already have been left in a locker. The girls would be visible to him, but not he to them. Having pointed out the girl of his choice, he would be taken to her room. The governess would then call the girl, who would peep through a spyhole at her admirer, and she would tell the governess if she did not fancy him, and then withdraw. She would not, however, return at once to the communal room so that the other girls should not know that one of their number had already found the man repugnant. The man would then return to the dark room, and the process would begin again. Old and deformed men would leave it to the governesses to find them women, and there would be special guards along the passages to deal severely with troublemakers who tried to upset the dignified peace of the Parthénion.

Children born in a Parthénion would be sent to wet nurses. Later they would be brought back to be educated in an annexe, where the mothers could visit them once a week. The women were to be present in the communal assembly room from eleven to one, four to seven, and from eight-thirty to eleven-thirty when they supped. When not sleeping or giving themselves to clients, they were to sit quietly in their rooms, reading or doing needlework. They would have daily dancing, singing and music lessons, attendance at which would not be obligatory, but if a girl absented herself too often, the governess in charge would sweetly and gently remonstrate with her, explaining what fun she was missing. Baths were to be taken every second day; no woman would be allowed to smell. Men who arrived drunk would be kept apart until they sobered up, when they could choose between going or staying. If they preferred to go, the price of the ticket would be refunded.

Boys born in a Parthénion would be brought up to be soldiers, thus repaying the mothers' debt to the state. Girls would be taught dressmaking, hairdressing and other trades fit for women. If they wanted to marry, even a dowry would be provided.

The women of a Parthénion, other than those born there, would not be allowed to leave unless they inherited, and if an heiress preferred to remain she would be allowed to enjoy her inheritance inside the Parthénion. On feast days the girls might go to the theatre accompanied by a governess; and since Restif de La Bretonne thought of everything, he prescribed a gauze curtain to be hung in front of their box so that they could see without being stared at.

In his personal life he held prostitutes in horror and denounced them to the police whenever he could.

In the 1780s and for four decades after the Revolution, the Palais Royal was the new Hueleu of Paris, except that the refinement and elegance of the girls who plied their trade in the gardens raised them in status far above the prostitutes of previous generations. They dressed well and with taste. In the afternoon, their promenading time, they strolled decorously, often in pairs. It was in the Grande Allée on September 22, 1787, that Lieutenant Napoleon Bonaparte made his first conquest.

However, the fame of the Palais Royal rested on the shops beneath the arcades. They were mostly milliners' shops, usually with a long counter, behind which stood the saleswomen whose goods were usually themselves. But the pretence was kept up. The customer entered, saluted the milliner, and asked for a hat with a blue, yellow or red ribbon. The answer was, "Go behind into the workroom, or if you prefer it can be delivered to your address."

The establishment of Mlle Brion, who liked to be addressed as Comtesse de Launai, was known to the uninitiated as a furniture shop. She had cards printed which advertised furniture of the latest style. Each piece could be hired for 6 livres a time.

In the gallery of the Café de Foy, directly above a restaurant, was a select brothel on five floors whose inmates were advertised on embossed paper. On the first floor hung out la Lamberti, five years in the trade, small, dark haired, piquante, price 5 livres. On the second floor was fat Adèle, only six months in Paris, price 2 livres, 10 sols. (Newcomers from the provinces were not appreciated by men of taste.) Rose, an interesting blonde, 1 livre, 10 sols, received on the third floor, and on the fourth Hortense, not pretty but intellectual; with twenty years' experience of whoring in Paris, she cost more than fresh Adèle. The most expensive was Saint-Julien on the fifth floor. She fetched 6 livres a time. She was described as twenty-eight, dark haired, thin, vivacious, vicious and frequently nasty.

Such brothels abounded in the Palais Royal, and were ably supported by the gambling dens, which sent them clients; in return the bawds sent their customers to the gaming rooms. Many found the Palais Royal irresistible, and it became the rallying point of foreigners, who named Paris the cloaca maxima of the world, though it was the foreigners who took greatest advantage of the facilities offered. The staunch burghers of the town avoided the area.

When the Allies entered Paris in 1815, they saw Divine chastisement in the French defeats, as though the Emperor had lost at Waterloo because of the Adèles and Roses of the Palais Royal. The Duke of Wellington declared that Paris deserved to be taught a moral lesson. His brothers in arms set a poor example to the Parisians. The Grand Duke Constantine spent 4,000,000 francs in a month on amusements connected with the Palais Royal, and Blucher lost 1,500,000 francs in one night at the gambling den at 113 Palais Royal, which he practically never left during his stay in

Paris. He had to mortgage all his property in Prussia. The presence of the Allies made the fortune of brothels, cafés, theatres and gaming rooms; in short, Paris waxed fat on the moralisers. The Palais Royal went out of fashion around 1830, and the boulevards took over.

From the nineteenth century onwards the prostitutes had to put up with the effects of bureaucracy. Their lives were no longer in danger, the curfew had long ceased to ring, and for those who preferred the rough and tumble of streets to the peace of the disorderly house, few streets were barred. They just had to keep away from the vicinity of churches and schools. However, there were in their view too many nagging regulations, such as those concerning medical visits and decorous behaviour. Until 1914, for example, no woman was allowed to solicit if she did not wear a hat, and one could not open a brothel without the Prefect's permission. In January 1832, a lady applied to the Prefect of the Seine department.

"Monsieur le Préfet, As I am responsible for my old and sick parents I am forced to look for an honest occupation so as to be able to make their old age happy. You are aware, Monsieur le Préfet, that it is the duty of children to give comfort in their decrepitude to those who have brought them into the world, and to repay them for all they have done for them when still of a tender age. Therefore, I hope that you will not refuse me permission to open a brothel. . . ."

One sincerely hopes that the Prefect appreciated her noble sentiments.

In the middle of the last century appeared the lorettes, so called because their favourite district was Notre-Dame-de-Lorette, named after its parish church. They were not prostitutes in the ordinary sense. They were recruited among women separated from their husbands, daughters of concierges who studied at the Conservatoire, and tradesmen's daughters who dreamed of freedom. They shunned work. They never made the first advances in their love affairs, and did not go out of their way to find the loves of their lives. Everything had to fall into their laps. A lorette merely permitted a man to give her presents. She did not refuse money; she accepted bank notes, without, as it were, provoking them. Generally, these women were stupid, which did not stop them from considering themselves witty and cultured. They were keen theatregoers, though they went not to watch the play but to have all opera-glasses fixed on them. If the males were too interested in the play, "There's not a soul in this theatre," they would say, "let's go." Lorettes moved in pairs.

In the days when Paris was not yet overpopulated, it was easy to find accommodation, particularly for the lorettes, who had one advantage over the bourgeois: they were ready to live in a newly constructed house without bothering if the paint were still wet. It became a custom, almost a right, for them to move into new houses and live there until plaster and paint had dried and the proprietors had found proper tenants. To keep up the pretence of culture, the lorette might hire a piano. There would always be one or two daguerrotypes on the wall to show her interest in the arts. She sang too: generally out of tune. She believed that she was the mistress of an ambassador or a minister. She thought that her father was an officer in the army or a diplomatist, whereas he was probably a baker or a greengrocer. She did not care for intrigue: if she tired of a lover, she found another.

On November 21, 1844, three months after he went to live at 58 rue Notre-Dame-de-Lorette, Eugène Delacroix, the painter, wrote to his friend George Sand, the writer, "This new district has arisen to make ardent men like me dizzy. On my arrival here the first object that struck the eyes of my virtue was a magnificent lorette dressed in black satin and velvet, who, getting out of a cabriolet, with the unconcern of a goddess let me see her leg up to her navel. . . ."

During the Second Empire, high police officials acted as welfare officers whose job was to dissuade young women from embarking on the career of prostitute. To such an official was taken an orphan of twenty who had applied for a prostitute's card. He tried to dissuade her. "Here," he said, "we are in communication with charitable ladies who have a deep understanding of all human frailties. You can read and write, which is a big advantage. Give us a little time and I promise we will find work for you either in a shop or as a housemaid in a decent family."

The girl looked disdainfully at him. "We don't touch that sort of bread in my family," she said.

In 1632 St Vincent de Paul installed in Saint-Lazare, in the Cour de la Ferme-Saint-Lazare, the Lazarists. Their function was to look after foolish persons and their kind whom their families had put into the care of "Monsieur Vincent". During the Revolution the house was turned into a prison, and it was there in 1793 that André Chénier wrote his last poems before being taken to the guillotine. In 1834 it became a prison and detention centre for prostitutes.

When they were arrested for soliciting without a police card, or infringing police regulations, they were taken to the dépôt of the Préfecture de Police. A police magistrate decided their fate. Once they understood that they would be sent to Saint-Lazare, they would often burst into tears and beg to be allowed to go to their lodgings to arrange food during their absence for their dog or cat or birds. (Most prostitutes, in common with other lonely people, are animal lovers. Before the Second Empire, they were permitted to take their pets with them, with the result that the prison became a menagerie and the privilege was stopped.) More often than not, they were allowed home to arrange with neighbours for the care of their animals, but they first had faithfully to promise to return next day. They did not always keep their promise.

Magistrates used to tell them how long they would be detained, until one day a prostitute threw a paper weight at the head of a police officer. Thereafter they were told only when they arrived in the panier à salade (Black Maria) at the prison, where their dresses were taken from them and they had to change into prison garb, black and blue striped dress and a black bonnet. They were not allowed the use of handkerchiefs. Those who were not ill were kept for about a fortnight. Nothing prevented them on their release from starting all over again, and they were often back in prison a month later.

Some of them led such a wretched existence in the outside world that prison was a kind of rest cure. Quite a few cried their eyes out when the day of release arrived. In 1869 the doyenne of Paris prostitutes was kept in Saint-Lazare purely as a guest. She was born in 1780. She no longer left her bed, and the other women, if in the mood to tease her, called her the mistress of Marat. She energetically denied that, and spoke of handsome Barras who had fancied her, adding, "Those were the days of the great wars."

In 1932 Saint-Lazare ceased to be a prison. It became a hospital for venereal diseases.

The maisons de rendez-vous were also on the list of houses tolerated by the police. In fact, they were tolerated more readily than ordinary brothels, for no one lived in them, and the women who ran them were sensible enough to choose their customers carefully and to hold scandal at arm's length. Moreover, they conducted their business in the afternoon only, from five to seven, as a result of which they were known also as maisons de cinq à sept. They were usually large flats or private houses, and the women were recruited among shopgirls, midinettes and their kind. Married women who were unsatisfied with their pin-money looked in occasionally to earn a little extra. The keepers of these establishments encouraged the rumour that society women were often to be encountered on their premises, but that can be taken with a pinch of salt since theirs was a world of false pretence or make-believe, according to how one looks at it. One house purported to provide only schoolmistresses, but a client recognised there a woman who two years previously had frequented a similar house where every woman was an officer's widow. (In the First World War when women bus conductresses appeared for the first time in Paris, it was claimed for a particular maison de rendez-vous that all its girls were conductresses.) The maisons de rendez-vous had their heyday during the Third Republic.

In the rue de la Victoire a Mme Gautier kept such a house. Hers was truly the realm of make-believe, and her audacity was unparalleled. There appeared in Paris a publication, *The American Register*, each number of which gave the names and the hotel addresses of Americans who arrived in the capital. The proprietor was Dr Evans, the American dentist who was instrumental in helping the Empress Eugénie to reach Sir John Burgoyne's yacht and escape to England on the fall of the Second Empire. Mme Gautier wrote to every American man whose name figured in *The American Register*. Even her girls warned her not to do so, but she was not the woman to listen to advice; she usually managed to land on her feet. She sent a letter to each new arrival, inviting him to her house between five and seven, saying that she had an important communication to make. It happened now and again that an entire American family arrived, father, mother and children. Mme Gautier was equal to the situation, explaining that she ran a theatrical agency—hence the presence of the young women—and that on reading the name in *The American Register* she had thought that the father was an actor whose fame had reached Europe. This approach was not unpleasing. Mme Gautier was so sorry for the misunderstanding, and would the family take refreshment?

Among her clients was a silly man eaten with snobbism. To please him, most of the girls were turned into marquises, but none the less his social appetite remained boundless. One day he confessed to Mme Gautier that his true ambition was to go to bed with the daughter of the President of the Republic. The snob certainly aimed high; the President was none other than Patrice de Mac-Mahon, Marshal of France, Duc de Magenta. "It will cost a lot of money," said Mme Gautier without batting an eyelid, "but I'll get her for you." Mademoiselle de Mac-Mahon, she explained, was a pupil at the Convent of the Sacré-Coeur. It would take time to contact her and persuade her to come to the establishment.

Mme Gautier had on her list a tall, distinguished-looking girl who, because of her blue eyes and fair hair, was known as Missy. She was presented to the snob as the President's daughter, and the man was so overcome that all he could do was to bow and kiss her hand. When the girl saw that even playfulness had no effect on him, she had practically to drag him to the sofa. "So you will really go to bed with me?" he timidly murmured. She nodded her assent and he burst into tears. Mme Gautier received a huge money present. At his next meeting with Missy, he approached the subject he had at heart. His valet, who had killed his faithless wife, was under sentence of death. Could Mlle de Mac-Mahon intercede with her father? Missy said she would try, but could hold out no hope as her father was an austere man who did not allow his family to interfere in matters of state.

Since coincidences do happen, a few weeks later the valet received the President's pardon. The snob hastened to Mme Gautier to thank Mlle de Mac-Mahon, who received his thanks graciously. "Mademoiselle," he cried, "will you marry me?"

That was going too far.

"I can't," she replied. "I am betrothed to King Alfonso XII of Spain who lost his dear Queen only recently. I am now very busy with my trousseau, which means I won't see much more of you. Soon my father will accompany me to Madrid, and after the wedding you will come out and I will make you a Grandee of Spain. In the meantime Mlle de Nemours of the House of France will take my place at your side."

Unfortunately Mlle de Nemours was not up to the mark. She was a simple girl and not good at lies. Mme Gautier was only too aware of this, but could find no other girl with the wit and presence of Missy. As the snob was hard of hearing, she decided to be present at the first meeting, and to whisper the answers from behind his back.

"Where were you born, Mlle de Nemours?" he asked, an understandable question since the Bourbons were exiled from France.

"During a short journey to France," instructed Mme Gautier.

"During a journey," said the simpleton.

"During a journey?" asked the snob. "I don't follow you."

"During a short journey to France, you idiot," shouted Mme Gautier.

"During a short journey to France, you idiot," said Mlle de Nemours.

Mme Gautier nearly fainted, but the snob was delighted to be called an idiot by a Royal Princess.

Business was brisk during the First World War. The brothels, which had closed at the outbreak of war, quickly reopened. When Big Bertha shelled or the redoubtable Zeppelins bombed Paris, the girls were sent to shelters, usually the métro stations. As the sirens sounded, so the girls in their flimsy dresses rushed into the stations. One evening a dance band also sought refuge in the métro, and the musicians decided to cheer up the crowd, among whom there were, of course, plenty of ordinary folk. Still, it was war-time with its mood of madness, so everybody danced, husbands at first with their wives, then with the lightly clad girls. Nobody minded; death lurked above, and conventions were thrown to the wind. In short, a good time was had by all, except the brothelkeepers, who even under the circumstances could not forget their vocation; and running from one dancing couple to the other, they distributed their business cards with the addresses of their establishments.

After the war the old complaint about amateurs was revived. In 1810 there were a hundred and eighty brothels in Paris; by 1924 their number had shrunk to twenty-nine. On the other hand, the number of maisons de rendez-vous had risen to three hundred. After the Second World War, in an upsurge of moral indignation, the Deputies passed an act closing all brothels for good. The result was the same when Glatigny was destroyed and Hueleu uprooted.

XIV

The Vendôme Column & the Napoleonic Cult

The ground on which the Place Vendôme was planned had originally been the property of César, Duc de Vendôme, natural son of Henri IV by Gabrielle d'Estrées. It was sold by his descendants to Louis XIV whom the Marquis de Louvois, Superintendent of Finance, had in 1686 persuaded to turn the site into a "grand ornament of the Town of Paris". Louvois ordered the construction of houses in the Corinthian style. He wanted to instal in them the Academies, the Royal Library and several embassies, but he died before his plan could be effected, and frightened by the expense, Louis XIV stopped further construction and assigned the land to the Town of Paris, which in turn sold the still vacant sites to private buyers, who had to conform to the original plan when building their mansions.

Jules Hardouin-Mansard and Germain Boffrand designed an equestrian statue of Louis XIV, to be erected in the centre of the square. The model was the work of François Girardin and cast in bronze by Balthazar Keller. It weighed over sixty thousand pounds, and twenty men could have sat around a table inside the horse's belly. The statue was unveiled in the presence of the Duc de Gesvres, Governor of Paris, and the square was named Place Louis-le-Grand.

The buildings, which now house the Ministry of Justice (numbers 11-13), were built by two revenue farmers (traitants), Bourvalais and Villemarecq, whom the Regent, Philippe d'Orléans, suspected of having manipulated sums due to the Revenue. He seized the houses, and in 1717 the Marquis de Dangeau turned them into the Paris residence of the Chancellors of France.

In 1763 the mountebanks from the fair of Saint-Ovide invaded the square and built booths and wooden stages. People of quality came to applaud Harlequin, visit the Café Royal to taste the wines of Burgundy, take part in chariot races and drive around in elegant coaches. Plebeians were not encouraged to join in the fun.

On August 10, 1792, the Assembly decreed the destruction of all royal statues. An eager, vociferous crowd appeared in the square to do their duty. It was not easy, for the heavy bronze resisted nobly, so ropes were thrown round the statue to which were harnessed men of revolutionary zeal. A woman called Rose Violet, who had been a vendor of Marat's *L'Ami du Peuple*, made herself conspicuous with her noisy encouragement of the work. When the enormous statue collapsed, part of it crashed onto her. Three days later Louis XVI, accompanied by the Royal Family, was forced to stop in his coach in front of the demolished statue of his forebear. The square had already been renamed Place des Piques.

On September 23, 1806, Napoleon laid the foundation stone of the Column of Austerlitz on the spot where Louis XIV's statue had stood. The column rose a hundred and forty feet and was decorated from top to bottom with the bronze of twelve hundred cannons taken in six weeks from the Austrians and Russians. It was an exact imitation of the Trajan Column in Rome with the difference that the Parisian monument was one-twelfth larger in dimension. Two hundred and seventy-four plates of bronze bore a set of bas-reliefs, exquisitely achieved, ascending in a spiral line, and representing the most famous actions of the Campaigns of the North. The pedestal was ornamented with ensigns and machines of war extremely well executed. The designs, on which thirty-one sculptors co-operated, were chiefly by Gérard, Renaud, Beauvellet and Bergeret. The Emperor dedicated the column to the glory of the Grande Armée. It was surmounted by his statue in a toga. With the erection of this statue the tribulations of the Column began.

On April 4, 1814, a crowd of zealous Royalists burst into the square, shouting, "Down with the Usurper, long live the King!" On this occasion the Marquis de Maubreuil took the place of the late Rose Violet. This was a better organised affair, however, and no one came a cropper. Horses were attached to the ropes, skilled workmen were used, and on the fourth day the Emperor's statue reached the ground. During the Hundred Days he refused to reinstall it, and it was melted down. After the Battle of Waterloo and during the years of the Restoration, the white flag of the Bourbons floated on top of the Column.

Yet the Column remained associated with the glory of the French army and the man who had led it. At the Congress of Vienna, Metternich asked Lord Dudley of Ward what he thought of Napoleon. "I think," he replied, "that he has made all past glory questionable and future impossible." The Parisians felt the same and even the best Royalist intentions could not overlook the past. In *A Tour Through Paris* (during the reign of Louis XVIII), the anonymous author writes:

"The French Military forms a distinct corporation in the state, and is governed by its own code. As the Romans, to evade the law that forbade the putting to death of a Roman citizen, declared him no longer a citizen before they inflicted extreme punishment, the French endeavour to save their military uniform from disgrace in the same manner, by first degrading the soldier into a private man. Accordingly, the first operation of punishment is to deprive the criminal of all that distinguishes the profession of arms. If he be an officer, they tear away his epaulettes and other military decorations. If a soldier, he is stripped of his regimentals and obliged to make his appearance in the dress of a convict . . . the Place Vendôme has been chosen as the theatre of these punishments, whether the offender be condemned to pay the forfeit of his life, or be consigned to the hulks, the place seems to have been chosen in order to render the punishment more exemplary and impressive.

"It is at the foot of the column, which excites an extraordinary degree of enthusiasm among the veteran military, that the culprit is expelled from the ranks of his late companions in arms."

Came the July Revolution and Louis-Philippe, King of the French, tried to bask in the sun of Austerlitz as though it shone on him too. He ordered a new statue, and the Emperor was again hoisted to the top of the Vendôme Column, this time wearing his redingote and the famous petit chapeau.

In 1865 his nephew Napoleon III, who was well acquainted with the Place Vendôme, so called since 1799, as he had stayed at the Hôtel du Rhin (numbers 4-6) before he became President of the Republic, thought that his uncle should again be represented as a Roman Caesar and not as the Little Corporal. Down once more came the Emperor, then up he went again, his new statue sporting a toga of such unfortunate cut that the surviving veterans of the Grande Armée who came to lay wreaths at the foot of the Column did not recognise their Emperor, dressed up, as some observed, as a laundryman. The statue of the Little Corporal was taken to Courbevoie (Seine-Saint-Denis) and set up at the Rond-point de la Défense.

The painter Jean-Désiré-Gustave Courbet, under whom Edouard Manet studied, developed an implacable hatred of Napoleon III. As early as September 1870, a few days after the defeat of Sedan, he wanted the Column to be taken down and re-erected at the Hôtel des Invalides minus the uncle of the hated man. At the time no one listened to him. However, when the Commune burst into being—

Punch published a drawing of Paris, a fair woman assailed by jackals while a Prussian soldier looks on with folded arms—Courbet was elected delegate of the Committee of Fine Arts, along with Manet, though he was then at Oléron and returned to Paris only towards the end of the Commune. On May 11, 1871, Courbet led a large mob to the Place Vendôme, where there had been a fusillade on March 22 among soldiers on their way to military headquarters. Fifty had perished in what was one of the curtain-raisers of the Commune. The inhabitants of the square barricaded themselves in their houses as Courbet and the throng arrived. There was no longer any argument about dismantling the statue. A carpet of dung and straw was prepared to receive the great Napoleon. As the statue came tumbling down, the head was badly damaged. The Column itself followed.

The crash could be heard as far as the Boulevard de Batignolles. An eyewitness from the rue de Rome saw the statue disappear. The crowd in the street duly celebrated the downfall of "military apotheosis, symbol of false glory". The bronze tablets were too heavy to be taken home as souvenirs, but the statuette of Victory, which Napoleon had held in his hand, vanished for good.

In 1873 Adolphe Thiers, President of the Republic, who had put down the Commune, ordered the Column to be raised again. Courbet was held responsible for having pulled it down and was sentenced to six months imprisonment and fined 350,000 francs, roughly the sum that its re-erection would cost. The fine ruined him, and when he left prison he sought refuge in Switzerland, where he died in 1877. It was not too difficult to repair the Column as most of the bronze had been left in the square, and the repaired laundryman still watches over the jewellers' shops in the Place Vendôme.

The statue of the Little Corporal at Courbevoie was lowered into the Seine on the orders of the Government of the Third Republic on September 17, 1870, the day the Prussians took Versailles. It was brought up in the following year and left in a mason's yard until

1911, when it was erected in the cour d'honneur of the Hôtel des Invalides.

In the 1830s and '40s, Bassero, a famous kettle drummer, kept his audience in thrall in a large booth in front of the Cirque-d'Hiver in the rue Amelot. The scenery on the stage consisted of old bits of sails painted in striking colours. There were twenty kettle-drums, and Bassero darted from one to the other. People from as far away as Ménilmontant and Montrouge joined the workmen of the neighbourhood and concierges and their families, to make up the audience, along with soldiers and servant girls. Bassero's outstanding solo performance was the Battle of the Pyramids. He beat the drums, then the battle began:

"Ladies and gentlemen, now you will hear the glorious battle. I beg you to give all your attention as I am the only man in the world who is capable of executing it.

"The camp awakes (crescendo rolling), the soldiers shoulder arms, General Bonaparte gives his orders, the soldiers rally round his grey redingote and little hat. (The drums imitate an army on the march.)

"'Soldiers! From the top of these monuments forty centuries and ten thousand nurserymaids watch you!'

"(The trot, the gallop, the thunder of cannons, the rolling of drums, collapse of houses.) Ladies and gentlemen, you hear the wailing of women, the shrieks of children, everything is in ruins, the massacre is general, the sun shines down on the field of carnage.

"The battle is won! I have the honour to thank you for your attention. Long live the Emperor!"

He gave a military salute to his swooning audience, which withdrew in deep silence. As the new spectators came in, he shouted, "On parade!"

In the last century the Boulevard du Temple was referred to as the Boulevard du Crime because its many theatres like l'Ambigu, la Gaieté, les Funambules, Cirque Olympique, le Petit-Lazari, Comique and Délassement produced crime plays when not bowing to the fashion of putting on plays with the Emperor as hero.

Actors like Gobert and Taillade made their fortune because they resembled Napoleon. Briand, a far from successful actor, remembered in his old age the days when he had played Sir Hudson Lowe in a play about Napoleon:

"In all my career as an actor I never had such reaction from the audience. After every performance they nearly lynched me before chucking me into the nearest fountain."

XV

Saint-Germain-des-Prés

When Childebert I returned in 543 from the Siege of Saragosa, he brought back a fragment of the True Cross and relics of St Vincent. Germain, Bishop of Paris, persuaded him to found the Abbey and Church of Saint-Croix-et-Saint-Vincent to house the relics. Childebert gave the Abbey the fief of Issy, which comprised all the land between the Petit-Pont and Meudon (Seine-et-Oise). The limits in Paris were the rue de la Huchette, the Carrefour Saint-Michel, and the rue de la Harpe as far as Porte Saint-Michel (Porte Gibart then); beyond the city gate, it took in Vanves, reaching the Seine above Meudon.

Germain was born in Autun or somewhere nearby. He studied in Avallon, then led a life of meditation at Lucey in Côte-d'Or. He was ordained priest, and when he was about forty years old he was elected Abbot of the Monastery of Saint-Symphorien in Autun. Childebert appointed him Bishop of Paris around 550, or perhaps earlier. He was over eighty years old when he died in Paris on May 28, 576, the only accurate date concerning him on record.

Already in his lifetime he was known for his miracles. He prayed once in front of a burning house and the fire subsided. Yet his most famous miracles came only after his death. On the day of his burial, as the procession passed in front of a prison, the coffin sank into the earth and could not be moved before all the prisoners were freed. He was buried in the Church of Saint-Croix-et-Saint-Vincent, which after his canonisation became the Church of Saint-Germain, des-Prés added to it because of another church of Saint-Germain in the Cité, Saint-Germain-le-Vieux.

In July 754 it was decided to transfer his coffin in the presence of King Pepin le Bref from the crypt to the sanctuary, but the sarcophagus remained stuck to the floor of the crypt. The King immediately promised to have the Abbey enlarged. The saint made no further difficulties.

By the first quarter of the ninth century the number of monks in the Abbey was one hundred and fifty. According to Abbot Hilduin his monks needed fourteen hundred muids of pure leaven a year, two thousand of wine, a hundred and eighty of vegetables, a hundred and sixty of cheese, four of butter and a hundred of salt; plus seven setiers of honey and two pounds of beeswax monthly, not forgetting an unspecified quantity of poultry and eggs for Christmas and Easter. A muid was an ancient French measure that varied in different regions. In Paris a muid of wine comprised eighteen hectolitres, a muid of oats about thirty-seven hectolitres, of salt twenty-four, and of coal and wood about forty-one hectolitres. A setier was about half a litre.

The monastery was self-supporting. All the labour of the serfs was dependent on it. As monks alone could read and write, they were the only people capable of undertaking and managing schemes on a scale beyond the ordinary man's conception for the exploitation of the land. In the Merovingian age a flourishing abbey like Saint-Germain was a direct descendant of the Gallo-Roman "villas" around which many French villages had developed.

The Normans first attacked Paris in 835. Each time they returned, they pillaged the monastery. In 863 the monks began to repair and rebuild the Abbey, but in 866, when all the churches of Paris were sacked, the Normans destroyed both Church and Abbey. In the first half of the tenth century Abbot Morard laid the foundations of the present church. He was the twenty-ninth Abbot of Saint-Germain. Church and Abbey were surrounded by high walls behind which lived about a thousand souls.

The domain of Saint-Germain, that is to say the Seigneurie de l'Abbaye, became known as the Bourg Saint-Germain. In the fourteenth century noblemen and burghers, drawn by the good air and the pleasant woods, built residences in the meadows, which were destroyed during the Hundred Years War, and during the sixteen years of English occupation (1420 to 1436) rebuilding was not encouraged. The area was still thinly populated when Nicolas Vauquelin, Seigneur des Yveteaux, chose around 1630 to build a house and lay out a garden in Saint-Germain, on the site of the present rue Visconti, formerly rue des Marais-Saint-Germain. His was the only house in the neighbourhood, and his friends nicknamed him the Last Man, also the Man who Lives at the End of the World.

Vauquelin was born in 1559 and lived to be ninety years old. He had been Lieutenant-General of Caen before he became tutor to the Duc de Vendôme. Vauquelin fell into disgrace, which decided him to exile himself from Paris, so he went to live at the end of the world!

His walled-in garden and park extended to the east beyond the present rue Bonaparte. Tallemant des Réaux described him in *Historiettes* as a grand seigneur in his seraglio. That was an exaggeration, as his sole vice was strolling in the garden with Jeanne du Poy, his harp player, a good-looking girl he had rescued from poverty. They enacted mythological scenes: she carried a shepherd's crook decorated with flame-coloured ribbons; in spite of his seventy years, he dressed as a young shepherd, wearing a straw hat lined with red satin; and guarding imaginary sheep they strolled in the garden, he reciting poetry, she playing the harp, and both of them fiercely defending the flock from imaginary wolves.

To the west of his garden extended the Pré-aux-Clercs. Two lanes cut across the fields, one leading to the Chapel of Saint-Pierre or Saint-Père (now rue des Saints-Pères, which separates the sixth arrondissement, that is Saint-Germain-des-Prés, from the seventh, the Faubourg Saint-Germain), the other used by carts bringing stones from the quarries of Vaugirard to be ferried across the Seine for the construction of the Castle of the Tuileries. The road leading to the ferry was called Grand Chemin du Bac, which after 1620 became the rue du Bac. Beyond Vauquelin's garden, the fields ran down to the Seine. Cows grazed in them, and ditches separated the small cultivated patches, but not a building was to be seen between house and river. Not far from his property, along the Chemin du Colombier (now rue Jacob), rose garbage heaps and refuse dumps. South of the property stood the imposing mass of the Abbey, surrounded by walls with turrets.

The Pré-aux-Clercs stretched from the Abbey to the Champs de Mars, taking in all the uncultivated land from the present-day rues de Seine and Bonaparte along the rues Jacob and de l'Université, the Quais Malaquais, Voltaire, Anatole France and d'Orsay to the Quai Branly. University students were called clercs (clerks), in the same way as ecclesiastics. There were two prés (fields): the Petit Pré near the Monastery, and the Grand Pré, which disappeared, so to speak, in the wasteland of the Champs de Mars. These fields belonged to the Abbey, but part of them had been ceded to the University, which noble gesture the monks were soon to rue, for with the students came noise, debauches, fights and duels. True that on summer evenings solid, peace-loving citizens were brought over in the ferry to enjoy a stroll and the country air; however, when the curfew chimed they hastened back to the ferry. It was not so much the students as the ruffians swarming all over the place who made life dangerous at night.

Until the sixteenth century the couvre-feu was chimed by the bells of every Paris church. Couvre-feu was originally the name given to one of Notre-Dame's church bells, because when it sounded one had to hasten home to bank up the fire and put out the lights. As the bell chimed the children chanted in unison: "Bonsoir mon père, bonsoir ma mère; le dernier couvre le feu." After the sixteenth century, curfew was rung in Notre-Dame only, at seven in the evening.

There were several Jeux de Paume (real tennis courts) in the Pré. Roistering and theatrical performances also helped to disturb the monks who, in accordance with the Rules of St Benedict, were enjoined to live in peace, prayer and study. The students loved fights and now and then came to blows with their benefactors. In 1163 the scholars and the monks had such a noisy quarrel that the matter was brought before the Council of Tours, where seventeen cardinals and one hundred and forty-four bishops had assembled. They decided in favour of the monks, and the scholars were condemned to perpetual silence. In 1192 came a new outbreak of fighting, and in a pitched battle a student was killed and several wounded. The sporadic fights continued until the Abbey withdrew the grant, and houses and gardens appeared in the Pré-aux-Clercs only after the University had been dislodged.

The students never accepted their defeat. In 1548 they appeared in the Pré, led by a certain de Ramus or de La Ramce, and rooted up trees and tore out vines. When evening came they withdrew with their booty, which they burnt in front of the Church of Sainte-Geneviève-du-Mont near the University.

The monks complained to the tribunals, but judgment this time went against them. The scholars had based themselves on some charter of Charlemagne, which they would certainly have been unable to produce, proving that the Abbey had usurped some of the land, including, of course, the Pré-aux-Clercs. The monks had to return half of their cultivated land in the Pré-aux-Clercs but in its pristine, uncultivated, unfenced state. Not content with their victory, the University's attitude remained belligerent, and six years after the judgment the war flared up again, this time led by another student, Baptiste Crocoezon, a native of Amiens. The students lost whatever sense of proportion they had and burnt down the houses of the substantial burghers who lived in the Pré. Unfortunately for the students, and especially for Crocoezon, one of the houses belonged to Jean Baillet, the King's Commissioner. Crocoezon was sentenced to be burnt, but as an act of mercy he was first strangled. His fellow students took his charred bones to the Chapel of Saint-Père, where several Masses were offered up for the salvation of his soul, and one of the students passed his hat round among the people who had witnessed the execution to collect enough money for Masses to be said for Crocoezon in perpetuity. The hat was filled.

Duellists found the Pré-aux-Clercs to their taste as there was little fear of being interrupted or arrested. In 1602 a duel was fought between two Protestant gentlemen, Villemor and La Fontaine, as a result of a quarrel they had had at tennis. They arrived in the field, put their swords on the ground, and searched each other for extra weapons; finding none, they shook hands, knelt and prayed together. They had with them a single witness, a lackey mounted on a fine steed. It was agreed that the survivor should take the horse after the duel. It was the lackey, however, who returned on horseback: the two duellists remained in the field, both dead.

After the Pont-Neuf was opened, more and more Parisians visited the Pré-aux-Clercs, much to the annoyance of duellists and students, and eventually Saint-Germain-des-Prés was attached to Paris in the reign of Louis XIV.

The pillory of the Abbey was situated where the rues de Buci du Four, des Boucheries (swallowed by the Boulevard Saint-Germain) and de Sainte-Marguerite (now rue Gozlin) met. The Abbey prison took up the whole length of the present houses in the Boulevard Saint-Germain between numbers 135-137 on one side and 166 on the other. It dated back to the fourteenth century and faced the main entrance of the Abbey. It was surrounded by some ramshackle buildings, one of them the Inn of the Chapeau Rouge.

In 1635 a transaction took place between the Abbot and the architect Gamard. Among other works for the Abbey, the architect undertook to build a new portal for the church and rebuild the prison. The new prison was a square building with turrets at each corner. If his aim had been to construct one of the most disagreeable prisons in Paris, Gamard certainly excelled at his work. The low-ceilinged dungeons were like oubliettes in which the prisoners could not stand up and so perished in a short time. By the eighteenth century the dungeons were no longer used, but the cells remained so abominable and damp that the soldiers—it had become a military prison—had on release to be taken straight to the Hospital of Val-de-Grace to recuperate. The walls were filthy and nothing was ever done to clean them. The courtyard, where prisoners were exercised, was so small that men stood pressed against each other, hardly able to move; and no fresh air entered it. The cells were overcrowded. One palliasse and one blanket were all a prisoner was given, and even the prison officials, whose rooms were comfortable, had no place for exercise. Before the Revolution the prison was mostly used for the detention of soldiers of the Gardes-Françaises, a crack regiment raised in 1563 which guarded the royal castles of Paris until the end of the old régime.

Room was also found in the overcrowded prison for debtors, whether noblemen or officers, who had not paid their debts of honour. Prison could, however, also be the jumping-off ground for the ambitious or the lucky. Pierre Broussel, Councillor to the Parliament of Paris, was put into the Abbey prison in 1648. In the following year he left it, nominated as Governor of the Bastille.

During the Revolution the Abbaye, as the prison was known, was filled with the unfortunate "enemies of the people". On September 2, 1792, sixteen persons were taken there in fiacres. The mob stopped the carriages at the Carrefour de Buci. Four of the passengers were killed even before they could leave their seats. The others were hauled out, and nine of them were butchered on the spot. Drunk with blood, the mob rushed to the Convent of the Carmelites in the rue de Vaugirard, where a hundred and sixteen souls were slaughtered. Not yet satisfied, the mob hurried back to the Abbaye, and formed a tribunal presided over by Maillard, a bailiff. Three hundred and fifty-seven prisoners were dragged before it; three hundred and fourteen of them were assassinated, some in front of the prison, the majority inside. The day became known as the September Massacres.

Among those held in the Abbaye during the Revolution were Mme Rolland, Clavières, Labédoyère and Charlotte Corday, who was taken there on July 12, 1793, but transferred to the Conciergerie a few days later. After her death a young man, Adam de Lux, Deputy Extraordinary of Mayence, published a leaflet in praise of her, proposing to have a statue erected to her with the inscription, "Greater than Brutus". He was locked up in the Abbaye. As he entered the prison he cried out joyfully, "I will die for Charlotte Corday." He did.

During the Restoration of the Bourbon dynasty, the Abbaye was used for the detention of soldiers waiting to be court-martialled. Five out of six detainees were acquitted. Those who were convicted left either for the gallows or to serve long sentences in irons.

On the same September day when the prisoners were being massacred, in one of the dungeons a poor parish priest awaited his turn to die. Suddenly a capital idea came to him, namely to make himself clothes with the rags lying around him. When Maillard's tribunal sent for him, he appeared before it wearing the rags. When asked why he was detained, he replied because he was a beggar who had been arrested while begging for his bread. He played his part so well, and the rags looked so convincing, that he was set free. He lived near the Louvre, and reaching his street he cried with joy. The first two people he ran into were neighbours of his, one of them a butcher.

"Congratulate me, my good friends, my dear neighbours, for I escaped the massacre," said the happy priest, then explained the stratagem he had used to bamboozle the awful tribunal.

"But you won't escape us, citizen," shouted the two men, and the butcher cut his throat on the spot.

On the site of the Institut de France stood a sinister tower, part of the Enceinte of Paris, and named after Philippe Hamelin, Provost of Paris. When Jean de Nesle built his mansion, the Hôtel de Nesle, in the rue Guénégaud, the tower was renamed Tour de Nesle. In 1308 Philippe le Bel bought the house from Amaury de Nesle. The King had three sons who married three cousins, Marguerite, Blanche and Jeanne de Bourgogne. The three women, who led licentious lives, received their lovers in the mansion. One day Isabelle, daughter of Philippe le Bel and wife of Richard II of England, recognised the aumônières, purses attached to the belt, worn by two noblemen at Court. The purses were presents she had given her sisters-in-law. She rushed to her father who locked up Marguerite and Blanche in the Castle of Gaillard des Andelys. Their lovers, Philippe and Gaultier d'Aunay, were drawn and quartered, then beheaded, and finally hanged by their shoulders and left to be pecked by birds. Jeanne was incarcerated in the Castle of Dourdan.

Ten years later Blanche took the veil in the Abbey of Maubuisson and Marguerite was killed on the order of Louis X, her husband, because he wished to remarry. Jeanne was set free and given the Hôtel de Nesle when her husband, Philippe V le Long, mounted the throne. Still young and pretty after her husband's death—his reign lasted only six years—she decided to take lovers, but having learnt from bitter experience that men were indiscreet, she had them killed once she tired of them. The form was to give the lover a good meal, then throw a sack over his head, take him up to the Tour de Nesle, and hurl him into the Seine. One of the lovers was

Jean Buridan, a shining light of the University. He too, according to legend, met his end in the river. Villon believed the tale:

> Où est la reine
> Qui commanda que Buridan
> Fût jeté en un sac en Seine?

However, Buridan survived the widowed queen, who died in 1329, and was, in fact, Rector of the University in 1348. Dismissing the entire legend in his *Paris* (six volumes, published between 1869-1875), Maxime Du Camp observes: "Nowadays husbands are so good-natured that great ladies no longer need to throw their lovers into the river."

The tower was pulled down in 1662. The legend persists.

"In the old days in Paris," wrote Henri Sauval, "there were two fairs at Saint-Germain. At present there is only one. All I know of the first is that in the twelfth century it opened fifteen days after Easter and lasted for eighteen days. The Abbot and the monks were the proprietors of it for reasons I am unaware of."

The second fair, which lasted until the second half of the eighteenth century, became the most important fair in and around Paris, and no Parisian, however rich or poor, failed to attend it. Provincials flocked to it from every corner of the land. The duration of the fair varied from age to age. In 1485 Charles VIII decreed that February 3 should be the opening date and that the fair should last for eight days. Eight years later he allowed it to open for the four days following the feast of St Mathew. In the troubled times of the League no fair was held, but in 1595, by consent of Henri IV, it remained open for three weeks. In Sauval's time in the seventeenth century, the fair started on February 1 and lasted as long as it pleased the King. By then Parliament, the Abbot and the Provost of Paris no longer had any say in the matter. The Court, the nobility and the rich were generally in Paris towards the end of winter and the beginning of spring during the bad weather, and consequently the fair did not close before their departure.

Originally the fair was held in a large field, teeming with booths and stalls, in the vicinity of the Abbey. Wine, horses and sheep were sold. Later two booths were built in the field, each a hundred and thirty feet long and a hundred wide, little pavilions on their own with shops and passages. The limits of the field were the rues Guisarde, du Four, des Boucheries, des Quatre-Vents, de Tournon and des Aveugles (rue Saint-Sulpice). There were seven doors of entry, each from the rue du Four. In front of the pavilions was a vast, empty square.

The first eight days of the fair were set aside for the sale of cloth, sheets, serge and their kind. The following week it was the turn of porcelain, crockery and similar merchandise. Then came the best, for crowds were at their happiest in the shops and booths of the goldsmiths, silversmiths, haberdashers, milliners and painters, who did a brisk trade until the fair closed. The painters were much sought after because of "the infinite number of their paintings". Linen, cotton and lace and all other objects "of vain luxury and sensual pleasure," says Sauval, "were assembled by merchants who at the risk of their lives went to find them at the extremities of the Indies, in China and the New World." The shops of the goldsmiths were like Aladdin's cave.

The type of visitor to the fair changed twice a day, as though there were two separate fairs. During the day the ordinary people filled it, but by nightfall they had vanished, their place being taken by the quality; even great ladies and the King himself appeared in the fairytale lights of lustres and torches.

The fair catered not only for the common people and their betters. Gambling dens and cabarets were filled with ruffians, mountebanks, jugglers, fortune-tellers and cardsharps. Turks sold rosewater and balm straight from Constantinople—so they said. Portuguese hawked amber and porcelain, and Armenians offered tea, coffee and chocolate. Among the attractions was a "huge devil of a woman", to quote Mme de Sévigné who saw her at the fair in 1671. In 1749 the star of the fair was a rhinoceros, the first that Parisian eyes had ever beheld. Theatrical performances became fashionable in the seventeenth century.

The fair closed its seven doors in 1786.

The ferry to the Louvre used to be tied up at the bottom of the rue des Saints-Pères. One evening in 1598, shortly after the signing of the Treaty of Vervins, Henri IV on his way back from a shoot and accompanied only by two gentlemen, appeared on the landing stage and hailed the ferryman, who did not recognise him because of the simple clothes he wore. While they crossed, the King asked the ferryman what he thought of the peace treaty. In a grumbling voice, the ferryman declared that he for one had no time to think of it as he had enough worries with the taxes he had to pay; not even his wretched boat was exempt. Henri IV asked him whether he had confidence in the King, who would surely right such matters now that the war had ended.

"The King," said the ferryman, "is a good fellow, but he has a mistress who needs fine dresses and it is we who have to provide the money for them." He added that she had other lovers beside the monarch.

The King was amused, and the next day sent for the ferryman and made him repeat his words in front of Gabrielle d'Estrées. The royal mistress became so angry that she wanted the man to be flogged. The King restrained her with the words, "You are mad. He is a poor, luckless wight whose ill-humour is caused by misery. I won't let him pay any more taxes, and tomorrow, I promise you, he will shout 'Long live Henri IV and charming Gabrielle'."

The ferryman, exempted from further taxes, left the Louvre with a purse containing 25 écus.

Until the middle of the sixteenth century Paris had only four bridges: Petit-Pont, Notre-Dame, Saint-Michel and au Change.

By then the need for a new bridge to connect the Right Bank with the Bourg Saint-Germain had become evident. Thus was born the Pont-Neuf. The first stone was laid by Henri III on the very day he attended the funeral of Quélus and Maugiron, his favourite Mignons. He came straight from the Church of Saint-Paul-des-Champs in the rue Saint-Paul, and was in such a lachrymose mood that Parisian wags wanted the bridge to be named Pont-des-Larmes, bridge of tears. The bridge was constructed between 1578 and 1607. Its buildings, and particularly its shops, which did not disappear until the 1850s, drew the people almost more than the prospect of visiting the fair at Saint-Germain or strolling in the Pré-aux-Clercs. If one wanted to find a friend, all one had to do was to spend an hour or so on the bridge, for no self-respecting Parisian let the day go by without putting in an appearance on the Pont-Neuf. Police agents and spies went straight to the bridge when searching for a person they wanted to arrest or trail. If on the fourth day he was still invisible, they reported that the quarry was absent from Paris.

Recruiting sergeants frequented the bridge, for colonels, as L. S. Mercier put it, needed men to sell to the King. The sergeants were up to any old trick, such as employing low women to entice the men or cabaret-keepers to get them drunk. On the eve of Shrove Tuesday and the feast of St Martin, they carried poles from which hung turkeys, chickens, quails and leverets, in the hope that where women and drink had failed ravenous hunger would succeed. They were seldom wrong. The poor dupes, loitering near the Fountain of the Samaritaine, who had not had a square meal in their lives, succumbed to the temptation. Another trick of the sergeants was to shake their moneybags, rattling the coins. "Who wants some?" they shouted. The price for a prospective hero was 30 livres, but if he were a hefty fellow he received more. Good profit could be made out of the sons of tradesmen. The recruiting officers or sergeants, having filled them with wine, signed them on, and it cost the desperate parents 100 écus to buy them out. The recruiting offices were actually in the vicinity of the bridge, and they flew their regimental flags, one of which was embroidered with a line from Voltaire:

Le premier qui fut roi, fut un soldat heureux.

But the message had no appeal, for most of the recruits could neither read nor write.

Until the reign of Louis XIII the statues of French Kings were to be seen only on their tombs or as decorations on church porches. Louis XIII broke with tradition when he erected a statue on the Pont-Neuf to his murdered father, Henri IV. The foundation stone of the monument was laid on June 20, 1614. The figure of the dead King was cast by Guillaume Dupré. The horse that bore him had been presented to Marie de Medici, his widow, by Giovanni di Bologna. As a work of art, the horse was superior to the rider.

On August 11, 1792, the mob destroyed the statue of the man who for nearly two hundred years had been regarded by the people of France as the best King they had ever had. In order to incite the mob the story was invented that Ravaillac had murdered him because the King had raped Ravaillac's sister. The smashed statue was thrown into the Seine. In 1809, with the Empire still in full bloom, the foundation stone of an obelisk was laid on the same spot. It was to be a hundred feet high and consecrated to the glory of the French nation, but the Empire passed without the obelisk being erected, and with the Restoration Henri IV returned to the Pont-Neuf in the shape of a plaster-cast. Public opinion clamoured, however, for a bronze statue, the money for which was raised by private subscription. Inside the pedestal were deposited documents relating to the inauguration of the first statue, documents relating to the new one, several books—among them *L'Henriade* of Voltaire and a life of Henri IV—the Charter of 1814, the Peace Treaty of 1814, and coins and medals. Moreover, Mesnel, a workman on the statue who was a rabid Bonapartist, inserted into the right arm of the King a statuette of the Emperor, and placed in the horse's belly anti-royalist writings and songs, which are still inside it. The statue was unveiled on

August 25, 1818, in the presence of Louis XVIII and the happy people who might easily have included some of those or their sons who had, in Restoration parlance, laid sacrilegious hands on the original. The new statue cost 350,000 francs.

The Cour de Rohan has no connection with the family of that name; it was the courtyard of the Paris mansion of the Archbishops of Rouen. Time had turned Rouen into Rohan. It joins the Cour du Commerce near the bookshop where Doctor Guillotin tried out his invention on sheep. Contrary to general belief, the doctor, who was described by his contemporaries as a quiet, sweet-natured man, did not invent the instrument; he simply brought it up to date. It had been used as far back as the fifteenth century in Italy and the south of France, when it was called mannaja, but the doctor's improvements made it far easier to operate. He was satisfied with his experiments on sheep. "A puff of air on the neck," he said, "and all is over." He called it a philanthropic engine. It started as a labour of love, for he did not see to what commercial advantage he could put it, yet he continued with his improvements and the heads of sheep rolled in the Cour du Commerce.

At number 9 lived a German carpenter named Schmidt who assisted the doctor in his philanthropic work. He was a willing helpmate, but when the Revolution put the guillotine to use, poor Schmidt took to drink, bitterly blaming himself for having helped the doctor, in whose defence it must be said that he too had not foreseen the consequences of his experiments. Schmidt died, during the Empire, of delirium tremens brought about by wine laced with remorse; and the mild doctor also, again contrary to general belief, never felt the puff of air on his own neck: he died in his bed in 1812 at the respectable age of seventy-four.

To the south of the Cour du Commerce stands the statue of Danton, on the Boulevard Saint-Germain in the exact spot where he had an apartment of seven rooms. He used to cross the courtyard on his way to the Café Procope to meet other revolutionaries of the neighbourhood.

Originally the rue Visconti was called the rue des Marais-Saint-Germain, and for a while it was referred to as Little Geneva because of the Calvinists who lived there. In the long narrow street between rues Bonaparte and Seine have resided several famous men, among them Bernard Le Bovier de Fontenelle, writer and Secretary of the Académie des Sciences, who in his hundredth year said to a pretty young girl, on being introduced to her, "If only I were ten years younger!" Marshal de Saxe, Voltaire and Jean Racine also lived in the street.

Racine lived and died at number 24, but it used to be believed in the street that he had lived at number 13 because he planted a vine there. The street was not yet as narrow as at the present time, and the playwright's house faced the gardens of the de la Rochefoucauld mansion. Racine was already fifty-three years old when he moved to the rue des Marais. He had given up the theatre fifteen years earlier, his only preoccupation now the salvation of his soul. He recollected with horror the days when he had frequented actresses and often sobbed over his "scandalous life", which had covered his great creative years. In the course of those fifteen years away from the theatre his wife, Catherine de Romanet, had given him eight children. In spite of the presence of the smaller ones, the house in the rue des Marais remained austere in its silence.

The house was on three floors. The walls of the rooms and even of the passages were hung with Flemish tapestries. Gloomy Racine loved red. When he went out, he wore a scarlet overcoat and short pink jacket. On his return he put on a red velvet cap and cried over his sins.

At the age of sixteen Jean-Baptiste, his eldest son, evinced a desire to go to the Opéra. Racine counselled him to read Cicero instead, and as an Easter present wrote him a sermon on death. He wanted Jean-Baptiste to enter a monastery: the boy ended up in the Ministry of Foreign Affairs. Racine was deeply influenced by the Jansenist Convent of Port-Royal, where his eldest daughter, Marie-Catherine, was brought up. Nanette, his second daughter, was educated in the convent of the Ursulines at Melun; the third, Babet, was with the nuns at Variville-en-Beauvaisis; the fourth, Fanchon, was waiting at the time of her father's death to be old enough to join Nanette in Melun; the youngest, Madelon, like Fanchon, lived in the parental home, together with the two small boys Lionval and Louis. Of amusements there were hardly any. Once the children were taken to the fair at Saint-Germain, where the sight of the elephant gave Lionval convulsions, an added reason not to indulge in outings.

In the summer of 1698 Racine fell ill. The medicos bled him copiously, and by October he was on his feet again, though he complained of feeling exceptionally weak. Still, he had the energy to travel to Melun to see Nanette take the veil. He sobbed throughout the ceremony. The following January he went for a stroll with his wife as far as the Tuileries, but acute pain in his back forced him home. He never left the house again, and died on April 21.

Sir George Brydges Rodney, Bart., Rear Admiral of Great Britain (elevated to the peerage as Baron Rodney in 1782), lived for a while in 1775 in the rue Visconti, driven to Paris by his creditors. He kicked his heels in his lodgings in the narrow street, thinking of the war raging in America while he, like a laid-up ship of the line, was anchored in peaceful Saint-Germain. He complained to his French friends, declaring that if only he could pay his debts and be on the high seas again, he would quickly put an end to French successes.

"If it only depends on that," said Marshal of France Baron de Biron, "I charge myself with their payment."

And he paid them. Soon it was the turn of the French Admiral, the Comte de Grasse, to complain.

In spite of all the other famous men who lived there, the rue Visconti seems most attached to the memory of Honoré de Balzac, who came to number 19 not to write, but to print and publish books. He had already done a stretch of four years as a writer, however did not feel there was enough money to be made in that profession. His mistress, Mme de Berny, who was twenty years his senior, set him up as a publisher. "Only a woman's last love can satisfy a man's first love," he wrote. He had an excellent idea, the only snag being that he thought of it before its time. He planned to publish the works of Molière, La Fontaine and other classic writers in single volumes, illustrated with woodcuts. His formula became enormously successful after he gave it up. There was not at the time a large enough public for cheap books. The literate still preferred their writers in six or more volumes. Madame de Berny paid his debts after the two-year venture failed. In 1828 Balzac went away and back to writing. The printing press remained, and can be seen at number 19 in the ground-floor workshop, now used for binding books.

In the rue de Bourbon-le-Château, which gives on to the market of the rue de Buci, a murder was committed in 1850 which, because of the rapid apprehension of the assassin, entered the annals of Saint-Germain-des-Prés. At number 1 rue de Bourbon-le-Château lived a Mlle Ribault, a spinster, who was draughtswoman at the *Petit Courrier des Dames*, edited by a Monsieur Thierry. She was killed in the afternoon of December 23 by her employer's assistant, Laforcade, while the happy throng was doing its Christmas shopping in the market. Loath to leave this life without denouncing her murderer, the old maid crawled to a screen and, with her finger dipped in her own blood, she wrote on it, "The assassin is the assistant of Monsieur Thi. . . ." Respectful to the last, she gave her employer his title though she lacked the time to complete his name.

XVI

Latin Quarter

When in 1855 the Boulevard Saint-Germain reached the Place Maubert, the square lost its personality and importance. The old houses were pulled down, and nowadays there is nothing but a circus where the Boulevard and the rues Monge and Lagrange meet. For seven centuries the square had been associated with the University, and, as one knows from an ordinance of 1546, a bread market was already established there at that date. Paris had four bread markets in all: Place Maubert, Halles, Cemetery of Saint-Jacques (Place Baudoyer) and rue Neuve-Notre-Dame (Place du Parvis-Notre-Dame). By the middle of the seventeenth century, the bakers who sold in these markets numbered one thousand five hundred and eighty. Roughly one-third of them baked their bread in Paris and the faubourgs; the rest of the bread came from surrounding villages, as far away as Saint-Germain-en-Laye.

On the Plan of Paris of Oliver Truschet and Germain Hoyau, drawn in 1552, the Place Maubert was marked with a little gibbet from which hung a little body, for the square was used for burning, drawing, quartering and hanging. To confess the condemned was the privilege of the Doctors of the University, but the Cordeliers thought it was their right too. A certain poor girl, who was to be hanged for theft, stood beneath the gallows. As a Cordelier began to confess her, an irate Doctor appeared, telling him that he had no business to do so. An unedifying row ensued. The Franciscan and the Doctor came to blows. The girl, watching them with detached interest, seemed to enjoy every brief second. The Doctor prevailed and the monk withdrew. The victorious Doctor then heard the girl's confession and gave her absolution. Then she was hanged.

The square owed its name to Jean Aubert, second Abbot of the Abbey of Sainte-Geneviève in 1161. The Abbey owned all the land in the district. The first colleges of the University were built around 1180, modest dwellings, providing roof and food for the scholars, who rose early and after Mass went to the Place Maubert and the rue du Fouarre where they listened to the lectures, sitting on the ground or on straw, beneath the open sky. Until the reign of François I the teachers were lodged and fed, but received no emoluments except from private pupils. In the colleges Latin alone was tolerated, execrable Latin spoken with a French accent. Even the servants had to speak in Latin. The custom persisted until the Revolution and earned the district the name of the Latin Quarter. In 1257 a college was founded by Robert de Sorbon for poor theological students. Later the whole faculty of theology came to be known as Sorbonne. Nowadays the whole University of Paris is called after him.

Philippe-Auguste established the organisation of the University, but the corporate body of teachers and scholars known as the University, which meant "Universality of the Sciences taught in Schools", did not come into being until the time of St Louis. It had four sections: three for the French and one for the English, Irish and Scots. The English College was given to German scholars during the Hundred Years War.

The students were a turbulent lot. In 1200 a German visitor sent his German servant to a cabaret in a street adjoining the Place Maubert. The servant was ill-treated. German students arrived to avenge their fellow countryman and gave the landlord an awful beating. Led by Thomas, Provost of Paris, the local burghers appeared on the scene and killed five German students. The Rector of the University complained to Philippe-Auguste who had the Provost and his friends locked up for life.

In 1221 the students were in trouble again. Considering themselves immune from persecution because of the privileges granted them by the King, they took to fornication, abducted married women, robbed and murdered. Guillaume de Seignelay, Bishop of Paris, excommunicated all students who carried arms. The ordinary citizens came to hate the students to the extent of fighting a pitched battle with them in 1223 in which three hundred and twenty students were killed, and their bodies thrown into the Seine. The Doctors took their complaints to the Pope; none the less the attacks on students continued until, led by the Doctors, they left Paris for a time, the colleges and faculties remaining empty. When they returned, trouble returned with them.

In 1275 on the feasts of SS Nicholas and Catherine the students marched through the streets of the Latin Quarter in the deep of night, carrying torches, dancing and shouting, and creating such disorder that further outings were finally forbidden by the Assembly of the University which met in the Church of Saint-Julien-le-Pauvre. A century later the rampaging started again. In 1367 the students chose a bishop from among themselves, dressed him up in ecclesiastical vestments and followed him through the streets with lighted torches, creating havoc. The Watch stopped them and one of the students was wounded. When Parliament heard of the affray, the Captain of the Watch was sent to the wounded youth, who not only banged the door in his face, though knowing that he was an emissary of Parliament, but set his friends on him. The Watch overpowered them and the students had to make penance in the Convent of the Mathurins (20–22 rue du Sommerard, demolished during the Revolution), and beg pardon on bended knees from the King, the Bishop of Paris and the Rector of the University.

In 1468 on the day after Epiphany the students elected a king whom they called the King of Fools and under whose aegis they made a terrible din, molesting people they met in the streets and keeping peaceful citizens awake. The following year, Kanedi, the Rector, assembled the Faculty of Arts in the Church of Saint-Julien-le-Pauvre and admonished the Doctors to keep their students in order. He sent representatives of the Faculty to wait on the Provost of Paris to ask him to arrest all students wearing a mask or carrying a stick in the street, and to send them back to their teachers who would mete out exemplary punishment. A year later, again on the day after Epiphany, the students misbehaved once more, but though they were punished, nothing seemed to stop them from indulging in scandalous behaviour during the feasts of Epiphany, SS Martin, Nicholas and Catherine. In 1488 a new order was issued by the Rector and the Faculty of Arts which permitted only decent recreations. On Sundays after Vespers the students were now allowed, even encouraged, to partake of innocent amusements, and if they felt the need of perpetrating practical jokes they were to ask the consent of their teachers who would grant permission only if they considered the jokes harmless.

In practice this decree had little effect. In 1525 on the feast of St Nicholas a woman was dragged along the narrow streets by students, some disguised as devils, others as Doctors of the University. François I was so incensed that he complained to the President of Parliament, who ordered such masquerades to be suppressed.

Excesses were not the prerogative of the Faculty of Arts. In a circular letter sent by the Faculty of Theology to all the Bishops of France, bitter complaint was made about theological students who went to church dressed as buffoons or even women, all wearing masks, singing bawdy songs, bringing their food with them and consuming it while the priest said Mass, playing dice in church, using foul language, and after Mass running round the streets like madmen. Now and then the students went even further. They elected a Pope of Fools who blessed the people he passed in the street. If someone remonstrated with them they spoke, says Henri

Sauval, "as though they were such good Christians that those who forbade their antics deserved to be excommunicated."

The colleges surrounding the Place Maubert included de Tournay, des Lombards, de Navarre, de Presles, de Boncourt, de Saint-Michel, de Montaigu, de la Marche and de Laon. In 1206 one of the first colleges of Paris was founded in the Impasse Maubert: the Collège Constantinople or Collège Grec. The Impasse Maubert, originally known as rue Sans-Bout, changed its name in the fifteenth century to Cul-de-sac d'Amboise after a private mansion of that name. It had an infamous reputation, for wherever students gathered, ruffians and prostitutes also made their appearance. The students hobnobbed and fought with them. In their wake came tramps and beggars. A low tavern in the Impasse Maubert, where one drank and slept until two in the morning when all clients were thrown out for fear of the police descending, acquired special fame in the eighteenth century because three female poisoners who practised there died from the fumes of the furnace in which they brewed their potions.

In the square the gibbet remained busy. On September 19, 1528, a young man of twenty was hanged, accused of having murdered his master with the complicity of a fellow servant. After dangling for half an hour on the gallows, he was cut down by the hangman, who pushed him into a cart to take him to the charnel house of Montfaucon. The young man moved his legs and tried to rise. The hangman took out a knife to cut his victim's throat; however, the women, who were always in the majority at executions, shouted "Miracle!" The young man began to shout too, claiming that he had been dead but was told to return to life by Notre-Dame-de-la-Recouvrance whose chapel stood on the south side of the square. He was taken to the Convent of the Carmelites, where he recovered within two days. A sergeant had remained at his bedside to arrest him the moment he could move. The Carmelites waited on François I, begging him to pardon the young man, which the King did, observing that he could not be less generous than Our Lady. A fresh investigation proved that the murdered man had been killed by his wife.

The square was used as a place of execution until the middle of the eighteenth century. One François Masson, who had stolen the goblets of the Church of the Cistercians, was hanged there on June 12, 1752. "It rained considerably and the gutters overflowed," said a police report, "none the less there was a large concourse of people."

In the nineteenth century the square was taken over by the needy and the homeless. Cigarette stubs, stale bread, leeches and fleas were sold. In the rue d'Ecosse and in houses adjoining the square, goats were raised. Cheap, dirty lodging-houses polluted the district until the coming of the Boulevard put an end to them. The poor of the Place Maubert moved into the streets between the square and the river.

The rue Maître-Albert, which until 1844 was called rue Perdue, took its name from the great theologian St Albert le Grand who, like St Thomas Aquinas, was one of the shining lights of the University in the thirteenth century. In 1815, at 13 rue Maître-Albert lived Zamor. He was Mme Du Barry's blackamoor, or more strictly he was a Bengali who had been brought to France when only seven years old by the captain of an English vessel. Blackamoors were much in fashion in the eighteenth century, and he became the Du Barry's possession. She educated him, spoilt him, lavished a fortune on him and dressed him up as a hussar. Because of the importance she attached to him, even Louis XV found him amusing. During the Terror, Zamor was the first to denounce her, and was one of the chief witnesses against her. "I often remonstrated with her because of the aristocratic world she moved in," he said. The story that he had been her lover when only a boy of ten is almost certainly untrue, for had it been the case, Zamor would have been the first to bring it up at her trial.

"One little minute more, Monsieur le bourreau," she pleaded on the scaffold.

In the rue Perdue, as it still was, Zamor eked out his existence giving lessons to children, whom he beat whenever he had a chance. "He was very nasty," said the local people, who yet went on sending their children to him. He taught them to read and charged little.

He paid 60 francs a year for his room. Charles Vatel, the historian of the Du Barry, called on Mme Lejeune, daughter of the proprietor of the house where Zamor had lived. He asked her to describe him.

"He was very small," she said, "no taller than I, less than five feet. He was a puny mulatto of a disagreeable yellowish colour with a flat nose and sparse greying hair. He would have had enough to live on had he not fallen in love with a milliner to whom he gave all his money, which she lost on a business venture."

One morning in 1820 a neighbour found him dead in bed. Three francs, all he possessed in the world, lay on his bedside table; and when he was buried not a single person accompanied his coffin to the Cemetery of Vaugirard. Twenty-seven years after the Du Barry had been guillotined, a long enough period, one would think, for a veil to have been drawn over the past, the people of the district said, "We are not going. He betrayed the Du Barry."

The rue de Bièvre already bore that name in the thirteenth century. It took its name from the river Bièvre which was linked to a canal dug about 1150 to carry water to the gardens of the Abbey of Saint-Victor. The canal, into which the inhabitants of the neighbourhood flung their refuse, ran parallel to the street, its water foul and smelly. The canal was covered in the seventeenth century to the displeasure of the local people, who demolished the brickwork in several places so as to be able again to throw their rubbish into it. Dante stayed in the street during one of his two visits to Paris.

Before the twelfth century medicine was taught and practised only in the monasteries. The physicians therefore were all monks. Their medical knowledge was not extensive, and was also limited by the celibate existence they led. In 1135 the monks were forbidden to continue practising medicine. Pope Alexander III threatened to excommunicate any monk whose studies went beyond purely theological subjects. As a result Paris remained for nearly a hundred years without physicians. In 1220 small lay schools of medicine opened their doors to lay students. In 1331 Philippe VI founded the Faculty of Medicine, which was attached to the University. The faculty's seat was at 13-15 rue de la Bûcherie which today houses offices of the department of the Seine. The street owed its name to the Port aux Bûches (port of logs) where timber for construction and wood for heating arrived. It was the most important port of Paris. The street, which then was no more than a lane, skirted the river.

At number 16 rue de la Bûcherie, Restif de La Bretonne died in 1806. Though his work comprised over two hundred volumes, he died in dire poverty. Even his small police pension had been suspended. As there was no money to pay for a decent funeral, men of the neighbourhood carried his coffin to the Cemetery of Sainte-Catherine (56-66 Boulevard Saint-Marcel). Today his books are obligatory reading in French lycées.

The oldest sign in Paris, the bas-relief at 42 rue Galande, mentioned as early as 1380 as "the house under the sign of Saint-Julien", shows Saint-Julien-le-Pauvre and his wife ferrying his Divine passenger across the river. The depth of mediaeval feeling is beautifully reflected in the bas-relief, which originally was above the portal of the Church.

Julian was of noble descent. One day, while hunting a stag, the stag suddenly stopped, turned round and spoke: "You who hunt me will one day kill your parents." Impressed by the speaking stag and frightened by the prophecy, Julian left his parents and exiled himself far from them. In the distant land where he took up his abode, he was befriended by the King, who gave him one of his castles. His parents, searching for him, found out where he was and hurried to him. They arrived at the castle while Julian was out hunting. Their daughter-in-law received them with great courtesy and gave them the conjugal bedroom. She then went out to find her husband. Night had fallen, and Julian came home without meeting his wife, and unaware of his parents' presence. He went straight to the bedchamber and in the darkness touched two strangers lying in his bed. In his fury he killed them both. When his wife got home she told him that he had killed his parents.

Julian gave up all his worldly goods, and with his wife went to live in a hut near a river, where he succoured the sick and the poor, and ferried them free of charge across the river. One evening a leper came to the hut and asked to be taken to the other bank. As Julian and his wife rowed him across the water, an aureole appeared over the leper's head. It was Christ, who had brought Julian remission of his sins. Gustave Flaubert relates the legend in his *Trois Contes*.

The Church of Saint-Julien-le-Pauvre existed as long ago as 507. Sacked by the Normans in 886, it was rebuilt in the twelfth century and given to the Abbey of Longpont. It became the parish church of the University in the days when lessons were given in the open air between Place Maubert and rue Fouarre. SS Albert le Grand and Thomas Aquinas worshipped there. The Assembly of the University was held in the church, the election of the Rector Magnificus took place there, and every two years the Provost of Paris came to Saint-Julien-le-Pauvre to swear to respect and uphold the privileges of the University. The great era ceased when new colleges were built on the Montagne-Sainte-Geneviève. The students became increasingly disenchanted with their rectors, who viewed them with dwindling indulgence, and since the rectors were elected in the church, in 1524 the students broke the windows and destroyed everything inside on which they could lay their hands. The Parliament of Paris decreed that future elections should be held in the Convent of the Mathurins.

In 1651 the Church was restored and attached to the Hôtel-Dieu. Under the Revolution it was used as a warehouse. It was restored to the cult in 1801. Robert Auget, Baron de Montyon, was a benefactor not only of the Church but also of the Paris hospitals and the poor of the city. He left large sums to charity when he died in 1820. First buried in the Cemetery of Vaugirard in 1838, he was reburied under the peristyle of the Hôtel-Dieu, and in 1877 found final rest most appropriately in the Church of Saint-Julien-le-Pauvre.

Nowadays it is the church of the Greek Catholics in Paris.

There were two saints called Séverin: one, Séverin, Abbot of Argaune in Valais, who was summoned in 504 to Paris by Clovis to cure him of a malignant fever; the other, Séverin the Solitary, who in the reign of Childebert I, son of Clovis, retired to lead a solitary, saintly life to the spot, then well beyond the southern city gate, where the Church of Saint-Séverin was to be built.

One knows that after a short stay in Paris the Abbot of Argaune left for Château-Landon in the Gatinais, where he died about 506. It seems unlikely that he could have had time in Paris to found a chapel on the left bank of the Seine. On the other hand, the Solitary lived there for a long time among fishermen and boatmen, setting them a shining example with the austere, pious life he led. They were witnesses to the miracles he performed after his death, and raised a chapel in his honour. The Normans burnt it down, but it was rebuilt in the eleventh century.

The present Church of Saint-Séverin was begun on the same site two centuries later. The clergy of Saint-Séverin found it difficult to choose between the two saints. In 1738 the parish priest tried to turn them into one: having been an anchorite in Paris, according to his version, the saint became the Abbot of Argaune. This theory had no success. Eventually both saints came to be venerated in the church and both their feast days celebrated, the Abbot's on February 11 and the Solitary's on November 23.

The clergy of Saint-Séverin took up their abode in the street which was first called rue de l'Archiprêtre, then rue aux Prêtres, and finally rue des Prêtres-Saint-Séverin. The street in front of the Church was referred to in the fourteenth century as a warren of women. A century later the College of Lisieux was installed there, but moved later to the rue des Grès (now rue Cujas), then to the rue Jean-de-Beauvais. The Cemetery and charnel house were beside the Church.

Because of the colleges and the narrowness of the streets (which included rues des Grands-Degrés, de l'Hôtel-Colbert, du Haut-Pavé, des Trois-Portes, de la Huchette, Saint-Séverin, de la Harpe, du Fouarre, du Petit-Pont and the alleyways round the Church of Saint-Séverin), life teemed in the Latin Quarter. The crowds in the neighbourhood were always dense. Monks begged in the streets in the name of "Jésus, notre Sire", itinerant vendors hawked their wares, and students and travellers pushed their way into cook-shops. The people were summoned by the bells of over twenty churches which called them to Mass or Vespers, to weddings or funerals, or to celebrate with a Te Deum the King's latest victory. But when the bell of Saint-Séverin rang out the curfew, everybody hurried home, closing the shutters and locking the doors against the night. One of the reasons why decent citizens so disliked the students was the young people's disregard of the dangers of the night to which, incidentally, they added with their turbulent roistering.

It was foolish to venture out at night in the unlit streets, for the Devil stalked them, and woe to the man he caught. Life was short and full of perils. The Devil did not reign alone in the dark: pestilence, assassins, robbers and other ruffians shared his rule. Moreover, carnal sin waited at every corner in the shape of prostitutes. Darkness was also the ally of death.

Even at home death did not leave you alone. The clocheteurs des trépassés saw to that. The bellringers of the dead, dressed in white, their coats embroidered with black skull and bones, ran through the streets ringing their hand bells until they were sure that all the inhabitants had been wakened, when they shouted:

Réveillez-vous, gens qui dormez,
Priez Dieu pour les trépassés.

The custom persisted well into the seventeenth century. There was no chance to forget or try to overlook the shortness of life and ever-present death.

The night, however, served medical students well. They used the hours after dark to steal corpses. Their purpose was not ghoulish: they were rarely given more than the odd corpse or two a year, and they could not study medicine without cutting up the dead. In that thick conglomeration of streets everyone knew about everybody's movements, including their deaths and burials. The medical students needed comparatively fresh corpses. Before nightfall an accomplice would hide among the tombstones of the Cemetery of Saint-Séverin who would later open the gate to his student friends. They did not need to take many precautions, for most of the people who were abroad at night were up to no good, and would not, therefore, interfere with them. The Watch seldom passed and if it came they could in any case hear it.

When the cemetery gate was unlocked, the students hurried to a fresh grave—they chose the graves of the poor, who had no coffins but were interred in shrouds—dug out the corpse, then carried it to the medical school, or in the seventeenth and eighteenth centuries to a house in the rue de la Harpe where many of them lodged. It goes almost without saying that one night Restif de La Bretonne followed such a procession to the rue de la Harpe, climbed the stairs unseen, and hidden in a dark corner, watched the students at work. He recognised the deceased, a girl of eighteen who had died the night before and whose parents he knew. Though filled with sorrow, he did not denounce the students. "Why are they not given the corpses of criminals?" was the pertinent question he asked himself.

However, there was an occasion when medical students saved a life by robbing a grave. A young girl had been duly buried, and the students had carried her away to be dissected, but by the time they reached their house the girl had revived. The students believed that the fresh earth on her shroud had brought her back to life. They gave her a drink, and as she had no idea where she was or what had happened, they tactfully explained that she had been very ill and that her parents had put her in their care, assuring her that she had recovered and was no longer in danger of death. They took her home before dawn. Her parents were out, for in their misery they had gone to spend the night with friends. The students put the girl to bed, told the servant maid to give her a hot broth as she had caught a chill in the grave, and at seven in the morning sent the servant to fetch the parents. While she was gone the students disappeared.

One was not always so lucky. At 12 rue Saint-Séverin lived for a time the Abbé Prévost d'Exiles of whose hundred and seventy works only *Manon Lescaut* is remembered. In 1763 he went for a short visit to Croix-de-Courtail, a small village in the forest of Senlis (Oise), where he died of a stroke. Death having come so suddenly, the authorities ordered a post-mortem. As the surgeon brought his scalpel to the Abbé's head, the Abbé came to life. The scalpel had struck the forehead with such strength however that a few minutes later he died of the wound.

At 33 rue Saint-Jacques stood the Chapel of Saint-Yves who was born near Tréguier in Brittany in 1253. As an ecclesiastical judge he acquired renown for his integrity and kindness to the poor. He gave up his office to become the protector of the poor, who referred to him as the father and defender of destitutes, widows and orphans. He died in 1303, and was canonised in 1347. The construction of the chapel began the following year under Philippe IV and was finished in the reign of Jean le Bon in 1357. It adjoined a college for poor scholars from Brittany, and was demolished during the Revolution.

Lawyers took St Yves as their patron saint, and on May 19 every year a Mass was celebrated in the Chapel for the eternal rest of the lawyers who had died the year before. Nowadays the Mass is celebrated in the Sainte-Chapelle. It is worth noting that the painters of Paris offer up a Mass on Ash Wednesday in the Church of Saint-Germain-l'Auxerrois for the souls of the painters who will die in the course of the year. But lawyers prefer to act on evidence.

There is a story that when St Yves arrived at the gate of Heaven, St Peter refused him entry, thinking that he was a professional lawyer. The saint waited for the next batch of arrivals, and, hiding among them, entered Paradise in their company. However, St Peter spotted him and told him to be gone. St Yves retorted that he would leave only if a huissier, a process-server, brought him an expulsion order signed by a judge. St Peter went in search of a hussier and a judge, but could find no one in Paradise belonging to the legal profession. So St Yves remained.

The Church of Saint-Etienne-du-Mont in the Place Sainte-Geneviève was built on the land annexed by Philippe-Auguste from the Abbey of Sainte-Geneviève in 1220, during the building of his Enceinte. The Church was first named Saint-Jean-du-Mont and renamed in the sixteenth century. When it became too small for the rising number of worshippers, it was pulled down, and construction of the present Church began in 1517, though it was not completed until the reign of Louis XIII. The first stone of the portal was laid in 1610 by Marguerite de Valois. The sarcophagus of St Geneviève was placed in the church, and on her feast, January 3, large crowds filled the church. By tradition on that day the sarcophagus was carried in procession as far as Notre-Dame. At first monks shouldered it, but from 1525 onwards, sixteen members of the Parisian high bourgeoisie were given the privilege of carrying the reliquary, which was so heavy that ten strong men were needed to lift it. Later twenty-four burghers who had held office as provost or alderman were granted the honour. Eventually their number rose to forty.

In 1793 the sarcophagus was melted down and the relics were burnt in the presence of happy sans-culottes, another victory over bigotry. In 1802 the original stone coffin in which the saint was buried in 551 was discovered in the crypt of the church of the Abbey of Sainte-Geneviève. Her bones had been removed from it and hidden by the monks at the time of the Norman invasion. Later a more ornate sarcophagus was made for them, so that the coffin was no longer needed. But now that there were no relics left, the original coffin was transferred to Saint-Etienne-du-Mont and surrounded by an imposing reliquary. On January 3 pilgrims still crowd the church and pray beside the coffin that the Normans failed to destroy.

The graveyard behind the Church was sold in 1784, but when the dead Mirabeau and the dead Marat fell in disgrace (the first in September 1794, the second in February 1795) and were expelled from the Panthéon (Church of Sainte-Geneviève before the Revolution) across the road, their coffins were taken to the graveyard. Mirabeau's coffin was delivered to his sister in 1798, but she refused to accept it, and it disappeared without trace, like Marat's.

The Church was restored to the Archdiocese of Paris in 1803. Its troubles were not yet over, for when on January 3, 1857, Marie-Dominique Sibour, Archbishop of Paris, arrived at three in the afternoon for the feast and novena of Sainte-Geneviève, an unfrocked, demented priest, Jean Verger, stabbed him to death.

XVII

From Montparnasse to the Jardin des Plantes

In the sixteenth and seventeenth centuries students of the University used to visit the hill south of the Sorbonne, where they read poetry and played music together. They gave it the name of Mont Parnasse. Montparnasse became one of the four districts of the fourteenth arrondissement when it was annexed to Paris in 1860.

In 1704 Louis XIV decided to urbanise the hill, which until then had consisted of meadows, orchards and fields, and boasted enough windmills to make Montmartre jealous. The plan of the present-day Boulevard du Montparnasse was traced in 1714; but construction did not begin until 1761. The knoll where the students used to meet—at the corner of Boulevards Raspail and du Montparnasse—was levelled down, though a small mound remained there until 1816.

The Boulevard du Montparnasse formed, with the Boulevards de l'Hôpital, Auguste-Blanqui, Saint-Jacques and des Invalides, the Boulevards du Midi, so called because they were south of the city. The Boulevard du Montparnasse stopped at the rue d'Enfer (Avenue Denfert-Rochereau) before the Avenue de l'Observatoire existed. The new thoroughfares were soon flanked by imposing private mansions with large gardens, among them the houses of Mademoiselle de Condé-Bourbon, Marshal of France Baron de Biron and the Ducs d'Orsay and Laval. During the early years of the Revolution, public feasts, dances, firework displays and "aeronautical experiences" were held in the gardens of those who had either succeeded in fleeing from, or had perished on, the guillotine. The Boulevard itself remained peaceful. In 1828 it was still described as an admirable but solitary place to promenade. It ceased to be solitary when guinguettes with arbours and swings, catering specially for lovers, came to line it.

In 1820, Choron, a theatrical impresario, established an academy of dramatic art in the Boulevard. He had the entry into several schools, where the masters introduced him to pupils who were making no headway in Greek and Latin. Such pupils were known as cancres (dunces). Choron took them under his wing. "They will soon be good for work," he said and carried them off to his academy. After a few lessons he called on their parents whom he persuaded to let their offspring embark on a theatrical career since they seemed no good for anything else. Nine out of ten agreed. When the pupils were, in his opinion, ready to be launched, he invited the aristocracy of the Faubourg Saint-Germain to witness their excellent performances. Now and again the pupils' first appearance was before empty seats, however, for the inhabitants of the Faubourg considered Montparnasse as the back of beyond.

There was another sort of academy on the Boulevard, its premises in a guinguette. The singer Anatole Lionnet gave this description: "At the other end of the room sat an aged man before a table, a small wooden hammer in his hand. He would call, 'The turn of our friend so and so . . .' and a man, usually a workman, rose in the audience, approached the table and sang a ballad or a song. Some did not sing badly and received thunderous applause. Others, naïve or pretentious, were laughed at, though also applauded. It was moving to see all those decent people who, after a day's hard work, came to that room to enjoy themselves simply and honestly, singing gay songs and sentimental ballads."

A dance hall, the Bal de l'Ermitage, was in 1848 the meeting place of female socialists and sans-culottes. Another dance hall, the Bal de l'Elysée-Montparnasse, was frequented by students and artists. Yet another, the Grande-Chaumière, was frequented by anybody who could get in.

The Grande-Chaumière began modestly enough: a few small thatched huts in a garden, where drink was served and dancing was allowed. It was started in 1783 by an Englishman called Tickson, who later took a tavern-keeper, Fillard by name, as his partner. They pulled down the huts, built a house two storeys high, and laid out the gardens; there were flower beds, an arbour, swings and a shooting-booth. Under the Restoration, the place became enormously fashionable. Admirers of Corot gave a banquet there for the painter in 1826. (Corot was not the first painter to climb Montparnasse: in the reign of Louis XIV, when it was still a wilderness, the painter Hyacinthe Rigaud used to hunt there.) Benoît, Fillard's son-in-law, inherited the Grande-Chaumière and installed a switchback. Lobster salad, switchbacks and the theatre were, according to a saying in the early nineteenth century, the three passions of the grisette.

After Benoît came père Lahire, another son-in-law, an old Grenadier of the Imperial Guard, a man of immense physical strength. He persuaded the authorities to leave the maintenance of order in the establishment entirely to him. The police, who used to irritate and provoke students, were no longer allowed in, and under his rule fights and tussles ceased. In 1843 the polka was danced for the first time in Paris in the Grande-Chaumière. When Jules Favre, Horace Vernet, Emile de Girardin and Adolphe Thiers were university students, they regularly frequented the place.

In 1855 the Grande-Chaumière closed its doors. The Closerie des Lilas took over its clientele.

Another dance hall, the Arc-en-Ciel, founded in 1800, reached the heights of fame in the 1830s. It had a good orchestra, and Laurent Filiberti, the landlord, was a composer of romances and waltzes, *Brise de Soir* and *Rosita* being the best known. However, Filiberti's fame was based neither on his work nor on the excellence of his orchestra, but on a popular tune that he did not compose:

> Toi qui connais les hussards de la Garde
> Connais-tu pas l'trombone du régiment?
> Il a l'air vaillant quand il vous regarde,
> Eh bien, ma chère, il était mon amant.

When Filiberti had done his military service, he had been first trombone in the fifth Hussars, so his customers sang the tune whenever he appeared among them. Associated with it in their minds, he became as popular as the tune.

Painters gravitated to Montparnasse, but they were still French painters until after the Franco-Prussian War. When Montparnasse became cosmopolitan, the old painters looked back nostalgically on the days when only French was heard there. They sighed as foreigners filled the cafés that had so completely been theirs. One night, a few years before the First World War, two Polish artists flew at each other's throats in a café in the Boulevard du Montparnasse. They could not be separated, and the police were called. The Poles were taken to the police station.

"Why did you fight?" asked the inspector in charge.

"To repay an old insult in Warsaw," said one of them.

"So that's why you travelled the whole way to Montparnasse," sighed the inspector.

The oldtimers had another grievance. On Sundays the military barracks of Lourcine, in the Boulevard de Port-Royal, disgorged its soldiers, who spent their day swaggering up and down the Boulevard du Montparnasse, pushing people out of their way, accosting women and filling the air with their country accents. These soldiers were from regiments from the reliable, traditionalist West (Sarthe, Anjou and Brittany), for the governments before the First World War still feared that another Commune might be attempted.

On the Boulevard de Montrouge (now Boulevard Edgar-Quinet) facing the rue de la Gaîté, stood for a time a long wooden hut, a wax museum, containing, it boasted, a hundred and sixty statues in wax. The life-size statues had been shown at the Paris Exhibition of 1855 and the Lyons Exhibition of 1872. "Everything here is magnificent, sumptuous and grand. The likenesses are perfect," declared a notice over the entrance door. The most striking statues and scenes were:

Marshal of France de Mac-Mahon, President of the French Republic and Madame de Mac-Mahon.

The Republic in all its glory, Goddess of Liberty, General Garibaldi offering her his sword.

The great reception given by Marshal of France Pélissier when he was appointed Governor of Algeria, and all the important people who assisted at the reception, including Madame la Maréchale.

The Treaty of Paris. In this group can be seen H.M. the German Emperor, M. de Bismarck, General de Moltke and a number of other Prussians.

The German Emperor's Dream.

The Indian Venus.

The Sultan Mohammed II entering his seraglio, where he finds his favourite Sultana poisoned by her jealous companions.

H.M. Victor-Emmanuel II; H.E. Count Cavour.

The unfaithful slave and the Pasha's vengeance.

Béranger, Voltaire and other poets.

The Imperial Families of Russia, Turkey and Brazil.

The Royal Families of England, Spain, Portugal and Belgium.

And a large number of other lifesize figures.

"Inside the Museum," the catalogue continued, "our employees will give all the explanations the visitors require. The Museum is lit by gas and worthy of receiving the best of Society.

"M. Serlin, the Manager, deserves the public's confidence and begs his esteemed clientele not to confuse his Museum with any other that has been set up in Paris, since his is beyond comparison!

"Anybody can visit this remarkable Gallery, where he will find nothing offensive to morals and decency. Open every day until 10 o'clock at night. Entrance fees: first-class 30 centimes; second-class 15 centimes.

"The Indian Venus is the masterpiece of the Academy of Florence, made of heavy wax, the Goddess lying on a bed. This masterpiece will not offend ladies. The masterpiece can be dismantled to satisfy the visitor's curiosity at a private session for 15 centimes."

In 1840 was built Montparnasse's first railway station, a humble building at the corner of the Boulevard de Vaugirard and the Avenue du Maine. It had one single-track line that connected Paris with Versailles. On May 8, 1842, a large crowd of Parisians travelled in several trains to Versailles to see the fountains play. At half past five the returning crowd filled eighteen small wooden coaches, too heavy a load for *Mathieu Mursay*, the little railway-engine. Instead of dividing the train into two sections, the stationmaster had a second locomotive—a real monster with six wheels—coupled to the train. Halfway to Paris *Mathieu Mursay's* axle broke and the large engine reared straight into the little one. A fire broke out in both engines and caught the wooden carriages, which were soon burning fiercely. There were hair-raising scenes inside the coaches. Most of the passengers were burnt to death. Among the few who managed to escape were a giant of a Prussian who broke open the door of his carriage and a blind man who carried his wounded brother to safety on his shoulder. When the débris was cleared a locomotive brought to Montparnasse Station a railway truck containing forty-two corpses, including those of Jules-Sébastien-César Durmont-d'Urville, sailor and explorer, and his family.

On October 22, 1895, towards four in the afternoon, a train was approaching the new Montparnasse Station in the Place de Rennes (now Place du 18 Juin 1940). It was the express from Granville, travelling at the imposing speed of sixty kilometres an hour. At the height of the rue du Château the brakes gave way, and despite the efforts of the engine driver, the train rushed at full speed into the station. The guard at the rear managed to apply the Westinghouse brake, saving the lives of the hundred and twenty-three passengers, for only the engine and the tender smashed through the glass wall and crashed into the Place de Rennes, killing a poor old woman who was selling Maurice Barrès's paper *La Cocarde* in which Barrès advocated "aesthetic nationalism". The hippomobile (horse-drawn tram) was passing as the engine—with its red apron, as André Salmon put it—broke through the glass. Luckily for the passengers, the frightened horses bolted with such speed that the engine missed the tram.

A postcard was issued depicting the accident. It sold remarkably well.

After selling his country seat, Vallée-aux-Loups, Chateaubriand returned to Paris with his wife, who, needing distraction and respite from his politics and love affairs, in 1819 founded at 86 rue d'Enfer (92 rue Denfert-Rochereau) a home, Infirmerie de Marie-Thérèse, called after the Duchesse d'Angoulême, who became its patron. It was for old priests and for widows and daughters of impoverished noblemen and of officers of the old régime. The fields and meadows belonging to this charitable institution contained a farm where cattle, goats and chickens were reared. Twenty-three cedars, two oaks and a drive flanked by chestnuts graced the property. Next to the home stood a chapel.

"I do not see a single house," wrote Chateaubriand. "At two hundred leagues from Paris I would be less separated from the world."

For financial reasons the Chateaubriands gave up looking after the home in 1838. In a letter to a friend, Madame de Chateaubriand boasted of having left it in a prosperous state. They went to live at 112 rue du Bac (now number 120), where they died, she on February 9, 1847, he on July 4, 1848. She was buried under the altar of the chapel of the Infirmerie de Marie-Thérèse, he in Grand-Bé at St Malo.

When the Boulevard Raspail was constructed, the house at 11 rue Notre-Dame-des-Champs (now number 27) was demolished. The newly married Victor Hugo lived there from the spring of 1827 until the spring of 1830. It was there that he wrote *Ballades, Cromwell, Les Orientales*, part of *Les Feuilles d'Automne*, *Marion de Lorne* and *Hernani*. Coming from the street, in order to reach the house, one went past a lodge, then under a dark ogival vault into a long open-air passage. The Hugos lived on the first floor, their flat comprising kitchen, dining-room, drawing-room, study and two bedrooms. The landlady, who lived on the ground floor, gave them the run of the garden. Young writers, painters and engravers, all belonging to the Romantic Movement, came continuously to visit the Hugos. A fortnight before *Hernani* came off the stage for the second time, the landlady bade her tenants be gone. She wanted less noise and bustle in her house.

"The corpses which the Hôtel-Dieu vomits up daily are taken to Clamart," wrote Louis-Sébastien Mercier in *Tableau de Paris*. A vast cemetery spread at Clamart (now in arrondissement de Sceaux), and the dead from the Hôtel-Dieu were wrapped in shrouds—no coffins for them—and as the hospital beds were urgently needed for new arrivals, the patients were lifted from them before they had time properly to expire, and, so the story goes, the hospital attendants in their hurry occasionally threw those still alive into the cart bound for Clamart. Some woke up or came round in the fresh air and shouted from among the corpses that they were not dead.

The cortège consisted of a cart pulled by twelve men, one priest, one bell and one cross. It left every morning at four. The bell awoke the good people who slept in the houses along the road. In times of epidemics, the cart made four journeys a day between the hospital and the cemetery. On All Souls Day relations of the dead visited Clamart, prayed at the nameless graves, then went to the taverns.

When the Cemetery of the Innocents was closed in 1785, Lieutenant of Police Lenoir hit on the idea of disposing of the bones in the old, disused quarries of Montsouris. A house called Maison de la Tombe Issoire was bought. Its deep well, which communicated with the quarry, was bricked up, and on April 7, 1786, with pomp and ceremony, the first bones arrived. The name Catacombes was given to the ossuary which was consecrated by the Archbishop of Paris. Many people protested against the name, including a journalist who was sent to the Bastille for a year to cool down. Over the gate was an inscription: "Memoria Maiorum"; on the door, "Stop, this is the empire of the dead."

Exaggerated figures have been given of the number of skeletons in the Catacombes, but six million seems a reasonable guess. The ossuary lies beneath the rues Dareau, d'Alembert, and Hallé and the Avenue du Parc-Montsouris, and is over eleven thousand square yards in size. Nightly a load of skeletons arrived, each convoy accompanied by a priest. They came not only from the Cemetery of the Innocents but also from the churchyards of Saint-Eustache, Saint-Etienne-des-Grès, Saint-Landry, Saint-André-des-Arts and others. At first the bones were simply dumped into the old quarry. During the Empire, they were grouped according to the cemeteries and churchyards from which they hailed. The bones were transported in funeral carriages, but this custom ceased in time, and they were taken in ordinary carts without priest or any form of ceremony. The last loads were delivered in 1859 following excavations and the closing of more cemeteries.

After the Catacombes stopped receiving new skeletons, the bones were arranged systematically, often in the shape of a cross, with the skulls mostly on the walls, in a straight line above them. A fountain near the gate leading to the rue Dareau was known either as the Fountain of Lethe or the Fountain of the Samaritaine. The Catacombes have a small stone chapel and a small monument, supposed to have come from the tomb of one Gilbert.

> Au banquet de la vie infortuné convive
> J'apparus un jour et je meurs!
> Je meurs, et sur la tombe où lentement j'arrive,
> Nul ne viendra verser des pleurs.

The Catacombes were opened to the public during the Empire, then closed for a time, but from 1874 onwards they could again be visited, though only twice a month.

When in May 1871 the Government troops from Versailles crushed the Commune, many of the insurgents tried to save themselves by hiding in sewers, quarries and in the Catacombes. They were all caught, most of them killed resisting their pursuers; those who surrendered were taken as prisoners to Versailles. The Battle of the Catacombes was fierce. One contingent of Versaillais entered from the Barrière de l'Enfer (Place Denfert-Rochereau), another from the Plain of Montsouris (Avenue du Parc-Montsouris). Carrying torches, they attacked the refugees, killing all who resisted. In the red light of the torches, the fight raged for several hours. The dead on that day did not enjoy the rest that had been promised them. "Here they rest, waiting for life eternal", was inscribed above one of the doors.

A more peaceful event was a concert given by fifty amateur musicians on April 1, 1897, in front of a hundred guests. The orchestra performed Chopin's *Funeral March*, Saint-Saëns's *Dance Macabre* and the Funeral March from Beethoven's *Eroica*.

The Avenue du Maine, so called since 1877, was previously known as the Chemin du Petit-Montrouge, and it led to Sceaux, originally Sceaux-du-Maine, the property of the Duc du Maine. Louis-Auguste de Bourbon, Duc du Maine, son of Louis XIV and Madame de Montespan, acquired the Château de Sceaux in 1699 from the Marquis de Seignelay, son of Colbert, who had spent a fortune on it and had several times acted as host there to Louis XIV.

The Duc du Maine was brought up secretly with his sister, who died in infancy, by Madame de Maintenon, the widow Scarron as she then was, in a house at 108-110-110 bis rue de Vaugirard, which Mme de Montespan rented from 1670 to 1674. It was on the estate of César de Vendôme, whose gardens reached as far as today's rue du Cherche-Midi. In 1692, at the age of twenty-two, the young Duke married Louise de Bourbon-Condé, the grand-daughter of the Great Condé. Sceaux became his small, personal Court. His wife gave many feasts, from which he escaped whenever he could, either going for a walk that was never long because he had a clubfoot, or hunting on horseback on his vast property, which skirted Paris. He was always happy when he reached the town where he had been brought up. In order to be even more on his own, he built the Château du Maine, more a shooting-lodge than a castle, on the very edge of his estate. The entrance was on the present site of 142-46 rue du Château. After his death in 1736, the Château du Maine slowly crumbled, changed hands several times, and was eventually demolished.

Around 1850, the grounds of the Château du Maine were taken over by a commercial enterprise with the aim of democratising the once ducal shoot. A few rickety stags and some bewildered hares were imported, to be loosed on shooting days for the benefit of the customers. The company was named Société des Chasses de Plaisance. The Nimrods of Paris gathered at the gate. There were two entrance fees: one for the guns, the other for the spectators. On Sunday afternoons, such was the din of hunting horns that one could imagine onself in the heart of the Forest of Fontainebleau. With hardly any game, and with their first excitement spent, the customers who, according to a contemporary, were more adept at hunting bedbugs than stags, ceased to patronise the place. The Société des Chasses de Plaisance went bankrupt, and thus ended the last cycle of the ducal shoot.

The Plateau de Montrouge was arid, waterless and honeycombed by quarries. Chateaubriand referred to it as a plain. He wrote in 1833, "When I tire of my gardens the Plain of Montrouge takes their place. Twenty-five years ago when going to the Vallée-aux-Loups I used to go through the Barrière du Maine; there were windmills right and left of the road, cranes at the openings of the quarries, and the nursery gardens of Cels, the old friend of Rousseau."

In time several guinguettes were built near the windmills, which stretched from the Barrière du Maine to the Barrière du Montparnasse. Acacias were planted on the plain, then travelling circuses set up their tents, and slowly a village came into being. Where today the Avenues du Maine and du Général-Leclerc meet, stood the hamlet of Petit-Montrouge, also surrounded by windmills and quarries, its inhabitants poor and living in wretched huts, and eager to rush to Paris whenever there was a chance to take part in a rising.

The hamlet of Montsouris, belonging to the parish of Montrouge, was another conglomeration of guinguettes near the Barrière Saint-Jacques. The Parc Montsouris was created by Napoleon III, who wanted to provide parks and public gardens to make Paris as green as the London he had known during his long exile.

The Parc Montsouris had its own philosopher, Emile Sauvage, who from 1872 onwards taught his disciples in the park. Seated on a bench, he discoursed on philosophy, mathematics and religion. He was a dreamer, a harmless anarchist and something of a dandy. He had no love for women, and he went home if a woman joined the open-air assembly. In winter as in summer he sat on the same bench, wearing a top hat and patent-leather boots. He defined himself as a psychologist and man of letters. He lived at 33 Avenue Reille, where he died in 1929 at the age of ninety-five.

The park was once associated with a political scandal. In 1891 a senator took a walk there. It was mid-winter and snow lay heavy on the ground. In one of the deserted lanes he came upon a statue of Marat. The senator was horrified. Who were the coarse, shameless men who had dared to erect in a public park a statue to a murderer? It later transpired that the statue had already graced the park for four years. The local authorities swore that they knew nothing about its existence. When the matter was raised in the Senate, the Government professed ignorance too. The senator persisted, however, and one night the statue was taken away in great secrecy and replaced by another—Tiger Fighting a Serpent by the sculptor Georges Guadet. Nevertheless, on March 4, 1891, the Government was censured in the Senate for having provoked decent citizens by inflicting on them the statue of Marat, which had in fact been found in a shed by the head gardener who, ignorant of history, had put it up in the park, which he considered short of statues.

In *Dames Galantes,* Brantôme relates the story of François I visiting the Royal Menagerie in the rue des Lions-Saint-Paul (now rue des Lions). He was accompanied by several noblemen and ladies, one of whom threw her handkerchief into the pit where two lions were fighting, then asked the Seigneur de Lorges, who was in love with her, to show his devotion by fetching it. He retrieved the handkerchief, and flung it into her face, saying he would never speak to her again. Brantôme got his site wrong, for the Royal Menagerie was no longer in the rue des Lions-Saint-Paul in the reign of François I: it had been removed to the Maison royale des Tournelles in 1490.

For centuries the Kings of France had owned menageries. They were less interested in plants. In 1626 Jean Hérouard, the botanist, succeeded in persuading Louis XIII to open a botanical garden in Paris, similar to the one in Montpellier, which had existed since the previous century. Hérouard's aim was to fill the garden with medicinal plants "for the use of those whose state of health required them", and to help the medical students of the University in their studies. Guy de La Brosse, colleague of Hérouard, was instructed by the King to purchase land for the garden. He did so from the Abbey of Sainte-Geneviève on February 21, 1633, for the sum of 67,000 livres. The land was outside Paris, on the edge of the Faubourg Saint-Victor (now 40 rue Geoffroy-Saint-Hilaire). It was first known as Jardin royal des Plantes médicinales, after the Revolution simply as Jardin des Plantes.

The University was opposed to the scheme, yet within ten years both botany and anatomy were being taught in the Garden, which began its career with sixteen hundred different plants. In time the University had chairs on twenty-one different subjects, including zoology, mineralogy, botany, anthropology and palaeontology.

In 1792, Bernardin de Saint-Pierre, Director of the Garden, decided to establish there a menagerie. He thought about the Royal Menagerie in Versailles, which Louis XVI wanted to get rid of, but since in all only one zebra, one buffalo and one rhinoceros were left, the deal collapsed. Next year the Commune de Paris came to the Director's rescue by having all wild beasts belonging to circuses and travelling menageries sent to the Garden. After the victories in Holland, the entire menagerie of the Stadtholder was brought there. In 1793 the Museum of National History was erected in the grounds.

Jack was the first orang-outang in the Garden. He came there in 1854, his fame having preceded him. Negroes, so Parisians were told, were convinced that orang-outangs were men who refused to speak because, if they did so, they would be forced to work. Jack arrived from Sumatra. On the voyage to France he was allowed to roam the ship, spending most of his time climbing the masts and helping the stokers. When they reached Le Havre the seamen were in tears at the thought of losing their Jack. In the Jardin des Plantes, Jack became everybody's favourite. Children doted on him and he on them. He took his meals with his keeper, using a spoon but he never mastered the fork. He was fond of women and of men's hats, and when he died Paris was heartbroken.

After him came Jacqueline, a young chimpanzee, as intelligent as Jack, and even more affectionate. She brushed herself before going to bed. She had a real bed with sheets and blankets which she shared with a dog and a cat, both of which she loved. A visitor to the Garden brought her a pair of gloves; she pulled the right one on the left paw, the left one on the right, but once her keeper had demonstrated how she should wear them, she never made the mistake again. She washed herself every morning in cold water. Her cleanliness was her undoing: she died one winter of pneumonia. She was stuffed like Jack before her, and given a place of honour in the Cabinet de Zoologie.

The Garden possessed two giraffes, the taller given in 1829 to Charles X by the Pasha of Egypt. There were two elephants, one called Marguerite, of an extraordinarily sweet disposition. The same could not be said of Martin, the brown bear, who killed two people, the first an Englishman, the second an old pensioner of the Invalides. The Englishman was in his cups and wanted to box with the bear. He jumped into the pit when nobody was looking. It was six in the morning and he lived but a few seconds longer. The pensioner's case was different: he had watched Martin playing from time to time with what he thought was a louis d'or that someone must have dropped into the pit. The old man could not resist the sight of it. Besides, it was of mighty little use to a bear. So he hid on the premises, and in the depth of night climbed noiselessly into the pit. Martin had already retired to his lair.

The old soldier picked up the shiny piece: it was a button. He cried out in his disappointment. This woke the bear, and the brave warrior, who had faced a thousand deaths at Wagram and Jena, found his swift end in the pit. A lament was written in his memory. The last verse went:

> Tout ceci doit vous apprendre,
> Enfants, vieillards, jeunes gens,
> De ne jamais, pour de l'argent,
> Chez un ours la nuit descendre.
> Car il ne respecte rien,
> Ni l' envie d'avoir du bien . . .

XVIII

Britons in Paris

In the mid-eighteenth century there lived in the rue des Cordeliers (now rue de l'Ecole-de-Médecine) a prosperous citizen who used to listen respectfully in the Luxembourg Gardens to a priest who was no friend of the English. The abbé had a simple formula. "Thirty thousand men must be raised, embarked, and disembarked in England. It might cost us thirty thousand men to take London. A bagatelle!"

The citizen fell ill and knew that his end was approaching. He remembered the dear abbé who had predicted the end of England. As he too disliked the English, he left the priest a legacy. "I leave to the Abbé Thirty-Thousand-Men 1,200 livres a year. I know him only by that name. He is a good patriot who proved to me in the Luxembourg Gardens that the English, a ferocious race who regularly depose their sovereigns, will soon be destroyed."

The benefactor died, and after the Courts had heard several witnesses who also frequented the Luxembourg Gardens, Abbé Thirty-Thousand-Men received his legacy.

After the Battle of Waterloo, when the Allies entered Paris, the Guards bivouacked in the Bois de Boulogne, which at the time was a wild, pathless, swampy, entirely neglected wood. The Prussians were under tent nearby, and did as much senseless damage as they could, cutting down the finest trees and setting the Bois on fire at several points. Three thousand Guards were the neighbours of ten thousand Prussians. "Our camp was not remarkable for its courtesy towards them," wrote Captain Gronow of the Grenadier Guards in his *Reminiscences*. He was one of the first of the British Army to penetrate into Paris. He had entered by the Porte Maillot and passed the Arc de Triomphe, which was then being built.

Scots regiments bivouacked in the Champs Elysées, which then contained only a few scattered houses. Parisian women were shocked by the kilts and did not hesitate to declare that the want of culottes was most indecent. The roads were ankle-deep in mud, and Gronow found the pavements imperfect. The stepping stones "were adopted to display the Parisian female ankle and boot in all their calculated coquetry," and the people in the streets appeared sulky and stupefied. He dined that day at the Café des Anglais on the Boulevard des Italiens, where to his surprise he found several brother officers. He had soup and fish, which was anything but fresh, then, according to English taste and predilection, "beef-steak and pommes de terre".

The Palais Royal was much visited by British and other allied officers, even if they went there in some fear and disgust. On the ground floor were jewellers' shops, where diamonds, pearls and emeralds were sold, it being the aim of a successful gambler to give these "to some female friend who had never appeared with him at the altar of marriage." Alongside a shop one might find a very dirty staircase that communicated with a café on the floor above, presided over by a very décolletée lady, laden with jewels, where the best of male society met, Britons included, holding long conversations exclusively about gambling and women. Next door might be a gaming-room. "Those gambling houses were the very fountain of immorality," wrote the captain, yet hurried daily to them with his brother officers.

An officer in the Grenadier Guards, on leave of absence, took apartments in the Palais Royal, at the time the only well-lit place in Paris. He was asked by his friends on his return to England whether it were true that he had never ventured outside. "Of course it is," he replied, "for I found everything I wanted there, both for body and mind."

The English flocked to Paris after the Restoration. There was a popular London song called *All the world's in Paris*. "Our countrymen and women," wrote Gronow, "having so long been excluded from French modes had adopted fashions of their own quite as remarkable and eccentric as those of the Parisians and much less graceful. British beauties were dressed in long, straight pelisses of various colours; the body of the dress was never of the same colour as the skirt; and the bonnet was of the bee-hive shape, and very small. The characteristic of the dress of the gentleman was a coat of light blue, or snuff colour, with brass buttons, the tail reaching nearly to the heels; a gigantic bunch of seals dangled from his fob, whilst his pantaloons were short and tight at the knees; and a spacious waistcoat, with a voluminous muslin cravat and a frilled shirt completed the toilette. The dress of the British military, in its stiff and formal ugliness, was equally cumbrous and ludicrous."

Fox, the Secretary of the Embassy, spent his days in bed, and his nights at the Salon des Etrangers at 6 rue Drouot, the most fashionable gaming-room in Paris, always full of British officers and officials. Fox was usually out of luck, but one night he won sixty thousand francs at dice, after which he was not seen again at the Salon. Gronow went to the Embassy with his passport, for a visa. He found Fox in bed in his room, which was crowded with Cashmere shawls, silks, Chantilly veils, bonnets, gloves and other articles of ladies' dress.

"Why, my dear Gronow," Fox explained, "it was the only

means to prevent those rascals at the Salon winning back my money."

The Salon des Etrangers was run by the Marquis de Livry, who presented an extraordinary likeness to the Prince Regent of England, who sent Lord Fife over to Paris "to ascertain that momentous fact".

The Hon. George T—— came regularly from London, bringing a substantial letter of credit, to gamble at the Salon des Etrangers. He contrived to lose his last penny at rouge et noir; and when he had lost all he possessed in the world he got up and exclaimed in an excited manner, "If I had Canova's *Venus and Adonis* from Alton Towers, my uncle's country seat, it should be placed on the rouge, for black has won fourteen times running."

German soldiers were much less popular than the British in Paris, where Bavarians and Wurtembergers behaved particularly badly. At Saint-Cloud, Blucher "bivouacked" his dog on Marie-Louise's sofa. The British and the Russians had better discipline than the Prussians. On November 24, 1815, on the frozen Canal de l'Ourcq, several English soldiers fell through the ice. Courageous Parisians rushed to their rescue and saved their lives. They might have felt less courageous had the soldiers been German.

Still, as Gronow relates, there was occasional trouble between occupiers and occupied. At the Théâtre des Variétés on the Boulevard de Montmartre, a piece entitled *Les Anglaises pour rire* was marvellously performed by two famous actors, Potier and Brunet. A number of Allied soldiers were admitted to the theatres free of charge. One night a party of Guards, composed of a sergeant and a few men, went to the Théâtre des Variétés. In the play, Englishwomen were ridiculed. This gave great offence to the Guardsmen, who decided to stop the show, which they did by hoisting themselves on the stage and chasing away the actors. The police were called, and wanted to imprison the men, but "they soon found to their cost that they had to deal with unmanageable opponents, for the whole posse of gendarmes were charged and driven out of the theatre."

"It must be remembered," adds Gronow, "that the only revenge the Parisians were able to take upon the conquerors was to ridicule them, and the English generally took it in good humour, and laughed at the extravagant drollery of the burlesque." Nevertheless, there were plenty of duels fought between the French and the English.

English soldiers generally walked about in parties of a dozen, and were quiet and well-behaved. Their favourite pastime was to gather in the Boulevard du Temple to watch the mountebanks and jugglers. Throughout the entire time that the British troops remained in Paris, only one of them was murdered in the streets, in sharp contrast to the fate of the Prussians.

Captain Rees Howell Gronow remained in Paris, in fact died there in 1865 at the age of seventy-one. He had become a friend of Shelley at Eton, and his mother was supposedly a friend of Mrs Jordan, mistress of the Duke of Clarence (King William IV), which was how he received his commission in the Grenadier Guards. In Paris he married a dancer from the Opéra. He was a short man with dyed hair, and was never seen without a gold-knobbed cane. Even among the snobs of his day he was considered an outstanding one. His life centred round the fashionable cafés and the boulevards. He is often mentioned in French memoirs of the last century, but without affection.

The Ecole Militaire was founded by Louis XV in 1751 for the education of five hundred young men whose fathers, in consequence of having sacrificed their fortunes in the defence of the realm, might find themselves unable to give their children an education becoming their rank and rendering them useful to the state. In front of the school was the Champs de Mars where Louis XVI took the oath to the Constitution, and where Napoleon reviewed his troops, at times as many as fifty thousand of them. The space was dug up in the shape of an amphitheatre in 1790 by the Fédérés, frightened by a rumour that it had been mined by the Royalists for the purpose of blowing them all up on the day of Federation.

On the other side of the river at the foot of Passy—the Highgate of Paris as English visitors called it—was the site intended for the palace of Napoleon's son, the King of Rome. It would have faced the Ecole Militaire, to stimulate the boy's imagination and to foster in his mind the love of military glory. When rising in the morning, he could have watched the evolution of troops in front of the school. After the Restoration, the government decided on the demolition of the foundations of the palace, which was as far as the building had gone. Tenders were invited, and an Englishman won the contract. French people accounted for this by observing that no Frenchman could have undertaken such an anti-patriotic task. As a matter of fact, the Englishman's tender was the lowest.

In the 1820s, British visitors formed part of the daily life of Paris. They liked strolling beside the Seine, admiring the washing-barges. "Through the lattice-looking openings," wrote a traveller, "one sees the flapping white caps, richly coloured handkerchiefs and bare, fleshy arms of hundreds of washerwomen, all dragging and dabbling their linen in the Seine, and casting sparkles of water up in their laughing eyes."

On the feast of St Louis the visitors observed the manners of the people, which, they regretted to see, stemmed from revolutionary habits. There was a lot of pushing at the wine fountains, where free wine was served to the masses. The gendarmes had often to expel from the crowd men who abused their superior strength in order to monopolise a good place. The expelled parties, however, were not long in forming again in column and returning to the charge. But if an old soldier, particularly an "invalide", appeared in the crowd, he was let through and at once given wine.

In the Tuileries Gardens, the Britons noticed that reading the

Public Journals was a major pastime of a Parisian. The original newspaper kiosk, which once had been sufficient to gratify the curiosity of all Paris, was established on the western side of the Gardens, and because it was exposed to the sun in all seasons, it acquired the name of Petite Provence. It had now become merely a meeting place of nurses and politicians of the lower class, fashion having abandoned it for the vicinity of the orange trees and the more frequented walks of the promenades.

"Of all the newspaper readers," wrote the anonymous author of *A Tour through Paris*, "there is not one upon whom this mode of commencing the day does not exert a great influence; but the Parisian cockneys are more fastidious than they used to be. In former times, if the Public Censor had but a poor devil of an author served up every morning to be devoured with his chocolate, he returned home perfectly contented; but now he requires the dishing up of Battles, Constitutions, Earthquakes, the Yellow Fever and the Elections. However, it must be admitted that we should get tired of newspaper reading, did not the complaisant Editors sometimes insert accidents in default of their being sent by Providence. Some offices have their portfolios for crimes and offences; the latter are put up for competition, and when they are well told, the insertion is paid to the last farthing. How many honest prose-grinders, who would not kill a fly if they could help it, live with perfect indifference on fires and murder?"

It would deeply have shocked the Britons strolling in the Gardens had they been told of the footman who in the reign of Louis XIV made a strange bet there. The Gardens were then frequented by people of quality, while their lackeys waited at the gates, at times as many as four thousand in number. The footman in question wanted to prove to his colleagues that he was a better man than they, so he bet a bottle of wine that he would raise the skirt of the first lady who emerged from the Gardens and whip her. He won his bet. Two ladies, Mlle d'Armagnac and the Marquise de Villequier, came out first. He raised Mlle d'Armagnac's skirt and whipped her, much to the merriment of the other footmen. Other ladies however ran to her rescue and held the footman until the Watch arrived. He was taken to prison. Just escaping the hangman's noose, he was condemned to the galleys.

John Scott in his *Picturesque Views of the City of Paris and its Environs* made some pertinent observations on the public gardens. ". . . public gardens are such favourites at Paris, and it must be admitted that they are, in general, handsomely embellished with casts from the antique, and ponds containing gold and silver fish. Their whole style is indeed very different from that of Hyde Park or Kensington Gardens; but the Parisians would not relish these latter. The walk to them would be found fatiguing; and when they had reached them the *picturesque* character of these noble spots would not be felt. The grandeur of the trees at Kensington would not be thought a compensation for the absence of the Apollo de Belvedere; and the free and open aspect of Hyde Park would be deemed too bare of ornament, too destitute of jauntiness and *agrémens*. The French, generally speaking, form their notions of what is fine and agreeable by some distinct reference to what is powerful, or curious, or celebrated; and without a recollection or a rule derivable from history or poetry, or present fact to guide them, their sense of the sublime and of the beautiful is at a loss. A happy combination of the effects of nature does not strike them so forcibly as the view of a palace, or of a pillar, or of a bust. As they know that an avenue has been cut out for the purpose of opening a grand vista; that a pond has been sunk to give the idea of coolness and magnificence; that a fountain has been contrived to sparkle and amuse; they are prepared at the sight of all such indications, to call up the corresponding sentiment, and to feel the due degree of delight and admiration. But, without such significant and intelligible hints, they would not know what to expect or what to experience: in candour, however, it ought to be stated, that no nation has a quicker sense of the acknowledged glories of history, of the accredited beauties of poetry, or pays the tribute of admiration more disinterestedly to the imposing circumstances of existing authority."

English travellers in the 1820s were obsessed by the Revolution which, they believed, had affected a considerable change in the French character, mingling gloom, austerity and suspicion with the politeness of the old régime, though, they admitted, a peculiar sort of politeness remained the most prominent feature of the Parisian. The dustman and the milkmaid saluted each other in the street with all the scrupulous and ceremonious punctilio that would be practised in an English drawing-room.

A drive through Paris made it obvious to the English that the French had no idea of comfort, but sacrificed everything to display. The most admirable feature of London was the excellent, constant supply of water, whereas the filth of the dwellings in Paris revealed the scarcity of supply of that necessary liquid. The English had a poor opinion of water carriers and their irritating shouts of "Eau-eau!"

Still, the boulevards exhibited a constantly enlivening scene, from an early hour in the morning until late at night. They abounded with theatres, coffee-houses, billiard halls, dancing-rooms, pleasure gardens and baths. The stalls sold toys, lace, earthenware, prints, drawings, fruit and poultry. Savoyards tormented the promenaders with their eternal strumming, but on the other hand hairdressers twisted the most wiry hair into pliant corkscrews. A "female professor" was ready for a fee to perform any given operation on one's dog. In places, chairs could be hired for a small sum per hour, and at times as many as a hundred well-dressed persons were seated in a row, some busily employed in staring or being stared at; others gossiping and indulging in the never-ending chit-chat for which the French were so renowned. The spectators themselves were part of the spectacle. They sat to be looked at, and none more so than the beaux, who with determined anxiety for the repose of their limbs, occupied three chairs at once.

The line of exhibitors in the boulevards was interminable, what with beggar bards, fortune-tellers, merry andrews, tragic actors, dancing children, performing dogs, white mice, learned monkeys and "militant canary birds". The dealers in tisane carried fantastic machines on their backs.

"Hurrah! Hurrah! Hurrah!" wrote National Guardsman Alphonse Balleydier. "The English offer us their hands, that is they offer them across the Channel. The immense English nation, that proud queen of the seas, this magnificent race of men now wants only one kind of rivalry between us, the rivalry of friendship. England is waiting for us on her happy shores; the wind is with us, the sky is blue and the sea calm. Let us go!"

And the French National Guard, twelve hundred strong, infantry, cavalry and sappers, not to mention pretty canteen-girls, set sail for Dover. It was October, 1848. The reception in Dover was most enthusiastic with loud shouts of "Vive la France!" answered by "Vive l'Angleterre!" Captain Gonnet, one of the leaders, an officer with many decorations, visited all the public houses, where at the sight of him everybody doffed his hat, and clasped his hand in burning, cordial friendship. At the banquet, toasts were drunk to the union of England and France. London was the final destination. Among the marvels of London, the French visitors saw real Chinamen, whom they found more impressive than the Turks of the rue Mouffetard in the fifth arrondissement.

They were received by the Lord Mayor. At a reception, M. Rougier, an old soldier of the Empire, met a one-armed Englishman. M. Rougier had a wooden leg.

"Where did you lose your arm?" the Frenchman enquired.

"At Waterloo."

"That's where I lost my leg. Let us embrace."

"Hurrah!" shouted One Arm, embracing Wooden Leg.

The French visitors were taken to Madame Tussaud's, which they praised, declaring that the wax figures were real works of art. Before their return to Paris they invited their English hosts, the Volunteers, to return the visit. An English committee was formed for the purpose. Its members were (as given by Balleydier):

MM Lloyd (Francis) esq; Beaufort Lodye Chelsea
Nind (Francis) esq; Sablonière, hôtel Leicester square;
Bulloch, esq; Chester street, Belgrave square;
Brown, esq; Martiham, square Chelsen;
Hible (Charles) esq; North Terrace Mount, grand Westminster nord.

At Easter the English contingent arrived in Paris, and their hosts were most anxious to show them the real Paris of their day, which, according to Balleydier, consisted of the boulevards, the rues de Richelieu and Vivienne, some streets of the Faubourg Saint-Germain, and the Chausée d'Antin, where virtue rubbed shoulders with vice.

In the Boulevard des Italiens, almost at the angle of the rue de Richelieu, stood the Hôtel des Princes. Though Paris could boast of two thousand hotels, yet the Hôtel des Princes was the only one worthy of the distinguished guests whom the National Guard awaited. Every reigning prince of Europe had visited the hotel, where incidentally Meyerbeer had written *Robert-le-diable*. In 1848 the hotel was the general headquarters of the committee formed to celebrate the new Constitution. Monsieur Privat, the hotel's admirable manager, had recently opened the sumptuous dining-room, which seated three hundred, and which was decorated in a striking Moorish style reminiscent of the Alhambra of Granada. Slender columns bore the coats of arms of all the European powers.

In the reading-room, newspapers of every country were displayed. There was a billiard-room, a smoking-room and bar, a salon de conversation, and a bathroom. There were large and small rooms for private banquets and intimate meals, and a ballroom for concerts and other fashionable gatherings. In the breakfast-room daily notices advised the guests on how to spend their day. Every evening the table d'hôtes, renowned for its perfect meals and choice wines, was filled with fashionable society. One reserved a place by inscribing one's name in the guest book during the course of the day, but tradespeople were not admitted to the table d'hôtes. The hotel boasted several interpreters.

The accommodation was in three sections, one reserved for families, the second for couples, or single people, and the third for the commercial travellers who were known as the nomads of the railway age.

A list of the most fashionable shops was drawn up for the English visitors:

"The elegant temple of Doucet, 17 rue de la Paix, for linen and cravats.

Humann, 83 rue Neuve-des-Petits-Champs (rue des Petits-Champs and rue Danielle-Casanova), tailor. No foreigner can afford to leave Paris without visiting his spacious premises.

Boivin, 8 rue Castiglione for gloves.

Ville, Passage de l'Opéra (Boulevard des Italiens) for inimitable boots. 'I have the honour of making boots for several crowned heads.'

Pinaud, the Caesar of Fashion, 87 rue de Richelieu for beautiful hats.

Audot, 81 rue de Richelieu, goldsmith, for travelling cases."

The hosts thought of everything. When the English visitors arrived, the reception committee established its headquarters in the Hôtel des Princes, where most of the English guests remained during their memorable stay. There were sixty male Britons, some of whom were accompanied by their wives and daughters. The clientele of the table d'hôtes became almost completely English. Claret and champagne flowed by the gallon, and one toast followed the other; yet, one is assured, there were no excesses, and decorum and exquisite politeness reigned. From the dining-room the English moved to the salon de conversation, where punch was drunk to the indissoluble union of the two nations.

On the second evening a causerie cordiale was given by the National Guardsmen who had been to London. At ten o'clock a large number of them, many in uniform, gathered in the Moorish Room to receive the distinguished guests. The admirable orchestra of the indispensable Monsieur Strauss was at the ready. As the Britons made their entrance, the signal was given, and the Moorish walls and ceiling echoed the magnificent tune of *God Save the Queen*. The British ladies joined with their menfolk in declaring their feelings of esteem and sincere friendship for France. All hands were grasped in deep affection, all eyes sparkled with happiness, and everybody expressed the same sentiments. At long last the Entente Cordiale had become a reality.

A speech from the English side contained the words: "It is supposed that the sea separates us. Perhaps it was so in the past, but I am glad to be able to say that now that our two nations know one another better, even the sea no longer separates us, and all the old prejudices which blinded us so often have ceased to exist. Oh, what state of happiness the English and the French have reached in witnessing this frank cordiality.

"We speak the language of Shakespeare, Walter Scott and Franklin, you the language of Voltaire, Rousseau and Fénelon, therefore no rivalry can exist any longer between us, and are we not all brothers and friends?"

Deeply moved, all those present drank to the union of North and South, meaning England and France.

After the speech and the toasts, the door of the dining-hall opened. Richly laid tables awaited the Britons. There was only one snag; not one Frenchman had brought his wife along. The English expressed their regret and disappointment, but during the whole week of festivities not a single French wife or daughter put in an appearance. An Englishman observed that it was probably better like that, since otherwise the bachelors among them might lose their heads and hearts. The French did not take the hint.

One Englishman became the hero of the party. When a National

Guardsman asked him whether he had seen the exiled French Socialist leader Louis Blanc in London he replied, "You mean that tiny fellow? I saw him between the legs of a Guardsman." The reception lasted until nine in the morning.

An Englishwoman asked Monsieur Strauss for his autograph. The next day he sent her an album of his prettiest waltzes.

The English were taken to a gala performance of the Opéra. The entire chorus sang *God Save the Queen*, which struck the French as a deeply religious anthem, and some of the National Guardsmen shed a tear for France, which had become a republic. "Vive la reine Victoria!" they shouted in unison.

On the following day the visitors were received by the Prefect of the Seine Department. Champagne flowed in the drawing-rooms of the Préfecture. The Prefect's toast was to the two most civilised people on earth. From the Préfecture the English were driven to the Café Tortoni, then back to the Hôtel des Princes, where they drank without excess until ten the following morning.

The last night of the visit was spent in friendly smoking and drinking punch and grog.

It was certainly not of the National Guardsmen's guests that Monsieur Charles de Forster was thinking when, in his *Quinze Ans à Paris*, published in 1849, he gave a picture of the foreigner in Paris, who, he said, never stopped in the streets to look at a building, for he found none worthy of his gaze, and in fact made a habit of noticing nothing, apart perhaps from throwing a cursory glance at a famous monument. The foreigner thought the royal palaces mean, the Arc de Triomphe de l'Etoile too low for him, and the Park of Versailles too small. If you showed him the Panthéon, he spoke of the Vatican; and as for the Louvre, everything was so much better in the British Museum. At the Opéra he put cotton wool in his ears, and thought of La Scala and San Carlo. If you spoke of David, Foyatier and Dantan, he would mention Thorwalden and

Flaxmann. In short, he came to Paris to praise other towns and their achievements.

After the Franco-Prussian War the English came back in even larger numbers. By then the British visitor was, as it were, under the aegis of the much admired Prince of Wales, the future King Edward VII. The Heir Apparent's popularity was such that every short and fat Parisian who had any self-respect tried to resemble him. Beards à la Prince de Galles were grown, frock coats were cut in the English fashion, and top hats had the same princely gloss. In a maison de rendez-vous frequented by just such a self-respecting Parisian, the manageress was aware that nothing gave her client more pleasure than being mistaken for His Royal Highness. Whenever the customer came to her establishment in the rue Taitbout, the manageress told the girl of his choice to ask him whether he were . . . she wouldn't dare to say who. A new girl who had no worldly manners put the question bluntly: "Are you the Prince of Wales?"

"Promise not to tell anyone?" he whispered. "Yes, I am. I hope I can count on your discretion because if it leaked out, it could lead to international complications."

In the eighties the English frequented mostly the Boulevard de la Madeleine. They wore yellow jackets, noted a boulevardier, had bandy legs and their faces reflected their spleen. They ambled from one railway or steamship agency to another. The Boulevard was in fact infested with travel agencies. There were so many Britons about that the poor boulevardier imagined himself in London on his way to Buckingham Palace. The sons of gay England, as he called them, were to be found also in large numbers in the rue Neuve-Saint-Augustin (rue des Filles-Saint-Thomas). The nearer you got to the Church of the Madeleine, the shabbier the Boulevard became. The cheap dairy shops and fruiterers in the area belonged to retired valets and cooks who had invested in them their life's savings; their customers were fellow servants, and at every step one encountered a man in a red waistcoat or wearing a white tie or dressed as a groom. These places were not for the British, but the flower market beside the Church which smelt of gardens and fields did give joy to the spleen-ridden sons and daughters of Albion.

There were many Fenians in Paris. They met at the Irish-American Bar near the Madeleine, and also at a cheaper place in the Faubourg Saint-Honoré known as the Irish Ambassadors. The Fenians' leaders were James Stephens, called the Head Centre of Fenian Brotherhood, and Eugene Davis, a writer and journalist. J. C. Millage, the Paris correspondent of *The Daily Chronicle*, wrote sensational articles on the Fenians in Paris who in fact led quiet lives, wanting only to earn a living. As a result of Millage's articles, Scotland Yard descended on Paris after the explosion in the Houses of Parliament in 1885, and since relations were excellent between England and France, Stephens, Davis and all other harmless, grousing Fenians were expelled without the slightest proof of complicity against them.

During the Exhibition of 1889, Sir James Whitehead, the Lord Mayor of London, gave a banquet in the Guildhall style at the Grand Hôtel. He was accompanied by Sir Polydore de Keyser and other celebrated City men. The Lord Mayor's banquet brought together W. T. Stead, fresh from his "Modern Babylon" campaign, Colonel Villiers of the British Embassy, the British press in Paris, and a crowd of Frenchmen, chiefly businessmen, but some from the fields of art and literature. When W. F. Lonergan of *The Daily Telegraph* entered the banqueting hall, "it was some moments before I could define to myself precisely whether the chairman or president of the function was the Lord Mayor, Monsieur Tirard, then head of the French Cabinet, or Mr W. Beatty-Kingston, the Special Correspondent of *The Daily Telegraph*. Mr Kingston, in truth, occupied a most commanding position at the table. He was able to see and to be seen by everybody." Then to his relief Mr Lonergan discovered that the powdered footmen stood not behind Mr Kingston but near the Lord Mayor and M Tirard. The banquet, thought Mr Lonergan, could not have been beaten in the City itself as far as food and wine were concerned. The speakers, though ponderous and dull, were fortunately brief in their utterances, and the banquet was a great success and a happy occasion.

Not so happy was the visit to Paris of the Sirdar, Sir Herbert Kitchener, after the Fashoda Incident in 1898, when Kitchener had ousted Major Marchand from the Sudan. A strong wave of Anglophobia came in the wake of the Incident. On October 26 Kitchener arrived in Paris from Marseilles, where he had landed on his return from Egypt. The entire British press in Paris went to the Gare de Lyons to see him arrive. To their surprise, they found the station crowded with enthusiastic Frenchmen, who had come however not to meet and applaud Kitchener but to acclaim Captain Baratier, one of Marchand's companions in the trek from West Africa to Fashoda. The British journalists were under the impression that it was not mere coincidence that Baratier was on the same train as Kitchener: it was a diabolic French machination to humiliate the English. Baratier and some of his brother officers were in the middle carriage, and were at the windows as the train came in. They were loudly cheered, the tempest of vivats continuing for a quarter of an hour. Kitchener, Sir Henry Rawlinson and Captain Rawson were in a carriage at the rear of the train, and when they alighted only the British press and Monsieur Lemoine, Thos. Cook & Son's agent, were there to receive them.

Kitchener looked curiously at the crowd of men and women who were cheering Baratier, then he turned away. Monsieur Lemoine swiftly took him and his party to one of Cook's hotels, the windows of which overlooked that outpost of England, the Gare du Nord.

Selected Bibliography

Alphand, A. *Les Promenades de Paris.* J. Rothschild, 2 vols., Paris, 1867-1873.
Andrieux, L. *Souvenirs d'un Préfet de Police.* Jules Rouff & Co., Paris, 1885.
Anonymous. *A Tour through Paris.* W. Sams, London (n.d.).
— *Notice sur les Prisons.* H. Fournier (n.d.).
Arbousse-Bastide. *Mes impressions à Paris.* C. Meyrueis, Paris, 1857.
Auberive, Ch. *Voyage d'un curieux dans Paris.* V. Sarlit, Paris, 1860.
Babize, E. *Le XVIIe arrondissement à travers les âges.* Published by the author, Paris, 1930.
Bachelin, H. *Collines et Buttes parisiennes.* Firmin Didot & Co., Paris, 1944.
Balleydier, A. *Visite rendue par l'Anglettere à la France.* Office général des chemins de fer et navigation, Paris, 1849.
Beaurepaire, E. *Paris d'hier et d'aujourd'hui. La chronique des rues.* P. Sevin & E. Rey, Paris, 1900.
Boisson, M. *Coins et Recoins de Paris.* Editions Bossard, Paris, 1927.
Boulenger, J. *Dans la vieille rue St. Honoré.* Firmin Didot, Paris, 1931.
Boutet de Monvel, R. *Les Anglais à Paris, 1800-1850.* Plon-Nourrit, Paris, 1911.
Brossays Du Perray. *Remarques historiques et anecdotes sur le château de la Bastille.* 1774.
Cain, G. *Coins de Paris.* Flammarion, Paris, 1905.
Cuisin, P. *Les Nymphes du Palais Royal.* Roux, Paris, 1815.
Deroye, L. *Le XIVe arrondissement, son origine, sa formation.* J. Mersch, Paris, 1898.
Deslys, Ch. *Paris historique, pittoresque et anecdotique. Le Jardin des Plantes.* G. Havard, Paris, 1854-1855.
Doniol, A. *Histoire du XVIe arrondissement de Paris.* Hachette, Paris, 1902.

Drumont, E. *Mon vieux Paris, hommes et choses.* Charpentier, Paris, 1878.
Du Camp, M. *Paris, ses organes, ses fonctions et sa vie dans la seconde moitié du XIX siècle.* Hachette, 6 vols., Paris, 1869-1875.
Dulaure, J.-A. *Singularités historiques, contenant ce que l'histoire de Paris et ses environs offre de plus piquant et de plus extraordinaire.* Baudouin frères, Paris, 1825.
Fegdal, Ch. *Choses et gens des Halles.* Athéna, Paris, 1922.
Fegdal, Ch. *Dans notre vieux Paris.* Stock, Delamain, Boutelleau & Co., Paris, 1934.
Forster, Ch. de. *Quinze Ans à Paris.* F. Didot frères, 2 vols., Paris, 1849.
Fournier, E. *Chroniques et légendes des rues de Paris.* E. Dentu, Paris, 1864.
Funck-Brentano, F. *La Bastille des comédiens.* A. Fontemoing, Paris, 1903.
Girault de Saint-Fargeau. *Les 48 Quartiers de Paris.* F. Didot frères, Paris, 1846.
Gronow, Captain Rees Howell. *Celebrities of London and Paris.* Smith, Elder & Co., London, 1865.
Gronow, Captain Rees Howell. *Reminiscences.* Smith, Elder & Co., London, 1862.
Hillairet, J. *Dictionnaire historique des rues de Paris.* Editions de Minuit, 2 vols., Paris, 1964.
Hillairet, J. *Gibets, piloris et cachots du vieux Paris.* Editions de Minuit, Paris, 1956.
Huysmans, J. K. *La Bièvre et Saint-Séverin.* P. V. Stock, Paris, 1898.
Laffitte, J. *Un coin de Paris.* Hachette, Paris, 1897.
Lenotre, G. *La Petite Histoire: Secrets du vieux Paris.* Grasset, Paris, 1954.
Lenotre, G. *Paris et ses fantômes.* Grasset, Paris, 1950.
Leroy, B. *Mémoires.* H. Kistemawckers, Bruxelles, 1895.
Leroy, J. *Saint-Germain-des-Prés, Capitale des lettres.* A. Bonne, Paris, 1952.
Lock, F. *Paris.* F. Didot frères, Paris, 1850.
Lonergan, W. F. *Forty Years of Paris.* T. F. Unwin, London, 1907.
Lurine, L. *Les Rues de Paris.* G. Kugelmann, Paris, 1844.
Mercier, L. S. *Tableau de Paris.* Virchaux, 2 vols.,Hambourg, 1781.
Mercier, L. S. *Le Nouveau Paris.* Fuchs, C. Pougens et C.-F. Cramer, Paris, 1798.
Minerath, M. *Histoire du XIVe arrondissement de Paris.* Lefebvre, Lille, 1928.
Pessard, G. *Paris nouveau et ancien.* Sauvaitre, Paris, 1892.
Piton, C. *Paris sous Louis XV.* Société du Mercure de France, Paris, 1908.
Poëte, M., Henriot, G., and Burnand, R. *Paris sous la République de 1848.* Bibliothèque historique de la ville de Paris, 1909.
Redesdale, Lord. *Memories.* Hutchinson, Vol. I & II, London, 1916.
Restif de La Bretonne, N.-E. *Le Pornographe.* J. Nourse, London, 1769.
Restif de La Bretonne, N.-E. *Les Nuits de Paris.* Smith-Lesouëf, London, 1788-1794.
Sauval, H. *Chronique scandaleuse de Paris.* H. Daragon, Paris, 1910.
Sauval, H. *Histoire et recherches des Antiquités de la Ville de Paris.* C. Moette, 3 vols.,Paris, 1724.

Sauvan, M. *Picturesque Tour of the Seine from Paris to the Sea.* R. Ackermann, London, 1821.
Scott, J. *Picturesque Views of the City of Paris and its environs.* Longman, Hurst, Rees, Orme & Brown, London, 1820.
Stern, J. *Lord Seymour dit Milord l'Arsouille.* La Palatine, Paris-Geneva, 1954.
Tallemant des Réaux, G. *Historiettes.* A. Levasseur, Paris, 1834.
Villemessant, H. de. *Mémoires d'un journaliste.* E. Dentu, Paris, 1873.
Virmaître, Ch. *Paris-documentaire: Trottoirs et Lupanars.* H. Perrot, Paris (n.d.).
Watin, fils. *Le provincial à Paris,* 1787.
Wiriot, E. *Paris de la Seine à la Cité universitaire.* Tolra, Paris, 1930.

Index

STREETS, SQUARES, ETC.

MONUMENTS, BUILDINGS, Etc.

INDEX